T0202921

Lecture Notes in Computer Science   13326

More information about this series at https://link.springer.com/bookseries/558

Norbert A. Streitz · Shin'ichi Konomi (Eds.)

Distributed, Ambient and Pervasive Interactions

Smart Living, Learning, Well-being and Health, Art and Creativity

10th International Conference, DAPI 2022
Held as Part of the 24th HCI International Conference, HCII 2022
Virtual Event, June 26 – July 1, 2022
Proceedings, Part II

Springer

Editors
Norbert A. Streitz
Smart Future Initiative
Frankfurt am Main, Germany

Shin'ichi Konomi
Kyushu University
Fukuoka, Japan

ISSN 0302-9743   ISSN 1611-3349 (electronic)
Lecture Notes in Computer Science
ISBN 978-3-031-05430-3   ISBN 978-3-031-05431-0 (eBook)
https://doi.org/10.1007/978-3-031-05431-0

This Springer imprint is published by the registered company Springer Nature Switzerland AG
The registered company address is: Gewerbestrasse 11, 6330 Cham, Switzerland

Foreword

Human-computer interaction (HCI) is acquiring an ever-increasing scientific and industrial importance, as well as having more impact on people's everyday life, as an ever-growing number of human activities are progressively moving from the physical to the digital world. This process, which has been ongoing for some time now, has been dramatically accelerated by the COVID-19 pandemic. The HCI International (HCII) conference series, held yearly, aims to respond to the compelling need to advance the exchange of knowledge and research and development efforts on the human aspects of design and use of computing systems.

The 24th International Conference on Human-Computer Interaction, HCI International 2022 (HCII 2022), was planned to be held at the Gothia Towers Hotel and Swedish Exhibition & Congress Centre, Göteborg, Sweden, during June 26 to July 1, 2022. Due to the COVID-19 pandemic and with everyone's health and safety in mind, HCII 2022 was organized and run as a virtual conference. It incorporated the 21 thematic areas and affiliated conferences listed on the following page.

A total of 5583 individuals from academia, research institutes, industry, and governmental agencies from 88 countries submitted contributions, and 1276 papers and 275 posters were included in the proceedings to appear just before the start of the conference. The contributions thoroughly cover the entire field of human-computer interaction, addressing major advances in knowledge and effective use of computers in a variety of application areas. These papers provide academics, researchers, engineers, scientists, practitioners, and students with state-of-the-art information on the most recent advances in HCI. The volumes constituting the set of proceedings to appear before the start of the conference are listed in the following pages.

The HCI International (HCII) conference also offers the option of 'Late Breaking Work' which applies both for papers and posters, and the corresponding volume(s) of the proceedings will appear after the conference. Full papers will be included in the 'HCII 2022 - Late Breaking Papers' volumes of the proceedings to be published in the Springer LNCS series, while 'Poster Extended Abstracts' will be included as short research papers in the 'HCII 2022 - Late Breaking Posters' volumes to be published in the Springer CCIS series.

I would like to thank the Program Board Chairs and the members of the Program Boards of all thematic areas and affiliated conferences for their contribution and support towards the highest scientific quality and overall success of the HCI International 2022 conference; they have helped in so many ways, including session organization, paper reviewing (single-blind review process, with a minimum of two reviews per submission) and, more generally, acting as goodwill ambassadors for the HCII conference.

This conference would not have been possible without the continuous and unwavering support and advice of Gavriel Salvendy, founder, General Chair Emeritus, and Scientific Advisor. For his outstanding efforts, I would like to express my appreciation to Abbas Moallem, Communications Chair and Editor of HCI International News.

June 2022   Constantine Stephanidis

HCI International 2022 Thematic Areas and Affiliated Conferences

Thematic Areas

- HCI: Human-Computer Interaction
- HIMI: Human Interface and the Management of Information

Affiliated Conferences

- EPCE: 19th International Conference on Engineering Psychology and Cognitive Ergonomics
- AC: 16th International Conference on Augmented Cognition
- UAHCI: 16th International Conference on Universal Access in Human-Computer Interaction
- CCD: 14th International Conference on Cross-Cultural Design
- SCSM: 14th International Conference on Social Computing and Social Media
- VAMR: 14th International Conference on Virtual, Augmented and Mixed Reality
- DHM: 13th International Conference on Digital Human Modeling and Applications in Health, Safety, Ergonomics and Risk Management
- DUXU: 11th International Conference on Design, User Experience and Usability
- C&C: 10th International Conference on Culture and Computing
- DAPI: 10th International Conference on Distributed, Ambient and Pervasive Interactions
- HCIBGO: 9th International Conference on HCI in Business, Government and Organizations
- LCT: 9th International Conference on Learning and Collaboration Technologies
- ITAP: 8th International Conference on Human Aspects of IT for the Aged Population
- AIS: 4th International Conference on Adaptive Instructional Systems
- HCI-CPT: 4th International Conference on HCI for Cybersecurity, Privacy and Trust
- HCI-Games: 4th International Conference on HCI in Games
- MobiTAS: 4th International Conference on HCI in Mobility, Transport and Automotive Systems
- AI-HCI: 3rd International Conference on Artificial Intelligence in HCI
- MOBILE: 3rd International Conference on Design, Operation and Evaluation of Mobile Communications

List of Conference Proceedings Volumes Appearing Before the Conference

1. LNCS 13302, Human-Computer Interaction: Theoretical Approaches and Design Methods (Part I), edited by Masaaki Kurosu
2. LNCS 13303, Human-Computer Interaction: Technological Innovation (Part II), edited by Masaaki Kurosu
3. LNCS 13304, Human-Computer Interaction: User Experience and Behavior (Part III), edited by Masaaki Kurosu
4. LNCS 13305, Human Interface and the Management of Information: Visual and Information Design (Part I), edited by Sakae Yamamoto and Hirohiko Mori
5. LNCS 13306, Human Interface and the Management of Information: Applications in Complex Technological Environments (Part II), edited by Sakae Yamamoto and Hirohiko Mori
6. LNAI 13307, Engineering Psychology and Cognitive Ergonomics, edited by Don Harris and Wen-Chin Li
7. LNCS 13308, Universal Access in Human-Computer Interaction: Novel Design Approaches and Technologies (Part I), edited by Margherita Antona and Constantine Stephanidis
8. LNCS 13309, Universal Access in Human-Computer Interaction: User and Context Diversity (Part II), edited by Margherita Antona and Constantine Stephanidis
9. LNAI 13310, Augmented Cognition, edited by Dylan D. Schmorrow and Cali M. Fidopiastis
10. LNCS 13311, Cross-Cultural Design: Interaction Design Across Cultures (Part I), edited by Pei-Luen Patrick Rau
11. LNCS 13312, Cross-Cultural Design: Applications in Learning, Arts, Cultural Heritage, Creative Industries, and Virtual Reality (Part II), edited by Pei-Luen Patrick Rau
12. LNCS 13313, Cross-Cultural Design: Applications in Business, Communication, Health, Well-being, and Inclusiveness (Part III), edited by Pei-Luen Patrick Rau
13. LNCS 13314, Cross-Cultural Design: Product and Service Design, Mobility and Automotive Design, Cities, Urban Areas, and Intelligent Environments Design (Part IV), edited by Pei-Luen Patrick Rau
14. LNCS 13315, Social Computing and Social Media: Design, User Experience and Impact (Part I), edited by Gabriele Meiselwitz
15. LNCS 13316, Social Computing and Social Media: Applications in Education and Commerce (Part II), edited by Gabriele Meiselwitz
16. LNCS 13317, Virtual, Augmented and Mixed Reality: Design and Development (Part I), edited by Jessie Y. C. Chen and Gino Fragomeni
17. LNCS 13318, Virtual, Augmented and Mixed Reality: Applications in Education, Aviation and Industry (Part II), edited by Jessie Y. C. Chen and Gino Fragomeni

39. CCIS 1582, HCI International 2022 Posters - Part III, edited by Constantine Stephanidis, Margherita Antona and Stavroula Ntoa
40. CCIS 1583, HCI International 2022 Posters - Part IV, edited by Constantine Stephanidis, Margherita Antona and Stavroula Ntoa

http://2022.hci.international/proceedings

Preface

The 10th International Conference on Distributed, Ambient and Pervasive Interactions (DAPI 2022), an affiliated conference of the HCI International Conference, provided a forum for interaction and exchanges among researchers, academics, and practitioners in the field of HCI for DAPI environments. The DAPI conference addressed approaches and objectives of information, interaction and user experience design for DAPI-Environments as well as their enabling technologies, methods and platforms, and relevant application areas.

The DAPI 2022 conference developed on topics and treatment of issues already discussed in previous years. Two tendencies were observed in this year's proceedings. On the one hand, there are papers addressing basic research questions and technology issues in the areas of new modalities, augmented and virtual reality, immersive environments, pattern recognition, blockchains, solar-powered beacons, smart furniture, etc. On the other hand, there was an increase in more applied papers that cover comprehensive platforms and smart ecosystems addressing the challenges of cyber-physical systems, human-machine networks, public spaces, smart cities, smart islands, theme parks, and even wildlife in the Himalayas. The application areas also include education, learning, culture, art, music, and interactive installations, as well as security and privacy, and the currently prominent topic of the COVID-19 pandemic.

Two volumes of the HCII2022 proceedings are dedicated to this year's edition of the DAPI Conference, entitled Distributed, Ambient and Pervasive Interactions: Smart Environments, Ecosystems, and Cities (Part I), and Distributed, Ambient and Pervasive Interactions: Smart Living, Learning, Well-being and Health, Art and Creativity (Part II). The first volume focuses on topics related to user experience and interaction design for smart ecosystems, smart cities, smart islands and intelligent urban living, smart artifacts in smart environments, as well as opportunities and challenges for the near future smart environments. The second volume focuses on topics related to smart living in pervasive IoT ecosystems; distributed, ambient, and pervasive education and learning; distributed, ambient, and pervasive well-being and healthcare; as well as smart creativity and art.

Papers of these volumes are included for publication after a minimum of two single–blind reviews from the members of the DAPI Program Board or, in some cases, from members of the Program Boards of other affiliated conferences. We would like to thank all of them for their invaluable contribution, support, and efforts.

June 2022

Norbert A. Streitz
Shin'ichi Konomi

10th International Conference on Distributed, Ambient and Pervasive Interactions (DAPI 2022)

The full list with the Program Board Chairs and the members of the Program Boards of all thematic areas and affiliated conferences is available online at

http://www.hci.international/board-members-2022.php

HCI International 2023

The 25th International Conference on Human-Computer Interaction, HCI International 2023, will be held jointly with the affiliated conferences at the AC Bella Sky Hotel and Bella Center, Copenhagen, Denmark, 23–28 July 2023. It will cover a broad spectrum of themes related to human-computer interaction, including theoretical issues, methods, tools, processes, and case studies in HCI design, as well as novel interaction techniques, interfaces, and applications. The proceedings will be published by Springer. More information will be available on the conference website: http://2023.hci.international/.

General Chair
Constantine Stephanidis
University of Crete and ICS-FORTH
Heraklion, Crete, Greece
Email: general_chair@hcii2023.org

http://2023.hci.international/

Contents – Part II

Distributed, Ambient, and Pervasive Well-Being and Healthcare

Smart Creativity and Art

Contents – Part I

Smart Artifacts in Smart Environments

**Opportunities and Challenges for the Near Future Smart
Environments**

Smart Living in Pervasive IoT Ecosystems

Augmented Reality Supported Real-Time Data Processing Using Internet of Things Sensor Technology

Alexander Arntz$^{(\boxtimes)}$ iD, Felix Adler, Dennis Kitzmann, and Sabrina C. Eimler iD

Institute of Computer Science, Hochschule Ruhr West University of Applied Sciences, Bottrop, Germany
{alexander.arntz,sabrina.eimler}@hs-ruhrwest.de,
{felix.adler,dennis.kitzmann}@stud.hs-ruhrwest.de

Abstract. Internet of things (IoT) devices increasingly permeate everyday life and provide vital and convenient information. Augmented reality (AR) enables the embedding of this information in the environment using visualizations that can contextualize data for various applications such as Smart Home. Current applications providing a visual representation of the information are often limited to graphs or bar charts, neglecting the variety of possible coherence between the subject and the visualization. We present a setup for real-time AR-based visualizations of data collected by IoT devices. Three distinct battery-powered IoT microcontroller systems were designed and programmed. Each is outfitted with numerous sensors, i.e. for humidity or temperature, to interact with the developed AR application through a network connection. The AR application was developed using Unity3D and the Vuforia AR SDK for Android-based mobile devices with the goal of providing processed and visualized information that is comprehensible for the respective context. Inspired by weather applications for mobile devices, the visualization contains animated dioramas, with changing attributes based on the input data from the IoT microcontroller. This work contains the configuration of the IoT microcontroller hardware, the network interface used, the development process of the AR application, and its usage, complemented by possible future extensions described in an outlook.

Keywords: Augmented reality · Internet of things · Data visualization

1 Introduction

Augmented Reality (AR) has become an effective way to contextualize data through spatial allocation and visual cues [2]. The origin of this data can vary considerably, ranging from internal sensors of the AR device to external sources, such as Internet of Things (IoT) devices [18]. Due to advancements in microcontroller technology that lowered prices and increased the capabilities of IoT devices, the usage of microcontroller-driven sensor data for visualization in AR

N. A. Streitz and S. Konomi (Eds.): HCII 2022, LNCS 13326, pp. 3–17, 2022.
https://doi.org/10.1007/978-3-031-05431-0_1

has become a promising field for various industries. This allows for easy interpretation of incoming sensor data, as visual cues and a contextual framework can help to better understand and interpret these data sets.

The objective of the project at hand was to combine AR with sensor-driven IoT devices to provide real-time data that are visually processed by the application for easy comprehensibility on the part of the user. Another goal is to ensure that information provided by the sensor can be accessed everywhere. For this purpose, we built a prototype concept, involving three distinct microcontroller systems equipped with sensor equipment that is able to relay the collected information towards a mobile-based AR application.

One possible usage of this concept would be a deployment in environments with demanding conditions that are required to be constantly monitored, such as industrial environments, laboratories, or a Smart Home. In a medical laboratory, for example, the temperature, as well as the humidity conditions, must be constantly monitored to prevent the degradation of samples. Microcontroller systems with the appropriate sensor attached would be suitable for this role and can be connected to a network via wireless LAN and constantly generate measured values. Anyone who wants to know whether the temperature or the light within the wine cellar is still appropriate can use their AR application to obtain the visually processed information in a comprehensible way.

The following chapters describe the development of this prototype framework, involving the used hardware components, the libraries, and network functions for the data exchange between the microcontroller systems and the mobile device as well as the mechanics of the AR application running on mobile hardware. In the end, a brief outlook is given regarding future applications that can be iterated from this prototype concept.

2   Hardware

2.1   Microcontroller Systems

There are a total of three individual microcontroller systems responsible for providing real-time sensor data. The essential component of each system is the NodeMCU1 ESP-12E module with a 32-bit ESP8266 microcontroller [14]. This chip is equipped with an 802.11 b/g/n wireless LAN module with a maximum data rate of 72.2 MBit/s and a transmit power of up to 20.5 dBm. As peripheral interfaces, the microcontroller offers a total of 17 GPIO pins for controlling sensors and actuators, an I^{2}C data bus [19], a micro-USB connector for external connection as well as optional power supply, and a 10-bit analog-to-digital digital converter (ADC). The provided RAM is 32 KiB for instructions and 80 KiB for user data. The flash memory of the ESP-12E module is a total of 4 MiB in size. While the 32-bit CPU clocks with a maximum of 160 MHz, the CPU clock was reduced to 80 MHz for this project, which is sufficient for WPA2 encryption and decryption of network data and to save power. The average power consumption of the ESP-12E module is about 80 mA [23].

NodeMCU is a modular open-source firmware that runs on the ESP8266 microcontroller [11]. Programs for NodeMCU can be written in Lua or C/C++ and allow easy access to the microcontroller's hardware. Due to the high level of abstraction, even a rudimentary web server can be run on the ESP8266 microcontroller with the appropriate modules, which is required for this project.

The SHT-31 sensor can measure temperatures in the range of -40 to $125\,^{\circ}\mathrm{C}$ with an accuracy of $\pm0.2\,^{\circ}\mathrm{C}$ [22]. The sensor measures humidity in the range of 0 to 100% with an accuracy of $\pm2\%$. The sensor is controlled via the $\mathrm{I}^2\mathrm{C}$ bus and supplied with $3.3\,\mathrm{V}$ voltage directly at the ESP8266. Each microcontroller system has a different sensor installed.

The TSL2591 sensor is a very high sensitive light to digital converter [12], which converts the measured light intensity into a digital signal. The sensor has two photodiodes, which allow measuring visible light as well as infrared light. The measuring range for the light intensity in Lux ranges from 188 µlx to 88,000 lx. The sensor is also controlled via the $\mathrm{I}^2\mathrm{C}$ bus and directly connected to the ESP8266 with $3.3\,\mathrm{V}$ voltage.

The YL-69 sensor is an analog soil moisture sensor [1]. The measuring range goes from 0 to 1023, because the sensor is connected to the 10-bit ADC of the ESP8266. The sensor is read out directly analog and supplied with $3.3\,\mathrm{V}$ voltage at the ESP8266. Table 1 gives an overview of the sensors used.

Table 1. The sensors used for the microcontroller

Sensor	Function
STH-31	Measure temperature and humidity
TSL2591	Measure infrared light and visible light intensity in Lux
YL-69	Measure soil moisture analog

2.2 Board Layout

Breadboards with $70 \times 50\,\mathrm{mm}$ dimensions were chosen for this project, as this size was optimal to accommodate all electrical components. To facilitate the replacement of defective components, headers were mounted onto the board as sockets for the electrical components. In accordance with the specifications listed in the data sheets [14], the sensors were connected to the ESP-12E modules [23]. A toggle switch enables the turning off and on of the board by either interrupting or restoring the battery power. A pair of LEDs were integrated into the circuit to indicate the status of the system, with a red LED signaling the system's operation status and a green LED for the active wireless connection. The Figs. 1, 2 and 3 show the schematics of the circuit board.

3 Software

The programs (sketches) for the ESP8266 microcontroller were developed by using the Arduino IDE5 v1.8.10 in the C++ programming language [7]. Table 2

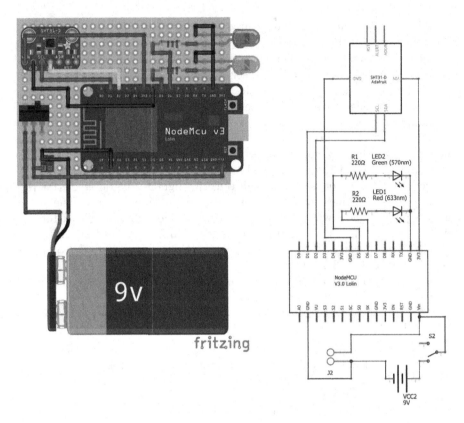

Fig. 1. Schematic board layout of the microcontroller system with the SHT31 sensor [16].

lists the additional libraries that are used within the sketches. The development of the sketches aimed for a modular design, to ensure that all three microcontroller systems share the same state behavior despite the different sensors attached.

3.1   Measurement Behavior

Once the microcontroller system has successfully initialized itself by detecting the attached sensor and establishing a wireless network connection, the system starts its periodic measurements. Every 250 ms a new measurement cycle begins, in which new sensor values are gathered and stored in the sensor object. In addition, the undercut duration of the lower threshold value or the overcut duration of the upper threshold value is calculated and also stored in the sensor object. To access the data, the attributes of the sensor object only have to be queried via the corresponding getter methods enabled by the EEPROM.

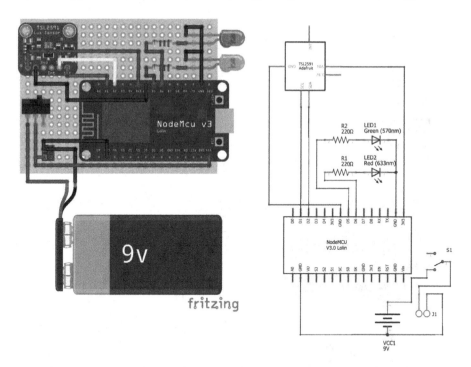

Fig. 2. Schematic board layout of the microcontroller system with the TSL2591 sensor [16].

3.2 EEPROM-Memory

An EEPROM (Electrically Erasable Programmable Read-Only Memory) is suitable for storing data even after the power supply of the circuit board is removed. While the used ESP8266 does not have a physical EEPROM, a 4 Kb flash memory on the board allows it to emulate this functionality. In this context, the EEPROM is used to persistently store the WLAN connection data, a user-defined microcontroller system name as well as the upper and lower threshold values. Each variable in the data structure has a maximum length that must not be exceeded, i.e. the optional user-defined name of the microcontroller system *(custom_name)* must not be larger than 64 bytes. If, for example, *custom_name* would

Table 2. Additional libraries used within the sketches

Library	Function
Adafruit SHT31 Library [4]	Controls the SHT-31 temperature sensor
Adafruit TSL2591 Library [6]	Controls the TSL2591 light sensor
Adafruit Unified Sensor [5]	Basic for Adafruit libraries
ArduinoJson [10]	Creates and reads JSON objects

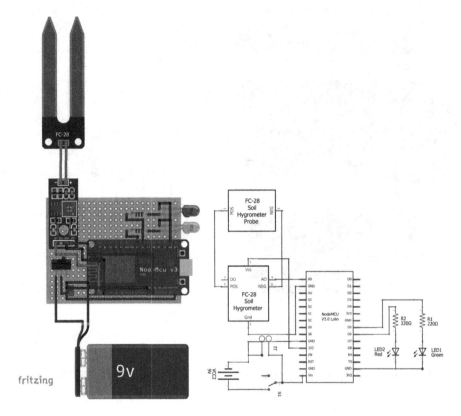

Fig. 3. Schematic board layout of the microcontroller system with the YL69 sensor [16].

be 80 Bytes, the next variable in the data structure *(threshold_lower)* would be overwritten. However, the microcontroller system recognizes this overflow and prevents data loss. The identification of the data structure serves, on the one hand, as an indicator of whether or not a data structure is in the EEPROM and, on the other hand, for the identification of the version of the data structure. If the data structure should change in the future, the readout of the EEPROM is prevented by the change of the identifier and the new version of the data structure is initialized in the EEPROM instead. The character string *undefined* for the attributes *custom_name, threshold_lower, and threshold_upper* indicates that these attributes have no value. This is important e.g. for the threshold values because the value ranges and data types (integer or floating-point number) depend on the sensor used. To write new access data for a WLAN network into the EEPROM, a method for the class *EEPROMStorage* was created, which has to be called once in the *setup()* function of a sketch. The microcontroller systems are configured for DHCP [20] and therefore receive their IP address from the DHCP server of the connected access point.

3.3 API

The API (Application Programming Interface) is based on the REST programming paradigm [15], which works with common HTTP GET and POST request methods. This open API allows easy integration into other applications or front ends that can handle HTTP. This allows via HTTP GET through a defined URL to access the real-time data of the specific microcontroller. The response of the microcontroller system indicates whether a request to the API was successful or not. The object schema is identical for each microcontroller system, except for the *data_*attributes*, which represent the sensor measurement data. The *threshold_lower* and *threshold_upper* attributes return the threshold values as a string for the following reasons: (1) The output of *undefined*, which signals that no threshold is defined. (2) The threshold values can be integers or floating point numbers.

3.4 Web Server

The web server is provided by the *ESP8266WebServer* module from the standard library of the ESP-12E module [8,9], running on port 80. If an HTTP GET request takes place on the path /, the web server calls the appropriate listener method for this path and returns the real-time data as a JSON object with the HTTP status code 200. This happens very fast because due to the periodic cycle only the attribute values of the sensor object have to be queried with no separate measurement started, which often takes 100 ms. This is a performance advantage with many simultaneous requests that also conserves energy. The web server behaves similarly when the user-defined designation of the microcontroller system or the threshold values are to be updated. If the new value is successfully checked, it is written directly to the data structure and then to the EEPROM itself. If an error occurs, an HTTP status code in the 400 range is returned; if successful, the HTTP status code 200 is always returned. If a path is called, which the webserver does not handle with a listener method an error page with the HTTP status code 404 is returned.

4 AR Application

The AR application was created using the Unity3D (v2018.4.15f1) development environment in conjunction with Vuforia (v8.6.10) [25,27], providing further access to AR-related functionality. For the AR application to work, a smartphone or tablet with a current Android operating system must be available. The device must also have a camera and a WLAN-network interface. In addition, the microcontroller systems must be on the same wireless network as the device running the AR application. Otherwise, the AR application cannot communicate with the microcontroller systems.

The AR application uses a total of three different AR markers, each representing a different microcontroller system. If an AR marker is targeted within the AR application using a camera, only the information of the microcontroller system that is hidden behind this AR marker is displayed. Figure 4 shows the AR marker for the microcontroller system with the temperature sensor.

Fig. 4. AR marker of the microcontroller system with the SHT-31 sensor. The symbol in the center of the AR marker is used for identification by the user.

The flowchart in Fig. 5 provides an overview of the main program flow of the AR application. For better clarity, the diagram has been simplified, since many processes within the AR application run in parallel or are triggered by events.

4.1   REST API Implementation

The AR application must strictly adhere to the API of the microcontroller systems. As soon as the sensor component belonging to an AR marker has been initialized and this marker has also been detected using a camera, an HTTP GET request to the path or the defined IP address is started every second. Since in this case, the API can only return a JSON object followed by the HTTP status code 200, no API-related error handling is required. The attributes from the JSON object are automatically copied to the sensor object that initiated the request. Attributes that are not in the class but are in the JSON object are automatically discarded.

The situation is somewhat different for HTTP POST requests to the /name and /thresholds paths. These are not executed until the user changes and saves

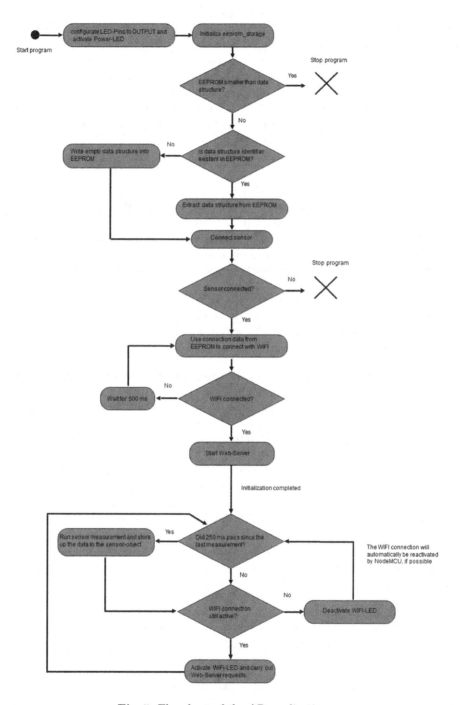

Fig. 5. Flowchart of the AR application.

the user-defined name or thresholds via the settings UI. For this request, a form must first be created that contains the data. If the microcontroller system accepts the new value and the AR application receives the HTTP status code 200 as a response, the respective action will be executed. If a value cannot be saved due to an error, status codes in the 400 range are returned. These error codes are taken into account by the AR application, but it is designed in a way to catch user errors in advance, if possible. For example, the AR application knows that the maximum size for a user-defined label must not exceed cannot exceed 64 bytes and truncates the string accordingly.

4.2   3D Models

As described earlier, the AR application uses several AR markers to display sensor data. Once the AR application receives the sensor data from the microcontroller system, a corresponding 3D landscape is displayed. For each sensor type, there are three different 3D landscapes that are displayed depending on the state of the sensor value. Each 3D landscape type corresponds to a specific sensor state:

- The temperature is too low, too high, or normal.
- Soil moisture is too low, too high, or normal.
- There is too little light, too much or normal.

A total of nine different 3D landscapes and two 3D text models were created (Figs. 6, 7 and 8). The 3D text models are displayed when the AR application connects to the microcontroller system and loads the sensor data or when no connection to the microcontroller system can be established. The 3D landscapes were created based on pre-built, free assets that can be obtained from the Unity3D Asset Store [3,13,21,26].

Each 3D landscape was composed manually without using any automatic tools. Individual prefabricated 3D objects were used and positioned in the right places by simple manipulations such as translation, rotation, and scaling. In general, all 3D objects can have such properties as color, shape, and size change. In addition, for various effects such as waves or light, ready-made scripts were used. The *LowPolyWater* script was used to create 3D water bodies as well as the appearance of waves. This script is located in the *LowPolywater* asset. The following variables can be used to configure the waves:

- Wave Height - adjusts the height of the waves.
- Wave Frequency - changes the frequency of the waves.
- Wave Length - changes the wavelength.

The standard spotlight object from the Unity3D library was used to create the light effect [24]. The spotlight object already contains an interface for configuration. This can be used to set the parameters such as range, color, and intensity for the light.

Once a complete 3D landscape was outfitted with the individual objects, this was then converted into a single prefab. In this way, AR application only needs to replace one prefab with another when the sensor state changes. The AR application places all 3D models centered and slightly above an AR marker. The 3D text models are rotated by an attached script at a static speed to rotate around their own axis.

4.3   User Interface

There are three user interfaces (UI) in total, which are only displayed during certain events. Since only one AR marker can be targeted at a time, all AR markers share the UI layout. The notification UI is only displayed if no AR marker has been targeted. Its purpose is to give the user an indication of what to do next with the AR application. The main UI (see Fig. 9) displays all real-time information about a microcontroller system associated with an AR marker. Because of this property, the main UI is only displayed when there is a connection to a microcontroller system and real-time data is received. If the sensor reading is below the lower or above the upper threshold value, the time since the threshold value was undershot or overshot is also displayed. Since the time is only given in milliseconds by the microcontroller system, the displayed time is converted into a more convenient format (e.g. 42 min or 28 s).

The settings UI (see Fig. 10) provides the option to set a user-defined name for the microcontroller system as well as custom threshold values to be defined. The sliders used to set the thresholds have been designed to be as error-tolerant as possible. The lower threshold value must be greater than the upper threshold and the upper threshold must not be smaller than the lower threshold if both thresholds are used. To comply with this convention, sliders can never be manipulated by the user in such a way that this criterion is not met. The settings UI gives the user the option to disable either or both thresholds by moving

Fig. 6. The 3D model that will be displayed when the soil moisture value is in the normal range.

Fig. 7. The 3D model which is displayed when the soil moisture value is too low.

Fig. 8. The 3D model which is displayed when the soil moisture value is too high.

the slider to the far left. In this case, the AR application would send the value *undefined* to the microcontroller system. When the user presses the Save button, an HTTP POST request is sent to each of the */name* and */thresholds* paths of the microcontroller system in question.

Fig. 9. The main UI contains all real-time information with the possibility to switch to the settings UI (Settings button top right).

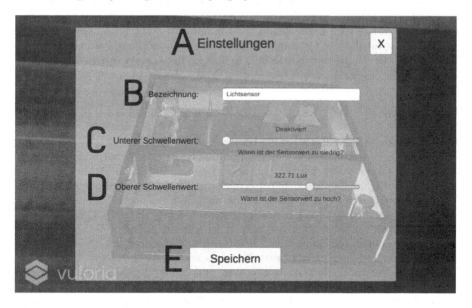

Fig. 10. The Settings UI provides the possibility to configure the individual microcontroller parameter. (Translation top to bottom: (A) settings, (B) designation - lightsensor, (C) lower threshold value - when is the sensor value too low?, (D) higher threshold value - when is the sensor value too high?, (E) save)

5 Outlook and Conclusion

The presented work is still in the prototype phase. Regarding the technical aspects of the implementation, it is of interest to reduce the usage of proprietary libraries, extend the supported microcontroller architecture and sensory equipment as well add the integration of dedicated AR devices such as the Microsoft HoloLens. Apart from the implementation, further evaluations are required regarding the usability of the application and the appropriate visualization of the information. Prior studies have shown [17], that the visualization of the information is a vital aspect for the comprehensibility of the displayed content and its placement in the appropriate context. While the current iteration of the AR application used pre-defined assets for displaying the content, the future application will incorporate bespoke visual representations of the displayed information, ranging from high fidelity 3D objects and animations to charts, graphs, and other suitable media.

The goal is to provide an open technical framework involving a variety of different microcontroller-based IoT devices that can be used for a wide spectrum of applications, to generate a benefit for emerging fields using AR technology such as Smart Home or industrial applications.

Acknowledgments. The presented work is partly supported by the Institute of Positive Computing funded by the Federal Ministry of Education and Research Germany. Equipment used has been partly funded by the initiative for quality improvement in teaching of the Institute of Computer Science. The authors thank Pasquale Hinrichs for reviewing the manuscript and Dustin Keßler for his support in the development process.

References

1. Abdelfattah, A.H., Sabirov, R.F., Ivanov, B.L., Lushnov, M.A., Sabirov, R.A.: Calibration of soil humidity sensors of automatic irrigation controller. BIO Web Conf. **17**, 00249 (2020). https://doi.org/10.1051/bioconf/20201700249
2. Aggarwal, R., Singhal, A.: Augmented reality and its effect on our life. In: 2019 9th International Conference on Cloud Computing, Data Science & Engineering (Confluence), pp. 510–515. IEEE (2019). https://doi.org/10.1109/CONFLUENCE. 2019.8776989
3. AndreyGraphics: Low Poly Pack (2018). https://assetstore.unity.com/packages/ 3d/environments/low-poly-pack-94605. Accessed 10 June 2021
4. Ardafruit: Adafruit SHT31-D Temperature and Humidity Sensor (2020). https:// github.com/adafruit/Adafruit_SHT31. Accessed 10 June 2021
5. Ardafruit: Adafruit Unified Sensor Driver (2020). https://github.com/adafruit/ Adafruit_Sensor. Accessed 10 June 2021
6. Ardafruit: Adafruit TSL2591 Library (2021). https://github.com/adafruit/ Adafruit_TSL2591_Library. Accessed 10 June 2021
7. Arduino: Arduino IDE 1.8.10 (2021). https://www.arduino.cc/en/software. Accessed 10 June 2021
8. Arduino: ESP8266 Web Server (2021). https://github.com/esp8266/Arduino/tree/ master/libraries/ESP8266WebServer. Accessed 10 June 2021

9. Arduino: Package ESP8266 (2021). http://arduino.esp8266.com/stable/package-esp8266com_index.json. Accessed 10 June 2021
10. bblanchon: ArduinoJson (2021). https://github.com/bblanchon/ArduinoJson. Accessed 10 June 2021
11. Componets101: NodeMCU ESP8266 (2021). https://components101.com/development-boards/nodemcu-esp8266-pinout-features-and-datasheet. Accessed 10 June 2021
12. Datasheet, A.: ESP-12EWiFi Module (2018). https://cdn-learn.adafruit.com/assets/assets/000/078/658/original/TSL2591_DS000338_6-00.pdf?1564168468. Accessed 10 June 2021
13. Dogan, E.: LowPoly Water (2018). https://assetstore.unity.com/packages/tools/particles-effects/lowpoly-water-107563. Accessed 10 June 2021
14. EspressivSystems: ESP8266EX Datasheet (2020). https://www.espressif.com/sites/default/files/documentation/0a-esp8266ex_datasheet_en.pdf. Accessed 10 June 2021
15. Fielding, R.T., Taylor, R.N.: Architectural styles and the design of network-based software architectures. Ph.D. thesis (2000)
16. Fritzing: Install Fritzing (2021). https://fritzing.org/download/. Accessed 10 June 2021
17. Kesler, D., Arntz, A., Friedhoff, J., Eimler, S.C.: Mill instructor: teaching industrial CNC procedures using virtual reality. In: 2020 IEEE International Conference on Artificial Intelligence and Virtual Reality (AIVR), pp. 231–234. IEEE (14122020–18122020). https://doi.org/10.1109/AIVR50618.2020.00048
18. Kucera, E., Haffner, O., Kozak, S.: Connection between 3D engine unity and micro-controller arduino: a virtual smart house. In: 2018 Cybernetics and Informatics (K&I), pp. 1–8. IEEE (2018). https://doi.org/10.1109/CYBERI.2018.8337531
19. NXP: UM10204I2C-bus specification and user manual (2014). https://www.nxp.com/docs/en/user-guide/UM10204.pdf. Accessed 10 June 2021
20. Droms, R.: Dynamic Host Configuration Protocol (1997). https://datatracker.ietf.org/doc/html/rfc2131. Accessed 10 June 2021
21. RunemarkStudio: PolyDesert (2020). https://assetstore.unity.com/packages/3d/environments/landscapes/polydesert-107196. Accessed 10 June 2021
22. Sensirion: Datasheet SHT3x-DIS (2017). https://cdn-shop.adafruit.com/product-files/2857/Sensirion_Humidity_SHT3x_Datasheet_digital-767294.pdf. Accessed 10 June 2021
23. Ai-thinker Team: ESP-12EWiFi Module (2015). https://components101.com/asset/sites/default/files/component_datasheet/ESP12E%20Datasheet.pdf. Accessed 10 June 2021
24. Unity Technologies: SpotLight (2021). https://docs.unity3d.com/ScriptReference/Experimental.GlobalIllumination.SpotLight.html. Accessed 18 June 2021
25. Unity Technologies: Unity 3D (2021). https://unity.com/de. Accessed 10 June 2021
26. ValdayTeam: Low Poly Nature Pack (Lite) (2015). https://assetstore.unity.com/packages/3d/environments/landscapes/low-poly-nature-pack-lite-40444. Accessed 10 June 2021
27. Vuforia: Getting Started with Vuforia Engine in Unity (2021). https://library.vuforia.com/articles/Training/getting-started-with-vuforia-in-unity.html. Accessed 18 June 2021

ForeSight – User-Centered and Personalized Privacy and Security Approach for Smart Living

Jochen Bauer[1(✉)], Reiner Wichert[2], Christoph Konrad[1], Michael Hechtel[1],
Simon Dengler[1,3], Simon Uhrmann[4], Mouzhi Ge[4], Peter Poller[5], Denise Kahl[5],
Bruno Ristok[3], and Jörg Franke[1]

[1] Institute for Factory Automation and Production Systems,
Friedrich-Alexander-Universität Erlangen-Nürnberg,
Egerlandstraße 7, 91054 Erlangen, Germany
jochen.bauer@faps.fau.de
[2] SageLiving GmbH, Borngartenstraße 10, 64319 Pfungstadt, Germany
[3] C&S Computer und Software GmbH, Wolfsgäßchen 1, 86153 Augsburg, Germany
[4] Deggendorf Institute of Technology, Deggendorf, Germany
[5] German Research Center for Artificial Intelligence (DFKI),
Saarland Informatics Campus, Saarbrücken, Germany

Abstract. With the emerging Internet of Things (IoT) techniques in smart home applications, artificial intelligence (AI), and highly interoperable IoT s ystems enable the development of context-sensitive multi-domain services in smart homes [1]. However, while such systems create enormous challenges regarding security and privacy, the IoT practitioners may overlook certain security and privacy concerns such as European Union (EU) General Data Protection Regulation (GDPR). This paper describes the necessities to consider privacy- and security-related challenges for smart living platforms. Core elements of this contribution are a user survey to detect key aspects to fulfill users' expectations and an in-detail description of a Gaia-X-compatible software technology stack for the smart living domain. The concept will be applied to a smart kitchen use case.

Keywords: Active assisted living · Gaia-X · Smart home · Smart living

1 Introduction

The world is getting more and more connected and the smart home market has proven its relevance [2,3]. In Germany there is a market potential of 129 billion EUR, and the scenario is similar for other European countries. Therefore the smart home is a core element in a connected world. Among smart homes

Supported by German Federal Ministry for Economic Affairs and Climate Action (ForeSight, Team-X), European Union (Activage (IoT-01-2016 - Large Scale Pilots Programme)), Bavarian State Ministry of Health and Care (Dein Haus 4.0).

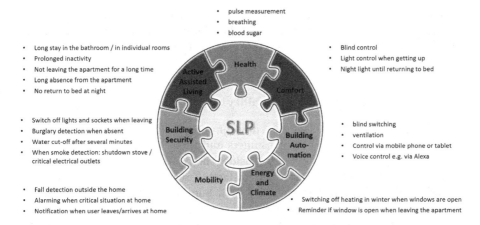

Fig. 1. Considered SLP use cases and relevant close-by domains that usually describe their own requirements.

and smart living several other domains are interwoven, e.g. energy management, health, and common smart home devices (see Fig. 1).

Future technological systems and their components need to be able to work together more closely to reuse solutions that have already been purchased and installed and to combine data for completely new applications. This requires open platforms that is capable of dynamically responding to changes. Once a system has been deployed, it adapts to different life situations and life phases. In order to be able to add dynamically, update or exchange offers from third-party providers, whether hardware or software, it is recommended to implement solutions on open semantic platforms. Such platforms need to consider and support privacy, security, and extendibility.

2   Challenges

According to the introduction several challenges arise in this heterogeneous field. The main challenges are related to the platform itself and the requirements regarding privacy and security.

2.1   Platform and Access-Management

Today's state-of-the-art situation is proprietary platform technologies that give one manufacturer power over all users. This lock-in effect is further coupled with opaque cloud architecture and a comprehensive consent form so that users can surrender their rights and data can be sold or used for marketing purposes accordingly. A solution for this is a user-individual and independent rights assignment system. This further enables both extensive context recognition and local execution so that the user's data is subject to a strict privacy and security code.

Due to the local nature of access management, the problem of decentralized trust also becomes omnipresent. As described by the European cloud initiative Gaia-X, this trust must be in place to allow local participants, detached from the cloud, to join a network.

2.2   Privacy, Security and Scalability

The EU regulates GDPR to set the rules for general data processing. The idea of GDPR is therefore to protect consumers and their data, so that a promising semantic platform approach needs to consider these privacy-related requirements [1,4]. Privacy cannot be achieved with a lack of security. It is especially challenging to ensure privacy and security in a home environment, where guests are often invited to the local network and many devices from different vendors are accessing these networks. Moreover, such networks are usually managed by nonprofessionals. For this user group, best-practice information security management strategies are hard to implement. In the end, there is a need for a solid identity and access management (IAM) routine that includes the local network and the cloud. Furthermore, such an IAM strategy should be user-centered and scalable to match the requirements for personal data, smart home data, smart building data, and smart city data. All these levels need their corresponding access rules. To enable the user as the owner of this data and the person in charge, a corresponding dashboard needs to be created and offered to everyone, that a user can track the frequency and the purpose of each data access event. Gaia-X as a decentralized cloud-based and service-oriented architecture seems to offer a promising approach for these requirements.

3   Approach

After the challenges have been described, we explain our approach in more detail. In this section, the subsections privacy and security, the platform components, the scalability, and the use case description are addressed.

3.1   Privacy and Security

The EU GDPR law [5] inevitably prescribes in Art. 25 GDPR Privacy by Design (PbD) with the wording "data protection by design and by default". For this purpose, suitable technical and organisational measures (TOM) must be taken both during the design phase and during subsequent data processing, such as strict data minimisation. In addition, data storage and use are subject to a general purpose limitation according to Art. 5 GDPR. A more precise interpretation of which TOMs must be taken in order to meet the requirements of the GDPR will only become apparent from future developments. Basically, PbD means that already in the design phase measures should be taken to minimize the risk of potential data loss and data misuse over the entire data life cycle – consisting of demand-oriented collection, processing, storage and deletion.

The four fundamental elements for sustainable compliance with data protection requirements are lawfulness of processing, risk management, TOMs and privacy friendly defaults (see Fig. 2). Ensuring the lawfulness of processing is the starting point. In the case of a SLPs, both a privacy policy and a declaration of consent as well as data processing agreements for third-party service providers are required as a legal basis. Besides the informed consent, the fulfillment of legal or contractual obligations and the associated legitimate interest may also be such a legal basis. Particularly in such a case, the purpose limitation and individual data erasure periods need to be observed. Due to the partly high protection requirements for the data to be processed, the data privacy aspects must be considered more carefully in the case of data transfer to third parties. According to Art. 35 GDPR, a data protection impact assessment must also be prepared by creating a structured risk analysis of the planned data processing based on the records of processing activities and examining the necessity and proportionality of the processing. Therefore, an accompanying risk management must be established by adapting the "IT-Grundschutz-Vorgehensmodell" (information technology (IT) basic protection procedure model) of the German Federal Office for Information Security (German abbreviation 'BSI') in the form of a data protection management system (DPMS). The organizational structure should be based on that of established information security management system (ISMS) such as ISIS12 [6] and VdS 10000 [7], so that the DPMS and the ISMS complement each other. Such a system can ensure the lawfulness, necessity as well as the fulfillment of data subjects' rights and data protection principles. According Art. 30 GDPR, a record of processing activities must also be kept in text form, containing the name and contact details of the responsible entity and, if applicable, the commissioner for data protection, the purposes of the processing, a description of the categories of data subjects and affected personals, categories of recipients, erasure periods and the categories of processing activities, as well as a description of the TOMs. This record, in turn, serves as the input parameter for risk management and represents the basis for fulfilling the documentation obligation, also with regard to the data subject's rights. It will also be able to transparently present the processing purposes. In order to comply with the data protection principles, aspects of data security, responsible data collection and processing, purpose limitation and transparency must be fulfilled. After identifying and assessing the risks, the objectives from a privacy perspective can be determined in addition to the data protection objectives in accordance with the Standard Data Protection Model (German abbreviation 'SDM') [8] of the committee of Independent German Federal and State Data Protection Supervisory Authorities – in abbreviated form German Data Protection Conference (German abbreviation 'DSK') – and addressed by specific countermeasures with suitable TOMs as part of a data protection concept. In this regard, it is possible to build on research conducted in the context of the telematics infrastructure, in which the data protection model was also applied, for example [9], the selection of TOMs in implementation is made in accordance with the "state of the art", whereby TeleTrust publishes a regularly updated guideline for this purpose [10].

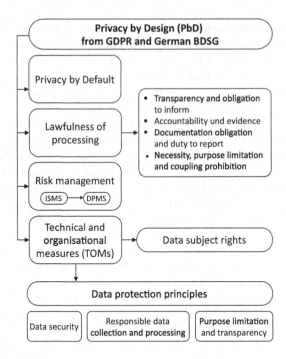

Fig. 2. Overview of the concept of PbD with the four basic elements for sustainable compliance and the data subjects' rights and data protection principles to be addressed.

For platform operators, there are some economical advantages: there is the reduction of risks in the area of IT security and the reduction of the effects of cyber attacks through distributed data storage and processing. In addition, data minimization would reduce compliance risks or at least make them calculable by reducing the complexity of data flows and strictly observing earmarking. This also applies to the overhead of complying with the prescribed documentation and evidence obligation. In addition to the preceding indirect advantages, a strict pursuit of PbD principles results in direct advantages for value creation and in competition with other platforms [11]. On the one hand, an adaptation of the architecture in responses to increasingly stringent legal requirements, if it is necessary to involve less effort and costs. An additional data abstraction, besides the desired semantic interoperability level, will also serve this goal. On the other hand, a feeling of insecurity has developed in a large portion of the population due to a loss of control and thus a more aware handling of personal data. By creating transparency in a central data protection control center and visualizing the generated data, both added value for the end user and trust in the provider can be strengthened and customer loyalty can be established [12,13], as is now also common with smartphone operating systems, for example. The current change in awareness could also lead to an increase in the willingness to pay, which in turn opens up new opportunities for monetization [12].

3.2   Platform Architecture

The ForeSight project follows the approach of a semantic platform that integrates solutions based on AI, interoperability, context-awareness, and smart home and smart building technologies into a flexible smart living platform [1,14]. ForeSight offers a flexible mechanism to handle requests, i.e. the requests are handled in the local network or, if necessary, will be offloaded to cloud services to increase performance. The core of ForeSight's architecture approach is the so-called thinking object (TO) – a device or group of devices that offers a specific service to the user or other TOs. There are three main modules, which are interacting to fulfill the system needs, here a service engineering module for service providers, e.g. a company of the housing industry, and an AI module to handle requests for computationally intensive operations, e.g. visually-based object identification, and an IoT module to connect to different smart home middleware systems, e.g. openHAB [15], which will connect to many different vendor-specific systems. In this work, ForeSight is connecting to openHAB to ensure interoperability on a syntactic level [14,20]. Besides, ForeSight will enable the usage of different smart home middleware systems like universAAL. To enrich this data with semantic information the Web of Things (WoT) approach is a key element.

IoT-Middleware. The openHAB is a smart home middleware, and it is possible to control different systems in one single graphical user interface (GUI) or app. The software uses specific components to offer an abstraction layer for all of its subsystems [14,16]. To connect to a third-party system like Homematic, it is necessary to create a binding. The binding coordinates the openHAB elements, here channels, items, and sitemaps to configure systems behavior. For automating event-driven tasks, there is the concept of rules, a script-like openHAB feature. There are several other smart living middleware systems or promising approaches apart from openHAB such as universAAL [17], HomeKit [18] and Matter [19].

Backend. In general, ForeSight tries to follow Gaia-X-compability (see Fig. 3) and explores several ways to achieve that, e.g. Sovereign Cloud Stack (SCS), Open Shift and Apache Kafka. Therefore we strive to identify challenges to gain Gaia-X-compatibility from a streaming platform to a common platform-as-a-service-provider.

Gaia-X offers users and providers of cloud services or cloud backends for on-premises applications the ability to negotiate securely and oligopolistically and to draft a user agreement without undesirable clauses. This offers the user the option to guarantee high scalability of the service without lock-in effects that would harm the end-users self-sovereign data usage (see Fig. 4).

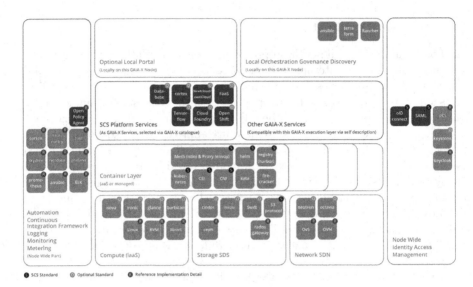

Fig. 3. Architectural overview of the SCS as used by Gaia-X with exemplary components [21]

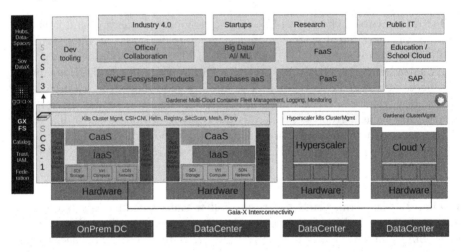

Fig. 4. Exemplary ecosystem overview of the SCS [21]

At the center of Gaia-X's decentralized trust model (see Fig. 5) is the user with his or her Self-Sovereign Identity (SSI). This identity is stored in a repository on a medium, such as a smartphone or an access card with built-in near-field communication (NFC). The user's SSI in turn consists of verifiable credentials issued by certified providers. This can be a citizens' office that verifies personal data from the identifier (ID) card. With the necessary credentials, users can then go to service providers and confirm their use with their SSI without having to disclose any specific data. The service provider thus trusts the verification by the provider of the verifiable credentials. However, it is important that there is a trust anchor that the service provider regards as trustworthy. This can be either the reputation of a company or a cryptographic check such as the eIDAS specifications.

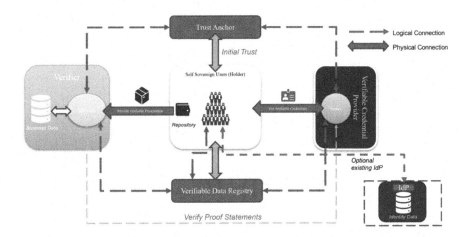

Fig. 5. Gaia-X-based concept of establishing trust in decentralized systems [22].

The Gaia-X Data Exchange Logging Service (see Fig. 6) allows traceability of transactions in the Gaia-X ecosystem without violating privacy and security requirements. The logging service is a stateless microservice that depend on other federation services, as it is directly coupled to a service [23]. The logging service is accessed by both providers and consumers to report changes to contracts. A token is used to validate if the contract exists and if the executing action is allowed. Likewise, it is possible for provider and consumer to talk to each other to retrieve accessible events. It is also foreseen that third-party providers are allowed to retrieve log messages. However, this must be approved by the service provider and provider/consumer. According to the specification, the stored log messages need to follow the W3C Linked Data Notification Protocol, which enables a very high level of interoperability, reusability, and decentralization of the notifications.

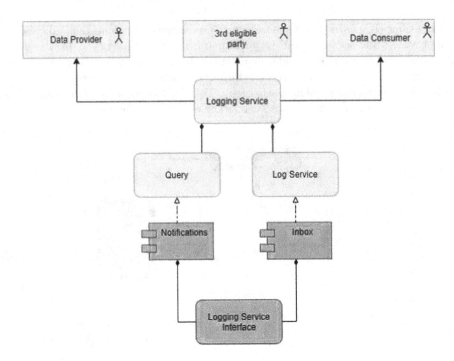

Fig. 6. Gaia-X logging mechanism to enable monitoring of service to service calls by granted users [24].

3.3 Scalability

To this end, architectures should be implemented either without cloud services, combined, or purely on the cloud side. According to this, Smart Living/Ambient Assisted Living (AAL) systems need to be structured so that they are able to combine and evaluate data both exclusively in the households and purely on the cloud side on a server. In addition, the merging and analysis of data should be distributed on both sides at the edge [25]. With this approach, users can decide where their data is collected and analyzed, giving a more secure feeling of data sovereignty. In solutions that are implemented together on client and server sides, the data is mirrored via a server-side gateway (digital twin), and thus services can be implemented on both sides. It should be possible to connect several platforms to implement cross-domain solutions. Since the user quickly loses control over who has access to the data with domain-overlapping applications and the merging of data, this leads to very high requirements for the protection of privacy and more complex requirements due to a large number of vulnerable accounts of IT security at each domain boundary. At the same time, systems are given the necessary flexibility for users to enable new business models for companies. For semantic platforms, there are completely new possibilities for recognizing specific situations and providing assistance in a variety of precisely tailored domains. Therefore, the installed sensors and actuators can be reused for other purposes and thus lead to cost savings [26] (see Fig. 1).

The merging of data across spatial boundaries can also generate additional added value such as building, facility, or quarter management, or enable optimized urban water and energy management and municipal traffic planning. Thus, the future platform systems should also enable scaling from the Smart Home, the building, the neighborhood (quarter), and finally to Smart City approaches [4]. Among the boundaries of these different spatial habitats and at all cloud connections, high-security requirements for data protection and IT security must be implemented so that the users would agree to the merging and extensive use of the data across living spaces. Different security levels have to be implemented at each of these borders, and the closer we get from the city to the apartment and the body space, the more stringent restrictions on privacy have to be implemented [26] (see Fig. 7).

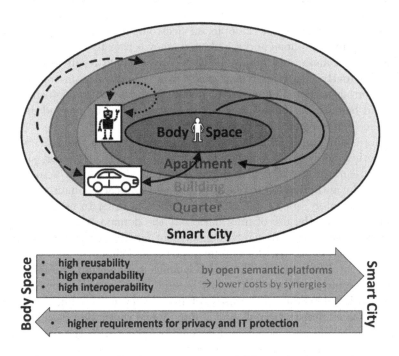

Fig. 7. High requirements for data protection and IT security between living spaces.

In order to meet this hurdle, software architectures need to build in such a way that they allow data to be merged across system boundaries to enable societal changes, the spread of diseases, and also linkage with other domains such as transport, energy, and water supply. This is to ensure optimal reusability, extensibility, and interoperability. The body space is to be understood as a mobile space that can move within the apartment. However, a user can also leave the apartment with his body space (close-to-the-body sensors and devices, e.g., blood glucose sensor for diabetes or his mobile phone) and enter other spaces, for example, other buildings, or be out in the city. He can also go to another mobile space like his car or public transport and move to other spaces. In this sense, a robot is also a mobile space that communicates with sensors and actuators in other spatial areas and with different users. There is also a sharp demarcation between the spatial areas from the point of view of privacy and IT protection. Otherwise, data across domain boundaries could not be appropriately delimited securely [25].

In the ForeSight project [27], these findings lead to the fact that a cross-domain use of data in the cloud must be subject to special attention both at the hierarchical levels in a spatial view and the merging and use of common data from different domains for aggregation. In many cases, it is no longer sufficient to consider the earmarked use required by the GDPR, because users can very rarely imagine what can be read from merged data. Suppose permission is given to use individual separated data, such as a motion detector to create movement profiles to switch on lights, for example, an electronic house access system to get easy access by mobile phone and a bed occupancy sensor to create a nice wake-up scenario with music and blinds. In that case, it could result in an analysis of who is currently in the apartment and what is happening in the bedroom, even the user has accepted only to use the data from the motion detector, access system, and bed sensor. Thus, any new application based on merged data need to allow the user to reconsider his consent.

Therefore, our approach is to make a direct request to the user, who can decide whether he wants to consent to this new purpose. However, since this information come from different domains and can also be used across spatial boundaries, the authorization for each spatial area and each domain must be set and stored separately in each piece of information in order to be able to define a control option for the use of information at the domain borders or a spatial area. For example, similar to rights management for apps on the mobile phone, which must be set explicitly, this can be implemented similarly for software services within the information. The rights management within the information determines the purpose for which it may be used. For example, movement data from the motion detector can be used for private services within the dwelling but not for the administration of the building, while ventilation data within the same dwelling would only be allowed for energy billing with the user's consent on a wider spatial scale. In return for consent to data use, a user could then be persuaded to agree to cheaper apartment rent. However, the decision-making authority must align with the user so that he can decide whether the information provided is of equal value, which conflicts with the most commonly used metaphor, "data is the new oil which possession can lead to great wealth. The profits generated from data resources belong to those who process the data, not those who originated it." [28] In contrast, with our approach, the decision-making authority should be returned to the user, where we believe that it will lead to a greater acceptance of the users.

3.4   Smart Kitchen Use Case

The Smart Kitchen use case contains a comprehensive assistance system in the area of nutrition, and includes a multitude of interconnected individual components, which continuously support the user over the course of a day. The ForeSight platform serves as a central data provision and exchange instrument based on semantically enriched information that can be accessed from anywhere. ForeSight-specific AI-driven services enable individually tailored assistance providing nutrition recommendations, nutrition preparation, household management, shopping support, and sporting activity recommendations, independent of the location and the devices used. Access to the individual services is based on authentication and the services themselves can be configured individually. This also means that the amount of personal data provided is entirely in line with the report-based privacy and security approaches presented. The more data a person provides about him or herself, the more efficient the individual services can be in providing support.

The core elements of the smart kitchen use case are the identification of food products based on image data, the digitization of purchasing data, intelligent household inventory management as well as two recommender systems, one for food selection and one for useful sports or recreation activities. The two systems intend to improve the client's health. In addition, the smart home system contains the integration of smart devices, e.g., a food processor, fridge, and pantry. The smart home also provides a small amount of context recognition, such as information about which person is in which room at runtime. Other necessary information comes from remote sources such as web services.

The household inventory management system combines food product identification and receipt digitization. After a purchase, the products are stored in the refrigerator or the pantry and automatically recorded by the camera. The shopping receipt is also photographed in a corresponding app and automatically digitized to a product list. The system then determines the new household inventory based on the last household inventory, the detected objects in the fridge and pantry, and the digitized receipt elements.

The food recommendation system provides the user with the ten most appropriate meals by taking into account the user's preferences. When proposing recipes, the availability of the ingredients and specific important details, such as weather conditions or the current side effects of team sport events, like the location or the organizing group, are taken into account. In addition to that, the system tries to reduce the overall waste by presenting a warning if a best consumption date is getting closer or indirectly by preferring recipes containing perishable products close to a best before date.

The following user story will describe one specific daily routine to increase the understanding of the smart kitchen use case. In the morning, the system detects that someone has entered the kitchen and determines who it is. Afterwards, a menu tailored to this person's preferences is recommended by the system based on his or her health related data, taste profile, food availability and established health goals. When preparing the meal, the person receives assistance from a smart kitchen such as the Cookit food processor. After having breakfast, the meal is evaluated by the scale of 5 stars. Additionally, the person can ask for a recipe recommendation for lunch. Out of the proposed recipes one is selected. A comparison of the ingredients of this recipe with the household inventory is performed and not available products are automatically added to the shopping list. When shopping, augmented reality (AR)-supported assistance in locating the products via a corresponding app is provided. Once at home, the household inventory is supplemented with the purchased products. After the products have been sorted, a comparison is made between the contents of the fridge, the contents of the pantry and the purchase receipt. After work, the person receives a recommendation for a sporting activity based on his preferences. When the activity is finished, the person evaluates it in the same way as he or she did before with the meal. The system can optimize the person's individual recommendations. In his or her absence, there is a maintenance message in the fridge and a corresponding dialog-supported data release for the installer or fridge owner. In the evening, the person displays the privacy report regarding the data generated by him and what services used what kind of data and how often they accessed this information. The interaction with the system takes place individually on the preferred channel, such as voice, mobile device or the computer. In addition to that, user's health related data are considered to improve recommendations or track the overall success of the health improvement process. Integrations of promising third-party approaches like the Gaia-X health projects [29], e.g. TEAM-X or HEALTH-X are currently considered to enable and improve health data management.

3.5 Implementation

In an intelligent kitchen environment, we demonstrate our current approach at the end of 2022. Due to the dynamic Gaia-X project progress and the decision that our efforts will be compatible with the Gaia-X ecosystem, we adapt to the current recommended technologies and semantically enriched information. To improve our development cycles dynamically, we are integrating users, external experts and experiences from other research projects continuously to carry out surveys and usability tests.

4 Methods

During the ForeSight project, usability tests, user surveys and expert interviews are happening. Out of a technical perspective, we are tracking Gaia-X-based recommendations and requirements. We strive to implement different technology approaches like Apache Kafka, OpenShift or SCS for the Backend and openHAB or universAAL as an IoT-module. After the implementation further tests regarding the technological robustness will be carried out.

To improve user-centered design and development, we carried out a survey to users of the universAAL system. Therefore the participants were used to smart home systems and everybody (n = 261) have been asked to rate the grade of importance (0 to 10 (highest importance)) and make an assumption how successfully this attribute is already implemented in the universAAL platform, so far (0 to 10 (very sophisticated)).

5 Results

Despite the complexity resulting from such vast integration of different domains, privacy protection is one of the most important aspects for humans and is extensively protected as a private retreat by Art. 13 GG of the German Constitutional Law. This has also been recognized by the Federal Ministry of Education and Research and demanded in the framework program "digital, safe, sovereign" through the focus on privacy, data protection, and self-determination of information. In order to find out the importance of privacy protection, the German deployment of the ACTIVAGE project [30] has been evaluated with 261 users, where the system evaluation is according to the importance of the system properties for the users, such as (1) privacy, (2) IT protection, (3) inconspicuousness, (4) maintainability, (5) costs, (6) interoperability, (7) reusability, (8) expandability and (9) accuracy [31]. It intended to find the importance of different quality characteristics the system has on the one side (in blue) and how the system has solved these characteristics (in orange) (see Fig. 8).

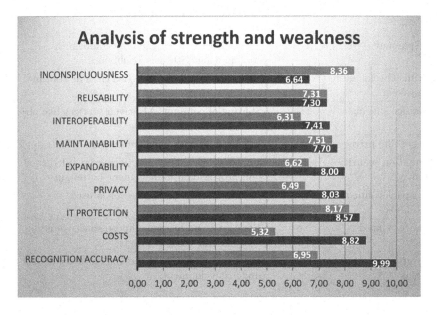

Fig. 8. Analysis of strengths and weaknesses of the ACTIVAGE project. (Color figure online)

This evaluation results showed that users consider a specific situation as the most important quality (9.99 out of 10). However, data protection and IT security (8.53/8.03) were observed as almost synonymous with the costs of the system (8.82). Therefore, these properties must be given special focus when implementing the system. This evaluation also showed that special priorities for further development had to be centered on privacy, security, costs, and accuracy. A reimplementation of the system by taking these four points into account had very positive effects for the acceptance due to the strict compliance with privacy by exclusively analysing data on the local controller, so that by the end of the project, the rejection rate of users in the apartments had been decreased from 11,7% to 5.3% [32]. Especially the younger residents with a higher technical understanding have very positive attitude towards such systems (0% rejection rate at the age of younger than 70).

The current technology stack and concept is evaluated based on reported requirements (see Table 1) of this paper.

Table 1. Fulfilled requirements regarding the here described technology stack.

Requirement	Fulfilled	Comment
GDPR-ready	Yes	Possible due to context-sensitivity (user-room-mapping at runtime)
Extendable	Yes	Service-based architecture offered by Gaia-X
Semantic layer	Yes	WoT-based approach to add semantic information
Transparency	Yes	Service-to-service logging mechanism in combination with user dashboard
Runtime checks and permissions	Yes	Users can grant access to services at runtime
AI-service sharing	Yes	Sharing of common AI-driven services like object identification are possible
User-specific privacy	Yes	IoT-module with cloud-mirrored IAM strategies
Information security system	Yes	Adapted ISMS best practices from ISIS12 for non professional management by tenants
Data space connecting capabilities	Yes	Eclipse Dataspace Connector is used
Distance-related privacy	No	Concept of body space, house space, building space is still work in progress
Integrations of other domains	No	Mobility, energy, health connectors are in still under development

After the user survey and the technical analysis we further investigate if an already running data acquisition project can benefit from this approach. The project DeinHaus 4.0 [33] focuses on equipping 100 households with smart home sensors and medical devices to enable elderly people to live as long as possible in their own house or apartment. In general the data has two origins: First the smart home sensors that are connected via Z-Wave and transmit the data via MQTT from the home to a database for later analysis; second are medical devices that transmit the data to the Withings cloud application from where it is mirrored to our data storage.

Privacy and security considerations are very important, because Dein-Haus 4.0 handles highly sensitive medical data. Thus, the ethics proposal of the project required a data protection impact assessment of multiple data sources. And again, the well established and easily adaptable architecture and designs like Gaia-X could make this less time-consuming. The approach in DeinHaus 4.0 was to pseudo-anonymized all data leaving the household [34].

Further, the processes of PbD of Gaia-X will reduce the error-prone organizational data protection first with a well-structured process and second with technical implementations like the logging mechanism. The standardized and decentralized backend architecture of Gaia-X will reduce the complexity to combine several data sources in a custom DeinHaus 4.0 app. The app has the goal of facilitating health competence by visualizing the gathered data and explaining the data in the corresponding videos. The explanation of the data might be included in openHAB. Summing up, several ideas of this approach can enrich the current DeinHaus 4.0 data handling procedures and add more flexibility and transparency.

6   Discussion

The analysis of the DeinHaus 4.0 project has shown that our approach is capable of creating beneficial effects for ongoing projects, because usually third-party clients can connect to Gaia-X-compatible data spaces and get in touch with people who explicitly want to share their data. Furthermore, it is possible to integrate specific parts of our approach for existing projects, for example, access existing AI-services or ask for interoperability and context-sensitivity to enrich a third party application.

The smart kitchen use case is suitable to demonstrate the successful implementation of the reported requirements, e.g. context sensitivity, Gaia-X-compatibility, and the user-centered development approach. It is an appropriate scenario to show specific properties of an advanced privacy and security system for the smart living domain.

The results of the survey show that privacy, security, and recognition accuracy are highly appreciated by the tenants. Therefore, context sensitivity and improved robustness will optimize recognition accuracy. Furthermore, our implementation efforts are focusing on the most important features due to the users' survey that will have positive effects on later system's acceptance. The latest interviews show that transparency regarding service-to-service communication is important for users and service developers and so the necessity for a transparency dashboard has been confirmed. The technological backbone needs to ensure that these service-to-service interactions are logged reliably.

Gaia-X compatible architectures are capable of meeting privacy and security-related requirements. Currently, the federated services are developed by the Gaia-X community. The quality and scope of these modules will determine the possibilities to use and extend these software components and therefore, there will be an impact regarding our necessary efforts to fulfill the mentioned requirements regarding the cloud backend, e.g., implementing our approach on a sovereign cloud stack. This approach creates a user-centric data ecosystem in which users have maximum control over how their data is used. Furthermore, Gaia-X is responsible for certifying suitable service providers and has very precise requirements for the infrastructure and software modules used, so that interoperability is largely guaranteed when changing providers.

7   Conclusion

In the context of the presented project, the approach for the presented cloud concept of Gaia-X and the model for privacy by design were exemplarily implemented. As shown, this demonstrator was evaluated by means of corresponding surveys and analyses, so that a derivation can be made for the following further developments and adaptations. The current approach will be further implemented and improved during the ForeSight, Team-X and other related projects. Simultaneously the possibility to adapt its strengths to other researching projects will be evaluated. Moreover we will analyse if and how our ideas can enrich live systems of the health, care and energy domain.

References

1. Bauer, J., et al.: ForeSight - platform approach for enabling AI-based services for smart living. In: Pagán, J., Mokhtari, M., Aloulou, H., Abdulrazak, B., Cabrera, M.F. (eds.) ICOST 2019. LNCS, vol. 11862, pp. 204–211. Springer, Cham (2019). https://doi.org/10.1007/978-3-030-32785-9_19
2. IDC Worldwide: Quarterly Smart Home Device Tracker (2019). https://www.idc.com/getdoc.jsp?containerId=prUS44971219. Accessed 18 Feb 2020
3. MarketsandMarkets: Smart Home Market by Product (Lighting Control, Security & Access Control, HVAC, Entertainment, Smart Speaker, Home Healthcare, Smart Kitchen, Home Appliances, and Smart Furniture), Software & Services, and Region - Global Forecast to 2024 (2019). https://www.marketsandmarkets.com/Market-Reports/smart-homes-and-assisted-living-advanced-technologie-and-global-market-121.html. Accessed 18 Feb 2020
4. Bauer, J., et al.: ForeSight approach to improve privacy and security in the smart living domain. Curr. Dir. Biomed. Eng. 7(2), 903–906 (2021). https://doi.org/10.1515/cdbme-2021-2230
5. European Parliament and Council: General Data Protection Regulation (GDPR). In: Schulz, M., Hennis-Plasschaert, J.A. (eds.) Official Journal European Union (OJ), L 119, pp. 1–88, Brussels (2016)
6. Moses, F., Kampmann, M., Struve, F., Wiesbeck, S.: Handbuch zur effizienten Gestaltung von Informationssicherheit für Kleine und Mittlere Organisationen (KMO). ISIS12. IT-Sicherheitscluster e.V., Regensburg (2020)

7. VdS Schadensverhütung GmbH: Informationssicherheitsmanagementsystem für kleine und mittlere Unternehmen (KMU). VdS 10000. Köln (2018)
8. UAG 'Standard-Datenschutzmodell' des AK Technik der Konferenz der unabhängigen Datenschutzbehörden des Bundes und der Länder: Das Standard-Datenschutzmodell, Version 2.0. In: Rost, M., Weichelt, R. (eds.) 98. Konferenz der unabhängigen Datenschutzbehörden des Bundes und der Länder. AK Technik der Konferenz der unabhängigen Datenschutzbehörden des Bundes und der Länder, Trier (2019)
9. Koch, M., Pawils, A., Weide, E.: Das Standard-Datenschutzmodell in der Telematikinfrastruktur. Datenschutz und Datensicherheit (DuD) **44**(2), 104–110 (2020). https://doi.org/10.1007/s11623-020-1232-1. ISSN 1614-0702
10. Bartels, K.U., Lawicki, T.: Guideline, State of the Art. IT Security Association Germany (TeleTrusT), Berlin (2021)
11. Kelber, U.: Datenschutz ist kein Hemmschuh für Innovationen. Gastbeitrag. In: Wettbewerb - Der Treiber für die Gigabit-Gesellschaft, VATM-Jahrbuch 2019, p. 76. Verband der Anbieter von Telekommunikations- und Mehrwertdiensten e.V. (VATM), Berlin (2019)
12. Thiel, C., Golle, D., Broy, M.: Privacy by Design als Win-win-Strategie für Wirtschaft und Verbraucher*innen. In: Höhne, N, Zimmer, K.B. (eds.) Digital Dialogue, Positionspapier. Zentrum Digitalisierung. Bayern, Garching (2019)
13. Pötzsch, S.: Privacy awareness: a means to solve the privacy paradox? In: Matyáš, V., Fischer-Hübner, S., Cvrček, D., Švenda, P. (eds.) Privacy and Identity 2008. IAICT, vol. 298, pp. 226–236. Springer, Heidelberg (2009). https://doi.org/10.1007/978-3-642-03315-5_17. ISBN 978-3-642-03314-8
14. Bauer, J., Hechtel, M., Konrad, C., et al.: ForeSight - AI-based smart living platform approach. Curr. Dir. Biomed. Eng. **6**(3), 384–387 (2020). https://doi.org/10.1515/cdbme-2020-3099
15. openHAB Homepage. openHAB Foundation e.V. https://www.openhab.org. Accessed 18 Feb 2022
16. openHAB: Concepts. openHAB Foundation e.V. https://www.openhab.org/docs/concepts/. Accessed 18 Feb 2022
17. universAAL IoT Homepage. Fraunhofer-Institut für Graphische Datenverarbeitung (IGD). https://www.universaal.info. Accessed 18 Feb 2022
18. Apple HomeKit Homepage. Apple Inc. https://developer.apple.com/homekit/. Accessed 18 Feb 2022
19. CSA Matter Homepage: The Foundation for Connected Things. Connectivity Standards Alliance. https://csa-iot.org/all-solutions/matter/. Accessed 18 Feb 2022
20. Bauer, J., et al.: ForeSight - an AI-driven smart living platform, approach to add access control to openHAB. In: Jmaiel, M., Mokhtari, M., Abdulrazak, B., Aloulou, H., Kallel, S. (eds.) ICOST 2020. LNCS, vol. 12157, pp. 432–440. Springer, Cham (2020). https://doi.org/10.1007/978-3-030-51517-1_40
21. Open Source Business Alliance e.V.: About, Technological Vision. https://scs.community/about/. Accessed 18 Feb 2022
22. GXFS.eu.: Gaia-X Federation Services for Identity & Trust, Architecture Overview (GXFS IDM.AO). eco - Association of the Internet Industry (eco - Verband der Internetwirtschaft e.V.), p. 24. https://www.gxfs.eu/specifications/. Accessed 18 Feb 2022
23. GXFS.eu.: Gaia-X Federation Services (GXFS) Toolbox. eco - Association of the Internet Industry (eco - Verband der Internetwirtschaft e.V.). https://www.gxfs.eu/set-of-services/. Accessed 21 Feb 2022

24. GXFS.eu.: Gaia-X Federation Service for Sovereign Data Exchange, Data Exchange Logging Service, Software Requirements Specification (GXFS SDE.DELS SRS). eco - Association of the Internet Industry (eco - Verband der Internetwirtschaft e.V.), p. 7. https://www.gxfs.eu/specifications/. Accessed 18 Feb 2022
25. International Electrotechnical Commission (IEC). Active assisted living (AAL) reference architecture and architecture model - Part 1: Reference architecture. IEC 63240-1 (2020)
26. Assisted Home Solutions GmbH (AHS) Homepage. https://assistedhome.de. Accessed 18 Feb 2022
27. Forschungsvereinigung Elektrotechnik beim ZVEI e.V.: ForeSight - Plattform für kontextsensitive, intelligente und vorausschauende Smart Living Services. https://foresight-plattform.de. Accessed 18 Feb 2022
28. Nolin, J.M.: Data as oil, infrastructure or asset? Three metaphors of data as economic value. J. Inf. Commun. Ethics Soc. **18**(1), 28–43 (2020). https://doi.org/10.1108/JICES-04-2019-0044
29. Bundesnetzagentur für Elektrizität, Gas, Telekommunikation, Post und Eisenbahnen: Gewinnerskizzen des Gaia-X Förderwettbewerbs. https://www.bundesnetzagentur.de/SharedDocs/Downloads/DE/Sachgebiete/Digitales/GAIAX/Gewinnerskizzen.pdf?-blob=publicationFile&v=6. Accessed 18 Feb 2022
30. European Commission, Horizont 2020: ACTivating InnoVative IoT smart living environments for AGEing well (ACTIVAGE). Community Research and Development Information Service (CORDIS). https://cordis.europa.eu/project/id/732679/de. Accessed 11 Feb 2022
31. Wichert, R., Tazari, S., Albrecht, A., Wichert, M.: The value of the user evaluation process in the European IoT large-scale pilot for smart living. In: Distributed, Ambient and Pervasive Interactions, 9th International Conference (DAPI), 23rd HCI International Conference (2021)
32. Wichert R., Albrecht A., Tazari S.: D9.6 DS7 WOQ final report. In: Work Package 9, LSP Deployment Sites Definition, Execution and Evaluation. Deliverable No. D9.6. ACTivating InnoVative IoT Smart Living Environments for AGEing Well (ACTIVAGE) (2020)
33. DeinHaus 4.0 - Länger Leben Zuhause Homepage. THD - Technische Hochschule Deggendorf. https://deinhaus4-0.de. Accessed 21 Feb 2022
34. Schiller, L., Wuehr, M., Poeschl, R., Dorner, W.: Concept for the large scale deployment of ambient assisted living systems. In: 2020 10th International Conference on Advanced Computer Information Technologies (ACIT), pp. 288–292 (2020). https://doi.org/10.1109/ACIT49673.2020.9208911

Improving Information Acquisition in City Tours via Simplified Virtual Scenes with Location-Based POIs

Yujia Cao[✉], Yiyi Zhang, and Tatsuo Nakajima

Department of Computer Science and Engineering, Waseda University, Tokyo, Japan
{mushishita,zhangyiyi,tatsuo}@dcl.cs.waseda.ac.jp

Abstract. Virtual city environments have been used widely in recent years as a substitute for physical travel in the form of mirrored worlds. This study aims to enhance user experience by providing better self-location and spatial knowledge acquisition during visits with simplified virtual city scenes and location-based floating information of points of interest (POIs). Our goal is to reduce redundant information disturbance by simplifying the overload of environmental information. Three experiments were conducted to explore the effect of simplifying overload redundant information and different information acquisition methods. We are hopeful that our study will assist users in better learning about specific areas in reality through their visits to virtual scenes and provide some reflection for further explorations of the demands of spatial knowledge and information acquisition during a city tour.

Keywords: Virtual reality · City exploration · Location-based service · Spatial learning

1 Introduction

Virtual city environments, which are generally considered a mirrored world, have been used widely in recent years. There are three main purposes for virtual city environment applications: arrangement purpose, social purpose, and travel purpose. For arrangement purposes [4, 8], a mirrored city in the virtual environment provides an ideal place for testing and modifying tasks having great impact. Communities, such as local government and researchers, could use such environments to collaborate on arrangement tasks such as city planning and threat assessment. For social purposes [2, 5], social information is combined into virtual city environments to build an immersive social media platform in 3D, where users pretend to visit specific points of interest (POIs) and gather comments or recommendations from their social acquaintances and friends without being there in person. For travel purposes [3], a virtual city environment provides convenience for users who are not able to physically visit and helps them explore the area with related information in an immersive city tour. This paper mainly focused on enhancing the user experience via virtual reality environment scenes for city travel.

© The Author(s), under exclusive license to Springer Nature Switzerland AG 2022
N. A. Streitz and S. Konomi (Eds.): HCII 2022, LNCS 13326, pp. 37–52, 2022.
https://doi.org/10.1007/978-3-031-05431-0_3

For the travel-oriented virtual city environment, the main research was devoted to mirrored scene reconstruction, the overlay of information of POIs based on actual locations and the design of engaging interaction to enhance the user experience. Spatial learning, which refers to the process through which users acquire a mental representation of the environment, plays an important role in navigating the scene, promoting the experience of exploration in an unfamiliar area. Studies [1, 7] have demonstrated the benefits of landmark cues that enhance spatial learning in a virtual environment; users can use landmarks as reference points in natural navigation of the environment [9]. However, sometimes a mirrored virtual world based on an actual location geographically displayed on a map may contain some redundant information; for example, similar buildings in blocks without regional characteristics would easily confuse users with their locations. Such extraneous information may lead the viewer to ignore it altogether; for example, unnecessary information may cause interference with navigation without leaving significant impressions of the are-as during the experience of the visit. Therefore, this study aimed to enhance user experience by providing better self-location and spatial knowledge acquisition during the visit. To reduce redundant information, help users enhance location awareness and acquire spatial knowledge from the surrounding major spots of the area, a simplified virtual city environment was proposed in this paper, where the majority of spots, such as landmarks, are kept as mirrored ones in reality, and unimportant in-formation without characteristics would be simplified as a few general models, while the area distribution would be kept for spatial learning. Users, like tourists who are not familiar with the city, and someone who is not able to visit in person can still experience and learn about the homologous destination area by visiting the simplified virtual city environment; with photo billboards and introductions provided in addition to models, users receive a general impression of the entire area without redundant in-formation disturbance. To help users better recognize their location in the area, we designed both an overview map with the corresponding user location viewer and location-based floating information of nearby POIs to help users acquire location-based information.

To study whether the simplified virtual city scenes and different methods of floating POI information can enhance user experience in specific city areas, two user study experiments were conducted. One is the comparison between the simplified virtual city environment and the mirrored virtual city environment of one specific area. In this case, Senso-ji, a typical tourism spot in Tokyo, was chosen as an example area. Another is the comparison between location-based floating information of POIs to show nearby spots and shops as an interest-based navigation guidance and an overview map viewer of navigation guidance. Through the user study experiments, we explored the effect of simplifying overload of redundant information and the demands of information acquisition methods during an immersive virtual city tour experience. A simplified environment and position-based information could contribute to an improvement in an interest-based virtual tour experience of users, while some limitations still exist. Furthermore, the provided information should be dynamic because the user navigation requests for POI recommendations may keep changing during the tour.

2 Related Work

2.1 Virtual City Environment and Mirrored Worlds

The development of virtual reality (VR) technology prompts the probability of build-ing mirrored worlds, which aim to provide an immersive experience for users leading them to pretend to be in an alternative reality. Various visual representations or textures are used to capture and visualize similar urban scenes as reality [10], such as getting textures from maps' street view [2] and using multiple cameras to build one model from different points of views. The key differentiator of our work is the provision of a simplified virtual city environment for users' exploration. We discuss challenges such as the choices of remaining mirrored areas and simplified areas in the virtual environment, the remaining area distribution and interactive capabilities during users' exploration.

2.2 Multiple Purposes for Virtual City Environment Applications

Generally, there are three main purposes for mirrored virtual city environment applica-tions: a) arrangement purpose; b) social purpose; and c) travel purpose.

Urban design is a typical example for applying virtual city environments in arrange-ment purposes [4, 8], as it affects people's experience of real-world cities, which need to be considered carefully. Developing the potential impact of urban design is important for urban planners and local governments. The virtual environment, which is a mirrored world as the reality, is an ideal platform to apply, test and modify the current design plan. Online application in a virtual city environment provides a feasible approach for collaboration between several departments and organizations as well, which is a great promotion for processing complicated affairs.

For social purposes, the virtual environment, as a mirrored world, provides a platform for combining social information with locations. For example, Geollery [2], which is an immersive social media platform in 3D, combines the social information in mainstream social media platforms into a virtual mirrored world with imaging from Google Street View. Users can walk in the virtual streets as mirrored ones in reality and obtain infor-mation from social acquaintances and friends, such as comments or recommendations of surrounding spots or shops. The improvement in immersion and location-based social information provision make it possible to be an ideal place for virtual family gathering and parties, as well as travel planning.

For travel purposes [3], a virtual city environment provides users with a place to explore and learn about the area with related information, especially for users who are not able to visit the area in reality. With a virtual traveling system, users are able to visit various destinations online without considering the arrangements for transportation and accommodations. It is a great chance for culture propagation, as more people would know a remote spot by visiting it in an online virtual environment. In this paper, the main research is designed for travel purposes, and is devoted to the overlay of POIs based on real locations with interesting interactions to enhance the user experience.

2.3 Spatial Learning in Virtual City Environment

Spatial navigation plays an important role in the virtual environment, which allows the active exploration of an unknown area without being lost through the use of spatial information and ensures efficient movement across well-known areas. Commonly used navigation supportive systems, such as Google Maps and Apple Maps, have benefits in daily navigation with efficient automatic orientation and route guidance. However, the spread of these navigation supportive systems may result in the ignoring of surrounding environment information [9] and decrease spatial knowledge acquisition. Users who are accustomed to such supportive systems gradually lose their navigation ability. Spatial learning, which refers to the process through which users acquire a mental representation of the environment, promotes users' exploration experience in an unfamiliar area.

Studies [1, 7] have shown the benefits of landmark cues that enhance spatial learning in a virtual environment and that users could use landmarks as reference points as a natural navigation skill. The interactive landmarks with related information pro-vide a natural method for users to learn about the current area. However, virtual city environments as mirrored worlds overlay landmarks that are visible to the users with redundant information making it difficult for users to be aware of the location of landmarks. To avoid such a situation, highlighting landmarks is necessary for users' spatial learning in their virtual city exploration. For example, providing virtual global landmarks [9] as references is a proper solution to improve users' spatial learning in mirrored virtual environments because the virtual global landmarks would be seen from any places without being overlayed by redundant information.

In this paper, we conduct a simplified virtual city environment, which is different from the mirrored worlds, to highlight the landmarks during users' exploration, im-proving their spatial learning. Our qualitative evaluation of comparative studies further reveals the strengths and weaknesses of a simplified virtual city environment and a mirrored virtual city environment.

3 System Overview

In this section, we present an overview of the simplified virtual city environment. Unity is used as a 3D platform, and the models are prefabs from the Unity accessory store. Google Maps is used as a reference for area distribution during construction.

3.1 Distribution of Simplified Virtual City Environment

Senso-ji is chosen as an example area for a simplified virtual city environment, which is a famous templet in Tokyo. Typical spots, such as Senso-ji, Kaminari Mon, and Hozou Mon, are constructed as mirrored spots in reality, as shown in Fig. 1 (Left), while other regions are simplified, such as shopping areas, as shown in Fig. 1 (Right). Related information is attached in addition to the typical spots, as well as introductions to several specificities.

Fig. 1. (Left) Comparison between: (a) real photograph of Kaminari Mon, (b) real photograph of Hozou Mon, (c) mirrored model of Kaminari Mon, (d) mirrored model of Hozou Mon, and (Right) Comparison between: (a) real photograph of shopping street, (b) simplified model of shopping street.

3.2 Location-Based POI Guidance

Maps are provided for better exploration experience, with a mini map, an integral map, and a local map, as shown in Fig. 2 (Top). The integral map shows the distribution of the whole area, providing a general impression of this area to users. The sur-rounding POIs are shown on the mini map and the local map for users to design their own routes for exploration based on their interests, as shown in Fig. 2 (Bottom). Users are allowed to teleport to the position they want to visit by simply clicking the map.

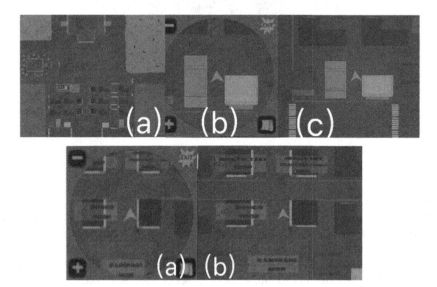

Fig. 2. (Top) Overview of maps: (a) integral map, (b) minimap, (c) local map, and (Bottom) Overview of POIs located on the maps: (a) POIs on the minimap, (b) POIs on the local map.

3.3 Virtual Representation of Reality

To help users gather information to learn about the same area in reality, we designed image billboards as a virtual representation of reality and separated them among the whole area to show users the reality information, as shown in Fig. 3. All photos are taken by the Canon camera in Senso-ji.

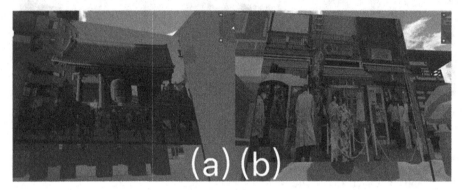

Fig. 3. Overview of image billboards located beside: (a) Kaminari Mon and (b) Meat cutlet shop.

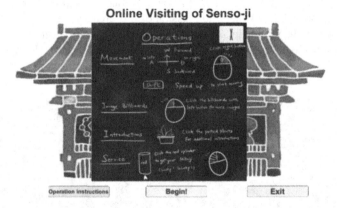

Fig. 4. Overview of operation instruction page.

3.4 Interactive Capabilities

Several interactive capabilities are available in this simplified virtual city environment.

Operation instruction. In the opening page of this system, an operation is provided for users to learn about the operation methods and interactive experiences inside the scene, as shown in Fig. 4.

Potted plants. Inside the scene, potted plants are placed beside the models, which could interact to show the related information of specificities, as shown in Fig. 5.

Online omikuji. At the omikuji corner, there is an interactive omikuji box, as shown in Fig. 6 (Left) for users to experience an online omikuji game, which is a typical event in Senso-ji. Users could test their fortune with seven different results: a) best fortune; b) regular fortune; c) medium fortune; d) a little fortune; e) fortune but finally; e) a little fortune but finally; and f) bad fortune, as shown in Fig. 6 (Right). We conduct this service to help users connect virtual city exploration with reality exploration to improve the attractiveness of their exploration in simplified virtual city scenes.

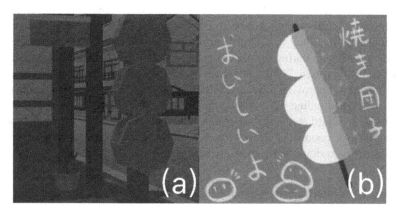

Fig. 5. Overview of (a) potted plants, (b) related information introduction.

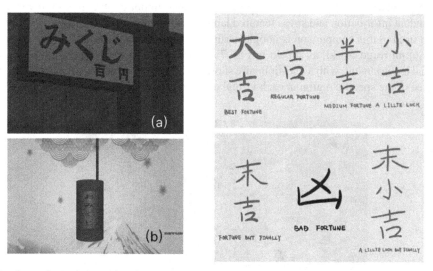

Fig. 6. (Left) Overview of (a) interactive item for omikuji, (b) online omikuji event, and (Right) Overview of various fortune results.

4   User Study

Two studies are conducted to investigate the environment and navigation influences during virtual city tours. In the first study, we wanted to directly compare the improvement in spatial learning using a simplified virtual environment instead of a mirrored virtual environment. We reasoned that the simplified virtual environment might be clearer and easier for users to learn about the area distribution and surrounding POIs. In the second study, two navigation approaches are compared, location-based POI guidance and simple guidance according to minimap information, to investigate a proper approach to provide information during virtual city tours in simplified virtual environments. We suspect that location-based POI guidance would help users design their touring routes based on interests, improving their virtual tour experience. These two comparison studies were performed online by watching demos since COVID-19 has spread recently. Furthermore, in a third study, the simplified virtual city tour system was implemented by participants for comments and advice. We believe these comments and advice will help us improve the simplified virtual city tour system in the future.

4.1   Study 1: Comparing the Virtual City Environment

Study Design. Our study has two environmental variables: the simplified virtual city environment and the mirrored virtual city environment. The simplified virtual city environment retains the main spots as mirrored regions and simplifies other regions to reduce redundant information and stress featured landmarks. The mirrored virtual city environment used in this comparison is google earth, which uses map information in reality to build a mirrored world, as shown in Fig. 7. A virtual tour demo is prepared for each virtual environment, with a questionnaire shown in Table 1 to investigate the exploration degree of the specific region in each virtual environment.

Fig. 7. Overview of mirrored virtual environment (Senso-ji).

Table 1. Questionnaire of exploration degree in virtual environment

Q1. Do you remember the name of the temple?
Q2. Do you remember what is been written in gate board?
Q3. Do you remember the mikuji corner?
Q4. What is your idea about getting your own mikuji online? (Be interested or not)
Q5. Please write down names of spots or specialties you remember

Depending on our concept and study design, we propose the following hypothesis:

H1: We expect that the simplified virtual city environment could help users focus on landmarks and have a better impression of area distribution.

H2: We expect that the simplified virtual city environment shows information more clearly, improving users' visiting experience.

Implementation. To implement the virtual city tour demo, senso-ji, a famous spot in Tokyo, is chosen as an example region for visiting. Image billboards and interactive icons are located near main spots in the simplified virtual city environment to help users learn more about this region and build connections between virtual and reality scenes. For better comparison, the same interactive icons are attached to Google Earth, the mirrored virtual city environment, as shown in Fig. 8, and two virtual tour demos are within similar time periods.

Fig. 8. Overview of POI locations in: (a) a simplified virtual environment and (b) a mirrored virtual environment.

Participants. We invited 15 volunteer participants for each environmental variable (30 in total). for the mirrored virtual city environment, 15 participants are invited (10 males and 5 females), aged between 20 and 30 years (average age = 24.3). We asked the participants to describe their experience in virtual tours and acquire POI Information during a tour, and 8 had virtual tour experience by using virtual maps or travel assistant apps. Recommendation systems (8 participants) and maps (6 participants) are their major approaches for POI information acquisition. generally, 15 participants were not familiar with Senso-Ji, including 10 participants who had not visited Senso-Ji and 6 participants who visited once without leaving many memories. For the simplified virtual city environment, 15 participants were invited (9 males and 6 females), aged between 20 and 30 years (average age = 24.5). We asked the participants to describe their experience in virtual tours and acquire POI information during a tour, and 7 had virtual tour experience by using virtual maps or travel assistant apps. Recommendation systems (8 participants), specific searches (5 participants), and maps (6 participants) are their major approaches for POI information acquisition. Generally, 15 participants were not familiar with Senso-Ji, including 13 participants who had not visited Senso-Ji and 2 participants who visited once without leaving many memories.

Results. The questionnaires included several questions to test the exploration degree for each environmental variable. accuracy is calculated for each question, as shown in Table 2. For the mirrored virtual environment, the accuracy for Q1 is 26.7% (4/15), the accuracy for Q2 is 33.3% (5/15), and the accuracy for Q3 is 53.3% (8/15). The aver-age number of main spots and specialties remembered after virtual tour is 0.67 per person (10 in total). For the simplified virtual environment, the accuracy for Q1 is 33.3% (5/15), the accuracy for Q2 is 86.7% (13/15), and the accuracy for Q3 is 80.0% (12/15). The average number of main spots and specialties remembered after the virtual tour is 1.4 per person (21 in total). For the online Mikuji event, 26.7% (8/30) of the participants showed their interest in getting their own Omikuji online, while 26.7% (8/30) of the participants showed no interest in this event. A total of 46.7% of participants (14/30) showed no preference for this event.

Table 2. The results for exploration degree questions in the questionnaire

Accuracy	Q1	Q2	Q3	Average number of main spots and specialties remembered
Mirrored virtual environment	26.7%	33.3%	53.3%	0.67
Simplified virtual environment	33.3%	86.7%	80.0%	1.4

Discussion. Based on our study results, the simplified virtual city environment shows a better exploration degree for participants within a similar time period (19.8% higher accuracy in Q1, 61.6% higher accuracy in q2, and 33.4% higher accuracy in Q3). Therefore, we can accept Hypothesis *H1*.

Most participants in the simplified virtual environment could name or describe at least 1 or 2 main spots and specialties, while most participants in the mirrored virtual environment stated that they forgot the details of the main spots and specialties, as well as their names (52.1% higher on average, the number of main spots and specialities remembered after the virtual tour). Therefore, we can accept Hypothesis *H2*.

Participants stated that they would use a virtual tour system for traveling assistants, for example, checking for information correctness, searching for routes in advance or visiting places that are difficult to visit in reality. However, mainstream traveling assistant applications and digital maps may contain redundant information, which confuses users remembering main spots in the region and prevents them from efficient spatial learning. Under such a situation, the simplified virtual tour system is more suitable for users who are not familiar with their destination region to learn about the general information of that region, such as distribution and surrounding POIs, and help their route planning efficiently during the tour.

An online omikuji event is a service that connects a virtual city environment and a reality city, which helps users become familiar with the reality event located inside the region. Since some participants showed their interest in this service, its gamification may improve users' experiences during visits.

4.2 Study 2: Comparing Navigation Approaches

Study Design. Our study has two navigation variables: location-based poi guidance and minimap information guidance. The simplified virtual city environment is used in this study. The location-based POI guidance approach provides floating information about surrounding POIs, which allows users to choose their next destination according to their interests. The click-to-teleport function is applied to the floating information map as a convenient and direct method for user movement in city tours. A virtual tour demo is prepared for each navigation approach, with a questionnaire shown in Table 3 to investigate the exploration experience of the specific region with each navigation approach.

Depending on our concept and study design, we propose the following hypothesis:

H3: We expect that location-based POI guidance provides clearer regional information during tours, which would be preferred by more users.

H4: We expect that location-based POI guidance provides more suitable route planning for users based on interests.

Table 3. User experience evaluation on different guidance approach

Q1. Which mode do you prefer for acquiring location-based Point-of-interests information?
Q2. Which one do you think is more interesting?
Q3. Which one do you think is more attractive?
Q4. Which one do you think is more helpful to learn about the surrounding POIs while visiting?
Q5. Which one do you think is clearer to show the general area distribution?

Implementation. To implement the navigation guidance demo, the simplified virtual city tour system is used as an example for virtual city tours. The location-based POI guidance approach allows users to click on the POIs they prefer to visit and teleport to their destination. The minimap information guidance provides the minimap and general map of this region, as shown in Fig. 9, so users can select their destination according to the area distribution. For better comparison, similar visiting routes are used for both navigation approaches.

Participants. We invited 19 participants (8 males, 11 females) aged between 20 and 56 years (average age = 27.4). We asked the participants to describe their experience in virtual tours and acquire POI information during a tour, and 7 had virtual tour experiences by using virtual maps. Recommendation systems (11 participants) and maps (11 participants) are their major approaches for POI information acquisition. Nine participants had not visited Senso-ji, while 10 participants had visited.

Fig. 9. Overview of minimap information guidance, includes: (a) minimap and (b) integral map

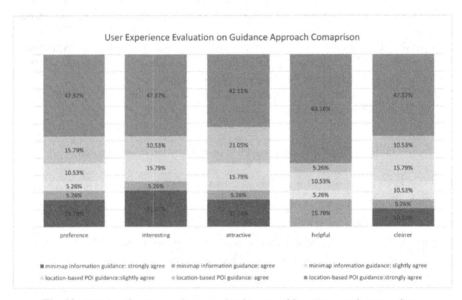

Fig. 10. Results of user experience evaluation on guidance approach comparison.

Results. The questionnaire included several questions, and investigated two users' preferences on different guidance approaches. As shown in Fig. 10, over 70% of participants (14/19) showed their preference for location-based POI guidance as a navigation approach during their virtual tour. None of the participants reported that they strongly agreed that the minimap information guidance approach is more helpful, while an extremely large number of participants (12/19) strongly agreed that location-based POI guidance is more helpful during tour.

Discussion. Based on our study results, location-based POI guidance is ahead in all ratings, especially in helpful aspects, where over 60% of participants strongly agreed that location-based POI guidance is more helpful during their tour. The majority of the participants preferred to use location-based POI guidance during virtual tours and said that this guidance approach is interesting and attractive. Therefore, Hypothesis *H3* is accepted.

Over 70% of participants agreed that location-based POI guidance is clearer to show surrounding information, which is more helpful to plan their routes based on interests and learn about the region as well. Therefore, our Hypothesis *H4* is accepted.

Participants stated that they would use a virtual tour system for travel planning, for example, learning about the region in advance for major spots and route planning. Some participants preferred to use a virtual tour system to visit some regions to decrease their cost in money and time and to learn about the introduction to the region. Under such situations, the location-based POI guidance approach is more suitable for users to learn about the surrounding POIs according to their locations and design routes step by step. They may have the chance to visit famous spots without actually being there, which would reduce the cost of transportation and accommodations.

4.3   Study 3: User Experience of a Simplified Virtual City Environment System

Study Design. To investigate the performance of the simplified virtual city tour system, we conducted a study of users trying virtual city tours with a simplified system to evaluate their virtual tour experience. Participants are allowed to explore the simplified virtual city in freedom for approximately 10 minutes and respond to the questionnaire shown in Table 4 about the user experience of this simplified system. Comments and advice are expected from users for future improvement.

Participants. An executable file is exported from Unity and is uploaded to the cloud platform for remote use by participants. An operation instruction is attached on the opening page with an interactive button to explain the common functions and operation methods in this simplified virtual city system. A 10-min exploration in freedom is required before answering a questionnaire to show users' comments and advice in this simplified virtual city tour system.

Implementation. Five volunteer participants are invited (4 males), aged between 23 and 25 years (average years = 24.0), to experience the practical use of the simplified virtual tour system. We asked the participants to describe their experience in virtual tours and ac-quire POI information during a tour, and 2 had virtual tour experience by using virtu-al maps and wandering virtual games. Recommendation systems (3 participants) and specific searches (2 participants) are their primary approaches to POI information acquisition. One participant had not visited Senso-ji, while 3 participants had visited.

Table 4. User experience evaluation of the simplified virtual city tour system

Q1. Do you think this simplified virtual scene with location-based POIs is supportive?
Q2. Do you think this simplified virtual scene with location-based POIs is easy to use?
Q3. Do you think this simplified virtual scene with location-based POIs is efficient?
Q4. Do you think this simplified virtual scene with location-based POIs is clear
Q5. Do you feel exciting when exploring in simplified virtual scene with location-based POIs?
Q6. Do you feel interesting when exploring in simplified virtual scene with location-based POIs?
Q7. Do you think this simplified virtual scene with location-based POIs is inventive?
Q8. Do you think this simplified virtual scene with location-based POIs is leading edge?
Q9. Do you think this kind of virtual tour would be helpful when you visit the same area in the reality?
Q10. Do you think this simplified virtual scene with location-based POI guidance could help you to plan exploration route based on your interests preference and need?

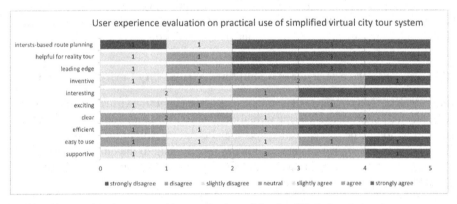

Fig. 11. Results of user experience evaluation of the simplified virtual city tour system.

Results. The questionnaire includes several questions to investigate user experience during their exploration in the simplified virtual city tour system. As shown in Fig. 11, all participants agreed that this simplified virtual tour system is supportive and is helpful for their reality tour. Leading edge and interesting aspects were also agreed upon by all participants. However, participants were shown to have some doubts about the ease of use and clarity of the tour system.

Discussion. Based on our study results, guidance clarity and ease of use are the main problems that affect the user experience of this simplified virtual tour system. Some comments from participants are as follows: *'The guidance to interactive items inside the system is not clear, and I need spend some time to find them...' (P3). 'Movement operations are quite different from other systems, which need to hold the right button* *to activate the movement functions. Users who skip the operation instructions on the opening page may not have chance to check for operations inside the system...' (P1). 'Information insides the scene is not enough for me to explore and design a route. I can only get introductions for specialties when exploring on the main shopping street. I hope more information would be attached for other parts of the scene...' (P4).* According to those comments, attention guidance for interactive items inside the scene is a major problem that needs to be addressed to improve user experience. Since some simple approaches to guide users' attention, for example, arrow or sur-rounding highlights, are proven to decrease immersion during the tour, immersion preserving attention guidance [6] should be considered in this simplified system. Information on other parts of the region should be added to future work for a better exploration experience.

5   General Discussion

According to our studies, the simplified virtual city environment showed better spatial learning than the mirrored virtual city environment, especially in remembering main spots and typical specialties. The simplified area stresses the main spots and reduces redundant information disturbance; participants were able to pay more attention to the mirrored spots remaining inside the scene. Participants showed their interest in exploring simplified virtual city tour systems for travel assistance and route planning with location-based POI guidance. The floating POI information around their location could help them choose their next destination based on their interests. According to the comments by participants, they preferred to use such a simplified virtual city system for route planning and leaning about the region in advance. Some participants preferred to visit some spots to reduce their costs on transportation and accommodations and acquire relevant information about the spots if they had difficulties visiting in reality.

However, some limitations still exist. The number and gender of participants in Study 3 may have some influence on the final results. The attention guidance to interactive items inside the scene also needs to be improved. Attaching icons of interactive items to maps may be a great idea to show users the distribution of surrounding interactive items. The immersion-preserving attention guidance method is also needed to guide users' attention to interactive items when they are not referring to maps. The information inside the scene is mainly located on the main street inside the scene, which may affect users if they want to explore other parts of the region.

6   Conclusion

In this paper, we propose a simplified virtual city tour system with location-based POI guidance to improve user experience in virtual city tours. We found that a simplified virtual environment could improve users' spatial learning by stressing landmarks, and location-based POI guidance could help users plan their route based on interests. We expected that this simplified virtual city tour system can be improved in future work, for example, a more convenient operation instruction access while virtual tours and more attention guidance to interactive items. We hope to find more participants of different genders for user experience as well.

References

1. Credé, S., Thrash, T., Hölscher, C., Fabrikant, S.I.: The advantage of globally visible landmarks for spatial learning. J. Environ. Psychol. **67**, 101369 (2020)
2. Du, R., Li, D., Varshney, A.: Geollery: a mixed reality social media platform. In Proceedings of the 2019 CHI Conference on Human Factors in Computing Systems (CHI 2019). Paper 685, pp. 1–13. (2019). https://doi.org/10.1145/3290605.3300915
3. Feng, J., Feng, X., Liu, X., Peng, J.: The virtual wandering system of Han Chang'an city based on information recommendation. In: Proceedings of the Symposium on VR Culture and Heritage - Volume 2 (VRCAI 2016), pp.75–78 (2016). https://doi.org/10.1145/3014027.3014028
4. Ingram, R., Benford, S., Bowers, J.: Building virtual cities: applying urban planning principles to the design of virtual environments. In: Proceedings of the ACM Symposium on Virtual Reality Software and Technology (VRST 1996), pp. 83–91 (1996). https://doi.org/10.1145/3304181.3304199
5. Kukka, H., Pakanen, M., Badri, M., Ojala, T.: Immersive street-level social media in the 3D virtual city: anticipated user experience and conceptual development. In: Proceedings of the 2017 ACM Conference on Computer Supported Cooperative Work and Social Computing (CSCW 2017), pp. 2422–2435 (2017). https://doi.org/10.1145/2998181.2998341
6. Lange, D., Stratmann, T.C., Gruenefeld, U., Boll, S.: HiveFive: immersion preserving attention guidance in virtual reality. In: Proceedings of the 2020 CHI Conference on Human Factors in Computing Systems, pp. 1–13. (2020). https://doi.org/10.1145/3313831.3376803
7. Lu, J., Wunderlich, A., Singh, A.K., Gramann, K., Lin., C-T.: Investigating the impact of landmarks on spatial learning during active navigation. In: 2019 Neuroscience Meeting Planner Society for Neuroscience, Washington, DC (2019)
8. Polys, N.F., Singh, A., Sforza, P.: A novel level-of-detail technique for virtual city environments. In: Proceedings of the 21st International Conference on Web3D Technology (Web3D 2016), pp. 183–184. (2016). https://doi.org/10.1145/2945292.2945322
9. Singh, A.K., Liu, J., Cortes, C.A.T., Lin, C-T.: Virtual global landmark: an augmented reality technique to improve spatial navigation learning. In: Extended Abstracts of the 2021 CHI Conference on Human Factors in Computing Systems (CHI EA 2021). Article 276, pp. 1–6 (2021). https://doi.org/10.1145/3411763.3451634
10. Zheng, J.Y., Zhou, Y., Shi, M.: Scanning and rendering scene tunnels for virtual city traversing. In: Proceedings of the ACM symposium on Virtual reality software and technology (VRST 2004), pp. 106–113 (2004). https://doi.org/10.1145/1077534.1077556

Mapless Indoor Navigation Based on Landmarks

Lulu Gao[1]([✉]) and Shin'ichi Konomi[2]

[1] Graduate School of Information Science and Electrical Engineering, Kyushu University, 744, Motooka, Nishi-ku 819-0395, Fukuoka, Japan
gao.lulu.648@s.kyushu-u.ac.jp
[2] Faculty of Arts and Science, Kyushu University, 744, Motooka, Nishi-ku 819-0395, Fukuoka, Japan

Abstract. With the increasing user demands for the ubiquitous availability of location-based services, and the acknowledgement of their substantial business prospects, researchers have extensively studied indoor navigation techniques that do not require extra infrastructures to provide accurate indoor navigation. Recently, Landmark, which is available in many scenarios without additional deployment cost, are integrated in plenty of works. However, existing feature extraction and selection methods to detect landmark involve manual feature engineering, which is time-consuming, laborious, and prone to error and additional Wi-Fi fingerprint is used to identify landmark. Therefore, this paper proposes an indoor navigation based on landmark, which is recognized by an unsupervised feature learning method to automatically extracts and selects the features, without extra deployment cost. The proposed method jointly trains denoising autoencoder implemented by convolutional neural network and LSTM neural networks produces a compact feature representation of the data to identify landmark. Besides, the relative distance between different landmarks is estimated by PDR to generate the indoor landmark map with the help of multidimensional scaling technique. The effectiveness of the proposed framework is verified through the experiments in the context of practical buildings. Experimental results show that the proposed method, which learns useful features automatically outperforms conventional classifiers that require the hand-engineering of features. We also show that the proposed method can build mostly correct indoor maps and provides efficient directions to users without extra infrastructure.

Keywords: Indoor navigation · Landmark · Autoencoder · Mobile sensors

1 Introduction

Navigation problems about how to reach the destination from the origin is often encountered in human daily life and work, especially in unfamiliar area. Depending on the target environment, it can be divided into outdoor navigation and indoor navigation. Global navigation satellite system (GNSS), such as Global Positioning System (GPS), Galileo Satellite Navigation (Galileo), BeiDou Navigation Satellite System (BDS) and other satellite systems can navigate us precisely and reliably in an outdoor open environment, which are widely exploited and broadly applied in our everyday lives [1]. Although outdoor navigation is well satisfied, indoor navigation is more challenging. Since GNSS does not perform well in urban canyons, underground environments, and indoor environments in which we spend most of the time and tend to lose position more easily because of the lack of a unified infrastructure and the weak signal strength of satellites due to the absence of line of sight, the attenuation of satellite signals as they cross through physical objects, especially walls, and noise interference, resulting in inaccurate navigation of us or devices [2, 3]. What's more, indoor navigation has played an important role in our routine, especially in a large building like a shopping mall or underground parking lot. Thus, in an effort to find an alternative technique that can provide indoor navigation service with high precision, a variety of approaches has been extensively researched in decades.

Many indoor navigation systems have been researched with the joint effort of researcher and engineer in the past few decades in recent years. For different scenarios, researchers investigate lots of technologies and techniques to build indoor navigation systems: radio frequency identification (RFID), Bluetooth, Zigbee, ultra-wideband (UWB), wireless local area network (WLAN), infrared ray (IR), ultrasound. Among these radio frequency-based methods, Wi-Fi is the most commonly used and extensively applied for indoor navigation systems using received signal strength and channel state information as the Wi-Fi settings are considered broadly distributed. While the Wi-Fi signals would not be accessed when the user is out of Wi-Fi coverage range, which are common in developing country due to poor information and communications technology (ICT) infrastructure [4], or the radio coverage have to be blocked sometimes. Therefore, the pre-deployment and special hardware hinder the wide adoption and practical application.

Meanwhile, mobile devices of all kinds are rapidly involving, and our daily life is significantly changed. The range of application, including indoor navigation, are efficiently growing with more and more advanced built-in sensors equipped. With the help of portable devices people usually carry around, pedestrian dead reckoning (PDR) based on built-in inertial sensors which are self-contained has been obtaining growing attention in different scenarios [6]. Nevertheless, PDR is prone to suffer from the accumulated error because of sensor drift, resulting in accuracy degradation. Combination it with Wi-Fi fingerprinting which are extensively adopted, Bluetooth, and some other localization methods to calibrate the trajectory are common remedies. In addition, a recent trend is to remove the requirements of infrastructure support.

Spatial context, such as maps and landmarks, which is available in many scenarios, can be another choice to calibrate the indoor navigation system based on PDR without additional deployment cost. Fusing spatial information which is easy to understand for successful wayfinding is an effective way to achieve indoor navigation with little or mostly with no need for complementary infrastructure [6]. As an pieces of important spatial information, landmark is a salient point in sensor readings when people pass the location, which can be detected by built-in sensors. There are many different proposed methods that integrated landmark in indoor navigation and positioning systems, in which landmark detection and matching are both involved to realize indoor navigation in works [7–9]. Currently, the manual designed features and threshold are extracted to detect different landmarks [10]. When there are multiple detected landmarks close, extra Wi-Fi fingerprints are widely adopted to identify [11].

In this paper, to reduce additional infrastructures demand in indoor navigation systems, we propose *mapless indoor navigation system based on landmark identification.* The motivation of this work is to provide navigation service to people with a typical smartphone equipped coming to a new area and without recourse to any additional deployment and spatial information in advance. The proposed methods can be divided into two phases: offline training and online navigating. In the former phase, dataset of mobile devices built-in sensors is collected to automatically extract features and train landmark recognition model after prepossessed, including filtering and segmentalizing, and construct the semantic map with the help of detected landmarks and PDR. In the later phase, realizing online navigation based on the location which be estimated with PDR and refined with landmark detected in sensor reading stream. The major contribution of this work consists of two aspects: the first aspect involves a novel extra infrastructure-free landmark-based indoor navigation systems without radio coverage to characterize landmarks without detailed floorplan ahead, which reduces the deployment without extra cost requirements and the cognitive load of people with a human-friendly navigation experience compared with physical coordinates to locate and navigate users. For the second part, a custom deep learning model is designed and implemented for landmark identification with the ability to automatically extract features through the raw signals to constructure indoor landmark map.

The remainder of this paper is organized as follows. Related work about indoor navigation, especially the landmark-based navigation is reviewed in Sect. 2. Section 3 introduce the theoretical methodology and the architecture of proposed mapless landmark-based indoor navigation system. Section 4 present the experimental methodology and results in datasets collected. Finally, conclusion and future work are presented in Sect. 5.

2 Related Work

There are three different modes to display the guidance in a navigation system: geographical coordinates, symbolic modes, and hybrid information [12]. Geographical coordinate is a detailed representation of location, a machine-friendly way, which is widely applied to navigation system in many professional devices. For indoor navigation, since the GNSS signal reception is degraded accuracy of the coordinates will be affected, therefore, representation via the earth coordinate system will be changed to a relative coordinate system, which is relative to a pre-defined location in the indoor environment. Symbolic modes denote the environment with the logical relationship of different area or location, which can generally navigate people both indoors and outdoors in a human-friendly way. These two representations are combined in the hybrid mode navigation systems.

In this section, a brief overview of relevant literature to this paper is discussed, which can be divided into indoor navigation based on geographical coordinates and landmark-aided navigation.

2.1 Indoor Navigation

With the help of indoor localization technologies and techniques promoted by the rapid development of wireless technology and pervasive computing, the theoretical research and practical application of indoor navigation systems has been efficiently broadened.

Multiple deterministic models are designed in combination of physical laws and mathematic, such as: Angle of Arrival (AoA), Time of Arrival (ToA), and Time Difference of Arrival (TDoA) [12]. Among them, from the received signal strength (RSS) of ambient radio signal sensed to derive the travel distance by log-distance path loss model (LDPL), which can predict the path loss a signal encounters inside a building, is the deeply researched approach [13]. While accuracy is greatly affected by noise and variation which are tackled in probabilistic method [14]. Additionally, a plethora of indoor positioning methods adopt the RSS as fingerprint to realize localization has been proposed. The core idea is to build up a fine-grained radio map consist of the fingerprint of each interested location, which the position can be achieved using matching algorithms. RADAR is the first attempt to apply the fingerprinting-based technique with k-nearest neighbors (KNN) matching algorithm in indoor localization, which utilize the Wi-Fi fingerprint [15]. Wi-Fi fingerprinting-based indoor localization can measure the RSSs from detected access points (APs) at target area to construct the detailed radio map on training phase, which will be used to determine the location via deterministic and probabilistic algorithms with different similarity metrics like Euclidean distance, Kullback-Leibler divergence and Jensen-Shannon divergence [16–19]. Therefore, the quality and quantity of radio map, which depend on the number of wireless devices installed and annotation accuracy, makes a significant impact on the performance of these Wi-Fi fingerprinting based positioning systems [20].

Simultaneous Localization and Mapping (SLAM) is a well-known technique dominate the robotic filed, which usually rely on the laser range sensor or cameras to build the map based on landmarks and simultaneously infer robot location in unknown area. SmartSLAM, as a modified algorithms based on smartphone, is proposed to gradually construct the indoor floor plan for anonymous buildings, employing inertial sensors to track user and using Wi-Fi signals as an indicator to find anchor point [21]. Sematic-SLAM uses the estimated landmark in the environment as reference point and combine the inertial sensors as an odometer to keep track of users [22]. Wi-Fi related fingerprint is also used in WalkSLAM and Wi-Fi-RTT-SLAM [23, 24].

DR (dead reckoning), as a radio signal-free localization method based on inertial sensors such as accelerometers, gyroscope, magnetometer, and barometer, are presented in many works. Given a starting point, locations can be continuously calculated by combing last position and the displacement inferred by the motion information which is provided by three parts: step detection, estimated strides length and heading changes. Because of no additional requirements and no coverage limitation of DR, it is popular in wireless blocked or denied area and emergencies [25, 26]. While, due to environmental contamination, vibration and temperature fluctuations, inevitable sensor drift causes the positioning error accumulated along movement, resulting in degraded localization performance. Wi-Fi fingerprint is commonly integrated to enhance the accuracy. Predefined Wi-Fi fingerprint as the reference point to When the Wi-Fi fingerprint whose corresponding location is known as the reference point is passed, the accumulated error can be eliminated by the absolute landmark position. Besides, with the ubiquitous mobile sensor rich device, DR is gradually extended to PDR.

Indoor addition to PDR, SLAM and Wi-Fi based localization approaches, plenty of research based on light Intensity, RFID, Bluetooth, Zigbee and other technologies realize the indoor positioning. However, extra infrastructure deployment or specific devices are required in the sensor-based approaches, even for the self-contained inertial sensor-based PDR methods, in which the absolute position of anchor point is needed to calibrate the positioning error.

2.2 Landmark Based Navigation

Landmark is defined as a spatial point with salient features and semantic characteristics from its near environment in indoor navigation systems, which can be used to calibrate the localization error based on the inherent spatial information. Fuqiang present the concept of sensory landmark with distinctiveness to distinguish, stability pattern to detect and identifiability to identify, categorizing the different landmarks based on the type of built-in sensor within the smartphone to assist indoor localization [27]. The location of these landmarks, presented by geographical coordinate or the relationship with other location/areas, where people perform specifical and predictable movement can be detected and correspondingly identifiable change displayed on the changes of the readings of at least one type of sensor, as an anchor point to correct the position we calculated.

To identify the landmark, plenty of features are manually calculated, and the special thresholds of different sensors within various kinds of landmark recognition are analyzed. For instance, the threshold of angular velocity produced by gyroscope usually used to detect the corner landmark, the acceleration changes can recognize the stairs. The combination of different thresholds of various sensors forms the decision tree can detect the standing motion state to further distinguish common landmarks, such as corners, stairs, and elevators [28]. However, the calculation, extraction, and selection of features of different sensors for various landmarks are heuristic with professional knowledge of the domain and time-consuming, laborious. To simplify the feature engineering and improve the performance, deep neural networks are applied in a variety of works. A convolutional neural network (CNN) is trained for the one-dimensional sensor data to learn the proper features automatically and landmark identification in [29]. The long short-term memory (LSTM) based deep RNNs (DRNNs) to classify the location mapped from variable-length input sequences of sensor data for landmark classification [30]. Wang et al. improve the LSTM neural network to recognize different kinds of spatial structure-related sensory landmarks [31].

To navigate people based on the landmark detected, in addition to the location, how to organize the landmarks precisely and effectively is also necessary. Multiple landmarks that the logical relationships are well displayed is an easy-understanding construction of indoor floorplan for indoor navigation. Although almost all buildings provide the indoor map at some conspicuous locations, it is still not easy for people, especially the spatial cognitive disability, children, to understand the map and reach the destination. ALMIC estimates the relative distance of all the landmarks detected and then generates the indoor floorplan using multidimensional scaling algorithms [11]. IndoorWaze calculate the movement trajectory with the help of PDR between different landmarks to construct the landmark graph to guide people, and the same fashion of the detected landmarks is also presented in many works [9, 32, 33].

3   Materials and Methods

In this section, the proposed indoor navigation system is presented, which only needs a smartphone, precisely the sensors in it. Both hardware sensors and virtual sensors are in a smart device. Hardware-based sensors derive their data by directly measuring specific environmental properties and physical attributes, such as the barometer, accelerometer, and gyroscope. Virtual sensors readings are calculated by one or more hardware sensors, such as the gravity sensor, linear acceleration, and rotation sensor. Here, the accelerometer, gyroscope, barometer, and rotation sensor.

3.1   Architecture

Figure 1 shows the architecture of proposed indoor navigation systems, which can be divide into two phases: offline training and online indoor navigation. In the offline phase, various sensors data flows for analyzing are firstly collected from handhold smartphone built-in sensors which record the changes of environment and body motion. Then, the signals need to be segmented into windows to detect landmark and perform the pedestrian dead reckoning (PDR) and preprocessed to reduce the noise for better feature extraction and motion state estimation, including data filtering and data scaling. Next, the with the help of PDR techniques, the locations and the trajectories are estimated to build the indoor landmark map, which to further assist the navigation on online phase. Besides, the preprocessed data are also used to extract the features and identify the landmark to aid online navigation. The same data collection module and PDR algorithms are utilized. On data processing, for timely navigation, the fixed sliding window with a degree of overlap is applied to generate the same inputs as the model trained in the offline phase. Therefore, the landmark identification model can distinguish the landmark and calibrate the location due to sensor drift and accumulative error simultaneously. What's more, in combination of the indoor sematic map constructed by landmark, user is navigated with accessible instructions based on their connectivity relationships.

3.2   Data Preprocessing

To combine the data from different sensors for landmark identification, the specific processing process is described below.

Data Interpolation. To fill the missing values, data interpolation, which is an approach of constructing new data point based on the known data points, is adopted.

Data Alignment. The same sampling rate for the four sensors are set to 50 Hz. While the sensor readings we collected are not following the same interval and even the same sensor, the sampling rate is different most of the time. The frequency is around 50 Hz

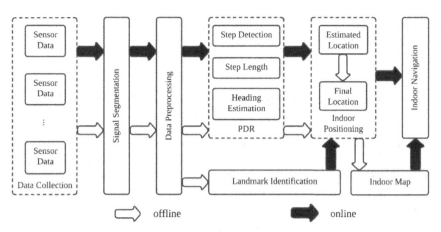

Fig. 1. Architecture of proposed approach.

on inertial sensors and 25 Hz on barometer. In order to obtain the same number of samples, linear interpolation and spherical linear interpolation is used to generate the sensor readings with the same sampling rate.

Data Segmentation. With the aligned sensor readings, a sliding window with a size of 2.56 s is applied to capture the samples of all the sensors we selected.

Data Scaling. Since the range of values of raw data varies widely, the model will not work properly without scaling. In the paper, max-min scaling method is applied to normalize the range of data we obtained.

3.3 PDR

Generally, PDR consists of three main components: step detection, stride length estimation and Heading estimation.

Step Detection. Peak detection is the most popular method for accurate step detection is employed in this paper, which relies on the repeat fluctuation patterns. The magnitude of acceleration on three dimensions instead of vertical part is used as the input to of peak finding approach to improve the performance. To further enhance the performance, the low pass filter is also applied to the magnitude to reduce the signal noise and an adaptive threshold technique of the maximum and minimum acceleration is adopted to fit different motion state with time interval between adjacent steps detected limitation.

Stride Length Estimation. Various of linear and nonlinear method are proposed to estimate step length which varies from person to person because of different walking posture. Therefore, it is not easy to precisely construct same step length estimation model. Some researchers assume that the step length is a static value affected by the individual characteristics of different users. On the contrary, Weinberg model estimate stride length according to the dynamic movement state, which is closer to reality. The model is present below:

$$SL = k \cdot \sqrt[4]{a_{max} - a_{min}} \tag{1}$$

where k is dynamic value concerned about the acceleration of each step and a_{max}, a_{min} are the maximum and minimum acceleration for each step [35].

Heading Estimation. Heading information is an important component for whole PDR implement, which critically affect the localization accuracy. As the accelerometer, gyroscope and magnetometer is already fused in rotation vector obtained by rotation sensor, the heading change can be calculated by a rotation matrix transformed from the vector. The rotation vector is defined as M, $M \in R^{3 \times 3}$:

$$M = \begin{bmatrix} M_{11} & M_{12} & M_{13} \\ M_{21} & M_{22} & M_{23} \\ M_{31} & M_{32} & M_{33} \end{bmatrix} = \begin{bmatrix} 1 - 2y^2 - 2z^2 & 2xy - 2zw & 2xz + 2yw \\ 2xy + 2zw & 1 - 2x^2 - 2z^2 & 2yz - 2xw \\ 2xz - 2yw & 2yz + 2xw & 1 - 2x^2 - 2y^2 \end{bmatrix} \tag{2}$$

the heading on three dimensions can be computed by:

$$\theta = \begin{bmatrix} arctan2(M_{12}, M_{22}) \\ arcsin(-M_{32}) \\ arctan2(-M_{31}, M_{33}) \end{bmatrix} = \begin{bmatrix} arctan2(2xy - 2zw, 1 - 2x^2 - 2z^2) \\ arcsin(-2yz - 2xw) \\ arctan2(2yw - 2xz, 1 - 2x^2 - 2y^2) \end{bmatrix} \tag{3}$$

3.4 Landmark Identification

Autoencoder is a type of unsupervised neural networks that can be used to learn feature representation of data. It learns the feature representation by training the network to reconstruct the data at the output layer. Each autoencoder consists of three parts: encoder, compressed features and output, whereby the compressed features extracted by encoder are sent to the decoder part to reconstrue the input. Many variants are proposed to solve different problems, such as the sparse autoencoder, variational autoencoder and denoising autoencoder [35]. Denoising autoencoder is a useful variant of vanilla autoencoder to learn a robust feature representation by introducing stochastic noise to the input data and the critical part will be reconstructed from the corrupted data [36, 37].

Usually, the denoising autoencoder are built by fully connected layers. Since the sensor data flow have a strong 1D structure that the previous state and the next state connect tightly. 1D convolution operation can efficiently capture the local correlation features by limiting the hidden units' receptive field to be local. CNN considers each frame of sensor data as independent and extracts the feature for these isolated portions of data without considering the temporal context beyond the boundaries of the frame. Due to the continuity of sensor data flow produced by user behavior, local correlation and long-term connections are both important to identify the landmark [38]. While LSTM with learnable gates, which modulate the flow of information and control when to forget previous hidden states, as a variant of vanilla Recurrent Neural Networks (RNN), allows

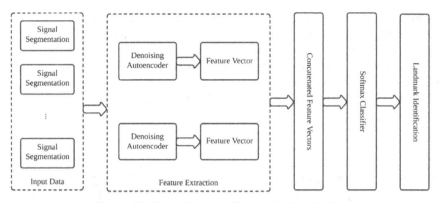

Fig. 2. The block diagram of landmark identification

a neural network to effectively extract the long-range dependencies of time-series sensor data.

The structure of landmark identification module is shown in Fig. 2. When preprocessed data segmentation of multiple sensors comes, features in different domains are automatically extracted by unsupervised featuring learning pipeline based on denoising autoencoders implemented by alternatively stacked 1D convolutional layer and 1D max-pooling layer and multiple LSTM layers, respectively. Denoising autoencoder extract the robust feature, both short-time correlation and long-term dependence from the sensor data corrupted by environmental noise. Finally, features extracted by encoder parts will be concatenated to train a classification model used in online predicting phase to identify landmarks to improve the localization accuracy and the performance of navigation based on the landmark map. The indoor landmark map can generate based on the relative distance of different landmark calculated by PDR, with the help of multidimensional scaling techniques which is commonly used to find the spatial relationship based on dissimilarity information, such as the relative distance in this work, between objects.

4   Performance Evaluation

In this section, we evaluate the performance of proposed methods on the dataset we collected on the fourth floors of the Building 1, at the Center Zone of Kyushu University campus.

4.1   Data Collection

For recording sensor data flow, we used the built-in sensors of a smartphone (Pixel 4a) and developed an Android application that periodically read and stored the readings. To collect the sensor dataset when the landmark passed and build the landmark map, five participants were invited to collect the data. During each collection, participants were required to keep their phones in hand and walk with them held to their chest level. They were also required to record the timestamp of passing by the landmark and the identification of landmark. Landmark information they passed are the type of scenario, the type of landmark, and the moment of passing by the landmark.

After data preprocessing, some statics with brief description of clean dataset is shown in Table1. There are 9271 samples in total for all 27 landmarks, including the almost all (toilet are not included, only one door selected of room 1401 and 1409, and no landmark on room 1410) the corners, stairs, elevators and two doors, which is assumed to be open during our experiment of each room of corridor, shown on Fig. 3.

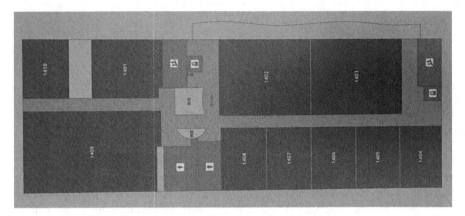

Fig. 3. The real floor plan in our experiment

Table 1. Dataset details

Users	S. Rate	# Landmark	# Samples	Sensors
5	50 Hz	27	9271	A,G,R,B

4.2 Hyperparameter Settings

The landmark identification model is trained on the collected data with different hyperparameters, which are listed on Table 2. Keras framework with TensorFlow backend is used for the implementation of the classifier to minimize the crossentropy loss. Both LSTM and 1D CNN share the same parameters, if not specifically summarized. The number of hidden layers represent the number of encoder layers, the same number of layers on decoder parts.

4.3 Results and Discussion

Visual Results. Figure 6 depicts the landmark graph generated by our system based on all the data we collected. The map presented on both Fig. 5 and Fig. 4 are very similar to the ground truth in Fig. 3. The difference between these two landmark maps are the doors landmark selected or not. Doors are usually not selected as a land-mark in existing

Table 2. Hyperparameter

Hyperparameters	
Optimizer	Adam
Batch size	64
Dropout rate	0.5
Filter size	5
Learning rate	0.002
Input vector size	128
Input channels	12
Number of epochs	800
Number of hidden layers	2
Units of hidden layers	64

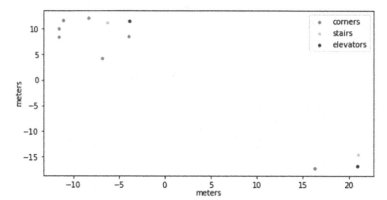

Fig. 4. The landmark-based indoor map without door

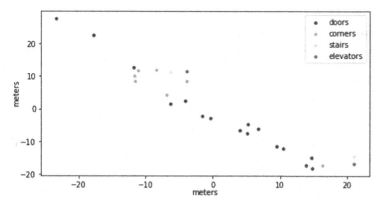

Fig. 5. The landmark-based indoor map with door

systems, while the building where we conduct our experiments is a 12 teaching building, and many people come to study or take classes in the classroom. Therefore, we spend triple time to obtain the landmark map with door in, as a frequently visited location, we still choose the doors of classroom as an important kind of land-mark, which make the map more comprehensive and guide people to the greatest extent possible.

Landmark Identification. The landmark identifications are performed using the collected data which were divided into training set and test set randomly without overlap between these two datasets. There are a total of 27 landmarks, and most of them are similar, which can be divided into four categories in total, including half-occupied doors, corners, stairs, and elevators

We evaluated the classification performance of proposed approaches for four kinds of landmark. The recognition result is presented by confusion matrix in Table 3. The confusion between the individual labels is small. Many other landmarks are misclassified as doors, which mainly because people have to make the same movement when entering and exiting the classroom as they do when go around corners, turning a corner and continuing to walk. The same situation occurs in elevator detection, mainly when entering and exiting elevators. Figure 6 is the classification confusion matrix on 27 landmark of the experiment conducted floor.

Table 3. Confusion matrix for the kinds of landmark classification

Truth	Prediction			
	Doors	Corners	Elevators	Stairs
Doors	1578	10	1	0
Corners	20	652	2	0
Elevators	13	18	280	0
Stairs	2	2	4	140

Indoor Navigation. We test the navigation service based on the generated landmark graph. In this experiment, four different routes are randomly selected from the real floor plan. We reached each destination by following the landmark based indoor relative map with different wrong steps. Most of the wrong steps are at the beginning to identify the landmark, which people have to move more than three steps to start the landmark identification model and plenty of space near the landmark. Additionally, if it is incorrect landmark detected, users will be misguided, which hap-pens in the fourth trail. There are three different directions near Room 1401 for user to start the walking and wrong direction is chose without landmark identification at the first serval steps. While it can be corrected during movement in a large area. Nevertheless, the results show that the proposed approach is accurate as an infrastructure-free indoor navigation system (Table 4).

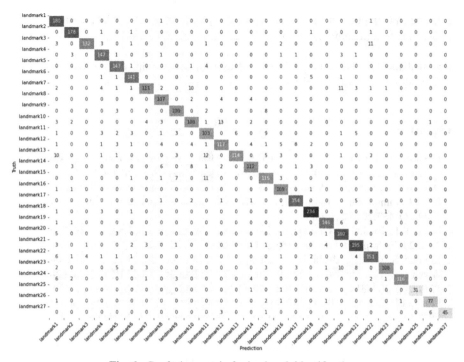

Fig. 6. Confusion matrix for landmark identification

Table 4. Navigation result

	Start point	End point	Total steps	Wrong steps
#1	Front door of Room 1404	Front door of Room 1401	77	2
#2	Elevator near Room 1404	Front door of Room 1409	96	3
#3	Stairs near Room 1401	Stairs near Room 1403	69	5
#4	Corner near Room 1401	Front door of Room 1404	41	12

5 Conclusion and Future Work

In this paper, based on the sensor data flow from built-in smartphone, including an accelerometer, a gyroscope, barometer, and a virtual rotation sensor fused by inertial sensor, the indoor navigation with the help of spatial landmark identification and PDR to generate the indoor map is achieved. What's more, the landmark, such as stairs, elevators, corners, and doors are distinguished by denoising autoencoder for automatically extracting the features without the requirement of extra infrastructure to significantly eliminate the laborious manual feature design. The effectiveness of this framework is demonstrated by extensive experiment based on the collected data. As part of our future work, we will keep collecting training data from more people with various attitudes of the device and conduct further research on the exploration of sensor data to improve the proposed method in combination of advanced deep neural networks.

Acknowledgments. This work was supported by CSC scholarship, JSPS KAKENHI Grant Numbers 20H00622 and 17KT0154.

References

1. Kunhoth, J., Karkar, A., Al-Maadeed, S., Al-Ali, A.: Indoor positioning and wayfinding systems: a survey. HCIS **10**(1), 1–41 (2020). https://doi.org/10.1186/s13673-020-00222-0
2. Davidson, P., Piché, R.: A survey of selected indoor positioning methods for smartphones. IEEE Commun. Surv. Tutor. **19**(2), 1347–1370, Secondquarter (2017). https://doi.org/10.1109/COMST.2016.2637663
3. Brena, R.F.: Evolution of indoor positioning technologies: a survey, J. Sensors **2017**, 2630413, 21 p (2017). https://doi.org/10.1155/2017/2630413
4. Konomi, S., Gao, L., Mushi, D.: An intelligent platform for offline learners based on model-driven crowdsensing over intermittent networks. In: Rau, P.-L. (ed.) HCII 2020. LNCS, vol. 12193, pp. 300–314. Springer, Cham (2020). https://doi.org/10.1007/978-3-030-49913-6_26
5. Lin, T., Li, L., Lachapelle, G.: Multiple sensors integration for pedestrian indoor navigation. In: 2015 International Conference on Indoor Positioning and Indoor Navigation (IPIN), pp. 1–9 (2015). https://doi.org/10.1109/IPIN.2015.7346785
6. Fellner, I., Huang, H., Gartner, G.: Turn left after the WC, and use the lift to go to the 2nd floor"—generation of landmark-based route instructions for indoor navigation. ISPRS Int. J. Geo-Inf. **6**, 183 (2017). https://doi.org/10.3390/ijgi6060183
7. Yao, G., Wang, W., Chen, X.: FreeNavi: landmark-based mapless indoor navigation based on WiFi fingerprints. In: 2017 IEEE 85th Vehicular Technology Conference: VTC2017-Spring. IEEE (2017)
8. Wang, H., Sen, S., Elgohary, A., Farid, M., Choudhury, R.R.: No need to war-drive: unsupervised indoor localization. In: Proceedings of the 10th International Conference on Mobile Systems, Applications, and Services (MobiSys 2012), pp. 197–210. Association for Computing Machinery, New York (2012). https://doi.org/10.1145/2307636.2307655
9. Gu, F., Valaee, S., Khoshelham, K., Shang, J., Zhang, R.: Landmark graph-based indoor localization. IEEE Internet of Things J. **7**(9), 8343–8355 (2020), https://doi.org/10.1109/JIOT.2020.2989501
10. Gu, F., et al.: Indoor localization improved by spatial context—a survey. ACM Comput. Surv. **52**, 64:1–64:35 (2019). https://doi.org/10.1145/3322241
11. Zhou, B., Li, Q., Mao, Q., Tu, W., Zhang, X., Chen, L.: Alimc: activity landmark-based indoor mapping via crowdsourcing. IEEE Trans. Intell. Transp. Syst. **16**(5), 2774–2785 (2015)
12. Xiong, J., Jamieson, K.: ArrayTrack: a fine-grained indoor location system. In: Proceedings of the 10th USENIX Conference on Networked Systems Design and Implementation (NSDI 2013), pp. 71–84. USENIX Association (2013)
13. Seybold, J.S.: Introduction to RF Propagation. Wiley-Interscience, Hoboken (2005)
14. El-Kafrawy, H., Youssef, M., El-Keyi, A.: Impact of the human motion on the variance of the received signal strength of wireless links. In: Proceedings of the 22nd Personal In-door and Mobile Radio Communications (PIMRC).pp. 1208–1212. IEEE (2011)
15. Bahl, P., Padmanabhan, V.N. RADAR: an in-building RF-based user location and tracking system. In: Proceedings of the Nineteenth Annual Joint Conference of the IEEE Computer and Communications Societies (INFOCOM 2000), vol. 2, pp. 775–784.Tel Aviv, Israel, 26–30 March 2000

16. Youssef, M., Ashok A.: The horus WLAN location determination system. In: Proceedings of the 3rd International Conference on Mobile Systems, Applications, and Services (MobiSys 2005), pp. 205–218, Association for Computing Machinery, New York (2014). https://doi.org/10.1145/1067170.1067193

17. Abdullah, O.A., Abdel-Qader, I.: Machine learning algorithm for wireless indoor localization. In: Farhadi, H. (ed.) Machine Learning -Advanced Techniques And Emerging Applications, IntechOpen (2018). https://doi.org/10.5772/intechopen.74754

18. Mirowski, P., Steck, H., Whiting, P., Palaniappan, R., MacDonald, M., Ho, T.K.: KL-divergence kernel regression for non-Gaussian fingerprint based localization. In: Proceedings of the International Conference on Indoor Positioning and Indoor Navigation (2011)

19. Abdullah, O., Abdel-Qader, I., Bazuin, B.: A probability neural network-Jensen-Shannon divergence for a fingerprint based localization. In: 2016 Annual Conference on Information Science and Systems (CISS), Princeton, NJ, USA, pp. 286–291 (2016). https://doi.org/10.1109/CISS.2016.7460516

20. Liu, T., Zhang, X., Zhang, H., Tahir, N., Fang, Z.: A structure landmark-based radio signal mapping approach for sustainable indoor localization. Sustainability 13 (2021)

21. Shin, H., Chon, Y., Cha, H.: Unsupervised construction of an indoor floor plan using a smartphone. IEEE Trans. Syst. Man, Cybern. Part C Appl. Rev. 42(6), 889–898. (2012)

22. Abdelnasser, H., Mohamed, R., Elgohary, A.: SemanticSLAM: using environment landmarks for unsupervised indoor localization. IEEE Trans. Mob. Comput. 15(7), 1770–1782 (2016)

23. Ma, L., Fang, T., Qin, D.: WalkSLAM: a walking pattern-based mobile SLAM solution. In: Liang, Q., Liu, X., Na, Z., Wang, W., Mu, J., Zhang, B. (eds.) CSPS 2018. LNEE, vol. 516, pp. 1347–1354. Springer, Singapore (2020). https://doi.org/10.1007/978-981-13-6504-1_160

24. Gentner, C., Avram, D.: WiFi-RTT-SLAM: simultaneously estimating the positions of mobile devices and WiFi-RTT access points. In: Proceedings of the 34th International Technical Meeting of the Satellite, September, pp. 3142–3148. Division of the Institute of Navigation (ION GNSS+ 2021), St. Louis (2021)

25. Chen, L., Wu, J., Yang, C.: Meshmap: a magnetic field-based indoor navigation system with crowdsourcing support. IEEE Access 8, 39959–39970 (2020)

26. Shang, J., Gu, F., Hu, X., Kealy, A.: Apfiloc: an infrastructure-free indoor localization method fusing smartphone inertial sensors, landmarks and map information. Sensors 15(10), 27251–27272 (2015)

27. Gu, F., Khoshelham, K., Shang, J., Yu, F.: Sensory landmarks for indoor localization. In: 2016 Ubiquitous Positioning, Indoor Navigation and Location-Based Services. IEEE. (2016)

28. Yuce, M.R.: Landmark-assisted compensation of user's body shadowing on RSSI for improved indoor localisation with chest-mounted wearable device. Sensors 21 (2021)

29. Zhou, B., Yang, J., Li, Q.: Smartphone-based activity recognition for indoor localization using a convolutional neural network. Sensors 19(3) (2019)

30. Bhattarai, B., Yadav, R.K., Gang, H.S., Pyun, J.Y.: Geomagnetic field based indoor landmark classification using deep learning. IEEE Access 7, 1–1 (2019)

31. Wang, Y., Zhang, J., Zhao, H., Liu, M., Niu, X.: Spatial structure-related sensory landmarks recognition based on long short-term memory algorithm. Micromachines 12(7), 781 (2021)

32. Li, T., Han, D., Chen, Y., Zhang, R., Hedgpeth, T.: Indoorwaze: a crowdsourcing-based context-aware indoor navigation system. IEEE Trans. Wirel. Commun. 99, 1–1 (2020)

33. Jiang, Y., et al.: Hallway based automatic indoor floorplan construction using room fingerprints. In: Proceedings of the 2013 ACM International Joint Conference on Pervasive and Ubiquitous Computing (UbiComp 2013), pp. 315–324. Association for Computing Machinery, New York (2013). https://doi.org/10.1145/2493432.2493470

34. Weinberg, H.: Using the ADXL202 in Pedometer and Personal Navigation Applications. Analog Devices Inc., Norwood (2002)

35. Vincent, P., Larochelle, H., Bengio, Y., Manzagol, P.A.: Extracting and composing robust features with denoising autoencoders. Machine learning. In: Proceedings of the Twenty-Fifth International Conference (ICML 2008), Helsinki, Finland, 5–9 June 2008

36. Jiang, J.-R., Subakti, H., Liang, H.-S.: Fingerprint feature extraction for indoor localization. Sensors **21**, 5434 (2021). https://doi.org/10.3390/s21165434

37. Garcia, K.D., et al.: An ensemble of autonomous auto-encoders for human activity recognition. Neurocomputing **439**, 271–280 (2021). https://doi.org/10.1016/j.neucom.2020.01.125

38. Zhao, Y., Yang, R., Chevalier, G., Gong, M.. Xu, X, Zhang, Z.: Deep residual Bidir-LSTM for human activity recognition using wearable sensors. Math. Probl. Eng. **2018**, 1–13 (2018). https://doi.org/10.1155/2018/7316954

WiHead: WiFi-Based Head-Pose Estimation

Yiming Liu[1]($\boxtimes$) and Shin'ichi Konomi[2]

[1] Graduate School of Information Science and Electrical Engineering,
Kyushu University, 744, Motooka, Nishi-ku, Fukuoka 819-0395, Japan
`liuyimingfirst@gmail.com`
[2] Faculty of Arts and Science, Kyushu University,
744, Motooka, Nishi-ku, Fukuoka 819-0395, Japan

Abstract. Due to the impact of Covid-19, people have started to conduct online courses or meetings. However, this makes it difficult to communicate with each other effectively because of the lack of non-verbal communication. Although webcams are available for online courses, etc., people often do not want to turn them on for privacy reasons. Thus, there is a need to develop privacy preserving way to enable non-verbal communication in online learning and work environments. WiFi as a sensor can be used to detect non-verbal gestures such as head poses, and has been increasingly valued due to its advantages of avoiding the effects of light, non-line of sight monitoring, privacy protection, etc. In this paper, we proposed an approach, which uses WiFi CSI data to estimate head pose. Our approach not only use the amplitude and phase data of raw CSI data, but also use the information in frequency domain. Our experiment with proposed approach confirmed the feasibility of head pose estimation based on WiFi CSI data. This has important implications for device-free sensing detection. Especially in today's world where web conferences and online courses are widely used, WiFi-based head recognition can give feedback to the other party while protecting privacy, which helps to improve the quality and comfort of communication.

Keywords: Device-free · Head-pose · WiFi CSI · CNN

1 Introduction

Head pose estimation refers to estimating the angle of the human head in three dimensions (i.e., pitch, roll, yaw) using various sensors (e.g., cameras, radar, etc.). By tracking the head, the machine can be controlled by head motion in the field of human-computer interaction; Good head pose estimation can help computers to perform human emotion recognition, facial recognition, 3D head reconstruction, line of sight detection, attention detection, etc. It also has an important role in the field of virtual reality or augmented reality. For example, head pose estimation is used for driver attention detection [11], and head pose is used for human-computer interaction [5]. Therefore, accurate estimation

N. A. Streitz and S. Konomi (Eds.): HCII 2022, LNCS 13326, pp. 69–86, 2022.
https://doi.org/10.1007/978-3-031-05431-0_5

of human head pose is particularly important. Nowadays, due to the restriction of travel by the new crown epidemic, the online ecology has been able to thrive, and people are more likely to choose online classes or work at home. Therefore, people's communication is more restricted to voice, which is not conducive to grasp other people's state and affect interpersonal communication due to the lack of information. Traditional image-based head pose estimation methods have been widely studied. However, there are also many drawbacks, such as difficulty in coping with facial occlusions, changes in head appearance, non-line-of-sight detection, etc., and the image-based methods do not adapt well to changes in lighting. Moreover, most of the existing image-based methods cannot estimate the head pose well for large angles because the face range needs to be detected before prediction. On the other hand, using cameras in work or study may cause serious privacy leakage and working under the camera may also cause stress to people's mind. Therefore, a method to effectively protect privacy and cost-effectively track human head movements is particularly important. Therefore, we propose a method for human head pose estimation using channel state information (CSI) of WiFi. In recent years, commercial WiFi devices have been increasingly studied as sensors. We can easily obtain CSI data from an IEEE 802.11n protocol compliant wireless device. Compared to image data, CSI data is not affected by light, occlusion, etc., and can be detected without even being in line of sight (e.g., through walls, etc.), and without privacy issues. In this paper, we use two hosts equipped with Atheros series wireless cards (as shown in Fig. 1). WiFi signals in 2.4 GHz operating mode (meeting the IEEE802.11 WiFi communication standard) can acquire CSI data for all 56 subcarriers. We also synchronize the image recording with a camera and extract the head pose. This recording is used as a token for the CSI data. We then developed a deep learning model to estimate the human head pose using WiFi data samples as input and the head pose obtained from RGB images as annotations to achieve the head pose estimation from WiFi data only. To the best of our knowledge, this is the first work to use WiFi data for head motion estimation on 3 degrees of freedom. Our contributions include: (1) proposal of a method for human head pose estimation using commercial WiFi devices, demonstrating its feasibility and filling a research gap, and (2) proposal of a deep learning solution to extract head motion information from highly superimposed CSI data.

2   Related Work

2.1   Camera-Based Head-Pose Estimation

RGB camera-based head pose estimation is popular among researchers because of its easy solution deployment, relatively mature machine vision technology, and visualization during the experiment. Many effective methods also exist. For example, the face keypoint-based approach in [19] estimates the head pose frame by frame for head tracking based on the detection of the center of both eyes, the tip of the nose and the center of the mouth. In contrast, in [14,21], and [12], facial features are extracted directly from RGB images for head pose estimation. Most

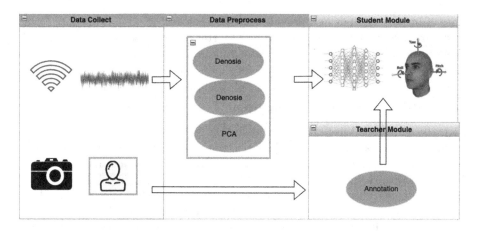

Fig. 1. We collect CSI data and image data simultaneously, and tag CSI data with images. That is, the image-based model is trained as a teacher module on the CSI-based student module.

of these methods require facial keypoints (e.g., eyes, nose tip, mouth corners, etc.) as features, or 3D to 2D mapping through a generic 3D face model, so the correct detection of the face and keypoints is crucial for head pose estimation, and if the detection fails, the head pose cannot be correctly track the head state. Therefore, this method is very sensitive to occlusion, light, etc. A different approach for head pose estimation involves 3D model registration techniques. First, Blanz and Vetter [2] propose a technique for modeling textured 3D faces automatically generated from one or more photographs. Cao et al. [4] exploited a 3D regression algorithm that learns an accurate, user-specific face alignment model from an easily acquired set of training data, generated from images of the user performing a sequence of predefined facial poses and expressions.

2.2 RGBD-Based Head-Pose Estimation

With the gradual development of disruptive technologies such as machine vision and autonomous driving, there are more and more applications that use 3D cameras for object recognition, behavior recognition, and scene modeling. Only the semantic analysis of the image can determine which objects are far away from us and which are close to us, but there is no exact data. The depth camera solves this problem. With the data obtained from the depth camera, we can know exactly the distance from each point in the image and the camera, and then add the (x, y) coordinates of the point in the 2D image to obtain the 3D spatial coordinates of each point in the image. By using the 3D coordinates, the real scene can be restored. In the article [3], a method is proposed to estimate head and shoulder pose based on depth images only. The method includes a head detection and localization module to develop a complete end-to-end system. The core element of the framework is called POSEidon +(CNN), which receives three types of images as input and provides the 3D angle of the pose as output. Their results show that their method overcomes several recent state-of-art works based on both intensity and depth input data, running in real-time at more than 30 frames per second.

2.3 CSI-Based Activity Recognition

With the widespread use of WiFi in daily life, people can receive WiFi signals in various settings, and as a kind of electromagnetic wave, it also has physical properties unique to electromagnetic waves. When humans move between WiFi transmitters and receivers, human activities affect the physical properties of WiFi signals (reflection, diffraction, etc.). In addition, the widespread deployment of commercial WiFi devices in public environments and the popularity of home use make it possible to use WiFi signals as sensors. Moreover, the use of WiFi signals as sensors for human activity recognition does not require taking any special sensors or wearing other devices, so the experimental environment can be easily set up and not cost much. Previously, signal strength indication (RSSI) of WiFi has been widely used for indoor localization, as in [9], and human activity recognition, as in [8,13], and Y. Gu et al. proposed a networked human activity recognition system by which different activities in daily life are learned, modeled, and a human activity fingerprint is generated, and this fingerprint is used to discriminate between different human activities. Although these methods have the advantages of passive recognition and easy to deploy and inexpensive equipment, the effectiveness of activity recognition is still very deficient. Firstly, RSSI is a coarse-grained data, which can record limited amount of information, and RSSI is relatively weak against random noise. Secondly, the indoor environment is complex. There are many different obstacles (furniture, walls) in the room, and the signal is not stable after multipath propagation superposition.

Therefore, when the IEEE 802.11 a/g/n framework is proposed, this OFDM-based framework divides the 20 MHz channel into 56 subcarriers and allows the extraction of CSI information on the supported wireless network cards. Compared to RSSI, which only provides power measurements over the entire channel bandwidth, WiFi CSI contains is a much more fine-grained data and can record more granular information, and so has replaced RSSI as the data for WiFi-based human activity detection. WiFi CSI-based human activity recognition has been widely studied. In [15], for the first time, they implemented the use of a home WiFi router to take the received 1D WiFi signal (CSI) as input and perform body segmentation and pose estimation in an end-to-end approach. In [17], they proposed E-eyes, which used the commercial WiFi devices to monitor human activity with one transmitter and multiple receivers. It examines channel features and identify both in-place activities and walking movements by comparing signal profiles. In [20], they proposed ViHOT, which uses phones to get CSI data to track driver's head pose in a lightweight design suitable for real-time driver assistance, but it can only track head pose in one direction. WiGest [1] can detect hand gesture by standard WiFi equipment. The main idea is to leverage the effect of the hand movement on the wireless signal to detect different gestures.

They also conducted experiments under different conditions (non-line-of-sight, different rooms). ABLSTM allows for passive human activity recognition [6]. It can automatically extract features from raw CSI data by deep neural networks and get good results. RT-Fall achieved the first motion segmentation from CSI signals and performed fall detection [16].

Although CSI data has the advantages of working in a dark environment, not being afraid of occlusion, protecting privacy, non-line-of-sight detection, etc., compared to traditional camera-based methods, there are some limitations, for example, compared to relatively mature machine vision, CSI as an emerging sensing data, although it can achieve a certain level of recognition accuracy, but there still are some gaps. The signal is susceptible to interference, how to effectively denoise is also an important issue. In addition, WiFi CSI as a one-dimensional data, is a highly superimposed data, how to build an effective model to extract features is also a problem that must be overcome.

3   Proposed Approach

We propose to estimate human head pose by collecting CSI data using WiFi as a sensor. The flow of the proposed approach is detailed in Fig. 1. In this chapter, we introduce the data types used in this experiment and describe our approach to label the training data and what pre-processing is performed for the data features to finally generate samples that can be fed into the model training.

3.1   CSI Data

In the field of wireless communications, so-called Channel State Information (CSI) is the channel property of the communication link. It describes the fading factor of the signal on each transmission path, i.e., the value of each element in the channel gain matrix H, such as signal scattering (Scattering), environmental fading (fading, multipath fading or shadowing fading), distance fading (power decay of distance), and other information. CSI allows the communication system to adapt to the current channel conditions and provides a guarantee for high reliability and high speed communication in a multi-antenna system. Equation 1 is the channel state information of the sub-channel of frequency f at the moment t. This is the case of single transmitting antenna, single receiving antenna:

$$H(f;t) = \sum_{i}^{N} a_i(t)e^{-j2\pi f\tau_i(t)} \tag{1}$$

where $a_i(t)$ refers to amplitude attenuation factor, $\tau_i(t)$ refers to propagation delay and f refers to carrier frequency. The channel can be described using the Channel Impulse Response (CIR) $H(f;t)$ in the time domain, or the Channel Frequency Response (CFR) $H(j,w)$ in the frequency domain as follows:

$$H(k) = \|H(k)\|\, e^{j\angle H(k)} \tag{2}$$

where $H(k)$ represents the CSI of the kth subcarrier. Each value in the CSI matrix is a complex number of the form $I + jQ$. Thus, the amplitude of the kth subcarrier $\|H(k)\|$ is $\sqrt{I^2 + Q^2}$, and the phase is $\arctan Q/I$. Each element in CSI describes the amplitude and phase of the corresponding subcarrier. Since we are using Atheros series NICs, which can acquire data for 56 subcarriers, the channel gain matrix is showed as Fig. 2.

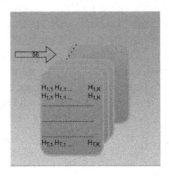

Fig. 2. The CSI data for each packet records 56 subcarriers and the matrix size is determined by the number of transmitter and receiver antennas.

3.2 Data Annotation

We used head image data captured by a camera for head pose annotation (Fig. 3). Among the various image-based head pose estimation methods, we chose WHENet [22] because it has good accuracy in head tagging at large angles as well. This is important to highlight the benefits of the WiFi-based approach, as the image-based approach is sensitive to light changes and does not work in dark environments, which facilitates the CSI-based model to perform head pose estimation at large angles even in dark environments.

3.3 Noise Reduction

Due to the limitations of commercial WiFi devices, there is a lot of noise through the raw WiFi channel state information, which is detrimental to the accurate prediction of the model. Therefore, noise reduction must be applied to the data. Since both signal strength and phase information recorded by CSI are used, the noise reduction process for both types of information is presented separately in the next section.

Amplitude. Due to the OFDM and the multiplex effect, the signal received by the receiver is a superposition of multiple signals, so the signal strength is not stable by the environment, and there is a lot of high frequency noise in the original signal. Since human activities are basically in the low-frequency part, we

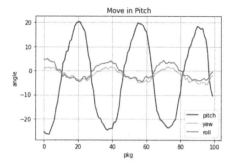

Fig. 3. A figure caption is always placed below the illustration. Please note that short captions are centered, while long ones are justified by the macro package automatically.

performed low-pass filtering to remove the high-frequency noise. Figure 4 shows the raw amplitude of one CSI subcarrier. We can easliy find there is a lot of high frequency noise. We thus use wavelet transform and smoothing methods to remove the noisy. Figure 5 shows the result.

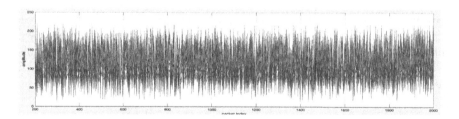

Fig. 4. Raw CSI amplitude information, containing a lot of high frequency noise.

Phase. The phase information obtained based on commercial WiFi devices is not very reliable and the accuracy is not up to the requirement. These errors consist of three main aspects: the offset of the sampling frequency, the time delay in detection, and the offset of the center frequency. This is because the carrier frequencies of the transmitter and receiver segments cannot be perfectly synchronized. The measured phase $\hat{\phi}_i$ for the ith subcarrier can be expressed as:

$$\hat{\phi}_i = \phi_i - 2\pi \frac{k_i}{N} \Delta t + \beta + Z \qquad (3)$$

where ϕ_i is the true phase, Δt refers to the timing offset at the receiver, β refers to the phase offset caused by the carrier frequency offset, Z is some measurement noisy, k_i is the subcarrier index of the ith subcarrier. In the Atheros series NICs, $i \in (1, 56)$ and N is the fast Fourier transform size. As a result, $\Delta t, \beta, Z$ ordinary WiFi NICs are unable to obtain the true phase. In our work, the original phase

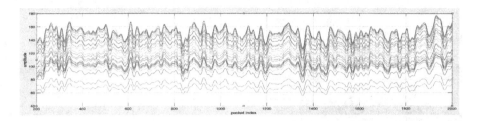

Fig. 5. We use wavelet transform, smoothing and other methods to remove the noise.

information is corrected by unwinding and then linearly changed to get the phase that can better reflect the position information of the reference point. The main idea is to eliminate $\Delta t, \beta$ by considering phase across the whole frequency band [16, 20]. First, we define two formulas a and b as follows:

$$a = \frac{\phi_n - \phi_1}{k_n - k_1} - \frac{2\pi}{N}\Delta t \tag{4}$$

$$b = \frac{1}{n}\sum_{j=1}^{n}\phi_j - \frac{2\pi\Delta t}{nN}\sum_{j=1}^{n}k_j + \beta \tag{5}$$

According to the IEEE 802.11n specification, the subcarrier frequency is symmetric, which indicates $\sum_{j=1}^{n}k_j = 0$. b can be expressed as $b = \frac{1}{n}\sum_{j=1}^{n}\phi_j + \beta$. Subtracting the linear term $ak_i + b$ from the raw CSI data's phase, random noise can be eliminated to some extent. As a result, we get a linear combination of true phases as follows:

$$\widetilde{\phi}_i = \hat{\phi}_i - ak_i - b = \phi_i - \frac{\phi_n - \phi_1}{k_n - k_1}k_i - \frac{1}{n}\sum_{j=1}^{n}\phi_j \tag{6}$$

Figure 6 shows the phase witch is denoised and not denoised.

3.4 Dimension Reduction

Since the Atheros series wireless cards we use can obtain channel state information of all 56 subcarriers at 2.4 GHz, and the transmitter and receiver each have 3 antennas, so the data we obtain has $56 \times 3 \times 3$ dimensions, and it is known from previous studies that although theoretically adjacent subcarriers should have similar responses to the same action. For avoiding dimensional disasters, We reduced the dimensions of raw data.

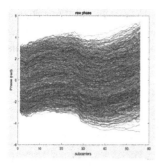 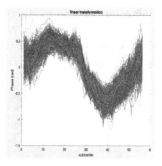

Fig. 6. Phase which is not denoisied (left) and denoisied (right).

Subcarrier Selection. A simple method is to select the antenna pair with the largest variance as the training data by calculating the variance of the 56 subcarriers for each antenna pair. It is known from the prior study [7] that since human activities interfere with WiFi signals, this tends to make CSI data have a larger variance. Therefore, the antenna pair with the largest variance is selected to obtain data that are more sensitive to head activity, which is beneficial for the model to learn the features of the head in different postures. Table 4 and Table 5 shows the variance of each antenna pair for various head motions in the dataset.

PCA. The weights of environmental information reflected by different subcarriers in different environments are different and dynamically changing. Also, we cannot simply superimpose all carrier signals together and then average them, because the decay of some carriers will weaken the drastic environmental information changes that some other carriers are responding to at that moment. Therefore, we have to extract the components of the data that contain a lot of information and compress the data dimension as much as possible without losing a lot of information, and principal component analysis (PCA) is a method that can be useful in this context. We perform principal component analysis on the amplitude and phase of CSI data respectively, and compress its dimensionality to 30 dimensions.

3.5   CSI Image Generation

CNNs have a significant role in deep neural networks, and although they are mainly used for feature extraction of images, they have also shown their superior performance in the direction of signal processing as research progresses. By moving convolutional kernels, CNNs can also extract time-dependent information. In [18], in order to extract features from CSI data using CNN, they cut the original CSI data using sliding windows and merge the phase and amplitude to form a CSI image such as [D, W, 2]. But in our work, we not only use raw CSI data to form the first two channels, but also use Fourier transform to get frequency information to form the third channel (see Fig. 7). This allows feature extraction of the CSI data using CNN. Also, a comparison experiment was done to determine the effect of sliding window size on feature extraction. This will be described in detail in Sect. 5.

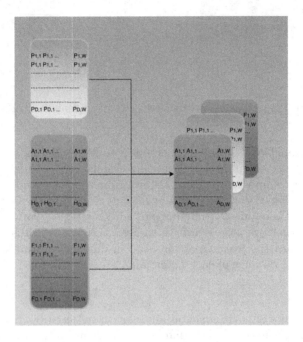

Fig. 7. We split the processed amplitude and phase data with a sliding window, move the window in steps of 5, and use Fourier transform to get frequency information to the same size and merge the amplitude, phase, and frequency information into a 3-channel image.

4   Experiment

In this section, we will detail the process of experimental head-pose estimation based on CSI data, including experimental environment construction involving equipment and tools, data collection methods, models, and some comparative experiments.

4.1   Experiment Setup

In our experiment, two desktop computers equipped with Atheros series wireless NICs are selected as transmitters and receivers. Compared with Intel 5300 wireless NICs, atheros series NICs can collect CSI data of all 56 subcarriers in 2.4 GHz operating mode. In addition, to ensure signal stability and collect more data, both devices are equipped with three antennas. Atheros CSI Tool, an open source tool, is installed for CSI data collection.

4.2   Data Collection

We positioned the receiver and transmitter 1 m apart, while the subject sat at the midpoint of the line of sight (LOS) between the two devices and about 50 cm away from the line of sight (LOS) for data collection. At the same time, a monocular camera was set up in front of the subject's head at an equal height to collect the image data. This will be used as important data for generating head pose data, which will be used as labels for training the CSI-based model. According to the method of [18], we let the transmitter send packets 100 Hz while recording image data. To ensure that the CSI data and image data are right for it, we did not receive 100 CSI data and let the camera take a picture, which means that the camera records image data 20 Hz. In time order, no 5 CSI data correspond to one picture, i.e., it corresponds to one head pose.

   In order to obtain head movements in various directions of the head, we spent 5 h collecting 1.5 million CSI packets, and the subjects were asked to rotate their heads in the directions of pitch, roll, yaw, and various combinations of directions, respectively, while also collecting head movements at rest, and at different speeds under normal conditions. In addition, since the reflection of WiFi signals varies from person to person and from static environment to static environment, a total of three subjects were asked to collect data in two different rooms, i.e., six domains, in order to improve the generalizability of the data (Table 1).

Table 1. Number of collected packets. The number refers to the number of the test subject. We asked three subjects to perform head posture collection in two different rooms.

People	1	2	3
Room1	350000	220000	220000
Room2	250000	220000	220000

4.3   Neural Network

Network Setting. After data preprocessing including noise reduction, PCA dimensionality reduction, etc. we get a picture-like sample that has three channels A, P, F, where A is the amplitude of the CSI and P is the phase of the CSI data and F is the frequency domain information obtained from A by Fourier transform. So the shape of 1 sample is $[W, K, 3]$, where W is the sliding window length and K is the number of subcarriers. We use a 6-layer convolutional neural network and connected to a SENet [10] to extract the features of the data, and then four fully linked layers for regression, except for the output layer, the rest of the network uses military relu as the activation function, and a layer is added before the last layer dropout is added before the last layer to avoid the problem of failure to converge. The detailed structure is shown in Table 2.

Table 2. Overview of the network structure. 1. The convolution kernel of CNN layers 1, 3 and 5 is 3×3, which is used to learn the relationship between time domain and sub-channel. 2. The convolution kernels of the CNN layers of layers 2, 4, and 6 eh 1×1 and are used to give the number of channels for data boosting only.

Network	Input size	Output size	Stride
Input	$40 \times 30 \times 3$	$40 \times 30 \times 3$	
Conv2d	$40 \times 30 \times 3$	$19 \times 14 \times 8$	(2, 2)
Conv2d	$19 \times 14 \times 8$	$19 \times 14 \times 8$	(1, 1)
Conv2d	$19 \times 14 \times 8$	$9 \times 6 \times 64$	(2, 2)
Conv2d	$9 \times 6 \times 64$	$9 \times 6 \times 64$	(1, 1)
Conv2d	$9 \times 6 \times 64$	$4 \times 2 \times 512$	(2, 2)
Conv2d	$4 \times 2 \times 512$	$4 \times 2 \times 1024$	(1, 1)
SE	$4 \times 2 \times 1024$	$4 \times 2 \times 1024$	
Flatten	8192	8192	
Dense	8192	1024	
Dense	1024	1024	
Dense	1024	256	
Dense	256	128	
Dropout	128	128	
Dense	128	3	

Loss Function. Since our network regresses the head pose in pitch, roll, yaw directly, we choose Huber Loss in the loss function. Huber Loss is a parameterized loss function for regression problems. It conbines the best features of MSE ans MAE and can reduce the interference of outliers. The Huber Loss L_H in our loss function is expressed as:

$$L_H = \frac{1}{T} \sum_{t=1}^{T} \frac{1}{N} - sum_{i=1}^{N} \left\| \widetilde{d_t^i} - d_t^i \right\|_H \tag{7}$$

where $\|.\|_H$ refers to the Huber norm, N refers to the number of direction demension, $\widetilde{d_t^i}$ and d_t^i means the predicted and real head pose at time t. It is defined as follows:

$$\|\widetilde{x}\|_H = \frac{1}{n} sum_{i=1}^{n} huber(x_i) \tag{8}$$

where:

$$huber(x_i) = \begin{cases} 0.5x_i^2, & if\, x_i < \theta \\ |x_i| - 0.5, & otherwise \end{cases} \tag{9}$$

4.4 Training

Since our data are generated based on sliding windows to segment, in order to determine the optimal sliding window size, we train the model on data generated from several different sliding windows. Epoch is taken as 40, and we also compare the results of PCA dimensionality reduction for the CSI data by directly selecting the maximum variance antenna pair, and for all antenna pairs, in order to determine the dimensionality reduction method. To evaluate the model performance, we use the k-fold method, where k is taken to be 10, to evaluate the model for training, and the results will be discussed in detail in Discussion part.

5 Discussion

5.1 Comparison of Different Sensors

We surveyed the commonly available sensors for detecting human activity, see Table 3. The most widely used approach in studies of head motion tracking is image-based. Monocular cameras are inexpensive, easy to deploy, and have a large research literature. But these sensors are sensitive to light, do not handle occlusion well, and often do not obtain good results for large angles of head posture. Depth cameras improve the accuracy to some extent because of the rich depth information they obtain, but are relatively expensive. And the vision-based approach carries the risk of privacy disclosure. Radar arrays can effectively protect privacy, but the equipment is also relatively expensive and not easy to deploy. Although gyroscopes can obtain accurate head angles, they require users to wear additional equipment, which is not convenient for real-time detection in daily life. Finally, we use WiFi sensors, which are not only inexpensive, but also CSI data can obtain rich environmental information to detect head posture. In addition, it can also work in the dark, non-visual distance, obscured, etc. And, CSI data can also effectively protect user privacy.

5.2 Comparison of the Variance of Each Antenna Pair

From Sect. 3.4, we tried to calculate the variance of each data in each antenna pair, and the antenna pair with the largest variance was selected since, in general, response data with large variance are sensitive to human actions and more likely to carry useful information. Table 4 and Table 5 shows the results.

As shown in the table, for the signal amplitude data, we choose the antenna pair of transmitter 2nd antenna and receiver 2nd antenna; for the signal phase information, we choose the antenna pair of transmitter 2nd antenna and receiver 3rd antenna. Because they both obtain the maximum variance in their respective fields, the signal of this antenna pair is more sensitive to the head activity and theoretically better responds to the head posture change.

Table 3. The table shows the characteristics possessed by the various sensors commonly used to detect human activity.

Sensor	Device free	NLOS	Work in darkness	Anti-obscuring	Low cost	Protect privacy
Monocular Camera	o	×	×	×	o	×
TOF Camera	o	×	×	×	×	×
Radar Array	o	o	o	o	×	o
Gyroscope	×	⟍	o	⟍	o	o
WiFi	o	o	o	o	o	o

Table 4. The average of the variance of the amplitude of each subcarrier for different antenna pairs.

RX/TX	1	2	3
1	1785.3	907.6	2341.4
2	33.7	4876.3	26.5
3	484.6	1997.0	3217.8

5.3 Effect of Sliding Window Size

Because our CSI data is a long temporal data, in order to align the CSI data with the image, we let every 5 CSI data correspond to one image. And then, we choose the 5 CSI data of current moment and the front 15 CSI data to form the first two channels of the CSI image. let X be a CSI sequence, then $X(s,t) = [H_1, H_2, ..., H_t]$, we take $t = 15$–45 (5 is the interval) for the experiments, respectively, and the results are shown in Table 6 From the results, 40 has a higher correct rate, which may be different from the amount of information stored in different lengths of time series.

5.4 Comparison of PCA and Subcarrier Selection

In the section of data dimensionality reduction, we just used two different methods for dimensionality reduction. In order to ensure that the reduced data retains as much information as possible, in the method of selecting antenna pairs, since our device has three antennas for both the transmitter and receiver, there are a total of 9 different antenna pairs, and we select the pair with the largest average variance for training by calculating the variance of the data between each antenna pair. PCA, on the other hand, finds the dimension that carries the most information over a total of 504 dimensions of the 9 antenna pairs and performs a projection transformation. The former speaks the data to 56 dimensions and the latter is reduced to 30 dimensions, and the results are shown in Fig. 9 (Table 7).

Table 5. The average of the variance of the phase of each subcarrier for different antenna pairs.

RX/TX	1	2	3
1	0.00050	0.00343	0.00453
2	0.17867	0.00017	0.7574
3	0.1682	0.00101	0.00059

Table 6. We change window size to search a better value.

Window	15	20	25	30	35	40	45
Acc	0.843	0.863	0.874	0.876	0.882	0.898	0.895

Table 7. Five-fold's result. And the last column shows the average accuracy.

	1	2	3	4	5	Average
PCA	85.88	88.17	88.98	89.54	90.39	88.60
Select	75.21	78.10	79.62	80.21	80.38	78.70

5.5 K-fold

From the above steps, we finally choose to use PCA for data compression on 504-dimensional data, and cut to size of 30 belonging to sliding window, and perform k-ford witnessing on the model, and we take $k = 10$. The results of cross-witnessing are shown in Table 8.

As can be seen from the table, our model can achieve an average correct rate of 88.93%, with the highest reaching 90.39%, which confirms the feasibility of our method. Information can be extracted from the CSI data of WiFi that responds to environmental conditions, from which the human head movement can be restored. The following figure shows the comparison of some data predictions with the real values.

The table shows that our model can achieve an average correct rate of 90, with the highest reaching 90, which confirms the feasibility of our method. The information that can be extracted from the CSI data of WiFi to respond to the environmental conditions can be restored from it to the human head movement. The following figure shows the comparison of some data predictions with the real values (Fig. 8).

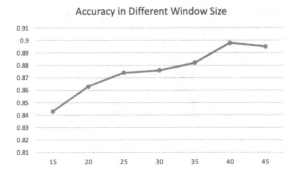

Fig. 8. This chart shows the relationship between sliding window size and correct rate.

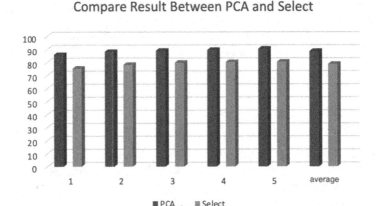

Fig. 9. This chart shows the accuracy between PCA and Select.

Table 8. The accuracy by k-fold. Then, we acculate the average of 10 results.

k-fold	1	2	3	4	5	6	7	8	9	10	Avg
Acc	85.88	87.57	88.17	88.98	89.17	89.40	89.84	89.54	90.31	90.39	88.92

6   Conclusion

We have presented method to track human head motion using channel state information (CSI) from WiFi. WiFi reduces deployment costs because it is already widely used, and the WiFi signal is independent of light, which makes the sensor effective even in a light-free environment. Also, there is no privacy leakage problem like images, which brings discomfort to people. Moreover, WiFi CSI is a kind of fine-grained data, which can do many things originally unimaginable if the right feature extraction method is found. Our experiment is to recover the orientation of the human head in 3D space from this WiFi signal, i.e., the angles of pitch, yaw, and roll in three directions. As CSI is an electromagnetic wave, it also receives interference from other waves, and CSI data is highly abstract, and the training process is not as intuitive as image visualization. We will continue our research in this direction.

Acknowledgement. This work was supported by JSPS KAKENHI Grant Numbers 20H00622 and 17KT0154.

References

1. Abdelnasser, H., Youssef, M., Harras, K.A.: WiGest: a ubiquitous WiFi-based gesture recognition system. In: 2015 IEEE Conference on Computer Communications (INFOCOM), pp. 1472–1480. IEEE (2015)
2. Blanz, V., Vetter, T.: A morphable model for the synthesis of 3D faces. In: Proceedings of the 26th Annual Conference on Computer Graphics and Interactive Techniques, pp. 187–194 (1999)
3. Borghi, G., Fabbri, M., Vezzani, R., Calderara, S., Cucchiara, R.: Face-from-depth for head pose estimation on depth images. IEEE Trans. Pattern Anal. Mach. Intell. **42**(3), 596–609 (2018)
4. Cao, C., Weng, Y., Lin, S., Zhou, K.: 3D shape regression for real-time facial animation. ACM Trans. Graph. (TOG) **32**(4), 1–10 (2013)
5. Chang, C.Y., Chung, P.C., Yeh, Y.S., Yang, J.F.: An intelligent bulletin board system with real-time vision-based interaction using head pose estimation. In: 18th International Conference on Pattern Recognition (ICPR 2006), vol. 1, pp. 1140–1143. IEEE (2006)
6. Chen, Z., Zhang, L., Jiang, C., Cao, Z., Cui, W.: WiFi CSI based passive human activity recognition using attention based BLSTM. IEEE Trans. Mob. Comput. **18**(11), 2714–2724 (2018)
7. Ding, J., Wang, Y.: WiFi CSI-based human activity recognition using deep recurrent neural network. IEEE Access **7**, 174257–174269 (2019)
8. Gu, Y., Ren, F., Li, J.: PAWS: passive human activity recognition based on WiFi ambient signals. IEEE Internet Things J. **3**(5), 796–805 (2015)
9. Hoang, M.T., Yuen, B., Dong, X., Lu, T., Westendorp, R., Reddy, K.: Recurrent neural networks for accurate RSSI indoor localization. IEEE Internet Things J. **6**(6), 10639–10651 (2019)
10. Hu, J., Shen, L., Sun, G.: Squeeze-and-excitation networks. In: Proceedings of the IEEE Conference on Computer Vision and Pattern Recognition, pp. 7132–7141 (2018)
11. Jha, S., Busso, C.: Analyzing the relationship between head pose and gaze to model driver visual attention. In: 2016 IEEE 19th International Conference on Intelligent Transportation Systems (ITSC), pp. 2157–2162. IEEE (2016)
12. Matsumoto, Y., Zelinsky, A.: An algorithm for real-time stereo vision implementation of head pose and gaze direction measurement. In: Proceedings Fourth IEEE International Conference on Automatic Face and Gesture Recognition (Cat. No. PR00580), pp. 499–504. IEEE (2000)
13. Sigg, S., Blanke, U., Tröster, G.: The telepathic phone: frictionless activity recognition from WiFi-RSSI. In: 2014 IEEE International Conference on Pervasive Computing and Communications (PerCom), pp. 148–155. IEEE (2014)

14. Vatahska, T., Bennewitz, M., Behnke, S.: Feature-based head pose estimation from images. In: 2007 7th IEEE-RAS International Conference on Humanoid Robots, pp. 330–335. IEEE (2007)
15. Wang, F., Zhou, S., Panev, S., Han, J., Huang, D.: Person-in-WiFi: fine-grained person perception using WiFi. In: Proceedings of the IEEE/CVF International Conference on Computer Vision, pp. 5452–5461 (2019)
16. Wang, H., Zhang, D., Wang, Y., Ma, J., Wang, Y., Li, S.: RT-fall: a real-time and contactless fall detection system with commodity WiFi devices. IEEE Trans. Mob. Comput. **16**(2), 511–526 (2016)
17. Wang, Y., Liu, J., Chen, Y., Gruteser, M., Yang, J., Liu, H.: E-eyes: device-free location-oriented activity identification using fine-grained WiFi signatures. In: Proceedings of the 20th Annual International Conference on Mobile Computing and Networking, pp. 617–628 (2014)
18. Wang, Y., Guo, L., Lu, Z., Wen, X., Zhou, S., Meng, W.: From point to space: 3D moving human pose estimation using commodity WiFi. IEEE Commun. Lett. **25**(7), 2235–2239 (2021)
19. Whitehill, J., Movellan, J.R.: A discriminative approach to frame-by-frame head pose tracking. In: 2008 8th IEEE International Conference on Automatic Face & Gesture Recognition, pp. 1–7. IEEE (2008)
20. Xie, X., Shin, K.G., Yousefi, H., He, S.: Wireless CSI-based head tracking in the driver seat. In: Proceedings of the 14th International Conference on emerging Networking EXperiments and Technologies, pp. 112–125 (2018)
21. Yang, R., Zhang, Z.: Model-based head pose tracking with stereovision. In: Proceedings of Fifth IEEE International Conference on Automatic Face Gesture Recognition, pp. 255–260. IEEE (2002)
22. Zhou, Y., Gregson, J.: WHENet: real-time fine-grained estimation for wide range head pose. arXiv preprint arXiv:2005.10353 (2020)

Participatory Sensing Platform Concept for Wildlife Animals in the Himalaya Region, Nepal

Daisuké Shimotoku[1]📷, Tian Yuan[2]📷, Laxmi Kumar Parajuli[1]📷, and Hill Hiroki Kobayashi[1(✉)]📷

[1] Information Technology Center, The University of Tokyo, Tokyo, Japan
{shimotoku,parajuli,kobayashi}@ds.itc.u-tokyo.ac.jp
[2] Graduate School of Frontier Sciences, The University of Tokyo, Tokyo, Japan
t.yuan@csis.u-tokyo.ac.jp

Abstract. Human Computer Biosphere Interaction (HCBI) is a relatively new academic discipline that acts as a critical juncture between the conservation biology and the Information, Communication and Technology (ICT). HCBI domain exploits the capabilities of the repertoire of available technological tools to remotely sense data from difficult geographical terrains in a secure and cost-effective manner. In this perspective paper, we highlight some of the bio-acoustic technologies that we have been using for our research in Fukushima prefecture, Japan. Learning from our experience in Fukushima, we provide our preliminary viewpoint on the possibility of incorporating HCBI research in Manang, Nepal. Our impressions are largely based on the site visit to Manang and informal interaction with locals and conservation specialists. The preliminary feasibility study will prove useful in future as we plan a full-fledged ICT based animal conservation study to assess how the application of ICT tools for wildlife monitoring can contribute to the economic empowerment of locals in Manang who depend on subsistence farming. In summary, this paper provides a preliminary overview of the potentiality of technology transfer from Japan to the remote hilly areas in Nepal for wildlife conservation by employing ICT tools and participatory sensing approach.

Keywords: Annapurna Conservation Area · Eco-acoustics · Fukushima exclusion zone · Human computation · Human computer biosphere interaction

1   Introduction

Recent decades have witnessed an explosion of plethora of computer-based technologies. In today's industrial and information age, it is becoming increasingly difficult to find a society which does not interact with digital technologies. Termed as the Human Computer Interaction (HCI), an open-ended interaction

N. A. Streitz and S. Konomi (Eds.): HCII 2022, LNCS 13326, pp. 87–98, 2022.
https://doi.org/10.1007/978-3-031-05431-0_6

between the human user and the computer has been made possible through the intervening interface medium. Among several examples of HCI, one of the popular examples is perhaps Siri, where computer responds to our voice interface. The concept of HCI has also been extended to the animal world in recent years. Monitoring locomotory behavior of pets, such as cats or dogs, through the GPS monitors or video cameras are some of the examples of the Human Computer Pet Interaction (HCPI). As a further extension of HCI and HCPI, the concept of Human Computer Biosphere Interaction (HCBI) has been put forward to study the interaction between humans and ecosystem using computer technologies. The concept of HCBI particularly pertains to auditory biosphere and as such it is complex, uncountable and non-linguistic in nature. The communication between humans and biosphere entails scenarios such as the interaction via computer interface between humans and the information that originates in the nature, for example, the sound of trees in forest or the sound of wild animals which are hard to decode and comprehend to human.

While preserving the ecological environment in its natural state *in situ*, research in the HCBI discipline ultimately aims to promote the interaction between humans and our ecology. This is particularly relevant in this modern era where urbanization is marked and rampant in nature, often interfering with the ecological pristine. The urban civilization has reached the pinnacle of development, but at the cost of the destruction of the nature. However, despite all the prosperity, nature is an indispensable component of mankind both from an emotional and aesthetic viewpoint. For this very reason, each country has allocated a portion of their territory for protected areas, conservation areas and national parks. Although the initial goal of these sort of protected areas is to conserve wild animals, ironically the influx of tourists and visitors in these sites may inadvertently cause destruction to the wildlife habitat. Furthermore, the vehicular movements in these areas also lead to roadkills of wild animals. One potential solution to this paradoxical problem is to employ the computer interface tools so that humans can experience a simulated feel of being in the nature itself. HCBI research also provides biologists an opportunity to study the behaviors of wildlife ranging from elusive, endangered to dangerous animals. A better grasp of the wildlife habitat and their behavior also aids societies to plan their urbanization and economic activities in an eco-friendly manner. In light of all these scenarios, HCBI envisages a sustainable society where humans can attain their economic prosperity while concurrently maintaining their co-existence with the nature.

Difficult geographical terrain and areas that are prone to natural and manmade disasters are not easily accessible to researchers. As it becomes difficult to conduct longitudinal studies of animal behavior in the physical presence of researchers in such areas, HCBI can be a powerful research tool in these circumstances. Storm, hurricane, landslide, earthquake, volcanic eruptions, nuclear accident, war, forest fires, pollution are some of the natural and man-made disasters that pose a great threat to the well-being and survival of wild animals. Australian bushfire in late 2019 and early 2020 can be a good example to depict the magnitude of damage that man-made disasters can inflict on wildlife.

A study commissioned by the World Wide Fund for Nature estimated that the number of animals that were either killed or displaced by the Australian bushfire could be as high as three billion [27]. Similar appalling scenario could be observed in other disasters as well. For example, two of the worst nuclear accidents in the history, namely, the Chernobyl nuclear power plant accident in 1986 in the then Soviet Union and the Fukushima nuclear disaster in Japan in 2011, have severely threatened the well-being of wildlife population. Research indicates that the nuclear radiation has caused an unprecedented genetic mutation and the potential genetic drift in the wildlife population in Chernobyl and Fukushima [13,14]. In fact, the damage and loss to the wildlife in the aftermath of disaster have often been overlooked and even the Post-Disaster Need Assessment (PDNA) from the government authorities puts a predominant focus on humans. This can place a risk to the human community in the disaster-affected areas as failure to monitor wildlife behavior and movement may even ultimately lead to the spread of zoonotic diseases to the human settlements in vicinity of the disaster hit areas. Similarly, imbalance in ecological pyramid due to the loss of wildlife by the disaster incidents will eventually have a detrimental effect in humans as well. Although the concept of post-disaster environmental need assessment to study the impact of disaster in wildlife has been gradually evolving, a firm need of HCBI discipline in the aftermath of disaster is yet to be widely incorporated by various stakeholders of ecological conservation. Remotely tracking animal behavior in real-time by the use of computer interface could be one of the best research disciplines to safely monitor wildlife population and devise possible intervention strategies for their survival and well-being in the aftermath of disaster incidents.

The nature of ecological destruction and the mitigatory approach differs depending on the topography and socio-economic status of each country. In industrial nations, as discussed above, the problem could even range in the scale of nuclear disaster accident. However, in the developing nations like Nepal, deforestation, forest fires, retaliatory killings of wild endangered animals by villagers and farmers when they prey on their livestock, and poaching or illegal trade of animals for fur and skin could be the major threats for the survivability of wild animals. It is estimated that forest fire alone could lead to the loss of as high as 40 % of animals in the affected area in Nepal [2]. Apart from the carelessness of the tobacco smokers and other passers-by in the forest, agricultural activities such as burning twigs and woods for ashes by farmers, intentionally setting forest fires by livestock owners to promote the growth of new grasses for grazing livestock could be ascribable to the forest fire incidents in Nepal [12]. This suggests that the mitigation strategy for the natural as well as anthropogenic disaster incidents could differ between the industrial and the developing nations. Encompassing the aspects introduced above, in this review paper, we highlight our research findings from the HCBI-based studies in the nuclear disaster hit area in Fukushima. Furthermore, based on our impression from the site visit and preliminary, informal discussion with the locals, we also discuss the feasibility to potentially extrapolate HCBI research for studying wildlife species in the hilly areas in Nepal.

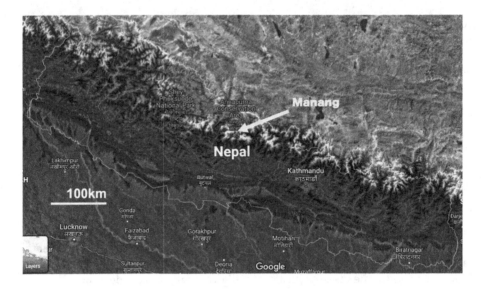

Fig. 1. Locality map of Manang, modified from the Google Map

2   Methods

Several methods are employed in conducting wildlife surveys. The presence of an animal in an ecological domain can be inferred either through the trace survey by humans or by the analysis of still images, movies and animal sounds. However, it is generally a labor intensive task to estimate the number and density of wild animals by employing these conventional methods. Although an aeronautical method could be utilized to survey a wider area, we cannot entirely depend on this method as well as it requires a significant cost. Thus, a good combination of several methods should be carefully adopted keeping in consideration of the cost and the throughput of the method involved. The speed of the research project can also be expedited by the help of trained ecological enthusiasts and citizen scientists. In the following paragraphs, we briefly discuss some of the ICT-based methodologies for animal research, including the involvement of citizen scientists for participatory sensing.

2.1   Visual Survey

Camera trapping is considered to be one of the most common and efficient survey methods for animal counting [3,16]. Camera releases the shutter in response to the animal motion and stores still or motion images on an internal SD card. However, the movement of leaves and light shadows can also cause the shutter to be triggered inadvertently for motion-triggered cameras. The latest model cameras are capable of running on internal batteries for about six months. Researchers generally visit the site once in every two weeks to collect data and confirm the normal operation of the camera. In some cases, if the conditions permit, images can also be sent directly from the camera to the cloud via 4G connection. As images are taken automatically in camera traps, a large number of images can be generated. Although these images used to be manually processed by human in the past, in recent years the application of deep learning approach have greatly eased the animal identification process. For example, Giraldo-Zuluaga *et al.* [9] have reported that up to eight mammal species could be identified with a 93% precision using convoluted neural network approach. Elias *et al.* [7] also reported the concept of edge computing to reduce communication with the cloud by putting the burden of this recognition on the edge side (camera side). Although this creates a pressure on battery life, it does make an effective use of low bandwidth lines to connect to the cloud system.

2.2 Acoustic Survey

Eco-acoustic surveys have been conducted to analyze the sounds produced by wild animals. The effectiveness of camera traps is generally limited in the forest due to the poor visibility caused by obstacles such as leaves, trees, and the terrain *per se*. Therefore, eco-acoustic surveys are often used for small animals, especially birds. Compared to the camera images, sound recordings generally consume low data volume and provides environmental information over the entire circumference, making it easier to conduct long-term monitoring. The data collected are either analyzed by using Fourier transformation in frequency decomposition or by employing machine learning approach. Farina *et al.* attempted to analyze these recordings using an eco-acoustic index [8]. Frequency decomposition are applied to the recording to measure the intensity of the sound components. For example, the NDSI, one of the most utilized indices [22], is expressed as the ratio of the high-frequency component of the recording, which contains animal sound, to the low-frequency part of the background. This method can identify sounds of biological origin with a relatively small computational load. Cai *et al.* [5] compared the identification performance among hidden Markov models, neural networks, and support vector machines, using Mel-cepstrum as input. The study showed that pre-processing of the sound has a significant impact on the accuracy, and the identification is more likely to fail when multiple birds are singing at the same time.

2.3 Satellite Imaging Survey

With the rapid technological developments and the increasing interaction between the satellite-based remote sensing and the Internet of Things (IoT)-based ground sensing methods, these two terms have often been used interchangeably. Although the distinction between these two has become gradually blurred, there does exists a sort of boundary between them. Satellite image sensing sensors convert the surface electromagnetic reflection features onto images. On the other hand, IoT-based sensors converts mechanical and electrical features at the ground to record physical attributes, such as the auditory, geographical, thermal attributes etc. Despite the high cost of the satellite images, satellite sensing does have definite advantages in comparison to the ground-based measurements.

In our potential future study, we conceptualize to use some of the geological and ecological parameters such as the elevation, slope, aspect, normalized difference vegetation index (NDVI) to understand the habitat preference of the wild animals in the Himalayas. The geo-ecological parameters can be obtained through the satellite images. However, as mentioned above, the satellite images are costly and as such it is desirable to combine satellite-based and IoT based methods.

2.4   Human Survey

In order to increase the breadth of the data collection, cooperation of ecological enthusiasts or local residents have also been sought in some projects. For example, Sullivan *et al.* [23] of the Cornell Lab of Ornithology used an online site named e-bird to solicit research reports from the public. Global bird migration reports have in fact been prepared through these citizen science methods. In Annapurna Conservation Area (ACA), community has been involved in making decisions for conservation-based activities. This concept is somewhat similar to participatory sensing. Bajracharya *et al.* [1] found that the abundance of barking deer and Himalayan tahr was higher in ACA, where community-based decision-making system exists for nature conservation, than in other areas.

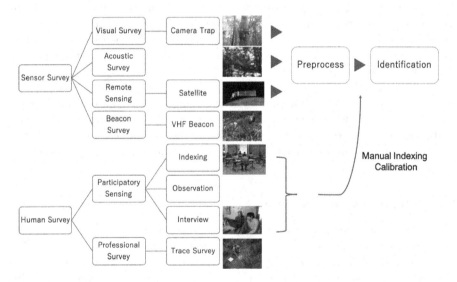

Fig. 2. Methods utilized for wildlife survey (some of the figures are adapted from [26]).

3   Results

3.1   Examples of Some HCBI Related Projects in Japan

In this section, we introduce some of the HCBI related studies that have been conducted in Japan. Saito *et al.* [18] have been operating an automatic monitoring system for forest observation since 1995 in a primary forest that lacks basic infrastructure. This system (called as Cyberforest) obtains environmental information from the entire circumference of the forest by capturing still images and the live sound. The forest environment is harsh, and it is not feasible to store data in the forest for a prolonged duration. Therefore, we made a constant live stream transmission to the university server to refrain from the possibility of data damage. Along with the live stream transmission, the records are archived at http://www.cyberforest.jp/ and it is continually made available to the public. Similarly, Kobayashi *et al.* [11] have continued to acquire live sound in the forest in Namie Town in Fukushima Prefecture, a restricted zone following the Fukushima disaster. The audio is publicly accessible from https:// radioactivelivesoundscape.net/. Animal sounds can be frequently heard in this audio as there is an animal pasture in the vicinity of our recording site. Similarly, Ueta *et al.* [25] have been working online simultaneously with other colleagues to remotely listen to the sounds of birds in a primary forest in Saitama Prefecture, Japan for bird identification.

With the participation of a large number of students, Nakamura *et al.* [15] took a series of time-lapse images over the span of years to study tree phenology (for instance, Casuarinas). It is expected that through this study, students will be acquainted with the natural environment and can intuitively feel environmental changes as they analyse these time-lapse images in their own classroom. During the course of image analysis, they may even discover hitherto unidentified objects. As the field has no capacity to accept a large number of participants simultaneously, participatory sensing by the public, even remotely as described in the above study, can engage a large number of people with the nature. Furthermore, this study also serves as a proof of concept that, apart from the ecological experts, amateurs and students with a minimal knowledge on ecology can also engage in participatory sensing.

3.2   Examples of Some ICT-Based Conservation Efforts in Nepal

Nepal has placed itself in the forefront of wildlife research by integrating latest ICT technologies. There exist several literature where camera tracking, radio collar, GIS (Geographic Information System), GPS (Global Positioning System) have been used for wildlife monitoring. These technologies coupled with geospatial modeling approach can provide insight into wildlife habitat, habitat use and selection. For example, satellite images were analyzed to construct habitat suitability maps for Tibetan wild ass in ACA in Mustang district [20] and for Asiatic black bear and red panda in Makalu Barun National Park in the eastern part of Nepal [21]. Time-lapse satellite imagery over years can also be used to deduce any alterations in the vegetation coverage, species abundance and transboundary movement of animals and their dietary pattern in relation to variables of interest such as temperature, humidity, global warming, pollution, tourism influx etc. As an example, in a study by Chaplin and Brabyn [6], the analysis of Landsat satellite images from 1999 to 2011 in ACA revealed a net reduction in forest around villages where tourist influx was high. Similarly, Thapa et al. [24] used Landsat images to compare the land cover changes and the habitat occupancy between 2002 and 2012 in Laljhadi-Mohana wildlife corridor, Nepal.

Largely owing to its topography, Nepal has a comparative advantage in studying mountain ecosystems. Nepal hosts eight of the fourteen mountains that are taller than 8000 m. In these last couple of decades, mountain ecosystems have been a matter of considerable research interest even from the perspective of global warming. Endangered species such as snow leopards, which can only be found in the mountains, can be considered as an indicator species of the high-altitude ecosystem because of the fact that these animals are highly sensitive to any slight changes in the environment. Latest ICT technologies have been of critical importance in remote, systematic study of snow leopards in Nepal for obtaining information on home range estimation, dietary pattern, survival data/mortality, body temperature, habitat selection etc. Rightly understanding the potential of cutting-edge technologies, Nepal has successfully completed satellite telemetry studies of eight snow leopards so far. For the first-time in the satellite telemetry studies of snow leopards in Nepal, four snow leopards were successfully studied by satellite telemetry between 2012–2017 in the Kanchenjunga conservation area in the eastern part of Nepal. Thereafter, two snow leopards were collared for satellite telemetry studies in 2019 in the Shey-Phoksundo national park that lies in Dolpa and Mugu districts. Again in 2021, two other snow leopards were collared in the Shey-Phoksundo national park. All these telemetry studies have been made possible by the joint effort of the Department of National Parks and Wildlife Conservation of the Government of Nepal, WWF Nepal, National Trust for Nature Conservation (NTNC), and the local stakeholders in the Kanchenjunga conservation area and the Shey-Phoksundo national park.

4   Discussion

The concept of human computer biosphere interaction (HCBI) has been gradually gaining its momentum. Although the very concept of HCBI is yet to be incorporated into many of the conservation action plans, the identification of ICT as a crucial component of wildlife management has been realized both in the developed and developing nations. We believe that the concept of HCBI and integration of ICT tools for wildlife monitoring is even more pertinent in mountainous areas, such as that in Nepal, which are generally difficult to access for researchers. Information and Communication Technology (ICT) policy of Nepal, 2015 also stresses on the necessity to use ICT for environment and natural resources management, including the installation of early warning systems for disaster risk reduction. Furthermore, it also mentions the need to build capacity of the stakeholders in using remote sensing technology and GIS software. Similarly, National Biodiversity Strategy and Action Plan and Species Conservation Action Plan are also in place for safeguarding wildlife in Nepal. Apart from the ecological perspective, protecting flora and fauna also has a great economic benefit both at the local and national level. For example, through biodiversity conservation and deforestation, Nepal aims to reduce 9 million tons of carbon dioxide (CO_2) emissions by 2025 and receive US$ 45 million financial incentive through Emission Reductions Payment Agreement (ERPA) program from the World Bank. The concept of HCBI can be instrumental in supporting Nepal's effort in biodiversity conservation.

The success of a conservation program highly depends on the participation of local stakeholders and the residents in the vicinity of the conservation areas. This is especially important in resource-limited countries where government or the other organizations involved in conservation may not be well-equipped with available ICT technologies to monitor wildlife in every nook and corner of the country. In Nepal as well, citizen science approach has also been undertaken for monitoring wildlife. With the support of the Government of Nepal and the organizations like NTNC and WWF, more than 400 community-based anti-poaching units are active in various parts of the country [4]. These units assist the responsible authorities for monitoring the well-being and the survival of the wildlife and rescue them when needed. Similarly, the Snow Leopard Conservation Action Plan for Nepal 2017–2021 prepared by the Department of National Parks and Wildlife Conservation, The Ministry of Forests and Soil Conservation has also acknowledged the involvement of more than 20 citizen scientists in participatory sensing in Kanchenjunga conservation area for snow leopard telemetry study.

In addition to being a biological problem, the conservation programs have social and economic dimensions as well [19]. When involving citizen scientists for participatory sensing, we need to motivate locals towards conservation by devising win-win strategy both from the environmental and socio-economic perspective. Around snow leopard conservation area, in the absence of a proper compensation scheme, locals may not show a great interest to participate as a citizen scientist. In fact, increasing the number of snow leopards will negatively affect locals, most of whom are subsistence farmers. Snow leopards' prey on their livestock and any loss of livestock incurs financial burden on the locals and as such locals' attitude towards snow leopards have been found to be mostly negative [10,17]. This scenario has also forced retaliatory killings of snow leopards by the locals. During our informal conversation with locals in Manang, they also expressed opinion that the existence of some sort of attractive insurance schemes for their livestock would greatly help them to sustain financial loss when snow leopard kills their livestock. Arranging soft loans, economic upliftment of locals by promoting eco-tourism and agro-tourism could be some of the mechanisms through which locals' participation in conservation and participatory sensing will increase in the context of Nepal. Moreover, the organizations involved in wildlife conservation should accordingly build capacity of locals to handle GPS, VHF devices, camera traps etc. Ultimately, through the awareness programs it will be important to educate locals about the necessity of wildlife conservation, and that protecting ecosystem is essential for human survival as well. Locals can be made aware of the conservation programs through mass media such as radio, television and even through the social networking sites. This will also prove beneficial to recruit conservation volunteers, especially the youths in the locality.

The experience that we have gained from several years of research in disaster hit Fukushima area in Japan can prove useful in Nepal as well. Fukushima and mountains areas in Nepal share commonalities in terms of the difficulty to access and the lack of well-developed infrastructure for ICT research. Apart from the technical aspects, winning the trust of local residents and the coordination with the local stakeholders were the key for the successful project implementation in Fukushima. Perhaps the same holds true in case of Nepal as well. In order to informally assess the feasibility of conducting HCBI based research, we had visited Manang in late 2019. Informal discussion was conducted with the local residents and the stakeholders about several ongoing efforts to conserve snow leopard. We had an impression that due to the geographical remoteness from Kathmandu, the country's capital and Pokhara, the Metropolitan city in Gandaki province where Manang is located; it is difficult to obtain repair parts if any ICT tools get damaged during the course of research. Thus, in all the instances, back-up accessories need to be stored in the research site. Moreover, the personnel in the conservation related organizations in Manang are dominated by ecologists, with hardly any representation of ICT related experts. As a result, they need to be trained beforehand to operate ICT tools. It also does not seem quite feasible to install high-performance computers in the research site in Manang due to the electric power constraints. Moreover, in order to protect the devices for the damage caused by the fine sand particles that are abundant in the dry fields in Manang, it is desirable to have dust-free ICT equipment for field research in Manang. Amidst all these technical challenges that one might need to overcome to perform ICT based research, the warmth of friendship that researchers receive from the locals will greatly help in research implementation in Manang.

Acknowledgements. This study is supported by the Coordination Funds for Promoting AeroSpace Utilization (2021–2023) grants from the Ministry of Education, Culture, Sports, Science, and Technology (MEXT) and a grant from the Tateisi Science and Technology Foundation.

References

1. Bajracharya, S.B., Furley, P.A., Newton, A.C.: Effectiveness of community involvement in delivering conservation benefits to the Annapurna conservation area, Nepal. Environ. Conserv. **32**(3), 239–247 (2005)
2. BBC: Nepal forest fires 'cause big wildlife loss'. https://www.bbc.com/news/science-environment-17937620
3. Beery, S.: Scaling biodiversity monitoring for the data age. XRDS **27**(4), 14–18 (2021). https://doi.org/10.1145/3466857

4. Bhatta, K., Bhattarai, S., Aryal, A.: Community based anti-poaching operation: effective model for wildlife conservation in Nepal. Poult. Fish. Wildl. Sci **6**(2) (2018)
5. Cai, J., Ee, D., Pham, B., Roe, P., Zhang, J.: Sensor network for the monitoring of ecosystem: Bird species recognition. In: 2007 3rd International Conference on Intelligent Sensors, Sensor Networks and Information, pp. 293–298. IEEE (2007)
6. Chaplin, J., Brabyn, L.: Using remote sensing and GIS to investigate the impacts of tourism on forest cover in the Annapurna Conservation Area, Nepal. Appl. Geogr. **43**, 159–168 (2013)
7. Elias, A.R., Golubovic, N., Krintz, C., Wolski, R.: Where's the bear?-Automating wildlife image processing using IoT and edge cloud systems. In: 2017 IEEE/ACM Second International Conference on Internet-of-Things Design and Implementation (IoTDI), pp. 247–258. IEEE (2017)
8. Farina, A., Lattanzi, E., Malavasi, R., Pieretti, N., Piccioli, L.: Avian soundscapes and cognitive landscapes: theory, application and ecological perspectives. Landsc. Ecol. **26**(9), 1257–1267 (2011). https://doi.org/10.1007/s10980-011-9617-z
9. Giraldo-Zuluaga, J.H., Salazar, A., Gomez, A., Diaz-Pulido, A.: Recognition of mammal genera on camera-trap images using multi-layer robust principal component analysis and mixture neural networks. In: 2017 IEEE 29th International Conference on Tools with Artificial Intelligence (ICTAI), pp. 53–60 (2017). https://doi.org/10.1109/ICTAI.2017.00020
10. Ikeda, N.: Economic impacts of livestock depredation by snow leopard Uncia Uncia in the Kanchenjunga conservation area, Nepal Himalaya. Environ. Conserv. **3**(4), 322–330 (2004)
11. Kobayashi, H.H., et al.: A real-time streaming and detection system for bio-acoustic ecological studies after the fukushima accident. In: Joly, A., Vrochidis, S., Karatzas, K., Karppinen, A., Bonnet, P. (eds.) Multimedia Tools and Applications for Environmental & Biodiversity Informatics. MSA, pp. 53–66. Springer, Cham (2018). https://doi.org/10.1007/978-3-319-76445-0_4
12. Kunwar, R.M., Khaling, S.: International forest fire news. Int. Forest Fire News **34**, 1–9 (2016)
13. Møller, A.P., Mousseau, T.A.: Strong effects of ionizing radiation from Chernobyl on mutation rates. Sci. Rep. **5**(1), 1–6 (2015)
14. Mousseau, T.A., Møller, A.P.: Genetic and ecological studies of animals in Chernobyl and Fukushima. J. Heredity **105**(5), 704–709 (2014)
15. Nakamura, K.W., Watanabe, R., Fujiwara, A., Saito, K., Kobayashi, H.H., Sezaki, K.: Plant phenology observation by students using time-lapse images: creation of the environment and examination of its adequacy. Environments **5**(1), 7 (2018)
16. O'Connell, A.F., Nichols, J.D., Karanth, K.U.: Camera Traps in Animal Ecology: Methods and Analyses, vol. 271. Springer, Tokyo (2011). https://doi.org/10.1007/978-4-431-99495-4
17. Oli, M.K., Taylor, I.R., Rogers, M.E.: Snow leopard Panthera uncia predation of livestock: an assessment of local perceptions in the Annapurna Conservation Area, Nepal. Biol. Conserv. **68**(1), 63–68 (1994)
18. Saito, K., et al.: Utilizing the Cyberforest live sound system with social media to remotely conduct woodland bird censuses in Central Japan. Ambio. **44**(Suppl. 4), 572–583 (2015). https://doi.org/10.1007/s13280-015-0708-y
19. Schaller, G.: Field of dreams. Wild. Conserv. September/October (1992)
20. Sharma, B.D., Clevers, J., De Graaf, R., Chapagain, N.R.: Mapping *Equus kiang* (tibetan Wild Ass) habitat in Surkhang, Upper Mustang, Nepal. Mount. Res. Dev. **24**(2), 149–156 (2004)

21. Su, H., Bista, M., Li, M.: Mapping habitat suitability for Asiatic black bear and red panda in Makalu Barun National Park of Nepal from Maxent and GARP models. Sci. Rep. **11**(1), 1–14 (2021)

22. Sueur, J., Farina, A., Gasc, A., Pieretti, N., Pavoine, S.: Acoustic indices for biodiversity assessment and landscape investigation. Acta Acust. United Acust. **100**(4), 772–781 (2014). https://doi.org/10.3813/AAA.918757

23. Sullivan, B.L., Wood, C.L., Iliff, M.J., Bonney, R.E., Fink, D., Kelling, S.: eBird: a citizen-based bird observation network in the biological sciences. Biol. Conserv. **142**(10), 2282–2292 (2009). https://doi.org/10.1016/j.biocon.2009.05.006

24. Thapa, A., et al.: Combined land cover changes and habitat occupancy to understand corridor status of Laljhadi-Mohana wildlife corridor, Nepal. Eur. J. Wildl. Res. **63**(5), 1–14 (2017)

25. Ueta, M.: Adequate survey periods and the utility of sound recording to census nocturnal birds in the forest. Bird Res. **4** (2008)

26. Wildlife Management Office Inc. https://wmo.co.jp/service/monitoring. Accessed Feb 2022

27. World Wild Life Fund: New WWF report: 3 billion animals impacted by Australia's bushfire crisis. https://www.wwf.org.au/news/news/2020/3-billion-animals-impacted-by-australia-bushfire-crisis

Research on the Application of Blockchain Technology in the Cross-border E-Commerce Supply Chain Domain

Fei Xing[1], Guochao Peng[2(✉)], and Zaipeng Liang[1]

[1] Suzhou Institute of Trade and Commerce, Suzhou 215009, China
[2] Sun Yat-sen University, 510000 Guangzhou, China
2021022006@szjm.edu.cn

Abstract. Blockchain technology is considered as one of the most important revolutionary technologies in human society after the Internet technology, which has been highly commended by academia and industry, but there is still insufficient understanding about what blockchain technology can exactly do for cross-border e-commerce. This paper aims to depict how blockchain technology can assist in the cross-border e-commerce supply chain domain. Through a comprehensive literature review, four major challenges were identified and discussed in the current cross-border e-commerce supply chain domain, namely: lack of security; high logistics transportation cost and long distribution time; complicated cross-border settlement procedures; and lack of product traceability. Afterwards, based on the features of blockchain technology, this paper discussed the feasibility and a number of scenarios to reveal how blockchain technology can be applied to improve cross-border e-commerce supply chain activities. In the end, four strategic recommendations were put forward to better promote the application of blockchain technology in cross-border e-commerce: 1) promote the research and application of blockchain technology actively; 2) accelerate talent training of blockchain technology; 3) establish a legal system for the blockchain technology application; and 4) develop an ecosystem of 'blockchain + cross-border e-commerce'. This paper will be of interest and value to practitioners and researchers who are concerned with blockchain technology usage in cross-border e-commerce contexts.

Keywords: Blockchain technology · Cross-border e-commerce · Supply chain application · Recommendations

1 Introduction

In the context of the development of the interconnection of all things, utilizing blockchain technology to enhance the competitiveness of cross-border e-commerce has become a key to achieving success for some trade enterprises. The essence of blockchain is a reconciliation system in which all participants can do recordings [1, 2]. In general, blockchain can be considered as a new chain data structure composed of distributed storage technology, time order, and the connection of head and tail. Cryptography technology was used in the whole blockchain system to make sure that it cannot be distorted and forged. Meanwhile, point-to-point transmission mode was used to share information in the internals of the blockchain system [3, 4]. Therefore, blockchain technology is considered to be shareable, programmable, reliable and trusted. Based on these characteristics, blockchain technology has a great impact on some industries, particularly on financial transactions, logistics service, e-government, etc., which has been highly commended by governments, industries, and scientific research institutions [5, 6]. For example, blockchain technology can be used in financial transactions, particularly in terms of payment and settlement. Under the blockchain distributed ledger system, multiple market participants jointly maintain and synchronize a 'general ledger' in real time, they can complete payment and clearing activities in just a few minutes. In this situation, complexity and cost of cross-bank transactions can be reduced greatly [7]. Moreover, blockchain technology can be used in e-government as it can make the data run and simplify the work process greatly. Specifically, the distributed technology of blockchain allows government departments to concentrate on one chain, and all work processes deliver smart contracts. In this way, all subsequent approvals and signatures can be completed in sequence as long as the clerk passes identity authentication and electronic signature in one department [8]. In addition, blockchain technology provides reliable support for medicine traceability, art and luxury anti-counterfeiting and other transactions [9]. Therefore, blockchain technology will become a disruptive application in the field of science and technology business in the future.

Cross-border e-commerce promotes economic integration and trade globalization because it breaks through the boundaries between countries. In recent years, cross-border e-commerce has developed rapidly and expanded greatly in scale. According to the data released by Accenture, Forrester and Goldman Sachs, taking cross-border on-line retail as an example, the global cross-border e-commerce B2C market reached 675 billion US dollars in 2018, and the average annual growth rate is close to 30%, which far exceeds the growth rate of traditional goods trade [10]. However, there are still many problems behind the continuous trading. For instance, as the cross-border e-commerce supply chain involves different countries, different laws and regulations, with different multiple circulation steps, there are many problems which need to be solved in cross-border e-commerce, such as the lack of security, low transportation efficiency and complex settlement procedures [11, 12]. Meanwhile, Artificial Intelligence, the Internet of Things (IoT), and other technologies have been fully applied in the supply chain industry; blockchain technology is in its infancy, which has a great potential in the development of different industries in the future. Therefore, it is of great significance to apply blockchain technology in the cross-border e-commerce supply chain domain to enhance its effectiveness and efficiency.

In light of this discussion, this paper aims to investigate potential applications of blockchain technology in the cross-border e-commerce supply chain through the analysis of literature. First of all, the essence and development of blockchain technology is introduced and discussed in Sect. 2. Besides, this paper discusses the current ch"allenges of cross-border e-commerce supply chains in Sect. 3. Moreover, a new pattern of blockchain-based cross-border e-commerce supply chains is put forward and a series of strategic recommendations are proposed. A conclusion is presented in the final.

2   Essence and Characteristics of Blockchain Technology

A completed decentralized electronic money trading system based on cryptography and distributed networks was put forward by Satoshi Nakamoto in 2008, which is the earliest application case of blockchain technology [13]. The essence of blockchain is a reconciliation system in which all participants jointly record transaction information. To be specific, block chain is a system that uses the consensus mechanism to establish distributed storage within the blockchain system, connects points, and obtains rights and interests through relying on data encryption algorithms [14]. Moreover, blockchain technology can be simply understood as a reliable public facility with super capacity. Each node in the blockchain system can participate in bookkeeping independently and all the transaction information that cannot be tampered with or deleted is stored in each page of a ledger. The data generated in the system is used to verify the validity of its content and link to the next page [15]. Therefore, blockchain technology has some major characteristics i.e. increased capacity, immutability, decentralization, openness.

The first - and an important feature of blockchain technology - is increased capacity, which can be considered as the most remarkable thing for this technology. With the demand of enterprises or individuals for computing resources, network capacity has become a key topic. The network capacity of the internet is limited when a single computer or only one server works. It may affect the working efficiency and reduce the computing power when running large projects. However, the most remarkable thing of blockchain technology is that it can increase the capacity of the whole network, because there are a lot of computers working together in blockchain which can offer great power collectively compared with each device working independently. For instance, one typical example of this increased capacity is that a supercomputer based on blockchain was created by Stanford University to stimulate protein folding in medical research [16]. In this situation, the problems caused by insufficient network capacity can be effectively solved.

The second feature of blockchain technology is immutability, therefore creating immutable ledgers is one of the main values of blockchain. Immutability can be considered as a permanent and tamper-proof record of transactions. Any centralized database is subjected to the possibility of getting hacked, and it is necessary to have a third party to keep the database secure. Therefore, it is easy to conclude that traditional payments have been prone to information leakage in the past. Blockchain technology is equipped with immutability because it uses cryptographic technologies such as asymmetric encryption and digital timestamp to encrypt transaction information and protect data from tampering and forgery [17]. As a result, due to its immutability, transactions of cross-border e-commerce can get better security through blockchain technology. Once a block is added, it cannot be altered, which therefore creates trust in the transaction record. Hence, immutability is one of the characteristics of blockchain technology.

Decentralization is the third characteristic of blockchain technology. In a blockchain system, point-to-point transmission can be realized. In this way, there is no centralized hardware or management organization for data storage in the blockchain system [18]. All data resource transmitted online are not stored in one or several data centers but scattered in all nodes participating in the blockchain system. Data transmission is carried out directly between nodes. The status and opportunities of any node are equal without the intervention of intermediate links, intermediaries or any servers. The data blocks in the system are jointly maintained by the nodes with maintenance function in the whole system [18]. As a result of this, the decentralized network transmission structure can ensure that each participant can record data in real time and update in each node, which greatly improves the security of data. Even if some nodes of the system meet problems like data loss or hacker attack, it will not affect the whole database system.

Last but not least, openness is also one of the features of block chain technology. The block chain system is transparent, so the full transaction history can be queried since the blockchain is an open file [19]. To be specific, the block chain system of a super capacity public ledger is open. The data of the blockchain is open to the public in addition to the private information of the transaction subject is added with a key. Any party or individual can get access to the block chain and audit transactions. This creates provenance under which asset lifetimes can be tracked. Hence, the information of the whole system is highly transparent.

3 Overview of Cross-border E-Commerce Supply Chain Development

Cross-border e-commerce transects the boundaries between countries, which enables the development of international trade and further promotes the global economic integration. However, with the continuous development of cross-border e-commerce, some problems have gradually emerged. This section mainly discusses the difficulties faced in the development of cross-border e-commerce. In detail, four major challenges were identified and discussed in the current cross-border e-commerce supply chain domain, namely: lack of security; high logistics transportation cost and long distribution time; complicated cross-border settlement procedures; and lack of product traceability.

The first problem of cross-border e-commerce is lack of security. When considering the cross-border logistics transportation, it is limited by the laws and regulations and logistics level of different countries, therefore the security problems will become more prominent. Specifically, on the one hand, cross-border transportation involves multiple organizations in different regions, therefore it is difficult to trace the product due to the information asymmetry between multiple organizations. On the other hand, many countries do not have the network conditions or legal protection for secure payment in the payment of logistics expenses, which causes payment vulnerability where some transactions cannot be supervised safely by authorities [20].

High logistic transportation costs and long distribution times are considered to be other problems faced by cross-border e-commerce supply chains at present. Many nodes are involved in the transportation of goods, and the distribution process is complex and its cycle is relatively long, which leads to an increase in the operational difficulty of customs and commodity inspection [21]. Therefore, the cost and distribution cycle of the cross-border supply chain will become longer and consequently result in an increase.

The complexity of cross-border settlement procedures is one of the problems faced by e-commerce supply chains. Traditional cross-border settlement involves domestic banks, foreign banks, domestic and foreign liquidating organizations etc. Therefore, it can be seen that the whole cross-border settlement procedures are complex, which makes it difficult for banks to review transaction data. At the same time, when faced with customs clearance, tax refund, payment and even returns, the cross-border settlement procedures will be more complex [21]. Therefore, cross-border e-commerce transactions can become cumbersome procedures.

The final challenge for cross-border e-commerce is the lack of product traceability. To be specific, products go through multiple links in the process of distribution such as package collection, warehouse transfer, export clearance, product transportation, etc. [22]. It becomes difficult to guarantee the integrity of the package and sometimes even causes the loss of it. Hence, this will reduce the buyer's sense of shopping experience and increase the operation cost of the seller to a certain extent.

4 Blockchain-Based Cross-border E-Commerce Supply Chains

Blockchain technology is a major innovation in the field of information technology. Based on the features of blockchain technology, this section mainly discusses three different scenarios for the application of blockchain technology in the cross-border e-commerce supply chain domain.

Blockchain technology can be used to monitor and record the logistics status of the cross-border e-commerce supply chain in real time due to its characteristics of distributed bookkeeping and decentralization. The whole blockchain system was made up of data perception layers, network link layers, distributed database and technology application layers [23]. In detail, transaction data was collected through the IoT system. The whole IoT system includes smart cameras and sensors so that the real-time status of transportation goods can be identified through RFID. Subsequently, the collected data was transmitted through the network link layer [24]. For example, as the goods are transported from manufacturer to distributor, the ownership of the goods has changed. Under this situation, digital signatures can be performed based on the distributed bookkeeping of blockchain technology, which not only hides the identity information but also ensures the traceability of goods. In the future, either party can query the logistics status in the blockchain system. Therefore, the blockchain-based cross-border e-commerce supply chain can ensure that the whole transaction information is recorded, which improves the transparency of logistics transportation.

Moreover, blockchain technology can be effectively used in order to improve the security of cross-border payment systems. The transaction bank, the third-party transaction platform, and the custodian bank involved in cross-border payment form multiple blocks that are connected in the block chain. Transaction information can be queried and the whole process will be monitored in the blockchain system, so as to make sure the information will not be leaked and to reduce the cost of data storage [25]. For example, if a customer buys a cosmetic item on a foreign shopping website, the transaction time, amount, logistics information and custom information of this order will form a block, so that both customer and the platform can keep track of the transaction progress in real time [26]. Therefore, it is easy to conclude that the application of blockchain technology can enhance the security of cross-border payment system.

In addition, the blockchain-based cross-border e-commerce supply chain can effectively avoid product quality problems. The quality of cross-border goods has always been a topic of concern in the field of e-commerce. The traceability of cross-border commodity quality can be divided into production segments in foreign countries, transportation segments abroad, and domestic transportation specifically [27]. The information generated in the above steps will be recorded in the blockchain in real time. As a result, as the customers encounter problems regarding product quality, they can quickly find the segment where the problem occurs and the corresponding director based on blockchain technology. Therefore, the blockchain-based cross-border e-commerce supply chain is helpful in providing an efficient and convenient information query channel for after-sales service of goods.

Although the application of blockchain technology can bring lots of benefits to the development of a cross-border e-commerce supply chain, there are still many difficulties needing to be dealt with. First of all, from the technical perspective, blockchain technology is still in the primary stage. At present, the blockchain technology platform is still immature and some security problems have not been completely solved and therefore it will take some time for it to be ready for large-scale use. At the same time, although digital signatures and encryption algorithms were used to ensure the safety of transactions, it also expands the probability of information infringement due to its distributed features [28, 29]. Secondly, the infrastructure of blockchain technology is not adequate. Concretely, the premise of the 'trustworthiness' of blockchain is the consensus of the whole network. If the number of information and users on the blockchain does not reach a certain level, that is, the number of nodes is too small, this will directly lead to the reduction of effective blocks on the blockchain [30]. As a result, the transaction data will become incomplete, so the data will be difficult to circulate in the whole supply chain. In addition to the technical deficiencies, the relevant legal system still needs to be improved in order to make the blockchain technology better applied. At present, as one of the countries that develops cross-border e-commerce rapidly, China has taken the lead in issuing normative documents. However, unified international conventions and rules have not yet been established on how to realize and manage blockchain technology [31]. Consequently, these technical and non-technical challenges still restrict the application of blockchain technology.

5   Recommendation

Blockchain technology can effectively improve the development of a cross-border e-commerce supply chain in the future. In order to better promote the application of blockchain technology in cross-border e-commerce supply chains, four strategic recommendations were put forward, namely: 1) promote the research and application of blockchain technology actively; 2) accelerate talent training of blockchain technology; 3) establish a legal system for the blockchain technology application; and 4) develop an ecosystem of 'blockchain + cross-border e-commerce'.

5.1   Promote the Research and Application of Blockchain Technology Actively

The implementation of any technology is inseparable from the effective guidance of the government and society. Some research from enterprise management and information systems showed that the government's effective management of technology is conducive to better implementation of the advanced technology [32, 33]. As discussed above in Sect. 4, blockchain technology is still in the early stages of development. The technology itself is not mature enough, thus there is still a certain gap from practical application. Therefore, research and the application of blockchain technology should be promoted actively. Firstly, it is necessary for governments to provide talents, sufficient funding and policies for the basic research of blockchain technology, which aims to promote the continuous improvement of blockchain technology. Secondly, local governments should take action to guide the application of blockchain technology, such as issuing qualifications to relevant enterprises so as to promote the standardization of technology application. Besides this, relevant government agencies should strengthen the publicity of blockchain technology in order to popularize its knowledge. For example, some public lectures can be given by university professors or corporate executives, which is helpful to increase the awareness and acceptance of blockchain technology for the public. Therefore, one of the strategic recommendations is to promote the research and application of blockchain technology actively.

5.2 Accelerate Talent Training of Blockchain Technology

With the development of advanced information technology such as big data, cloud computing and artificial intelligence, etc., talents of enterprise have become the core element in market competition. Hence, there is no doubt concerning the importance and urgency of accelerating talent training in blockchain technology. Blockchain technology involves the computer, network communication, encryption technology, chip technology, law, finance and other subjects, which is viewed as a typical interdisciplinary technology [34]. Therefore, the development of blockchain technology requires a large number of compound talents with multi-disciplinary knowledge. Under this situation, there are three specific suggestions on talent training. Firstly, the education department within the government should set up related majors for blockchain technology as soon as possible. At the same time, the corresponding curriculum system need to be established. Consequently, a group of talents engaged in the research and application of blockchain technology can be trained quickly and on a large scale, so as to promote the development of blockchain technology. Secondly, in addition to the effort made by education departments, universities and colleges should set up optional, general courses aimed at popularizing the blockchain technology, so as to cultivate the interest of students. Thirdly, scientific talents and applied talents should be diverted through the specific talent programs. For example, research universities need to strengthen the research and development of blockchain technical difficulties. However, the application-oriented universities or colleges need to train blockchain technical talents according to the demand of e-commerce enterprise.

5.3 Establish a Legal System for the Blockchain Technology Application

A mature and reasonable regulatory mechanism is a fundamental guarantee for the effective utilization of technology [35]. In order to ensure that the development of blockchain technology is on the right path, a legal system should be founded. Government departments still play an important role in this process. Specifically, the establishment of 'blockchain + cross-border e-commerce' is mainly divided into the following aspects. On the one hand, laws and regulations need to be improved, particularly for individual users. Only in this way can the behavior of users be monitored effectively and mostly avoid crimes being committed by taking advantage of the existing technical loopholes in the blockchain. Research from information systems presented that regulations are the key to successful applications of new technology in society. On the other hand, governments should formulate unified technical standards for blockchain, especially for 'blockchain + cross-border e-commerce supply chain'. Only once a legal system is established can e-commerce enterprises have evidence and guidance to depend on and follow the technical standards, so as to promote the development of blockchain-based cross-border e-commerce. As a consequence, it is essential to establish a legal system for the blockchain technology application.

5.4 Develop an Ecosystem of 'Blockchain + Cross-border E-Commerce'

As discussed in Sect. 5.1, the research and development of blockchain technology is the technical support for the implementation; the establishment of 'blockchain + cross border e-commerce' is the social environment support. Adner considered that no organization or individual can survive without an ecosystem [36]. For instance, any manufacturing enterprise needs to have raw materials from upstream organizations and orders from downstream customers to survive. Similarly, the application of blockchain technology in cross-border e-commerce needs a complete and ecological environment for sustainable development [37]. Hence, it is significant to develop an ecosystem of 'blockchain + cross-border e-commerce'. Specifically, the first thing is to guide and encourage those large scale cross-border e-commerce enterprises to take the lead in adopting blockchain technology in cross-border transactions. The purpose of this is to drive small and medium-sized cross-border e-commerce enterprises to upgrade their businesses by using blockchain technology. Secondly, cross-border e-commerce enterprises should be encouraged to try to actively apply blockchain technology in other fields besides the payment and supply chain. In the end, an information platform for blockchain technology communication should be built. Based on the platform, users can discuss the deficiencies and existing problems in technology application, which is helpful to promote the improvement of technology and application. Therefore, blockchain technology can be effectively implemented in the field of cross-border e-commerce supply chains through developing an ecosystem.

6 Conclusions

Blockchain technology is a new Internet Technology which can effectively solve the problems of cross-border e-commerce in payment, logistics, quality traceability, etc. In this paper, a blockchain-based cross-border e-commerce supply chain pattern is proposed by combining blockchain technology with cross-border e-commerce. At present, blockchain technology is still in the initial stages of its development. The application of blockchain technology in various fields is not mature enough. However, it is undeniable that blockchain technology has great application value, which provides strong support for the digital development of a cross-border e-commerce supply chain. As a result, based on the challenges faced by blockchain technology, combined with the characteristics of it, four strategic recommendations were put forward in this paper in the end, namely 1) promote the research and application of blockchain technology actively; 2) accelerate talent training of blockchain technology; 3) establish a legal system for the blockchain technology application; and 4) develop an ecosystem of 'blockchain + cross-border e-commerce'.

References

1. FossoWamba, S., KalaKamdjoug, J.R., EpieBawack, R., Keogh, J.G.: Bitcoin, blockchain and fintech: a systematic review and case studies in the supply chain. Prod. Plann. Control **31**(2–3), 115–142 (2020)
2. Chen, Y., Gu, J., Chen, S., Huang, S., Wang, X.S.: A full-spectrum blockchain-as-a-service for business. collaboration. In: 2019 IEEE International Conference on Web Services (ICWS), pp. 219–223. (2019)
3. Liu, Z., Li, Z.: A blockchain-based framework of cross-border e-commerce supply chain. Int. J. Inf. Manage. **52**, 102059 (2020)
4. Niranjanamurthy, M., Nithya, B.N., Jagannatha, S.: Analysis of Blockchain technology: pros, cons and SWOT. Clust. Comput. **22**(6), 14743–14757 (2018). https://doi.org/10.1007/s10586-018-2387-5
5. Ali, O., Ally, M., Dwivedi, Y.: The state of play of blockchain technology in the financial services sector: a systematic literature review. Int. J. Inf. Manage. **54**, 102199 (2020)
6. Carter, L., Ubacht, J.: Blockchain applications in government. In: Proceedings of the 19th Annual International Conference on Digital Government Research, Governance in the Data Age, pp. 1–2 (2018)
7. Albayati, H., Kim, S.K., Rho, J.J.: Accepting financial transactions using blockchain technology and cryptocurrency: a customer perspective approach. Technol. Soc. **62**, 101320 (2020)
8. Li, S.: Application of blockchain technology in smart city infrastructure. In: 2018 IEEE International Conference on Smart Internet of Things (SmartIoT), pp. 276–2766. IEEE (2018)
9. Behnke, K., Janssen, M.F.W.H.A.: Boundary conditions for traceability in food supply chains using blockchain technology. Int. J. Inf. Manage. **52**, 101969 (2020)
10. Mou, J., Cui, Y., Kurcz, K.: Trust, risk and alternative website quality in B-buyer acceptance of cross-border E-commerce. J. Global Inf. Manage. (JGIM) **28**(1), 167–188 (2020)
11. Wang, Y., Jia, F., Schoenherr, T., Gong, Y.: Supply chain-based business model innovation: the case of a cross-border E-commerce company. Sustainability **10**(12), 4362 (2018)
12. Nuruzzaman, M., Weber, A.N.: Supply chain in cross-border e-commerce. In: Cross-Border E-Commerce Marketing and Management, pp. 54–77. IGI Global (2021)
13. Hariguna, T., Durachman, Y., Yusup, M., Millah, S.: Blockchain technology transformation in advancing future change. Blockchain Front. Technol. **1**(01), 13–20 (2021)
14. Zheng, Z., Xie, S., Dai, H., Chen, X., Wang, H.: An overview of blockchain technology: architecture, consensus, and future trends. In: 2017 IEEE International Congress on Big Data (BigData Congress), pp. 557–564. IEEE (2017)
15. Efanov, D., Roschin, P.: The all-pervasiveness of the blockchain technology. Proc. Comput. Sci. **123**, 116–121 (2018)

16. Shae, Z., Tsai, J.J.: On the design of a blockchain platform for clinical trial and precision medicine. In: 2017 IEEE 37th International Conference on Distributed Computing Systems (ICDCS), pp. 1972–1980. IEEE (2017)
17. Bashynska, I., Malanchuk, M., Zhuravel, O., Olinichenko, K.: Smart solutions: risk management of crypto-assets and blockchain technology. Int. J. Civil Eng. Technol. (IJCIET) 10(2), 1121–1131 (2019)
18. Treleaven, P., Brown, R.G., Yang, D.: Blockchain technology in finance. Computer 50(9), 14–17 (2017)
19. Francisco, K., Swanson, D.: The supply chain has no clothes: technology adoption of blockchain for supply chain transparency. Logistics 2(1), 2 (2018)
20. Chen, C.M., Cai, Z.X., Wen, D.W.M.: Designing and evaluating an automatic forensic model for fast response of cross-border e-commerce security incidents. J. Global Inf. Manage. (JGIM) 30(2), 1–19 (2021)
21. Shuyan, C., Lisi, X.: Research on the overseas warehouse construction of cross-border e-commerce. In: Association for Information Systems AIS Electronic Library (AISeL) WHICEB 2013 Proceedings (2013)
22. Luo, Y., Xie, C.: Traceability system construction of agricultural products cross-border e-commerce logistics from the perspective of blockchain technology. In: Sugumaran, V., Zheng, X., Zhou, H. (eds.) MMIA 2020. AISC, vol. 1233, pp. 105–111. Springer, Cham (2021). https://doi.org/10.1007/978-3-030-51431-0_16
23. Chen, J., Lv, Z., Song, H.: Design of personnel big data management system based on blockchain. Futur. Gener. Comput. Syst. 101, 1122–1129 (2019)
24. Zhang, G., Li, T., Li, Y., Hui, P., Jin, D.: Blockchain-based data sharing system for ai-powered network operations. J. Commun. Inf. Netw. 3(3), 1–8 (2018)
25. Deng, Q.: Application analysis on blockchain technology in cross-border payment. In: 5th International Conference on Financial Innovation and Economic Development (ICFIED 2020), pp. 287–295. Atlantis Press (2020)
26. Liu, Q., Li, K.: Decentration transaction method based on blockchain technology. In: 2018 International Conference on Intelligent Transportation, Big Data and Smart City (ICITBS), pp. 416–419. IEEE (2018)
27. Su, W., Wang, Y., Qian, L., Zeng, S., Baležentis, T., Streimikiene, D.: Creating a sustainable policy framework for cross-border e-commerce in China. Sustainability 11(4), 943 (2019)
28. Helo, P., Hao, Y.: Blockchains in operations and supply chains: a model and reference implementation. Comput. Ind. Eng. 136, 242–251 (2019)
29. Choi, D., Chung, C.Y., Seyha, T., Young, J.: Factors affecting organizations' resistance to the adoption of blockchain technology in supply networks. Sustainability 12(21), 8882 (2020)
30. Ølnes, S., Jansen, A.: Blockchain technology as s support infrastructure in e-government. In: Janssen, M., et al. (eds.) EGOV 2017. LNCS, vol. 10428, pp. 215–227. Springer, Cham (2017). https://doi.org/10.1007/978-3-319-64677-0_18
31. Tan, A.W.K., Zhao, Y., Halliday, T.: A blockchain model for less container load operations in China. Int. J. Inf. Syst. Supply Chain Manage. (IJISSCM) 11(2), 39–53 (2018)
32. McClure, C.R., Jaeger, P.T.: Government information policy research: importance, approaches, and realities. Libr. Inf. Sci. Res. 30(4), 257–264 (2008)
33. Liu, S., Wang, L.: Understanding the impact of risks on performance in internal and outsourced information technology projects: the role of strategic importance. Int. J. Project Manage. 32(8), 1494–1510 (2014)
34. Ahram, T., Sargolzaei, A., Sargolzaei, S., Daniels, J., Amaba, B.: Blockchain technology innovations. In: 2017 IEEE Technology and Engineering Management Conference (TEMSCON), pp. 137–141. IEEE (2017)
35. Zhang, L., Long, R., Chen, H., Huang, X.: Performance changes analysis of industrial enterprises under energy constraints. Resour. Conserv. Recycl. 136, 248–256 (2018)

36. Adner, R.: Ecosystem as structure: an actionable construct for strategy. J. Manag. **43**(1), 39–58 (2017)
37. Nam, K., Dutt, C.S., Chathoth, P., Khan, M.S.: Blockchain technology for smart city and smart tourism: latest trends and challenges. Asia Pacific J. Tourism Res. **26**(4), 454–468 (2021)

Investigation of Enterprise WeChat Development Modes Based on a SWOT-PEST Model

Fei Xing[1], Guochao Peng[2(✉)], and Zengjian Huang[1]

[1] Suzhou Institute of Trade and Commerce, Suzhou 215009, China
[2] Sun Yat-sen University, Panyu District, Guangzhou 510000, China
2021022006@szjm.edu.cn

Abstract. Today more than ever before, the issues of communication and information sharing are much more closely linked to economic effect and quality of employees' work of enterprise, which is causing an increased interest for researchers from the information systems (IS) and management field. With the development and popularisation of network communication technologies and mobile devices, enterprise instant messaging (EIM) is set to improve information sharing and communication among employees as a result of integrating instant messaging and collaborative office. As one of the EIM tools, Tencent product Enterprise WeChat has been made publicly available and is gradually being extended and applied in organisations. Currently, Enterprise WeChat has a certain amount of market share and promotes the capabilities of overall communication and information sharing in enterprise. In this paper, the strategic analysis tools derived from the SWOT (strengths, weaknesses, opportunities and threats)-PEST (political, economic, social and technological) model has been adopted to investigate the development mode of Enterprise WeChat in organisations. Subsequently, on the basis of analysis results, several corresponding recommendations have been put forward in an attempt to achieve the rapid and sound development of Enterprise WeChat in organisations in the future.

Keywords: Enterprise WeChat · SWOT-PEST model · Strategic analysis · recommendation

1 Introduction

The demand for effective communication and information sharing in organisations has witnessed its role and significance in the development of enterprise for a long time. Effective communication and information sharing among employees are essential for a company to achieve success from a management perspective, since it can facilitate decision-making capabilities in the workplace, promote experience and tacit knowledge exchange amongst employees, build learning organisations particularly through a long-term mutual learning routine, and ultimately stimulate cultural change and innovation of enterprise [1]. Therefore, it is obvious that high-quality information sharing and effective communication can bring a lot of benefits to a company where teamwork, remote working and advanced information technology are increasingly common.

However, in reality, poor communication and information sharing deficiency in organsations are a common sight and they are gradually becoming major issues that seriously affect the efficiency and productivity of enterprises, particularly in such sectors of enterprise as research and development (R&D), production, and logistics where these multi-department employees need to make concerted efforts to achieve business goals [2, 3]. To be specific, failure to share information and poor communication highly bound with data inconsistency and retardance can obviously affect the operating efficiency of enterprises and is thought of as a key factor giving rise to problems in the process of enterprise operational management, which, in turn, probably resulted in low production efficiency, slow response to raw material supply, even slow product delivery, particularly for some manufacturing companies [4, 5]. According to the research conducted by McKinsey & Co., the results showed that a failure to share information and poor communication can be catastrophic at the corporate level [6], in particular, due to the lack of information sharing mechanisms in business management, employees from various departments potentially find it difficult to communicate well with each other in terms of routine work, thus resulting in the disjunction of logistics, capital flow and information flow of enterprise [7]. In this case, it can further lead to such serious problems as out-of-control planning, excessive inventory, poor connection between procurement and sales, and ultimately causing the incalculable loss of enterprise [8, 9]. In addition, Six and Skinner [10] considered that effective communication and information sharing can have a positive and healing effect that facilitates employees to be engaged and closely connected to their organisations, and when they are, they will be happy, work hard in their workplace and be more proactive.

In response to confront the poor communication and failure of information sharing, instant messaging (IM), as a real-time and text-based internet service, has been developed and is being put into practice due to the prevalence of mobile devices and advancement of network communication technology. Faulaber [11] defined IM as a text-based means of near-synchronised information exchange and communication between users who have registered for the service. On the other hand, instant messaging as a communication application which allows employees to send and receive real-time messages to connect with their co-workers in organisations [12, 13], therefore describes instant messaging as one type of information technology to facilitate communication and enhance work productivity. There are a number of instant messaging tools by different brands currently on the market, for instance, MSN Messenger by Microsoft, Yahoo Messenger by Yahoo, WhatsApp Messenger from Facebook, AOL Instant Messenger owned by AOL, and most of them were intended for personal use originally. However, promotion and application of instant messaging tools at a corporate level is much more urgent and significant [14]. Peng et al. [15] considered that the use of EIM tools to help employees to communicate in organisations is more efficient than email because it allowed messages to appear on the recipient's screen automatically, saving enormous amounts of time. Moreover, it can also reduce interruptions. Employees can communicate with one another while continuing with current work, because it does not require them to stop work to answer the phone or have a face-to-face conversation, and, more importantly, it is not subject to workplace restrictions [16]; enterprise users can log on to internal servers as long as they have the network to communicate within a specific range of work.

As one type of instant messaging tool for organisational use, Enterprise WeChat has received a lot of attention from both academia and industry [17–20]. Enterprise WeChat, known in Chinese as "企业微信", is a foremost messaging app for sending text, voice, video and files to internal colleagues and external business partners. Enterprise WeChat was launched in 2016 by Chinese technology company Tencent, one of the world's most valuable technology conglomerates and one of the largest social media companies worldwide [17]. Enterprise WeChat has become the second largest organisational service market share in China and it is used to help employees stay connected with colleagues and customers and help companies to improve their operating efficiency, so as to increase the core competitiveness of the enterprise [21]. Therefore, Enterprise WeChat has important strategic significance in China, even in the world. For the moment, little research has been studied due to the short release time of Enterprise WeChat, wherein most of the research concentrates on technical aspects like system modelling and algorithm optimization [22] and user behaviour dimension [21, 23, 24]. However, no study has been found so far reporting the development modes of Enterprise WeChat from a strategic perspective using the integrated SWOT-PEST model. In this paper, the strategic analysis tool stemming from the SWOT-PEST model has been adopted to explore the development modes of Enterprise WeChat. The results of this research have a great significance for strategic development of Enterprise WeChat in the future, which can help organisations enhance communication effectiveness in the workplace.

In what follows, the SWOT-PEST model is introduced and reviewed first. Subsequently, development modes of Enterprise WeChat are investigated and discussed in depth. Finally, the recommendations of its future development strategy and conclusion are put forward.

2   SWOT-PEST Model

SWOT is a strategic planning tool to help organisations gain a better insight of their internal and external business environment by evaluating four areas: strengths, weaknesses, opportunities and threats [25]. Strengths and weakness can be considered as two internal factors that support or hinder organisations' growth and these two factors are controllable. Nevertheless, opportunities and threats are two external factors that enable and disable organisations from achieving their mission, they are comparatively uncontrollable [26]. Specifically, S (strengths) represents the advantages that the organizations have; W (weaknesses) are properties of stopping an organisation from performing at an optimum level; O (opportunities) refer to favourable external elements that can bring advantages to organisations; T (threats) define the negative factors that do harm to an organization [27].

PEST is a measurement tool that is used to assess markets for a specific product or application within a given time frame. PEST has political, economic, social and technological dimensions [28]. In PEST analysis, P (political) refers to how and to what degree the government regulations influence organisations' economy; E (economic) is associated with external economic factors like interest rates, economic growth, inflation rate and exchange rates; S (social) refers to social factors that form the macro environment, including population growth, working attitude, age distribution, etc.; T (technological) is related to technological aspects, such as factors of technology incentives, technological innovation rate, and automation [29].

SWOT mainly concentrates on the internal micro-environment analysis in an organisation whereas PEST is more commonly adopted and implemented in analysing external macro-environmental regions [30]. Analysis results are not comprehensive when they are used separately. However, the SWOT-PEST model can be integrated from a comprehensive point of view to better analyse the current and prospective advantages, disadvantages, opportunities and threats in the field of political, economic, social and technical dimensions, the integrated analysis matrix is illustrated in Table 1. To date, some research has been undertaken using this type of model to do analysis from a top-level strategic point of view. For instance, Ha & Cogill [29] determined the development situation of e-government in Singapore. Zhu et al. [30] explored the development modes of the bioenergy industry in China based on the SWOT-PEST model. Andoh-Baidoo et al. [31] investigated the e-government readiness in Ghana through a SWOT and PEST analysis. Therefore, the SWOT-PEST model can, without doubt, help to identify determinants of facilitating Enterprise WeChat development in a strategic manner.

Table 1. SWOT-PEST analysis matrix.

SWOP-PEST model		Political	Economic	Social	Technological
Internal factors	Strengths	SP	SE	SS	ST
	Weakness	WP	WP	WS	WT
External factors	Opportunities	OP	OE	OS	OT
	Threats	TP	TE	TS	TT

3 SWOT-PEST Model Analysis of Enterprise WeChat

According to the current status of Enterprise WeChat and its existing issues, the main elements that have an impact on the development of Enterprise WeChat have been identified and summarised as shown in Table 2. Based on the analysis results of the SWOT-PEST model, from an internal point of view, it is easy to draw the conclusion that the advantages of Enterprise WeChat are obvious, such as policy support, rapid progress in the Tencent R&D research team and low cost for enterprise users. Several disadvantages like lack of publicity, long product revenue return cycle, individual or enterprise-level information security problems can be minimised or even dealt with by taking appropriate strategies through the development of national policy and advanced technology in the future. On the other hand, in terms of external factors, the opportunities co-exist with the threats, a series of uncertain and uncontrollable factors might increase. At the same time, the main barrier of Enterprise WeChat use in China is the habits of enterprise users; to be specific, users in enterprise are more accustomed to communicating with their colleagues through the personal WeChat platform.

4 Development Modes of Enterprise WeChat

With the development of economy and increasingly fierce business competition, it is crucial for enterprise employees to break through the limitations of time and space to realise mobile office, that is, employees can deal with anything related to business at anytime and anywhere. As one of the mainstream products in collaborative office and mobile office, Enterprise WeChat has a large market share due to its rich and distinctive functions. This section discusses the current development modes of Enterprise WeChat based on the SWOT-PEST model, as shown in Table 2.

Table 2. SWOT-PEST matrix model analysis of Enterprise WeChat

SWOT-PEST model		Political	Economic	Social	Technological
Internal factors	Strengths	• Adequate internal investment • Integrate enterprise account into Enterprise WeChat • High level of openness	• Sufficient funds for R&D • Attractive third-party APP market award policy • Subsidy support for new enterprise users	• Rich human resource • Low cost for users' learning • Complete company's business ecosystem	• Strong technical team • Strong scalability • Mature interworking technology with WeChat
	Weaknesses	• Lack of teamwork • Conservative product function development • Lack of publicity	• Long product revenue return cycle • Overlap with enterprise QQ business	• Users expansion takes a long time • Low acceptance of enterprise decision-makers	• Information security problem • Function update is limited by WeChat • Imperfect chat function
External factors	Opportunities	• Strategic direction of national digital economy development • Paperless office in enterprise • Strong demand of enterprise users	• Big quantity of companies • Strong demand for refinement management	• Public willingness to distinguish between work and life • Great influence of WeChat	• Good communication network equipment • Obvious trend of home office
	Threats	• Information security risk of enterprise • Overseas enterprises cannot pass the certification	• Slow economic development • Large number of competitive products	• Entering the market late • Many alternative products	• Slow product function update • Users' information security needs cannot meet with high quality

5 Recommendations

(1) Relying on internal advantages to seize external opportunities

Enterprise WeChat depends on their internal advantages to seize external opportunities, in order to look for the best development opportunities and strategies. To be specific, Enterprise WeChat was released as the strategic product of Tencent, meanwhile, Tencent has integrated multiple internal resources to fully support the development and promotion of Enterprise WeChat. It should be noted that the successful application of small programmes in 2017 gave WeChat more possibilities, and, therefore, brought more development opportunities to Enterprise WeChat. As Hao et al. [32] discussed, the lightweight characteristics of small programmes fully facilitate personal use, that is to say, users can have multiple applications through one-stop App, which gives Enterprise WeChat a broader application scenario.

In recent years, the development pattern of enterprise has changed greatly. Specifically, some enterprises have changed from high-speed development to high-quality development, which, thus, puts forward new requirements for enterprise production efficiency and employee work efficiency. As a result, Enterprise WeChat should fully tap its internal advantages in order to explore more functions and broaden the scope of business applications rooted in many scenarios such as enterprise production, management and other external business.

(2) Take advantage of external opportunities to adjust internal disadvantages

Mobile office has become an unchangeable trend and fact for most enterprises, especially for commercial companies [33]. At present, WeChat has been most widely used in enterprise users' daily work because of its convenience. As a result, many people add a lot of colleagues to their personal WeChat platform, mixing together their working and personal lives. However, considering the strong social attributes of WeChat and the difficulties of collaborative office access, which leads to the inadequacy of WeChat as the main communication tool for office. With the increasing willingness and demand to separate work and life, Enterprise WeChat has huge advantages in the acceptance of enterprise users due to its similar user experience. Therefore, the entry threshold of Enterprise WeChat is low, employees at any level of enterprise can realise barrier-free communication in the applications.

As the development and dissemination of network communication, mobile office has existed for a long time. Before the official release of Enterprise WeChat, some high-quality products have gradually entered the market and affected users' working habits [34]. As a result, enterprise instant messaging tools already have a certain market awareness, which is helpful to the promotion of Enterprise WeChat. In order to deal with the existing problems of internal disadvantages of Enterprise WeChat, the opportunities in the external environment can be made full of to adjust. For instance, information security problems can be improved and solved by applying for a variety of internationally recognised network information security certificates, or drawing support from the combination of third-party evaluation and authentication to improve their own information security assurance [35]. At the same time, Enterprise WeChat should give full play to the media influence for publicity, so as to obtain public psychological recognition.

(3) **Utilise internal advantages to overcome external threats**

Based on the results derived from the SWOT-PEST model analysis, it is apparent that several external threats hinder the development of Enterprise WeChat to some extent. For example, first of all, in addition to the basic instant messaging function, most of the applications that meet the enterprise office usage scenarios are developed and accessed by third-party partners. In this case, information security will become the most obvious problem. Secondly, the cooperation mode between enterprises and third-party partners is complex and changeable, and it is obvious that several large Internet companies are incompatible with each other, which results in low acceptance of common mobile office products.

As a consequence, faced with the external threats discussed above, Tencent utilised several internal advantages to overcome them. To be specific, firstly, 'Enterprise WeChat' was officially promoted as a strategic plan in April 2018 [36]. As the most important product to open up the enterprise level market, a large number of high-level talents are gathered to work together in terms of Enterprise WeChat's technology development or business expansion. Besides this, the operational team of Enterprise WeChat was established separately, the independent team can, therefore, expand the new user group of Enterprise WeChat with the strong influence of Tencent. Secondly, in order to meet the changeable needs of different enterprises and effectively deal with the relationship between enterprises and third-party partners, the operational team of Enterprise WeChat attracts more excellent and influential application developers to work together through industry salon and public speaking [37]. At the same time, the Enterprise WeChat operational team can formulate personalised products according to the different needs of enterprise. Finally, the information security of enterprise has attracted extensive attention; for instance, as Steinbart et al. [38] discussed, failure of data or information protection can result in the loss of key customers and even lead directly to the loss of businesses' confidential documents. Therefore, in some industries like finance, banking and high-tech, enterprises put forward higher requirements for information security. In this situation, Tencent can give full play to its influence and social recognition to eliminate users' doubts by establishing a perfect and reliable information security system, which aims to escort all kinds of information for enterprise users.

(4) **Overcome internal weaknesses to respond to external threats**

Based on the results of the SWOT-PEST model analysis, in recent years, there have been many substitutes in the external competitive market. These alternative products are developing rapidly and they are dividing the market with obvious intention. To be specific, in view of the development path of Enterprise WeChat, there is no advantage for it to enter into the market, it lags behind the 'Nail' of Alibaba and is known in Chinese as "叮叮", which is the main competitive product for recent years in terms of time [39]. Besides this, in terms of product functions experience, Enterprise WeChat is far less than the 'Cloud Home' developed by Kingdee Group that focuses on enterprise collaboration. According to this, Enterprise WeChat is confronted with a huge threat from similar external products. At the same time, Enterprise WeChat is also facing some difficulties and challenges within the organisation such as lack of close cooperation between different departments, lack of product popularity, long business development cycle of enterprise users, low acceptance of enterprise decision-makers, etc.

In this situation, when facing the external threats above mentioned, Enterprise WeChat needs to take timely measures to overcome their internal weaknesses and make more efforts to improve product functions. First of all, the product function of Enterprise WeChat was relatively weak in the early stage. However, with continuous product updates and gradual opening of the third-party application market, Enterprise WeChat has also realised the transformation from a single internal communication tool to an enterprise level collaborative office tool. Therefore, it can be concluded that the continuous upgrading of product functions and versions is one of the most effective measures. Secondly, Enterprise WeChat's operational team should make full use of the influence of advertising and media to expand its popularity. In addition, the needs of enterprise users should be fully considered in the development process of Enterprise WeChat, which aims to provide a personalised mobile office service for enterprises based on their business process. Eventually, cooperation between different departments within the company should be strengthened, which is beneficial to product development. As Ernst et al. [40] discussed, a successful product involves the research team, manufacturing team, market team, service team and finance team, etc. Innovative products can be created only through hard work. Therefore, Enterprise WeChat's operational team should coordinate the internal resources of the company to the greatest extent.

6   Conclusions

The emergence of the Internet provides human beings with new technologies, new approaches and new media for information exchange. With the development and popularisation of network communication technologies and mobile devices, enterprise instant messaging (EIM) is set to improve information sharing and communication among employees as a result of integrating instant messaging and collaborative office. In order to promote EIM technology and tools to better serve enterprise in the world, one of the world-class EIM tools developed by Tencent, Enterprise WeChat, was investigated and analysed based on the SWOT-PEST matrix model. A SWOT-PEST matrix model analysis of Enterprise WeChat was built up (see Table 2), several current problems and issues of the Enterprise WeChat product were explored and discussed from the internal micro perspective and the external macro environment. In general, from the internal point of view, policy support, rapid progress in Tencent R&D team, low cost for enterprise users, etc. are the main advantages of Enterprise WeChat. However, several weaknesses like lack of publicity, long product revenue return cycle, individual or enterprise-level information security problems can be minimised or even dealt with by taking appropriate strategies through the development of national policy and advanced technology in the future. On the other hand, in terms of external factors, some uncertain factors might increase, the main barrier of Enterprise WeChat use in China is the habits of enterprise users. In this regards, the Enterprise WeChat operation team should increase product exposure, so as to gradually develop user habits.

Enterprise strategy is a long-term and overall plan made by an enterprise for continuous development in the future. Enterprise WeChat is a strategic product for Tencent in their future plan. As one of their most competitive products, Enterprise WeChat is not only a key product that helps Tencent to enter the enterprise market, but it is an efficient tool that transforms Tencent from an individual level to business level market. Therefore, the following points should be considered in the future development of Enterprise WeChat, 1) build a more perfect partner ecosystem to make up for shortcomings in the enterprise market; 2) explore potential customer groups and become a service tool for the whole scene of the enterprise; 3) establish product advantages in the fierce competition, particularly in the future intelligent era.

References

1. Carr, A.S., Kaynak, H.: Communication methods, information sharing, supplier development and performance: an empirical study of their relationships. Int. J. Oper. Prod. Manag. **27**(4), 346–370 (2007)
2. Zhou, H., Benton, Jr. W.C.: Supply chain practice and information sharing. J. Oper. Manag. **25**(6), 1348–1365 (2007)
3. Leonardi, P.M.: Social media, knowledge sharing, and innovation: toward a theory of communication visibility. Inf. Syst. Res. **25**(4), 796–816 (2014)
4. Pandey, V.C., Garg, S.K., Shankar, R.: Impact of information sharing on competitive strength of Indian manufacturing enterprises: an empirical study. Bus. Process. Manag. J. **16**(2), 226–243 (2010)
5. Chen, P.T., Kuo, S.C.: Innovation resistance and strategic implications of enterprise social media websites in Taiwan through knowledge sharing perspective. Technol. Forecast. Soc. Chang. **118**, 55–69 (2017)
6. Wolfe, C., Loraas, T.: Knowledge sharing: The effects of incentives, environment, and person. J. Inf. Syst. **22**(2), 53–76 (2008)
7. Patnayakuni, R., Rai, A., Seth, N.: Relational antecedents of information flow integration for supply chain coordination. J. Manag. Inf. Syst. **23**(1), 13–49 (2006)
8. Luo, X., Gurung, A., Shim, J.P.: Understanding the determinants of user acceptance of enterprise instant messaging: an empirical study. J. Organ. Comput. Electron. Commer. **20**(2), 155–181 (2010)
9. Hasan, N., Miah, S.J., Bao, Y., Hoque, M.R.: Factors affecting post-implementation success of enterprise resource planning systems: a perspective of business process performance. Enterp. Inf. Syst. **13**(9), 1217–1244 (2019)
10. Six, F., Skinner, D.: Managing trust and trouble in interpersonal work relationships: evidence from two Dutch organizations. Int. J. Hum. Resour. Manage. **21**(1), 109–124 (2010)
11. Faulhaber, G.: Network effects and merger analysis: instant messaging and the AOL–Time Warner case. Telecommun. Policy **26**(5–6), 311–333 (2002)
12. Cameron, A.F., Webster, J.: Unintended consequences of emerging communication technologies: instant messaging in the workplace. Comput. Hum. Behav. **21**(1), 85–103 (2005)
13. Ogara, S.O., Koh, C.E., Prybutok, V.R.: Investigating factors affecting social presence and user satisfaction with mobile instant messaging. Comput. Hum. Behav. **36**, 453–459 (2014)
14. Ou, C.X., Davison, R.M.: Shaping guanxi networks at work through instant messaging. J. Am. Soc. Inf. Sci. **67**(5), 1153–1168 (2016)

15. Peng, X., Zhao, Y.C., Zhu, Q.: Investigating user switching intention for mobile instant messaging application: taking WeChat as an example. Comput. Hum. Behav. **64**, 206–216 (2016)
16. Sheer, V.C., Rice, R.E.: Mobile instant messaging use and social capital: direct and indirect associations with employee outcomes. Information & Management **54**(1), 90–102 (2017)
17. Liu, S., Zhang, Y., Chen, L., Guo, L., Yu, D.: Enterprise WeChat groups: their effect on work-life conflict and life-work enhancement. Front. Bus. Res. China **9**(4), 516 (2015)
18. Tian, M., Xu, G.: Exploring the determinants of users' satisfaction of WeChat official accounts. In: 2017 3rd International Conference on Information Management (ICIM), pp. 362–366). IEEE (2017)
19. Gong, X., Lee, M.K., Liu, Z., Zheng, X.: Examining the role of tie strength in users' continuance intention of second-generation mobile instant messaging services. Inf. Syst. Front. **22**, 1–22 (2018)
20. Huang, H., Yang, H., Piao, Y.: Improving the satisfaction of hospital staff: an attempt at Enterprise WeChat. Ch. J. Hospital Adm. **34**(10), 872–876 (2018)
21. Tsai, W.H.S., Men, R.L.: Social messengers as the new frontier of organization-public engagement: a WeChat study. Public Relat. Rev. **44**(3), 419–429 (2018)
22. Pan, X., Chen, C., Wang, F.: WeChat Wisdom Medical treatment process based on the hall three-dimensional structure. In: Karwowski, W., Ahram, T. (eds.) IHSI 2019. AISC, vol. 903, pp. 148–154. Springer, Cham (2019). https://doi.org/10.1007/978-3-030-11051-2_23
23. Bai, H., He, S.: Understanding the behavior of sharing information of WeChat users: an integrated model. In: 2016 6th International Conference on Management, Education, Information and Control (MEICI 2016). Atlantis Press (2016)
24. Cheng, A., Ren, G., Hong, T., Nam, K., Koo, C.: An exploratory analysis of travel-related WeChat mini program usage: affordance theory perspective. In: Pesonen, J., Neidhardt, J. (eds.) Information and Communication Technologies in Tourism 2019, pp. 333–343. Springer, Cham (2019). https://doi.org/10.1007/978-3-030-05940-8_26
25. Phadermrod, B., Crowder, R.M., Wills, G.B.: Importance-performance analysis based SWOT analysis. Int. J. Inf. Manage. **44**, 194–203 (2019)
26. Dyson, R.G.: Strategic development and SWOT analysis at the University of Warwick. Eur. J. Oper. Res. **152**(3), 631–640 (2004)
27. Bell, G.G., Rochford, L.: Rediscovering SWOT's integrative nature: a new understanding of an old framework. Int. J. Manage. Educ. **14**(3), 310–326 (2016)
28. Gupta, A.: Environment and PEST analysis: an approach to the external business environment. Int. J. Mod. Soc. Sci. **2**(1), 34–43 (2013)
29. Ha, H., Coghill, K.: E-government in Singapore-a SWOT and PEST analysis. Asia Pac. Soc. Sci. Rev. **6**(2), 103–130 (2008)
30. Zhu, L., Hiltunen, E., Antila, E., Huang, F., Song, L.: Investigation of China's bio-energy industry development modes based on a SWOT–PEST model. Int. J. Sustain. Energ. **34**(8), 552–559 (2015)
31. Andoh-Baidoo, F.K., Babb, J.S., Agyepong, L.: e-Government readiness in Ghana: a SWOT and PEST analyses. Electron. Govern. Int. J. **9**(4), 403–419 (2012)
32. Hao, L., Wan, F., Ma, N., Wang, Y.: Analysis of the development of WeChat mini program. In: Journal of Physics: Conference Series, vol. 1087, No. 6, p. 062040. IOP Publishing (2018)
33. Wu, F., Wang, Z.M., Yao, G., Miao, Z.M.: The research on cloud mobile office system development for enterprise application. In: Applied mechanics and materials, vol. 596, pp. 123–126. Trans Tech Publications Ltd. (2014)
34. Ding, Q., Wang, X., Tian, J., Wang, J.: Understanding the acceptance of teaching method supported by enterprise WeChat in blended learning environment. In: 2019 International Symposium on Educational Technology (ISET), pp. 211–214. IEEE (2019)

35. Li, D., Cai, Z., Deng, L., Yao, X., Wang, H.H.: Information security model of block chain based on intrusion sensing in the IoT environment. Clust. Comput. **22**(1), 451–468 (2018). https://doi.org/10.1007/s10586-018-2516-1
36. Li, L.: Wechat Service of University library under the mode of O2O reading promotion. Adv. J. Commun. **8**(2), 49–58 (2020)
37. Yang, S.: Research on WeChat marketing strategy. In: 6th Annual International Conference on Social Science and Contemporary Humanity Development (SSCHD 2020), pp. 624–629. Atlantis Press (2021)
38. Steinbart, P.J., Raschke, R.L., Gal, G., Dilla, W.N.: SECURQUAL: an instrument for evaluating the effectiveness of enterprise information security programs. J. Inf. Syst. **30**(1), 71–92 (2016)
39. Li, Y., Wang, H.: The Future of remote conferencing platforms in China's online education market. In: 2021 2nd International Conference on Big Data and Informatization Education (ICBDIE), pp. 545–552. IEEE (2021)
40. Ernst, H., Hoyer, W.D., Rübsaamen, C.: Sales, marketing, and research-and-development cooperation across new product development stages: implications for success. J. Mark. **74**(5), 80–92 (2010)

**Distributed, Ambient, and Pervasive
Education and Learning**

TSSP: A Toolkit to Broaden the Possibilities Transmedia Content Creation

Jie Hao[1], Chawchen Ting[1], Zhilu Cheng[1], and Huan Wang[2(✉)]

[1] Beijing Institute of Fashion Technology, Beijing 100029, China
jhaohj@126.com, ding@bift.edu.cn, zhilucheng@qq.com
[2] Capital Normal University, Beijing 100048, China
whuan@cnu.edu.cn

Abstract. What challenges do designers face when working on different disciplinary backgrounds? Disciplinary integration based on new media design is increasingly flourishing. However, in most projects, due to the differences between disciplines and the time constraints of cooperation, consensus needs to be reached quickly in cooperation for work output, making the consensus communication toolkit particularly important. Can designers do responsible work apart from hardware and software design? This toolkit was initiated in 2018 in the college course of Design of a Digital Lifestyle one, which I presided over, and so far, it has been updated for four versions. The audience has been gradually completed as the progressive structure of students studying in the department of new media - students majoring in design - junior designers working in companies. In order to construct a complete teaching system of the school and link it to the talent cultivation for the market, a toolkit called TSSP was initiated in the context of new media design, aiming to facilitate the integration of different disciplines for fast output of demos. The toolkit is composed of two core stages, personal fabrication laboratory and interaction transition. It broadens the cooperation path of enterprises and accelerates technological iteration, realizing convenient and efficient demo output, test and work output. It thus enables designers of different stages to grasp the relationship between lifestyle design, media and practice, thus realizing clear structures, so as to enhance the matching performance of interaction prototypes. It helps them to get familiar with the solution of design projects from multiple perspectives, including user research, concept design and technical analysis, etc., thus solving part of the lifestyle issues in an in-depth manner. It reflects on our relationship with space, and tries to create methods to design objects and their environment.

Keywords: Transmedia content · Toolkit · Personal fabrication laboratory

1 Introduction

With the extensive application of cross-professional cooperation in various industries, the acceleration of information iteration has brought great potentials for the integration of various disciplines, and the members of design research teams have shifted from single

© The Author(s), under exclusive license to Springer Nature Switzerland AG 2022
N. A. Streitz and S. Konomi (Eds.): HCII 2022, LNCS 13326, pp. 123–136, 2022.
https://doi.org/10.1007/978-3-031-05431-0_9

to multi-disciplinary talents to meet multiple challenges. Consequently, research teams studying the blend of disciplines are faced with challenges from various aspects. They, from different disciplines, need to not only undergo a long process from strangers to familiar working partners than similar majors but also understand each other's disciplines and clearly explain their discipline overview. 'The nature of work and its organization has evolved from being hierarchical and top-down, to multidirectional and collaborative. As a result, companies must reinvent their culture and engagement model with their workforce if they want to successfully harvest the benefits associated with their digital transformation' [1]. The trend of all industries and teaching environments tends to be the disciplinary integration to reshape the way of participation, which is reflected in the teaching environment as various workshops integrating multiple disciplines. However, the new media discipline plays an essential role in this rising trend of cooperation. Both social practice and teaching research are under the development of a general education tool kit. As a digital platform, new media broadens the idea for the construction of the toolkit.

Based on the above three aspects, a tool kit-TSSP is analyzed in this paper to expand the possibilities of cross-media content creation. The name of TSSP consists of the abbreviations of four core workshops that constitute the toolkit. After four times of iteration, the workshop has been gradually improved in terms of core theoretical basis and expected results, involving Tool Research, Size, Spatial and Perception, respectively. Hereinafter, the toolkit is simply referred to as TSSP.

Its audiences will gradually develop into the following three categories: (1) students majoring in new media, (2) students majoring in design, and (3) junior designer teams in companies. The possibility of cross-media content creation can be motivated through practicing various aspects of the TSSP toolkit. Thus, the interaction, communication, symbiosis and integration between media can be broadened, and the user-centered innovation can be investigated. Content creators include two major subjects: users and designers. The scope of designers' content creation can be broadened through participatory design, reflective practice, and action research. This stage is composed of two parts: manual manufacturing and intelligent manufacturing. First, it lays a foundation for the demonstration knowledge of building large structures. Then, the latest information of the industry, technology media platforms, and investigation methods are understood. It can visually or structurally indicate its function through simple hand exercises. Besides, its function can be realized through investigation and analysis and knowledge structure optimization. Gradually, exercises related to mechanical structure extension can be expanded. Afterward, the criticality of the human body, dimension, and space is developed through basic technology space experiments and integrated into the digital field at a later stage. The TSSP toolkit can assist in the rapid production of results at different stages of interdisciplinary integration and bring crucial feedback.

2 Purpose

Based on the college course Digital Lifestyle Design I, four series of core workshops were generated in this paper. Besides, the TSSP tool kit was initiated by the background of new media design and assisted the integration and rapid communication of different disciplines to produce a demo, paving the way for the complete construction of the college's teaching system. As an essential link in the information age, industrial personalization makes machine shops return to people's daily life. 'When interacting with the environment, with others, and with the artefacts of technology, people develop internal mental models of themselves and the things with which they are interacting' [2]. Meanwhile, personal manufacturing is also the improvement and redesign of information itself, contributing to the generation of a series of chain reactions that make technology be more deeply integrated into the digital lifestyle. Additionally, it is a point of communication connecting with the times, requesting designers to extend and design the objects or things that cannot be classified or defined.

Intelligent manufacturing can help increase the value of intelligent manufacturing, which is based on the transformation of individual manufacturing achievements. As for the process of manufacturing, intelligent manufacturing can play a role in partially replacing manual supervision and executing intelligent strategy, which however is dependent on the direction of output as determined by personalized manufacturing

Inspired by the idea 'Chemical kinetics studies the speed of converting compounds from reactant species to products' [3], the rate of transformation products is stimulated by chemical reaction. Meanwhile, the draft in the design process should have the source power of its conversion rate. In other words, the design draft produced in the implementation process of the toolkit has the corresponding conversion rate evaluation criteria to present its value tendency. According to the Cambridge dictionary, the meaning of transformation is 'the process of changing completely the character or appearance of something in order to improve it' [4]. The core element of evaluating the value of the TSSP toolkit is transformation rate. Inspiring the standard intended for evaluating the core value of TSSP, the above "rate of conversion products" is referred to as transformation rate. As for the process of design, it is also supposed to be transformed in different links. The outcomes of this design are assessed against five elements, which are audience, structural, functional, modular, and visual, respectively. The quantity of different elements converted is recorded according to the standard of unit time for inferring the level of transformation rate. If the transformation rate is low for an element, it is suggested that the element should be redesigned.

Challenges faced by the toolkit:
Whether can it solve the desired problems, such as improving effectiveness, reducing worthless communication, and broadening the audience?
Whether can it improve the conversion rate from draft to mature design?
Whether can it assist in determining the conversion value at the initial design stage?

3   TSSP

TSSP is a toolkit to broaden the possibilities for transmedia content creation. This toolkit is based on the real information feedback of practical teaching and broadens the research from three aspects. Firstly, students majoring in new media can broaden the possibility of media diversification to prepare for cross-major cooperation and company practice. Secondly, TSSP, as one of the ways for students majoring in design to learn about other majors, can simulate the trend of cross-major cooperation in the future and understand the responsibilities of different majors in the team. Thirdly, it is oriented to junior designers for the company or new junior designers for the company's mature team as a transition or adjustment status toolkit. The toolkit can be employed to achieve fast output design demo, observe and explore its design conversion rate, and broaden the design output path. "There is a difference between cooperation and collaboration that must be acknowledged. Cooperation means that I help you when you ask. Collaboration means that I understand and appreciate others' role to the point of actively looking at ways to involve them in the development process" [5]. The workshop supports the designer in the creation of fast feedback loops with the participants; it provides the designer with an opportunity to empathise with the users during the entire design research process.

The following series of workshops reflects the full exploration process and attempts of the toolkit.

Workshop1: Tool Research. Tool Research mainly includes tools, technologies, platforms, equipment, and media for intelligent manufacturing. Workshop 1 focuses on new or mature technologies based on the framework research discipline background. The framework includes name, application fields, use case, technical principle, and simple quote. In the research tool stage, the number of team members is not limited while the team is required to share several tools following the above framework within a fixed time (the recommended time is less than 2 hours). The workshop aims to quickly build a tool collection through crowdsourcing [6], allowing participants to quickly understand the new tools.

Workshop2: Size. Measuring tools and estimated dimensions, body sensation space.

1. Select space
2. Estimate the space size
3. Restore space to sketch based on the estimated size
4. Assist in the measurement of the space with any size of the body
5. Precisely measure with a ruler
6. Repeat the measurement
7. Compare the error of 2 and 6
8. Repeat steps 1 to 7 above

In repeated modular exercises, different venues can be selected to reinforce participants' concept of size. The classroom is the realization of the innovation of teaching mode, making the course feedback form a cycle. Firstly, they let the students wander in the class. For example, each student in the study of the size needs to check his or her previous guesses about size with a tape measure, instead of just teaching the importance of size. Secondly, it involves periodic reports and mutual evaluation of the academic achievements of the student group. From finding units for reference to the measurement for reporting, students are arranged around desks in the classroom. This suggests that there will be a space in the middle to form a similar atmosphere of reporting desk during the reporting stage of students' works. For example, students can learn from the half-arm length to walk in a given space to measure how many half-arms the space length is composed of, or even the height of participants. They can measure the space size with body height by lying down. Particularly, practice and teaching can be closely linked since the visibility of teaching organization in class can be maximized, and the communication of each group of students can be emphasized. In the technical investigation stage, the possibility of applying the technology at the present stage is investigated in detail with the technology by keeping up with the development of science and technology of the times, laying a foundation for broadening the design ideas. Besides, the progressive construction of different sizes is established by combining course content with teaching methods to consolidate design thinking. It needs to start from the basic concept of size to complete the conception transformation of the third workshop from two-dimensional to three-dimensional.

Workshop 3: Spatial. Understand the concept of space and dimension, and introduce the concept of space and dimension through the practice of exploring the information conveyed by different media. The workshop is an exercise in mystery boxes of one cubic meter. It is built by selecting one of ten mood phrases, such as cold, hot, adventurous, and enthusiastic. The appearance of each group is uniform, and no other design can be performed. Moreover, one or two holes can be left for touching with both hands or a single hand. Regarding perception, only retaining the sense of touch requires de-signers to maximize the particularity of materials and media to convey emotional perception. As illustrated in Figure 1, part A is the preliminary sketch modeling, in which the selected materials are added. Based on the deconstruction and material experiment of part A, detailed 3D model construction is conducted (Part B). The blind box is fitted in Part C. After the completion of several blind boxes in the group, the 28 people in the student team will guess and score the words in each group and choose one word from the ten words provided.

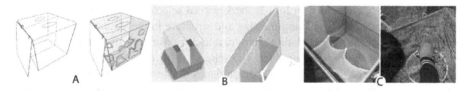

Fig. 1. Perceptual training-The process of fitted blind box

Objective:(1) To make designers understand the relationship between design and media and practice implementation and clarify the structure and enhance the matching degree of interaction prototype. (2) To reflect on the relationship between us and space and creative ways of designing objects and their environments. (3) To understand design tools as the dominants of the design, concretely analyze design tools and design media, realize perceptual changes through the use of different materials, and build large structures. 4) Develop the integration of the human body, dimension, and space through space experiments of basic technologies and integrate it into the digital realm in the later stage.

Workshop 4: Perception. At present, the commercial activities of new media mechanical devices are frequently faced with too many but difficult-to-implement new ideas. The state model should be designed to facilitate the implementation. Therefore, this workshop connects the transition from students' states to professional designers while assisting in the construction of the model. The application of model practice can intuitively demonstrate the device model of equal scale reduction. This not only lays a model foundation for its implementation but also expands the manipulative ability of students. The first three workshops are mainly about the combination of the body, which is a part of the design. Workshop 4 is the combination of body and media and adopts small wooden strips with a cross-section of one square centimeter to conduct a series construction. The raw materials are small wooden strips, basic hardware, and basic tools with a length of one meter and a cross-section of one square centimeter.

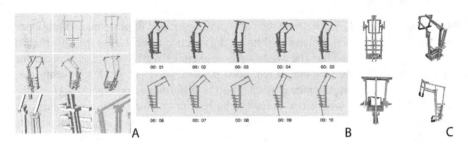

Fig. 2. The wearable device design process

The core of Workshop 4 is to pave the way for students to become professional designers and build expansion structures based on modular raw materials. The keywords of structure construction contain support, stability, rotation, movement, pull, and bearing. The construction practice of each keyword lasts for 24 h, and the participation of each group can be improved in the stage of mutual evaluation of the construction results of each keyword. As revealed in Fig. 2, the keyword selected is "movement"; part A is the modeling accurately shaping the size and structure in the virtual model; part B is the simulated dynamics simulating the dynamic demonstration of real scenes in the software; part C is the finished product. The scheme is a wearable dynamic structure, which is worn on legs to simulate the characteristics that clothes cover body structure. This workshop limits the raw materials since the materials with a cross-section of one square centimeter are relatively thick. Concerning the construction of fine structures, it is necessary to enlarge the structure ten or even ten times. Thus, students can observe the dynamic structure in life and redesign it.

Figure 3 illustrates the workshop framework of body and media based on the above Workshops 1–4. Body-led Workshops 1, 2, 3 and body-media-led Workshop 4 jointly constitute the workshop series.

Corresponding design drafts can be produced, and manual models can be constructed. The malleability of the results of the series of workshops is reflected in the following three aspects:

1 The achievements are easy to be understood and can be used for the expansion research of various majors.
2 The combination of media and body contributes to multiple possibilities of creation.
3 The broad scope of mechanical interaction and diverse forms of expression of new media.

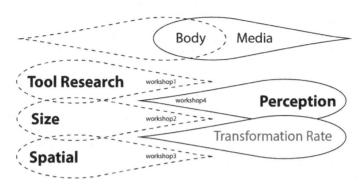

Fig. 3. Workshop framework based on Body and Media.

Due to the variable size and dynamic deduction, the mechanical movable structures produced by the series workshops would be transformed into other designs. In the design process, preliminary investigation, user research, sketch drawing, scheme deepening, and other links should perform design transformation. Methods and tools that can broaden the creation way of designers should be determined to improve the conversion rate of each link to promote redesign. From one perspective, this series of hand-built workshops allow people to use enlarged materials to manually build this series of workshops instead of being limited to virtual drawing. From another perspective, the size of the original is conducive to carefully dismantling and assembling the infrastructure, so as to discover the extension between the subtle structure in life and body medium.

4 Characteristics of TSSP

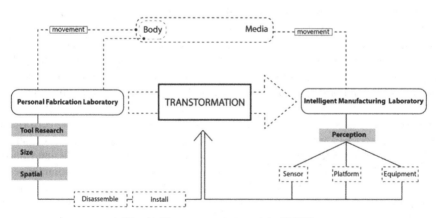

Fig. 4. The construction model of TSSP.

Furthermore, as shown in Fig. 4, Based on the series workshop, the way to find the critical points of collaboration has been completed, we expand the transmedia content creation into the toolkit, namely, TSSP. The toolkit is composed of two core stages, personal fabrication laboratory and interaction transition. Through the practice in various links of TSSP, possibilities of transmedia content creation are stimulated, thus broadening the interaction, dissemination, co-existence, and integration between media, researching on user-centered innovations, and the content creators include two subjects: users and designers. It broadens the scope of content creation by designers through participatory design, reflective practice, action research, etc. This stage is composed of two parts, namely manual manufacturing and smart manufacturing. First, the knowledge basis is prepared for the construction of large-scale structures; learning the latest information of the industry and technological media platforms, etc., including methods of surveys. It enables them to express functions through visual means or structures on the basis of simple handicraft practice; optimize such expression through investigation & analysis and knowledge architecture; broaden relevant practice through mechanical structure relevance. Then, through basic technical space experiments, the human body, dimensions and criticality are developed, which will later be integrated into the digital domain. Creative practice has moved from material to multidisciplinary expertise. Recent research revolves around this changing context, with an increasing number of professionals and academic researchers engaging in collaboration to explore interdisciplinary research in areas of creative practice [7]. The TSSP toolkit can facilitate interdisciplinary integration and realize fast outcome production at different stages, thus bringing great feedback.

5   Testing Model

Case1: Research on the Transformation from Personal Manufacturing to Intelligent Manufacturing. The modular form of the workshops can broaden the ideas for the initial interaction designers. Traditional methods of presentation and display focus on the construction ability of infrastructure and hardware guarantee. According to five core concept of Fab Lab:1 .Digital and personal fabrication; 2. Everyone can be a designer; 3. Technology/STEM education; 4. Maker movement; 5. Third Industrial Revolution [8]. The traditional exhibition is faced with complications such as poor timeliness and failure to update information in real-time. Meanwhile, traditional interaction stresses functionality, communication efficiency, and procedural aesthetic classification. These two aspects should be combined to achieve better conceptual integration. Information lag will be caused by the visual promotion and publicity based on this kind of information when a certain kind of data or information is no longer the focus of the moment. The innovations of the testing model are described as follows. Firstly, design and innovation on the basic structures such as eccentric circles, bearings, and sliding rails are performed based on this series of workshops. Secondly, the modular mechanical structure can be applied in most exhibition platforms, without a lack of individuality. This innovation point is the right combination of the characteristics of individuality and commonness. Finally, an information update closed-loop is integrated and formed to handle the diversity of implementation forms of new media interactive devices in the fashion presentation and display. Then, the identity of the brand value is enhanced through various dynamic mechanical structures.

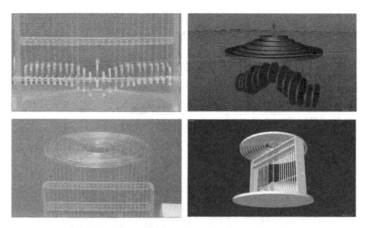

Fig. 5. Jewelry brand mechanical interaction device

As presented in Fig. 5, this device designs and produces mechanical device models for jewelry brands to provide a dynamic display of small-volume jewelry. Its first-level trigger is composed of 25 eccentric circles with different centers of the circle. Ascribed to the different center distances, the connecting rod will push the big and small circles at the top to float dynamically when the fixed shaft of the circle drives the connecting rod in the middle. The jewelry is placed in the center of the top of the device, which is triggered by people at a close distance. The device intervened by someone in the area with a radius of 0.5 m suggests that the device will float up and down in layers and stop when the person leaves.

The construction objectives of the testing model are detailed as follows. Firstly, it intends to expand the possibilities of new media presentations. Virtual cooperation projects with brands can extend to the direction of mechanical device exhibition, so as to explore a better interactive mechanical form carrier to spread its brand information. Secondly, it will build the way of cross-disciplinary cooperation of the college. This new form of mechanical interaction and academic achievements of fashionable exhibitions and displays can help fashion professionals better present their information. For example, such achievements contribute to the improvement of the construction form of showcases or the way of T-stage shows and the display state of fashion products. Thirdly, it boosts the conversion rate from draft to mature design. 'The difference between the general and the professional approach to design thinking is reflected in the current focus in design thinking studies on how designers and practitioners of design thinking think and act in processes' [9]. Moreover, the basis for the implementation of basic structures can be provided through the iterative continuation of the workshops, such as eccentric circles and gravity. Thus, students can transform this structure into mechanical devices with different difficulties under the research of the workshops and thus broaden the thinking for exploring new fashion exhibition cities.

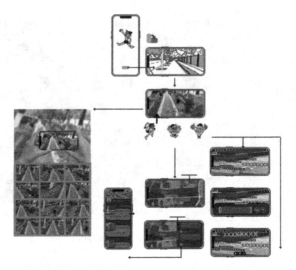

Fig. 6. Virtual digital technology games active streets

Case 2 Virtual Information Construction

Based on the application of interactive design to explore the composition of future communities, the designed research of case 2 is aimed at the road program to vivify urban streets with virtual digital technology. The exploration of cities to update their interactive prototypes by new media should break through the concept of time, suggesting that retaining historical information can run simultaneously with updating real-time data. Figure 6 illustrates a game application for making friends and vivifying streets. It requires the real locations and geographic points, indicating that users can walk in public areas with their mobile phones to find preset game characters while the characters can walk in the virtual world in sync with the finders. One user can leave a message at a point where he/she stays, with the words floating dynamically on the screen; the other can reply or revise the message at the same place. In this way, a virtual dialogue scene crossing time and space is created to strengthen people's ability to feel the space and enable them to cross space and experience the novel way of information transmission, contributing to the improvement of urban vitality by steering people walking outside.

For this situation, we try to test with TSSP shown as Fig. 7. Ten-minute conversion rate verification is conducted from the five perspectives of audience, structure, functionality, modularity, and vision. The radius of the circular area represents the expansion possibility per unit time (every ten seconds). The area of the circle denotes the local conversion rate of the design case. The circular area of the five perspectives overlaps, as exhibited in the red areas of the figure. This demonstrates the overall conversion rate of this case. The larger the red area, the higher the conversion rate, and the more the

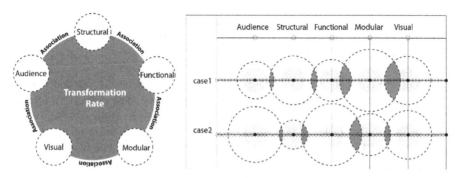

Fig. 7. Evaluation of the Listed workshops by TSSP Mode transformation rate

future expansion direction of iterative redesigns regarding designed works. Case1 aims to explore the direction of new media mechanical interaction forms and fashion exhibitions and improve the audience recognition of new media professions. The audience does not have an accurate visual definition of the mechanical interaction forms of new media. Consequently, too many undefined interactive forms in the current market are classified as the mechanical interaction of the new media. Therefore, the recognition understood by the audience is first strengthened in this type of designed research to make the audience realize that the fashion exhibition contains the form of mechanical interaction. Different from sculptures or other artistic works made by artists, plug-in interactive mechanical devices break the conventional form and attempt to abandon or combine traditional media to maximize the flexibility of visual movement while ensuring the safety of the devices. They reorganize and strengthen cross-media cooperation, redefine the display form of fashion exhibitions, and enable the audience to travel cross space or perform flexible visual tracking.

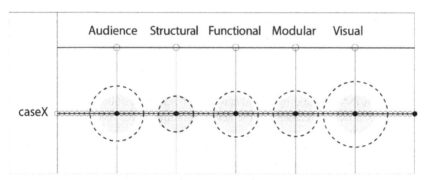

Fig. 8. Casex is an example evaluation of the Listed workshops by TSSP Mode transformation rate

What kind of design case has a low conversion rate and is recommended to re-examine and re-design?

Case x shown in Fig. 8 is taken as an example. Its conversion rate related to the audience is 5 per unit time (every ten seconds), and 3, 4, 4, and 6 for the others, respectively.

The overall absence of overlapping areas implies that the design can achieve substantial transformation in five aspects. The conversion rate of case x is 28%. Therefore, it is recommended to improve the whole features or strengthen individuals according to different cases.

Overall, the conversion rates of case 1 and case 2 are (34/60) 56.7% and (34/60) 56.7%, respectively. The critical value for distinction is 50%. The conversion of case 12 is higher than 50%, which is acceptable. The workshop procedure for the overall design or its details would be repeated to upgrade the transformation of the details. The core values of the workshop series are presented as follows. The first of all is to raise the participation in the design process and maximize the acceptance of participants by transforming from new media students in school to professional designers or even designers just starting to work, learning the means of discipline integration from other working fields, and increasing the diversity and coordination of the team. Secondly, workshop series can be a transition in the early design stage and the bottleneck period since teamwork is a regulator to improve efficiency. The third point focuses on the review method of the design value. Regarding the calculation of conversion rate, related recommended parameters can be provided for product transformation or iteration.

6 Discussion

6.1 Broaden the Scope of Cross-professional Cooperation

For the new media major, workshop series rebuild the concept of mechanical interaction of new media, improve the defect that traditional information carriers cannot update data in real-time, and make the best use of existing location characteristics to create modular and variable-sized interactive device carriers without changing their original form. Besides, the definition of business forms is updated. The possibility of interactive media devices requires to be expanded based on the existing fashion industry form. For example, traditional store windows are composed of partial narrow windows and flat walls. Sufficient research should be conducted on the decoration of the windows and the iterative update of the content. The seasonal update of brands will involve redecoration of windows, continuous high cost of products and workforce. In response to the above situation, this kind of modular mechanical structure will bring a new development path for the fashion industry due to the advantages of zero limitation of the space size to the new modular device realized by the new media interactive mechanical devices and timely updated vision. Concerning students majoring in design, the workshop series can be used as primary teaching methods for various majors in terms of the innovation of curriculum design. Hence, different subjects can be output rapidly in stages to maintain the attractiveness of courses and the initiative of students. The short-term small-scale construction can be performed by individuals or groups, and modular project exercises can be conducted in a short time to consolidate design thinking. Students gave positive feedback and demonstrated significantly strengthened initiative when the mutual evaluation was added during the workshop report period, contributing to shaping collective design and collaboration consciousness.

6.2 Possibility of the Modular Toolkit

In the initial stage of toolkit construction, it is necessary to preset multiple short-term subjects for user research and repeatedly explore the value of a certain toolkit through the results of short-term subject research. The research should be conducted to explore a method to organize and integrate the toolkit by efficiently applying the basic model structure. After the construction of the TSSP toolkit, it can be applied as exercises for the output method of subsequent applications in other scenarios, including models of simple mechanical structures. 'Designers today are faced with a multiplicity of choices in a cultural context that often appears to be without direction and where the results of their actions can have unforeseen consequences. They are in need of new creative methods to make sense of the world, to assist in giving form and meaning to modern culture. Designers need design orientation' [10]. Based on the single material and simple process, the toolkit composed of this workshop series can quickly adapt to audiences of various professional backgrounds. Furthermore, the products of the conversion rate can provide a reference for the opening of other new toolkits.

6.3 Possibility of the Creation Trend in the Future

With the rapid development of media information, technology and other means are employed as support points to transform virtual information into other forms of value expression and make future creations people-oriented through design methods. This paper focuses on a toolkit for broadening transmedia content creation. Toolkit and its core conversion rate possess a complementary relationship. The characteristics of cooperation, integration, efficiency, and iteration can drive future creation trends. 'Only orderliness makes design useful to us' [11]. TSSP toolkit can more efficiently and accurately evaluate the design and strengthen cooperation efficiency, laying a foundation with workshop series for the improvement of the conversion rate of designs.

References

1. InfoQ. https://www.infoq.com/articles/Digital-Transformation-Guide-1/. Accessed 2 Nov 2021
2. Petra, B.S., Andre, N., Kristina, L., Susan, M.:Mental models in design teams: a valid approach to performance in design collaboration? Int. J. CoCreat. Des. Arts 3, 5–20 (2007). https://doi.org/10.1080/15710880601170768
3. Science Direct. https://www.sciencedirect.com/topics/chemistry/rate-of-transition. Accessed 12 Nov 2021
4. Cambridge Dictionary. https://dictionary.cambridge.org/dictionary/english/transformation. Accessed 12 Nov 2021
5. CIO. https://www.cio.com/article/3292919/why-design-thinking-hasn-t-saved-your-digital-transformation-yet.html. Accessed 8 Nov 2021
6. Bella, M., Bruce, H.: Universal Methods of Design, Rockport Publishers, Inc. (2012)
7. Nithikul, N., Camilla, G., Oscar, T., Julia, V.N.: Knowing together – experiential knowledge and collaboration. Int. J. CoCreat. Des. Arts 16, 267–273 (2020). https://doi.org/10.1080/15710882.2020.1823995
8. Massimo, M.: FabLab: Revolution Field Manual. Niggli Verlag, Salenstein (2017)

9. Thames, H.: Quick Guide to Design Thinking. Strandberg Publishing, Copenhagen (J2021)
10. Maurice, B.: Design, Creativity and Culture: An Orientation to Design. 1st edn. Black Dog Press, London (2011)
11. Cees, W.D., Klaus, K., Erik, M., Jorrit, M., Dieter, R.: Ten Principles for Good Design. Prestel, Munich (2021)

Designing a Distributed Cooperative Data Substrate for Learners without Internet Access

Shin'ichi Konomi[1]($\boxtimes$), Xiangyuan Hu[2], Chenghao Gu[2], and Doreen Mushi[3]

[1] Faculty of Arts and Science, Kyushu University, 744, Motooka, Nishi-ku, Fukuoka 819-0395, Japan
konomi@artsci.kyushu-u.ac.jp
[2] Graduate School of Information Science and Electrical Engineering, Kyushu University, 744, Motooka, Nishi-ku, Fukuoka 819-0395, Japan
[3] Institute of Educational and Management Technologies, The Open University Tanzania, Dar es Salaam, Tanzania

Abstract. The increased use of Internet-based tools in education can create a problematic situation for those without Internet access. In this paper, we propose a distributed cooperative data substrate (DCDS) that allows learners without Internet access to use digital learning tools on their mobile devices. DCDS combines delay-tolerant networking (DTN) mechanisms, Web 3.0 technologies such as blockchains and InterPlanetary File System (IPFS), and human computation to support reliable and secure data access in a decentralized manner.

Keywords: Developing regions · e-learning · Data substrate · Blockchains · DTN · Web 3.0

1 Introduction

Internet-based digital tools can improve access and quality of education in many countries and communities. However, limited Internet connectivity can pose a major challenge in adopting such tools. Without Internet access, it is extremely difficult to use the learning tools that rely on centralized servers. It is also difficult for instructors to monitor and understand what's going on with the learners without the ICT infrastructure for collecting, storing and using educational data.

In this context, we propose a distributed data substrate that allows learners without Internet access to use digital learning tools. The data substrate we propose combines mobility-based data sharing mechanisms, Web 3.0 technologies such as blockchains and InterPlanetary File System (IPFS), and human computation to support reliable and secure data access in a decentralized manner.

We next motivate our design by examining the current status, opportunities, and challenges of technology-enhanced learning in Tanzania, and discuss the importance of providing data substrate for learners without Internet access.

N. A. Streitz and S. Konomi (Eds.): HCII 2022, LNCS 13326, pp. 137–147, 2022.
https://doi.org/10.1007/978-3-031-05431-0_10

1.1   Technology-Enhanced Learning in Tanzania

Current Status and Opportunities

The need for deploying technology in improving access and quality of education has been a prioritized agenda in both governmental and institutional levels in Tanzania. The government recognizes that quality education is fundamental for attainment of national sustainable development and it has been making substantial efforts in making sure that the target is realized. One way of supporting this was the formulation of National ICT Policy (United Republic of Tanzania, 2016) which (through its objectives), clearly stipulates the intent to use ICT to improve the quality of education delivery in all fields.

Tanzania has a population of 58.01 million as of 2019, out of which, 35.6% resides in urban areas and 64% in rural areas [1]. Usage data report by the Tanzania Communication Regulatory Authority indicates that Tanzania had a total of 29.01 million Internet users in March 2021 and it had reached service penetration by 50% compared to 46% in 2019 [2]. The rise of Internet users is evidently correlated with the increased use of mobile phones [3]. However, despite this advancement in Internet access, there is still a huge gap in Internet accessibility between rural and urban dwellers. For the case of Africa, reports by International Telecommunication Union (ITU) mention that only 15% of rural dwellers have Internet access. Recalling the fact that Tanzania has over 37.1 million people living in the remote area, this proves the need of innovative offline solutions to support delivery of content to users in remote areas [4].

E-learning is a permanent agenda in the country and in response to this, the education sector, from primary to tertiary level, has been embarking on finding avenues of integrating ICT in teaching and learning activities. In the case of higher education sector, universities have put in place ICT infrastructure, corresponding mediums and developed virtual learning environments to enhance learning experiences and access to content. The rise of mobile technology is also a significant contributor to the demands pertaining to e-learning development.

The developments in e-learning in Tanzania have so far brought a plethora of advantages including improved access to learning materials, self-paced and flexible learning, reduced educational costs and improved teaching and learning practices. The current status of e-learning in Tanzanian higher education sector is in its fundamental stages with ample room for potential development. There has been an increasing deployment of virtual learning environments, to engage in online teaching and learning at both distance and on-campus institutions [5]. Universities are acquiring learning management systems and invest in supplementing technologies such as mobile learning to ensure students get access to learning materials. However, further developments such as learning analytics and game-based learning are under exploited.

Information service in Tanzania is operated from the National Fibre Optic Cable Network named the National ICT broadband Backbone (NICTBB); and two submarine cables namely Eastern Africa Submarine Cable System (EASSY) and Southern and Eastern Africa Communication Network (SEACOM). The broadband provides leased connection to Mobile network operators, Internet service providers, local television and radio stations and data service providers [6].

Challenges
Despite the policies and initiatives to establish the ICT infrastructure, the e-learning sector in Tanzania is still faced with problems: As in other African countries, the key challenges facing e-learning implementation include poor ICT infrastructure, lack of facilities and lack of Internet connectivity. According to World Bank, by 2017 only 16% of total Tanzanian population has access to the Internet as compared to Japan which is at 91%. There is a huge gap in terms of urban and rural access to ICT Services. In rural areas problems such as lack of reliable electricity and limited access to computers intensify the issues exponentially. For the case of the Open University of Tanzania which provides service through 30 regional centers across the country, this problem has been evident. Most students from remote areas do not have access to the Internet and hence cannot access resources in Moodle [7]. In this regard, students have been supported by interactive CDs that are equipped with learning materials. Furthermore, lack of skilled human resources, technical skills and motivation amongst academic staff are identified as challenges as well.

1.2   Data Substrate for Learners, or the Lack Thereof

Educational data about learners, teachers and learning contents can be used to visualize and analyze educational successes and failures. Such data can also provide resources for reflecting on the past, present and future of educational environments, and allow for the introduction of advanced data-scientific approaches such as predictive analytics and educational recommender systems. These approaches could be used to improve the satisfaction and performance of students, and also reduce dropouts.

   Our experiences [8] suggest some of the attributes that can be useful for analyzing and predicting dropouts and academic performance:

- demographic information,
- attendance,
- scores of quizzes,
- submissions of assignments,
- access logs of learning materials,
- learning journals,
- responses to surveys (e.g., course evaluation surveys), and
- grades

   Additionally, contextual attributes such as location and time are important when learning activities take place at different times and at different places inside and outside the classroom.

   Although digital devices such as mobile phones are pervading the world, many cannot access the Internet easily due to various obstacles including the high cost of wireless broadband services. Also, aforementioned types of attributes cannot be collected, stored and used easily without the reliable and secure data management infrastructure in place.

In this paper, we discuss the design of a *distributed cooperative data substrate (DCDS)* as an alternative data management substrate for learners without Internet access. Building on our earlier work on the platform for offline learners [9], DCDS integrates *cooperative mechanisms among the carriers of digital devices* and *a secure decentralized data sharing mechanism* to collect, store and use educational data about learners, teachers, and learning contents to improve the satisfaction and performance of learners without reliable and secure Internet access in developing communities. The sociotechnical nature of the proposed environment requires us to perform the design and development in context, in particular, the contexts of developing communities in countries including Tanzania.

2 Related Works

2.1 Mobile-Phone Sensing

Mobile-phone sensing [10], as a means of participatory or opportunistic data collection, allows us to collect data "anywhere at anytime" without relying on embedded data-collection mechanisms in physical spaces. Several projects have deployed mobile-phone sensing environments in developing regions. For example, Singh et al. developed an SMS-based prototype that provides real-time notification and information gathering capabilities [11]. Gupta et al. developed a mobile crowdsourcing platform that exploits SMS, making it accessible from a low-end mobile phone [12]. Their platform allows participation by people who do not own high-end mobile phones, thereby offering employment opportunities to low-income workers. There are many smartphone users in developing regions. Open-source tools such as Open Data Kit (ODK) [13] enables flexible and powerful data collection using web forms, cameras, microphones, sensors, GPS, and databases. ODK allows for an asynchronous means of data transfer, thereby supporting pervasive crowdsensing regardless of the availability of Internet connectivity. These mobile crowdsourcing technologies could be extended and integrated with digital learning environments.

2.2 Intermittent Networking

Researchers have proposed networking technologies for challenging environments such as disaster events and developing communities. Brewer et al. discussed intermittent, delay-tolerant networking (DTN) technologies for the education of children in developing regions. The applications they propose include a local content repository where students and teachers can store and retrieve digital stories, games, and other digital content that they create by using easy-to-use authoring tools. The Digital Study Hall system [14] exploits intermittent networking technology, thin-client displays, and educational content repository to support usage scenarios such as lecture capture and replay, homework collection and feedback, and question-answer sessions in resource-starved village schools in rural India. However, these proposals focus on networking mechanisms without fully considering its integration with mobile sensing or support for secure data sharing in decentralized environments.

2.3 Decentralized Data Sharing Infrastructure

Niavis et al. propose DEON, a decentralized data infrastructure for off-grid networks using state-of-the-art Web 3.0 technologies [15]. InterPlanetary File System (IPSF), which is also used in DEON, is a peer-to-peer distributed file system upon which one can build versioned file systems, blockchains, and permanent Web [16].

Edutech researchers have explored uses of blockchains in recent years. Chen et al. discuss potential educational applications of blockchains, including management of credentials and historical records of learning [17]. Turkanovic et al. (2018) propose a credit platform for higher education based on the blockchain technology [18]. Bore, et al. describe a school information system based on the blockchain technology to collect, store and manage school records involving information about students, teachers, and assets [19]. Kwok and Treiblmaier discuss potential of the blockchain technology for social inclusion based on a literature review [20]. Steiu discusses benefits of applying blockchains in education, including learner empowerment, security enhancement, and efficiency improvement [21]. Educational blockchain applications are yet to mature, and the potential of Web 3.0 in general seems still underexplored.

Community networks are decentralized telecommunications that people build and operate themselves [22] and they may provide local platforms that is closely related to the idea of distributed cooperative data infrastructure. One can design local platforms for communities based on distributed ledger technologies such as blockchains by considering some design dilemmas [23].

3 Mobility-Based Data Sharing

To address the limitations of the existing approaches, we propose a mobility-based data sharing mechanism that integrates mobile tools and embedded devices based on spatial analytics. The proposed mechanism is based on Delay Tolerant Networking (DTN), and lays a foundation for a novel distributed data substrate.

3.1 Mobile Tools

Our preliminary mobile tools are based on Open Data Kit [13] and allows for collection of various types of data including the ones from sensors, web forms, cameras, and microphones. The collected data can be easily uploaded and visualized on a cloud server. The data collection form we designed records contextual information (location and time) as well as student's demographic information (ID, gender, age) and feedback (perceived difficulty and satisfaction, and comments). It can also capture student's handwritten learning journal entries. All of the data can be captured offline without requiring Internet connectivity. The captured data will be uploaded to a server when the mobile tool becomes online.

3.2 Embedded Micro-servers

The data collected by mobile tools are shared through intermittent *ad hoc* peer-to-peer exchange of data across mobile devices in proximity. To cope with the sparsity of mobile devices in unpopulated areas, we introduce embedded micro servers that receive, store, and send data to/from mobile devices in proximity, thereby enabling asynchronous communications across mobile devices. Embedded micro servers are small devices with computing, storage and wireless networking capabilities that can be embedded in public spaces. We use Raspberry Pi to develop a prototype micro server that can communicate with our ODK-based mobile tools.

3.3 Mobility-Based Data Sharing Mechanism

Figure 1 show the mobility-based data sharing mechanism using *ad hoc* peer-to-peer communications across mobile devices in proximity as well as embedded micro-servers (MS). Zones Z1 and Z2 represent local communities without Internet access. Embedded micro-servers (MS) are deployed at key locations in the community and can communicate with each other wirelessly (provided that they are within a certain communication range), which is represented by solid blue lines between micro-servers.

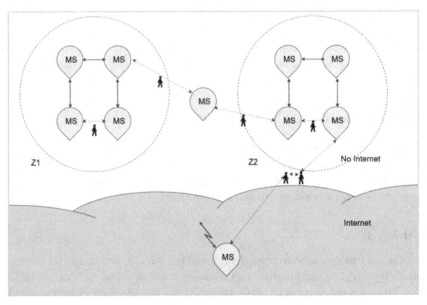

Fig. 1. Mobility-based data sharing mechanism (Color figure online)

Micro-servers that cannot communicate with each other wirelessly can still exchange data with the help of a person who carries a mobile phone and travels between the micro-servers' locations, which is represented by dotted blue line between micro-servers. Communications between zones Z1 and Z2 can be mediated by people who travel across these two zones. They can be also mediated by people who travel to the micro-server in-between Z1 and Z2, which can store and forward data from/to nearby mobile phones. A person traveling from Z2 towards the Internet-covered area pass-by someone. When they meet, their phones can exchange data.

This type of data sharing mechanism can be applied to an educational institution which has a headquarter office in the Internet-covered area, and satellite local-zones without Internet access to enable the use of networked digital learning tools in no-Internet zones. Making this mechanism work requires the deployment of micro-servers at appropriate locations based on the mobility patterns of people in and across different zones.

3.4 Spatial Analytics

We design proximity-based data communication environments based on the analysis of human mobility patterns in the geographical space of concern. Spatial analytics of human mobility patterns supports the processes of finding optimal locations to instrument micro servers.

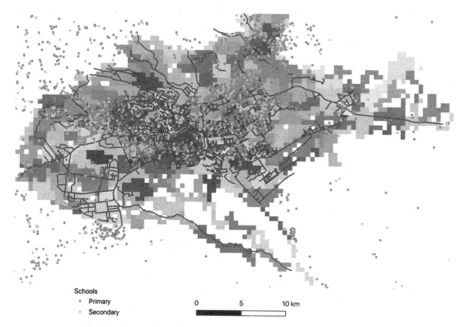

Fig. 2. Result based on the people flow 2013 dataset in Nairobi.

Figure 2 shows a preliminary result of our spatial analysis process based on a human mobility dataset from the Nairobi metropolitan area. Although we intend to extend and employ our spatial analytics process for other areas in the East-African region including different areas in Tanzania when relevant datasets are available, we present the sample visualization here to demonstrate our spatial analytics process using the currently available datasets from the broader geographical region of our concern. The spatial analytics of human flows can inform the design of a crowd-powered information delivery environment that supports teachers and learners without easy access to the Internet. The intended information delivery environment is based on a computer networking approach called Delay-tolerant networking (DTN) which can exploit pervasive devices, such as mobile phones and embedded micro servers, moving in and across local communities.

We use the *People Flow 2013 Nairobi Metropolitan Area (spatially reallocated)* dataset provided by the center for spatial information science at the University of Tokyo as well as the *Kenya-Schools dataset in 2020* provided by the Kenya Ministry of Education [24]. The analysis approach we employ is based on Colocation networks [25], which is based on people's colocation in space-time cubes during the time period between t_0 and $t_0 + T$. We have constructed an undirected Colocation network from the mobility dataset of Nairobi, and applied a community detection algorithm to detect groups of relevant spaces [26]. Our current analysis is based on rectangular spaces with their width and height being 500 m and 500 m, respectively.

We have identified 225 groups of spaces, each of which is indicated with a different color. Compared to a similar analysis of human flows in Tokyo [27], the shapes of the grouped spaces look more like pieces of Jigsaw puzzles than a radial web. This may reflect the differences of the structures and uses of transportation environments in Nairobi and Tokyo, and suggests a need of a different approach to enable an effective crowd-powered information delivery environment in different countries. The shape of each colored area suggests a pattern of geographical spread of data based on peer-to-peer exchange across nearby mobile phones. One may modify the shapes of colored areas by strategically deploying embedded micro-servers.

4   A Distributed Cooperative Data Substrate

The proposed mobility-based data sharing mechanism can be used to collect data from local zones and send them to a centralized server on the Internet(, or deliver learning contents from a centralized server to the mobile phones in local zones). However, this type of centralized data flows can involve a single point of failure, and thus can make the data substrate fragile and unreliable. In addition, the proposed mobility-based data sharing lacks a means of secure and private data exchange across distributed devices.

We next propose a distributed cooperative data substrate based on the mobility-based data sharing mechanism (see Fig. 3). Our data substrate employs blockchains and InterPlanetary File System (IPFS). The blockchain mechanism enables secure and private data exchange across distributed networks based on an identity management mechanism, and IPFS provides a resilient, peer-to-peer distributed file system. The DCDS architecture also provides the Local Crowdsourcing component for increasing the resilience of the data substrate based on a human-computational approach [28]. In doing so, we consider to extend our previous preliminary work on mobile community question-answering (CQA) system [29] and active learning-based crowdsourcing [9]. Learners and teachers can use various applications to share learning materials, submit assignments and quizzes, and manage badges and learning logs. Anonymous location information can be stored in the location DB to perform spatial analytics and optimize DCDS.

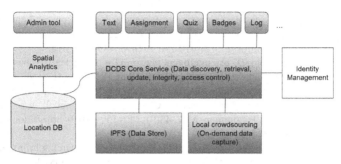

Fig. 3. Architecture of Distributed Cooperative Data Substrate (DCDS)

5 Discussion and Conclusion

In this paper, we presented our design of a distributed cooperative data substrate that allows learners and teachers without Internet access to use mobile phone-based learning applications. The data substrate we propose combines multiple mechanisms including mobility-based data sharing, spatial analytics, blockchains, IPFS, and human computation in order to support reliable and secure data access in distributed environments.

Our future work includes technical implementation based on the proposed design, and the test of feasibility to collect, store and use educational data for the support of learners in East African region including Tanzania.

Acknowledgement. This work was supported by JSPS KAKENHI Grant Number 20H00622.

References

1. The World Bank, "World Bank Open Data. https://data.worldbank.org/country/TZ. Accessed 11 Feb 2022
2. TCRA: Quarterly Communications Statistics January-March 2021 (2021)
3. Alexander, H., Leo, J., Kaijage, S., Alexander, H., Leo, J., Kaijage, S.: Online and offline android based mobile application for mapping health facilities using google map API. Case study: Tanzania and Kenya Borders. J. Softw. Eng. Appl. **14**(8), 344–362 (2021). https://doi.org/10.4236/JSEA.2021.148021
4. Mahenge, M.P.J., Msungu, A.C.: A strategy towards cost-effective content delivery in the higher learning institutions of Tanzania. In: Ubiquitous Technologies for Human Development and Knowledge Management, pp. 271–287 (2021). https://doi.org/10.4018/978-1-7998-7844-5.CH013
5. Mtebe, J.S.: Examining user experience of eLearning systems implemented in two universities in Tanzania. Interact. Technol. Smart Educ.**17**(1), 39–55 (2019). https://doi.org/10.1108/ITSE-05-2019-0025/FULL/XML
6. NICTBB: Status of the NICTBB and prospects for local contents development in Tanzania. http://www.nictbb.co.tz/news.php. Accessed 11 Feb 2022
7. "Moodle - Open-source learning platform|Moodle.org. https://moodle.org/. Accessed 11 Feb 2022

8. Okubo, F., Yamada, M., Oi, M., Shimada, A., Taniguchi, Y., Konomi, S.: Learning support systems based on cohesive learning analytics. In: Emerging Trends in Learning Analytics, pp. 223–248, April 2019. https://doi.org/10.1163/9789004399273_012
9. Konomi, S., Gao, L., Mushi, D.: An intelligent platform for offline learners based on model-driven crowdsensing over intermittent networks. In: Rau, P.-L. (ed.) HCII 2020. LNCS, vol. 12193, pp. 300–314. Springer, Cham (2020). https://doi.org/10.1007/978-3-030-49913-6_26
10. Lane, N.D., Miluzzo, E., Lu, H., Peebles, D., Choudhury, T., Campbell, A.T.: A survey of mobile phone sensing. IEEE Commun. Mag. **48**(9), 140–150 (2010). https://doi.org/10.1109/MCOM.2010.5560598
11. Singh, A., Li, Y.(, Sun, Y., Sun, Q.: An intelligent mobile crowdsourcing information notification system for developing countries. In: Huang, X.-L. (ed.) MLICOM 2016. LNICSSITE, vol. 183, pp. 139–149. Springer, Cham (2017). https://doi.org/10.1007/978-3-319-52730-7_14
12. Gupta, A., Thies, W., Cutrell, E., Balakrishnan, R.: mClerk: enabling mobile crowdsourcing in developing regions. In: Proceedings of the SIGCHI Conference on Human Factors in Computing Systems, pp.1843–1852 (2012). https://doi.org/10.1145/2207676
13. Brunette, W., Sudar, S., Sundt, M., Larson, C., Beorse, J., Anderson, R.: Open Data Kit 2.0: a services-based application framework for disconnected data management. In: Proceedings of the 15th Annual International Conference on Mobile Systems, Applications, and Services, pp. 440–452 (2017). https://doi.org/10.1145/3081333
14. Wang, R., et al.: The digital StudyHall (2005). https://www.cs.princeton.edu/techreports/2005/723.pdf. Accessed 11 Feb 2022
15. Niavis, H., Papadis, N., Reddy, V., Rao, H., Tassiulas, L.: A blockchain-based decentralized data sharing infrastructure for off-grid networking. In: 2020 IEEE International Conference on Blockchain and Cryptocurrency (ICBC), pp. 1–5 (2020). https://doi.org/10.1109/ICBC48266.2020.9169441
16. Benet, J.: IPFS - Content Addressed, Versioned, P2P File System, July 2014. http://arxiv.org/abs/1407.3561
17. Chen, G., Xu, B., Lu, M., Chen, N.-S.: Exploring blockchain technology and its potential applications for education. Smart Learn. Environ. **5**(1), 1 (2018). https://doi.org/10.1186/s40561-017-0050-x
18. Turkanović, M., Hölbl, M., Košič, K., Heričko, M., Kamišalić, A.: EduCTX: a blockchain-based higher education credit platform. IEEE Access **6**, 5112–5127 (2018). https://doi.org/10.1109/ACCESS.2018.2789929
19. Bore, N., Karumba, S., Mutahi, J., Darnell, S.S., Wayua, C., Weldemariam, K.: Towards blockchain-enabled school information hub. In: ICTD 2017: Proceedings of the Ninth International Conference on Information and Communication Technologies and Development, pp. 1–4 (2017), https://doi.org/10.1145/3136560.3136584
20. Kwok, A.O.J., Treiblmaier, H.: No one left behind in education: blockchain-based transformation and its potential for social inclusion. Asia Pac. Educ. Rev. **2021**, pp. 1–11 (2022). https://doi.org/10.1007/S12564-021-09735-4
21. Steiu, M.-F.: Blockchain in education: opportunities, applications, and challenges. First Monday (2020). https://journals.uic.edu/ojs/index.php/fm/article/view/10654/9726. Accessed 10 Feb 2022
22. Bidwell, N.J.: Wireless in the weather-world and community networks made to last. In: PervasiveHealth: Pervasive Computing Technologies for Healthcare, vol. 1, pp. 126–136, June 2020. https://doi.org/10.1145/3385010.3385014
23. Cila, N., Ferri, G., de Waal, M., Gloerich, I., Karpinski, T.: The blockchain and the commons: dilemmas in the design of local platforms. In: CHI 2020: Proceedings of the 2020 CHI Conference on Human Factors in Computing Systems, pp. 1–14, April 2020. https://doi.org/10.1145/3313831.3376660

24. Kenya Ministry of Education: Kenya - Schools | The World Bank Data Catalog. https://dat acatalog.worldbank.org/search/dataset/0038039. Accessed 11 Feb 2022

25. Konomi, S.: Colocation networks: exploring the use of social and geographical patterns in context-aware services. In: UbiComp 2011 - Proceedings of the 2011 ACM Conference on Ubiquitous Computing, pp. 565–566 (2011). https://doi.org/10.1145/2030112.2030215

26. Hu, X., Konomi, S., Gao, L., Sezaki, K.: Analysis of human flow to inform the design of a crowd-powered information delivery environment in developing communities. Res. Abs. Spatial Inf. Sci. CSIS DAYS **2021**, 60 (2021)

27. Sasao, T., Konomi, S.: The use of colocation and flow networks in mobile crowdsourcing. In: Proceedings of the 2015 ACM International Joint Conference on Pervasive and Ubiquitous Computing and Proceedings of the 2015 ACM International Symposium on Wearable Computers - UbiComp 2015, pp. 1343–1348 (2015). https://doi.org/10.1145/2800835

28. Franklin, M.J., Kossmann, D., Kraska, T., Ramesh, S., Xin, R.: CrowdDB: answering queries with crowdsourcing. In: Proceedings of the 2011 international conference on Management of data - SIGMOD 2011, pp. 61–72 (2011). https://doi.org/10.1145/1989323

29. Hu, X., Konomi, S.: QFami: an integrated environment for recommending answerers on campus. In: Stephanidis, C., Antona, M., Ntoa, S. (eds.) HCII 2021. CCIS, vol. 1498, pp. 119–125. Springer, Cham (2021). https://doi.org/10.1007/978-3-030-90176-9_17

Ways of Experiencing Technology in a Smart Learning Environment

Pen Lister[✉] [ID]

University of Malta, Msida MSD 2080, Malta
pen.lister@penworks.net

Abstract. This paper discusses ways of experiencing digital technology and digital interactions in 'smart learning journey' activities. Smart learning journeys can
be considered as ad-hoc smart learning environments outside in the real world,
offering a wide range of opportunity for empowering local populace engagement
in issues relevant to a neighbourhood area. Activities may often be associated
with urban citizen communities, enhancing quality of life and life-long learning in urban digitally connected 'hyperlocal' spaces. Activities discussed in this
paper used freely available smartphone apps and consisted of a series of digitally
augmented real-world local features that together formed a journey of points of
interest related by topic.

Research discussed in this paper investigated how people experienced 'Technology' as one of four conceptualised system elements of a smart learning journey activity, the others being Place, Knowledge and Collaboration. Utilising
the methodology of phenomenography and analysing participant semi-structured
responsive interviews with a structure of awareness analytical framework approach, four categories of Technology experience variation emerged. These were
Easy, Helper, Novel and Problematic. These categories were formed by noting the
commonality and variation across all interviews at collective level, while retaining the individual participant context. This paper reflects on these categories of
experience variation, positioning discussion in further context of the socio-cultural
technological, 'post digital' world that smart learners may find themselves in future
urban smart learning environments.

Keywords: Human-computer interaction · User experience · Augmented
reality · Presence · Post digital · Smart learning environments

1 Introduction

This paper discusses aspects of research carried out during 2018–2020 investigating
experiences of participation in 'smart learning journey' activities, here reflecting specifically on how participants in these activities expressed their experiences of Technology. This follows on from previous publications discussing this work from pedagogical
aspects of interest and formation of pedagogical guidelines for smart learning design in
these activity contexts [30, 31, 33]. Smart learning journeys are considered as ad-hoc
smart learning environments located outside in the real world, offering a wide range of

N. A. Streitz and S. Konomi (Eds.): HCII 2022, LNCS 13326, pp. 148–164, 2022.
https://doi.org/10.1007/978-3-031-05431-0_11

opportunity for empowering local population engagement with issues relevant to their neighbourhood area. Activities may often be associated with urban citizen communities, enhancing quality of life and life-long learning in urban digitally connected 'hyperlocal' spaces, e.g. [28, 31]. Hyperlocal is a useful term to define a small local area of closely related places or specific communities, arising from a term originally describing 'hyperlocal media' such as blogs and local news websites [60]. Carroll et al. [8] and others, e.g. [36], have used this term in relation to learning situated in a closely localised area. Participants in these activities often take part voluntarily, and choose what they might find of interest, using their own mobile devices to digitally interact with aspects of an activity. Smart learning journey activities discussed in this paper used freely available smartphone apps and consisted of a series of digitally augmented real-world local features that together formed a journey of points of interest related by topic.

To determine the variation in how participants experience taking part in an activity, the smart learning journeys discussed in this paper were researched using the methodology of phenomenography, and research participants were drawn from groups of undergraduate and postgraduate students who took part voluntarily in smart learning journeys in their own time. Participants were interviewed according to the phenomenographic method of eliciting deep emergent reflections of their experiences during open responsive interviewing [1]. Interview transcripts were analysed using a phenomenographic structure of awareness framework [12]. This facilitates deeper understanding of the focal awareness of participants and what may form the figure and ground in the continuously reconstituting range of a participant's experience that constructs meaning and context for an activity [37, 39]. Zerubavel elaborates: "(a)lthough originally conceptualized specifically within the context of sensory perception, the figure-and-ground model is nevertheless applicable to non-sensory modes of cognition ... (to) capture the essence of the process of mental focusing" [63, p. 11]. Additionally, Lister [34] discusses figure and ground in relation to understanding of focal awareness for learning through self-reflection.

Focus in this paper is on examining participant experiences from the perspective of thinking about a smart learning journey activity as a system, conceptualising broad system elements that may assist in delimiting aspects of participant experience. This thereby further enables analysis and discussion of relationships between system element experiences as well as variations within them. These relationships might in some ways be considered as the functions, purposes and interconnections of system elements according to the systems thinking terminology of Meadows [42]. Four broad smart learning journey 'system elements' of Place, Knowledge, Collaboration and Technology were utilised, both to provide focus in interviews, and additionally to act as alternate lens perspectives of analysis for the focal awareness of structure and meaning in participant interview experience reflections. This offered a mechanism for delimiting analysis interpretations related to each system element (SE), yet retained potential analogous contexts. Four system element phenomenographic outcome spaces [25, 40] of experience variation were therefore formed, each including several relational categories of experience variation. This paper focuses on the Technology outcome space experience variations discovered in the analysis, and seeks to highlight possible ways that people experience aspects of interacting with the technological mediations of their participation in a smart learning activity and environment. Discussion explores reflections on the nature of experiencing real-world and digital realities in co-existing socio-temporal spaces [57, 4, p. 141], and potential relationships of digitally mediated reflective and affective intra-active [4, p. 168] perceptions in smart learning environments.

2 Summary of Research

Two smart learning journeys were investigated, located in the City of London, UK (a route of 2 km), and central Valletta, Malta (a route of 650 m), with themes of heritage, history and literature. Real-world points of interest (PoI) features such as statues, monuments or building plaques were digitally augmented with augmented reality (AR) interfaces offering a choice of context-aware digital knowledge content to click on via a series of icon triggers. This was achieved using the HP Reveal[1] web-based 'Studio' app, high-resolution photographs and image based recognition to recognise and trigger the AR augmentations. Early in the study experiments with geo-fenced image recognition proved technically successful, however during the period of research HP Reveal withdrew their AR geo-fencing functionality, leaving the research to use the simpler image based recognition as the AR method. This was sufficient to create a 'future-present' [18, 24] version of a digitally augmented real-world environment for users at each of the PoI locations. A custom map was created using Google MyMaps[2] which showed each augmented feature location (PoI), additionally providing basic instructions in the information panel at each PoI for what to focus on and how to trigger the AR. The Edmodo[3] app was used to provide participants with a group online area for uploading content they had created either during or after the journey (photographs, written notes or web links related in some way, with some group commenting). Digital knowledge content provided for each PoI in the AR triggers consisted of video, image galleries or custom webpages authored by the tutors of classes participating in the journeys, plus third party content sourced from WikiMedia[4] or other open knowledge content. Original knowledge content webpages were hosted on a WordPress custom website[5], where webpages were only accessible via the AR triggers, otherwise hidden from website menus. All mobile apps used were free to use, available in the Apple App Store or Google Play store.

2.1 Methodology

Phenomenography [37, 39] was selected as the methodology most suited to this investigation, as other relevant qualitative research studies had benefited from its utilisation. Studies involving learning with technology and studies in user experience have increasingly looked to phenomenography to understand more about what users and learners do and why they do it. For example, Souleles, Savva, Watters, Annesley & Bull [53]

---

[1] HP Reveal, formerly Aurasma, defunct link and app as of 2020 [https://www.hpreveal.com].

[2] Google MyMaps [https://google.com/mymaps].

[3] Edmodo app [https://edmodo.com].

[4] WikiMedia [https://commons.wikimedia.org/wiki/Main_Page].

[5] Smart Learning Journey website [http://smartlearning.netfarms.eu].

examined art and design student experiences of using iPads in their studies, describing the phenomenographic approach as allowing for a "bottom-up investigation, ie, from the perspective of learners". Kaapu & Tiainen [23] investigated experiences of consumers and their understanding of virtual product prototypes, "to get an idea of users' subjective experience", aiming to "support customers' participation in product design process". The aims of these studies were somewhat reflected in my research, therefore phenomenography was considered a 'good fit' for investigating participant experiences of smart learning activities, and to "observe the phenomenon of 'learning' from their perspective" [3].

Phenomenography is 'non-dualist' [38] in nature, making an epistemological assumption that there is only one world as experienced by the learner, "where there is an internal relation between the inner world and the outer world" [19]. Here we are interested in the reality concerning phenomena of interest to the research as experienced by individuals being researched. Phenomenography analyses learner experience at collective level, looking at the experience variation itself rather than the individual context, though context is retained. Drawing on Gurwitsch's [17] ideas about theme, thematic field and margin, experience is analysed using a 'structure of awareness' analytical framework [12]. Significantly, phenomenography takes a 'second order' perspective to analysis [37, p. 2; 38, p. 183; 52, p. 340]. This means that the researcher accepts the participant self reported experience without attaching latent interpretation, that is, the analysis does not seek to explain why a participant may state something, simply that they do. Therefore, the outcome space and categories of description are developed by the researcher, yet are emergent and consist of the experience variation as noted in the manifest content only, described by Bowden as "if it is not in the transcript, then it is not evidence" [6, p. 15].

2.2 Sampling

The sample of research participants was purposive and convenience [48, p. 6, 53, p. 4], recruiting undergraduate and postgraduate students on a voluntary basis between 2017–2019. Student cohorts were drawn from Education and the International Master in Adult Education for Social Change degree programmes based at University of Malta, plus an additional cohort from London Metropolitan University studying English Literature and Creative Writing. Phenomenography does not require large amounts of data, only sufficient to permit the widest possible (or likely) variation of experience to be found [62, p. 8]. Taking into account practical limitations as well as iterative estimation for different variations to emerge, twenty-four participants were considered sufficient, giving a snapshot of variation [2, 58] that included different demographics and subject disciplines. A possible limitation was gender representation, with nineteen females and six males. This might be because of a paucity of males in the degree programmes or simply the voluntary nature of recruiting participants for interviews. However, Reed considers gendered distinction of experience as a potentially artificial construct within the terrain of phenomenographic inquiry and 'individuals most likely to provide… variation in ways of experiencing' [49, p. 6].

2.3 Analysis

A brief description follows of the overall smart learning journey system element analysis, with subsequent discussion specifically focusing on the Technology system element, the topic of this paper. Further commentary on pedagogical analysis is found in [30, 32].

Adopting a phenomenographic analysis approach, categories of experience variation emerged to form outcome spaces [25, 40] for each of the conceptualised system elements. Through reflecting on analysis in each system element of a smart learning journey it was possible to broadly delimit aspects of experience as separate yet related parts of a system. Experience was analysed using a phenomenographic structure of awareness framework, discovering units of meaning [40, 49], noting commonalities and difference variations across the utterances at collective level in the interview transcripts. The phenomenographic structure of awareness (SoA) analysis framework conceptualises awareness based on Gurwitsch's theme, thematic field and margin [12, 17]. The 'referential' aspect of the SoA is the theme, the central focal awareness, where meaning is formulated from the closest focus of attention in relation to the immediate or most relevant context of surroundings. This referential meaning is seated within the thematic field of a structural 'internal horizon' of the focus, formed through interpretation of it. The internal horizon surroundings extend outward until they reach the margin, the structural 'external horizon' which is articulated as the perceptual boundary [62] of what may still be relevant to the referential and internal horizon. In other words, as the focal awareness extends outwards it becomes less related to meaning and close focus, steadily fading from perceptive awareness into the background. Analysis findings are reviewed by a co-judge [5, p. 68] to confirm or challenge analysis interpretations, and to enhance communicability and interpretive awareness [12, 50]. The system element outcome spaces of a smart learning journey that arose from this analysis are described in more detail in following sections.

3   The System Elements of a Smart Learning Journey

The purpose of the system element analysis was to help define the delimited nature of the experience perspective positions, as this enabled an articulation of those differences. By analysing from the perspective of each SE it was possible to look at how participants viewed and thought about their experience of particular broad aspects of the smart learning journey (SLJ) without having prompted them directly in the interviews, which may have risked influencing their responses. Noting that the phenomenographic method is to adopt a second order position, the researcher/analyst always attempting to bracket their own assumptions about *why* participants might be saying things, simply to take it 'at face value'. Therefore, phenomenographic outcome spaces were discovered in the commonality and variation of how participants expressed their experiences of each of the broad SE's of the SLJ, namely Place, Knowledge, Collaboration and Technology. These SE outcome spaces formed categories with delimited structure of awareness (SoA) perceptual boundaries, being delimited by the element itself, defined by (analytically) asking the question, "experiencing place in a smart learning journey as…", "experiencing knowledge … as …", and so forth.

The categories in each SE outcome space derived from the most obvious commonalities of experience variation, so aspects that show variety of experiences within those commonalities across multiple transcripts that are given prominence or emphasis in the context of individual transcripts. Analysis was kept to an overview of possible experience variations, not seeking to define these beyond a first level of complexity for a possible SE structure of awareness. This was because in a smaller scale study of this size there is risk of duplication, and additionally, the main focus of the questions in the study were on relationships of learning and development for pedagogical understanding in the experience of a smart learning journey, not to analyse deeply the experience of place, knowledge, collaboration or technology within it. In this paper however, it is of interest to attempt to highlight the Technology SE outcome space to potentially uncover useful understanding that may be of relevance to others who develop SLJ or similar activities in urban connected spaces. To provide context for the Technology outcome space discussion, here I give brief outlines of all the SE outcome spaces, to describe the other SE categories in relation to the Technology SE. Subsequent sections will then describe the Technology structure of awareness analysis process and categories in more depth.

3.1 Place

The Place SE enables thinking about aspects of being at locations, points of interest on the SLJ, or the journey as a whole. Here the analysis statement is "experiencing place in a smart learning journey as....". It is therefore more possible to delimit the variations of the position place occupies in the awareness of the learner. The categories in 'Place' were Being at the place; Being outside; A tour, a trip, a game.

3.2 Knowledge

The Knowledge SE looked for how information was experienced in terms of content provided in the SLJ activities. Here the analysis statement is "experiencing knowledge in a smart learning journey as....". Commonality with related variation in perceptions of information were observed as either interesting, or not interesting, or that there was just too much content (even though this can be interesting or not interesting). Analysis of how information was experienced by participants is especially useful when considering learning activities, as may have bearing on how technology mediates knowledge content to learn how to learn [35] in these scenarios. The categories in 'Knowledge' were Of interest; Not of interest; Too much.

3.3 Collaboration

The 'Collaboration' SE was a way to acknowledge the direct or indirect impact between people in a SLJ activity. Here the analysis statement is "experiencing collaboration in a smart learning journey as....". It could be argued that people form part of all aspects of a smart learning journey system, that is, elements, functions, purposes and perhaps especially interconnections [42, pp. 11, 13]. However, 'Collaboration' created a sufficiently broad category with focus on narrowing down the experiencing of 'people' in these activities. The categories in 'Collaboration' were Distracting; Sharing; Social, engaged (sociable).

3.4 Technology

The Technology system element permitted a drilling down of the structure of awareness for 'Technology' in a SLJ activity. Here the analysis statement is "experiencing technology in a smart learning journey as....". Technology topics nearly always emerged completely naturally in conversations but appeared to not be at the forefront of most participants' minds. Comments relating to the experience of technology were about how augmented reality (AR) worked, and this caused both a sense of 'wow factor' as well as frustration when things didn't work. Other comments were about the potential of AR for interacting with the environment for both civic and learning experiences in future professional work scenarios, so seeing the possibilities in wider context. Remembering again that participant comments emerge naturally (not specifically prompted for), it was notable that not everyone remarked on technology in any way, it merely seemed to form an unacknowledged aspect of background or assumed context. There were four categories in the 'Technology' SE, these were Easy; Helper; Novel; Problematic.

4   The Technology System Element 'Outcome Space'

The focus of this paper is to unpack the findings of the Technology system element (SE) phenomenographic outcome space, and reflect on possible areas of understanding that might be derived from what was discovered. The categories of 'Easy', 'Helper,' 'Novel' and 'Problematic' are described here, illustrating each category with key quotes drawn from interview transcripts, with brief contextual reflections. These categories offer clues about the range of variation in experiencing technology in smart learning environments, acknowledging that this range of experience variation can be concurrently present in a single individual, as well as between individuals. Experience variation will fluctuate according to the interests and motivation of each individual and additionally be impacted by multiple other factors such as peers, other persons, the sociocultural context or other issues.

The Technology SE analysis looked at all participant expressions that related in some way to technology, and analysed them for meaning by using an approach of first establishing individual context for emphasis, significance and position in transcript discussions, then looking for commonality and variation across all participant expressions concerning technology (somewhat after descriptions in [51, 52]). 'Technology' was interpreted as any app or technical service that might have been mentioned by a participant relating to their participation on a SLJ. Technologies were not limited to only those that might have been used 'on the day' but any other that a participant felt relevant to mention, for example discussion using WhatsApp[6] or Facebook Messenger[7] before or afterwards,

---

[6] WhatsApp [https://www.whatsapp.com/].

[7] Facebook Messenger [https://www.messenger.com/].

using Edmodo to upload content to group areas, or using wifi and phones generally in relation to the activity. However, the majority of mentions concerned the AR app, HP Reveal.

To reiterate, the structure of awareness analysis framework [12] considers the structural (context and boundary) and referential (meaning) aspects of perceptual awareness. Meaning is formed of the 'internal horizon' of the structural, those aspects that hold the most significance from the closest focal awareness. The surrounding context extends out finally to the perceptual boundary or 'external horizon' of awareness. The four categories of variation are now described:

4.1 Category: Easy

- Referential (Meaning): Simple, easy to use, fun
- Structural/Internal Horizon: Fast, normal, straightforward, works
- Structural/External Horizon: The (assumed) normality of it, ease of using, 'it was great'

Quotes

1. "If you have to check about it before you would get it, it's a simple technology but on the day on the task they couldn't set it up or whatever… because *they haven't paid attention"; (P8) (*referring to classmates)
2. "… I was quite scared of it at first but like now it makes more fun, You know it's fun going into different things and just pressing a button and, and saying oh my like wow a video popped up"; (P11)
3. "I think its much easier with technology (…) I said this, that you are immersed in the technology, you are not just there. You are immersed in the visual sphere"; (P13)
4. "… it was very easy to tap on individual things, erm, and my data was working well, so I had a really quick internet response, so when I clicked on the links, I was able to load pretty quickly, erm, so, I, er, yeah, thought it was great."; (P23)

The 'Easy' category consisted of what participants said about their ease of use, or learning to operate the technology, particularly the AR. Though quotes may hint at other interrelated relationship aspects such as being immersed, not just 'there', or the 'wow' of things popping up, the meaning in the experience of technology is attempted to be analysed separately, delimiting it from further meaning or structural categorisations - such as novel, or helper, or other system elements such as place or knowledge. Quotes show a selection of how participants appeared to think of the technology as easy, fun or simple, sometimes compared to others not finding it easy.

4.2 Category: Helper

- Referential (Meaning): Guide, helping, convenient
- Structural/Internal Horizon: Convenient, right there, personal assistant
- Structural/External Horizon: Providing content you would not know about, sparking ideas and interest

Quotes

1. "what it does is in putting you in the place it almost gives you another level of access to something that really we don't have anymore, get a deeper understanding of what that part would've been like at a certain time and what was going on around that time. I think, I think it did help."; (P3)
2. "It's more alive, It's like you're a tourist and seeing the sights of Malta and at the same time learning about them it's like you have a person but a personal digital assistant telling you about the place, the historical background about the things you are seeing..."; (P7)
3. "the most significant part was using our smartphones in this learning experience like you could access the content that's very important just by taking a photo of that monument for example"; (P15)
4. "... without your phone, you're looking at a building, which is pretty, and there's a couple of statues, and a small plaque, but that's all you get. Whereas with the phone there are like all these other facts and figures and videos and pictures and stuff and impulses for questions to ask and answer"; (P21)

The 'Helper' category was how I categorised meaning for a range of comments that referred to convenience, guidance, digital tour guides. The sense that a participant had when they accessed content about the location they were at which perhaps then prompted discussion or further awareness and reflections about the historic significance of the place. Comments in Helper covered a range of variation demonstrating interrelated relationships between this category and others, notably the 'Problematic' category in the Technology system element.

4.3 Category: Novel

- Referential (Meaning): Novel, new, futuristic
- Structural/Internal Horizon: Sci-fi, modern, new, different
- Structural/External Horizon: Expectations of new technologies, potentials

Quotes

1. "I really liked the idea because I've never done a kind of augmented tour before. I liked the idea of going to a place and even though it's mediated and you have to do it on your phone it's as close as you're maybe get to going to a place like, which isn't going to provide you with kind of a document of its history."; (P4)
2. "I guess to *capture their emotions like how they looked when they were revealing the content like it was something unusual so they were like wooaaa oh my god"; (P16) (*refers to taking photos of classmates)
3. "the interactions that the app provides with the environment, that to me was very interesting. Feels a little ... sci-fi?"; (P17)
4. "... when it worked we were like oh that's actually quite cool, like, I don't know because it's a bit like magic, you know, like tschoo (makes sparkly noise) and suddenly it's there. That's kind of cool."; (P18)

Aspects of novelty that formed the 'Novel' category were recognised quite early in the analysis process, appearing in slightly different ways in participant transcripts, with remarks on the 'sci-fi' or 'new' nature of the AR. Though it might have been a likely presupposition by the researcher (and therefore potential bias) to assume that participants would think of the AR as significant to discuss, especially as novel or futuristic, only some participants articulated this, sometimes interrelated with the 'easy' category. Perhaps for others it was seen as a kind of assumed given, a normal expectation by them that there would be AR and it was simply 'there'. It didn't seem that special to them, so often participants didn't even remark on it at all. This in itself was surprising and of interest to the research as it indicated that some people were not attentive to the technology *of itself*, but only to any resulting mediation outcome or possibility, whether positive or negative.

4.4 Category: Problematic

- Referential (Meaning): Not working, not good
- Structural/Internal Horizon: Not working, no wifi, no data, no battery
- Structural/External Horizon: Overwhelming, too complicated, difficult, tiring, obstructive, self conscious, tech zombies

Quotes

1. "... on the app I think I remember that things were quite layered they was kind of quite a lot of information on the screen at once so it was a little bit overwhelming"; (P1)
2. "... but like I hate that because it's like people walking around and looking just like zombies and not paying attention to anything or anyone you know like they're in this beautiful park and all they're doing is like looking at their phones"; (P22)
3. "... we did run into a couple of issues at the very end being we, I wanted to continue doing the walking tour but all of our phones were dying. And I didn't have a power bank or anything"; (P23)
4. "I was trying to make it happen, and, like, it did pop up at the beginning and then when I er, clicked on one of the icons, that's where it started hanging, started crashing and went crazy."; (P24)

Comments in the 'Problematic' category spanned a wide range of issues relating to using technology. Many quotes concerned access and use of AR triggers or issues regarding availability and access to WiFi. Other quotes refer to either technology in general, to using Edmodo or Google Maps, or to suitability of phones, including battery power. However, the vast majority of quotes are about AR and related issues of WiFi access. This may be because what is uppermost in participants minds is how they interacted on the journey itself, not the activity as a whole, which might have included Edmodo or creating digital content. It is clear that some participants thought access to the AR triggers (using HP Reveal) depended on quality of phones, while others said it was not about 'brand', and others said they thought it was about up-to-date mobile operating systems. P22 makes an interesting comment about 'zombies' and clearly indicates that the more phones are used to interact with reality, the less reality itself is being interacted with.

5 Interpreting Technically Mediated Interactions

The combination of apps and services that provided the technically mediated interactions and functionality of the smart learning journey activities were in general found to be fairly easy and understandable to use. The AR triggers offered an 'AR interface' of choices, not the more common approach of triggering one piece of content only, such as opening a video or single webpage. This was to accommodate the choices of content desired by the tutors, and created an impression of being *smarter*. The aim was to create the future in the present moment, and though this may not have been an accurate representation of a future digitally interactive experience, it was a potential way to conjure an assimilation of a smart digitally augmented and interactive integrated city. Therefore the technology used was a 'future-present' representation [18, 24, 34] of what may happen more seamlessly in the future but as such was still somewhat primitive. However, participants either realised this and accepted it, or did not particularly notice it and accepted it. For example, it was noticeable that participants did not talk about the icons and the AR interface used in the AR triggers, as seemed to know how to use them, and what the icons represented. Even though participants had never used augmented reality and context-aware content triggers, there appeared to be an implicit understanding of what it was or could be.

This implicit understanding may be part of what Thompson describes when she states "technologies and people fold into each other. Human and non-human actants are in a co-constitutive relationship […] co-constituted in webs of relations with other actants" [56, p. 160]. It is in this context that Latour [26, pp. 133, 134] declares "from now on, everything is data", and whether something is 'digital' or not "no longer matters". Jones describes "knowledge and capacities as being emergent from the webs of interconnections between heterogeneous entities, both human and non-human… sociomaterialist approaches offer the prospect…that encompasses people and machines in a symmetrical way" [20, p. 47]. In more simple terms (though no less technological) Morville [45] contends that "we are what we find", indicating the influence of the technical networked system on the individual's perception and 'wayfinding' in knowledge and understanding. Though it was noticeable that technology was not at the forefront of a majority of participants minds in terms of the emphasis and context of what they talked about, many reported some experience focus where the AR technology provided a structural aspect of experience variation that contrasted with another referential theme of meaning. For example, it may have been that an AR content trigger (structural) created an opportunity for (referential) meaning to occur regarding personal reflections or memories about a place. However, technology also appears to have provided (referential) meaning *of itself* for some, for example the feeling of 'wow factor' to be in a place and trigger an AR content experience. It was up to participants how they may have chosen to talk about technology, some emphasising its role, others hardly mentioning it at all.

Contextualising the experience variations of Technology with the other three system element outcome spaces of Place, Collaboration and Knowledge can support reflections on potential relationships between digital interactions in related contexts. For example in relatedness of knowledge and place, by 'hypersituating' access to knowledge and a user's location [44, p. 68]. Access to digital augmentation and interaction with context-aware knowledge content (as described in [27]), may impact perceptions in relation to real-time presence in place, memory or personal reflective value, e.g. [21]. Likewise, experiencing technology in relation to synchronous, asynchronous, face-to-face or virtual dialogic contexts of activities may alter how dialogic experiences form, and how the value of them is perceived, e.g. [10].

Technology mediates participant experience between these terrains, in cognitive, social and affective intra-active, co-constitutive relationships of awareness, communication, learning or value, mingling with externalised physicality of weather, light and heat, buildings, peers and the real-world and (potential) virtual conversations going on [4, 48]. These relationships may further inform perceptual interpretations within individual and social socio-cultural experience of place and the nature of the activity, or be influenced by presuppositions and expectations about the technologies themselves, e.g. [14, 29, 46, 47].

6 Technology in a Post Digital World

Considering the post digital world of Latour [26] where "whether something is 'digital' or not "no longer matters", what can human experience variation of technology tell us? Jordan defines two key conditions of post digitality as "the pervasiveness and consequent normalisation of computationalism; in other words a complex enmeshment of digital technology with everyday life, to the point where to describe something as 'digital' becomes almost meaningless" [22, p. 176]. This is Morville's 'intertwingled' daily life of pervasive knowledge networks and activities [45, p. 75], the 'multidimensionalities' of smart cities described by McKenna, where, referring to the work of Streitz [55], "the computer disappears into the background and environments are more generally infused with technologies" [41, p. 6]. Yet, participants experience this variously, both within internal and externalised contexts.

Post digital debate has been going on for some time [9, 11], perhaps with renewed resonance in the hybridity of real world augmented reality and its various connotations of location-aware or vision-based digital interactivity as described by Dede in 2005, and then later [13, 15]. This scope of AR has developed over the past decade to potentially involve embedded sensors or smarter content delivery in some instances, though essentially remains as Dede indicated. The impact of new 3D virtual network worlds such as Metaverse[8] or AltspaceVR[9] may yet create new kinds of AR, though some might consider these as more 'sociotechnical imaginaries' better suited to venture capital investment than any useful or purposeful technical innovation [61]. These fluctuating mixtures of human face-to-face and virtual presence and glocality, e.g. [43, 59], mediate the participant experience of their real-time world through the interplay of technological interface, digital augmentation and multiple socio-material, spatio-temporal [57] and cultural intersections [7]. Sense of being in place in smart learning digital augmented

---

[8] Metaverse (Facebook) on Wikipedia [https://en.wikipedia.org/wiki/Metaverse].
[9] AltspaceVR (Microsoft) on Wikipedia [https://en.wikipedia.org/wiki/AltspaceVR].

environments is reconfigured as intertwined layers of physical real-time presence, virtual telepresence [16, 54] toward hypersituationism [14]. Further, socio-cultural glocalities of multiple time zones, languages and personal cultural connotations may impact senses of place [43].

Traxler describes an 'erosion of physical place' by multiple mobile virtual spaces as 'absent presence', that "(p)hysical space in fact is emptied of significance, becomes less dense as thickness, as the dimension of virtual space is grafted on to it" [57, p. 198]. Further reflecting on temporal and spatial contexts as "spatio-temporal capital, ... or space-time as a commodity" [57, p. 199], which may be a way of considering how participants in smart learning activities focus engagement directed at differing digital and real-world domains as interest or motivation occurs. Clearly, participants gave voice to uncertainty regarding the impact of AR interactions in relation to how their 'real world' was perceived. Notably, P22 remarked passionately on her observations that no one was 'present' in the moment at the location their group was at, that "all they're doing is ... looking at their phones". Others remarked on the phone interactions being an obstacle to engaging with place (P1, P5) or that amounts of knowledge content provided were 'overwhelming' or 'boring' (P1, P17), though others enjoyed the contrast and potentially enhanced understanding that both digital and real offered (e.g. P3, P7, P12, P14, P23). Yet, many participants did not remark in any significant or emphasised way about any of the technology being utilised to mediate the smart learning journey activity they had taken part in. It simply did not seem remarkable or unusual, and if probed further was greeted with a shrug of the shoulders, a kind of 'yeah, it was fine'. Only some participants offered reflections of their own volition on the impact of using apps or about using the AR in real world places, however if the AR app did not work then participant reflections were more readily expressed. This appears to suggest that if technology just 'works', there is an implicit general understanding and expectation of what it does and how it is used, even if it isn't that efficient, at least within this study and these kinds of activities. It becomes somewhat transparent in its affect, it is merely part of 'doing', like getting on a bus with contactless payment, or sending a text. This appears to describe the commonplace intertwingled, multidimensional [41, 45] post digitality that forms a smart learning environment.

7 Conclusions

This paper has discussed the ways participants experienced technology in smart learning activities positioned as journeys in ad hoc smart learning environments. Considering the categories of 'Easy', 'Helper', 'Novel' and 'Problematic' as the four categories of experience variation most commonly appearing in participant interview reflections, a further aspect of note was the absence of technology as a significant topic of reflection for many participants. Discussion further considered the possibility of a tacit assumption of post digital normality amongst participants implied in this absence.

In the near future, real world AR interactivity will likely become a much more streamlined set of technical interactions [41], and this evidently increasing ordinariness of technological experiences may well lead to activities such as those discussed in this paper becoming a regular feature of learning or in citizen led urban initiatives, supporting numeric ideas and purposes. For example, apps such as Google Lens[10], What3Words[11] and others may seamlessly integrate with a Virtual Learning Environment (VLE) through related Application Programming Interface (API) connectivity[12]. Though AR or other digital interactivity with the real world may still be somewhat of an unusual experience, in the post digital city many participants already appear to greet it with an urbane nonchalance. Yet while they may not be explicitly acknowledging their interpretations of technical mediations, citizen learners experience technology in multilayered ways, continuously reconstituting their interpretative awareness of the world around them in socio-spatio-temporal meaning and context. Acknowledging this spectrum of variations both within and between individuals and non-human actants can perhaps contribute towards improving design for more effective and useful activities, creating a more level playing field for a wider and more diverse range of users and communities.

References

1. Åkerlind, G.: Learning about phenomenography: interviewing, data analysis and the qualitative research paradigm. In: Bowden, J., Green, P. (eds.) Doing Developmental Phenomenography, pp. 63–73. RMIT University Press, Melbourne (2005)
2. Åkerlind, G., Bowden, J., Green, P.: Learning to do Phenomenography: a reflective discussion. In: Bowden, J., Green, P. (eds.) Doing Developmental Phenomenography, pp. 74–100. RMIT University Press, Melbourne (2005)
3. Badie, F.: Knowledge building conceptualisation within smart constructivist learning systems. In: Uskov, V.L., Bakken, J.P., Howlett, R.J., Jain, L.C. (eds.) SEEL 2017. SIST, vol. 70, pp. 385–419. Springer, Cham (2018). https://doi.org/10.1007/978-3-319-59454-5_13
4. Barad, K.: Meeting the Universe Halfway: Quantum Physics and the Entanglement of Matter and Meaning. Duke University Press, Durham, NC & London (2007)
5. Booth, S.: Learning to Program: A Phenomenographic Perspective. Goteborg Studies in Educational Sciences, vol. 89. Acta Univesitatis Gothoburgenis, Goteborg (1992)
6. Bowden, J.: Reflections on the phenomenographic team research project. In: Bowden, J., Green, P. (eds.) Doing Developmental Phenomenography, pp. 11–31. RMIT University Press, Melbourne (2005)
7. Buell, L.: Space, place, and imagination from local to global. In: Buell, L. (ed.) The Future of Environmental Criticism: Environmental Crisis and Literary Imagination, pp. 62–96. Blackwell, Malden; Oxford (2005)
8. Carroll, J.M., Shih, P.C., Kropczynski, J., Cai, G., Rosson, M.B., Han, K.: The internet of places at community-scale: design scenarios for hyperlocal neighborhood. In: Konomi, S., Roussos, G. (eds.) Enriching Urban Spaces with Ambient Computing, the Internet of Things, and Smart City Design, pp. 1–24. IGI Global, Hershey (2017). https://doi.org/10.4018/978-1-5225-0827-4.ch001
9. Cascone, K.: The aesthetics of failure: 'post-digital' tendencies in contemporary computer music. Comput. Music J. 24(4), 12–18 (2000). http://www.jstor.org/stable/3681551
10. Chappell, K., et al.: Dialogue and materiality/embodiment in science\arts creative pedagogy: their role and manifestation. Think. Skills Creat. 31, 296–322 (2019). https://doi.org/10.1016/j.tsc.2018.12.008

---

[10] Google Lens [https://lens.google/].
[11] What3Words [https://what3words.com/].
[12] For example, Vision API [https://cloud.google.com/vision] or What3Words API [https://developer.what3words.com/public-api].

11. Cramer, F.: What is 'post-digital'? In: Berry, D.M., Dieter, M. (eds.) Postdigital Aesthetics: Art, Computation and Design, pp. 12–26. Palgrave Macmillan, London (2015)
12. Cope, C.: Ensuring validity and reliability in phenomenographic research using the analytical framework of a structure of awareness. Qual. Res. J. 4(2), 5–18 (2004)
13. Dede, C.: Planning for neomillennial learning styles. Educ. Q. 28(1), 7–12 (2005)
14. Dinello, D.: Technophobia! Science Fiction Visions of Posthuman Technology. University of Texas Press, Texas (2005)
15. Dunleavy, M., Dede, C.: Augmented reality teaching and learning. In: Spector, J.M., Merrill, M.D., Elen, J., Bishop, M.J. (eds.) Handbook of Research on Educational Communications and Technology, pp. 735–745. Springer, New York (2014). https://doi.org/10.1007/978-1-4614-3185-5_59
16. Gorman, T., Syrjä, T., Kanninen, M.: Immersive telepresence: a framework for training and rehearsal in a post- digital age. In: The Online, Open and Flexible Higher Education Conference 'Blended and Online Education within European University Networks', pp. 237–252 (2019). https://conference.eadtu.eu/previous-conferences
17. Gurwitsch, A., Zaner, R. (eds.): The Collected Works of Aron Gurwitsch (1901–1973). Volume III, The Field of Consciousness: Theme, Thematic Field, and Margin. Springer, Heidelberg (2010). https://doi.org/10.1007/978-90-481-3346-8
18. Ireland, C., Johnson, B.: Exploring the FUTURE in the PRESENT. Des. Manag. Instit. Rev. 6(2), 57–64 (1995). https://doi.org/10.1111/j.1948-7169.1995.tb00436.x
19. Ireland, J., Tambyah, M.M., Neofa, Z., Harding, T.: The tale of four researchers: trials and triumphs from the phenomenographic research specialization. In: Jeffery, P. (ed.) Proceedings of the Australian Association for Research in Education (AARE) 2008 International Research Conference. Changing Climates: Education for Sustainable Futures, pp. 1–15. The Australian Association for Research in Education (2009). https://eprints.qut.edu.au/20457/
20. Jones, C.: Experience and networked learning. In: Bonderup Dohn, N., Cranmer, S., Sime, J.A., de Laat, M., Ryberg, T. (eds.) Networked Learning. Research in Networked Learning, pp. 39–55 (2018). Springer, Cham. https://doi.org/10.1007/978-3-319-74857-3_3
21. Jordan, S.: Writing the smart city: "relational space" and the concept of "belonging". Writ. Pract. J. Creative Writ. Res. 1 (2015). http://eprints.nottingham.ac.uk/32234/1/WritinginPractice_Version2.pdf
22. Jordan, S.: Totaled city: the postdigital poetics of ben lerner's 10:04. In: Evans, A.-M., Kramer, K. (eds.) Time, the City, and the Literary Imagination, pp. 169–185. Palgrave MacMillan, London (2021)
23. Kaapu, T., Tiainen, T.: User experience: consumer understandings of virtual product prototypes. In: Kautz, K., Nielsen, P.A. (eds.) SCIS 2010. LNBIP, vol. 60, pp. 18–33. Springer, Heidelberg (2010). https://doi.org/10.1007/978-3-642-14874-3_2
24. Kitchin, R.: The timescape of smart cities. Ann. Am. Assoc. Geogr. 109(3), 775–790 (2019). https://doi.org/10.1080/24694452.2018.1497475
25. Larsson, J., Holmström, I.: Phenomenographic or phenomenological analysis: does it matter? Examples from a study on anaesthesiologists' work. Int. J. Qual. Stud. Health Well Being 2(1), 55–64 (2007). https://doi.org/10.1080/17482620601068105
26. Latour, B.: Reassembling the Social. An Introduction to Actor Network Theory. Oxford University Press, Oxon (2005)
27. Lister, P.J.: A smarter knowledge commons for smart learning. Smart Learn. Environ. 5(1), 1–15 (2018). https://doi.org/10.1186/s40561-018-0056-z
28. Lister, P.: Smart learning in the community: supporting citizen digital skills and literacies. In: Streitz, N., Konomi, S. (eds.) HCII 2020. LNCS, vol. 12203, pp. 533–547. Springer, Cham (2020). https://doi.org/10.1007/978-3-030-50344-4_38

29. Lister, P.: What are we supposed to be learning? Motivation and autonomy in smart learning environments. In: Streitz, N., Konomi, S. (eds.) HCII 2021. LNCS, vol. 12782, pp. 235–249. Springer, Cham (2021). https://doi.org/10.1007/978-3-030-77015-0_17
30. Lister, P.: The pedagogy of experience complexity for smart learning: considerations for designing urban digital citizen learning activities. Smart Learn. Environ. **8**(1), 1–18 (2021). https://doi.org/10.1186/s40561-021-00154-x
31. Lister, P.: Applying the PECSL: using case studies to demonstrate the pedagogy of experience complexity for smart learning. Smart Learn. Environ. **8**(1), 1–19 (2021). https://doi.org/10.1186/s40561-021-00158-7
32. Lister, P.: Understanding experience complexity in a smart learning journey. SN Soc. Sci. **1**(1), 1–13 (2021). https://doi.org/10.1007/s43545-020-00055-9
33. Lister, P.: Measuring learning that is hard to measure: using the PECSL model to assess implicit learning (2022, submitted manuscript)
34. Lister, P.: Future-present learning and teaching: a case study in smart learning. In: Sengupta, E., Blessinger, P, (eds.) Changing the Conventional Classroom, Innovations in Higher Education Teaching and Learning (IHETL). Emerald Publishing, Bingley (2022, in press)
35. Liu, D., Huang, R., Wosinski, M.: Characteristics and framework of smart learning. In: Liu, D., Huang, R., Wosinski, M. (eds.) Smart Learning in Smart Cities. LNET, pp. 31–48. Springer, Singapore (2017). https://doi.org/10.1007/978-981-10-4343-7_3
36. Martin, J., Dikkers, S., Squire, K., Gagnon, D.: Participatory scaling through augmented reality learning through local games. TechTrends **58**(1), 35–41 (2014)
37. Marton, F.: Phenomenography - describing conceptions of the world around us. Instr. Sci **10**, 177–200 (1981). https://doi.org/10.1007/BF00132516
38. Marton, F.: Cognoso ergo sum – reflections on reflections. In: Dall'Alba, G., Hasselgren, B. (eds.) Reflections on phenomenography: Toward a methodology?, pp. 163–187. Acta Universitatis Gothoburgensis, Gothenburg (1996)
39. Marton, F., & Booth, S.: Learning and Awareness. Lawrence Erlbaum Associates, Mahwah (1997)
40. Marton, F., Pong, W.P.: On the unit of description in phenomenography. High. Educ. Res. Dev. **24**(4), 335–348 (2005). https://doi.org/10.1080/07294360500284706
41. McKenna, H.P.: Human-smart environment interactions in smart cities: exploring dimensionalities of smartness. Future Internet **12**, 79 (2020). https://doi.org/10.3390/fi12050079
42. Meadows, D.H.: Thinking in Systems, A Primer (edited by D. Wight). Sustainability Institute, Earthscan (2008)
43. Meyrowitz, J.: No Sense of Place. The Impact of Electronic Media on Social Behaviour. Oxford University Press, Oxon (1985)
44. Moreira, F.T., Vairinhos, M., Ramos, F.: Conceptualization of hypersituation as result of IoT in education. In: Mealha, Ó., Rehm, M., Rebedea, T. (eds.) Ludic, Co-design and Tools Supporting Smart Learning Ecosystems and Smart Education. SIST, vol. 197, pp. 67–73. Springer, Singapore (2021). https://doi.org/10.1007/978-981-15-7383-5_6
45. Morville, P.: Intertwingled: Information Changes Everything. Semantic Studios, Ann Arbor (2014)
46. Nestik, T., et al.: Technophobia as a cultural and psychological phenomenon: theoretical analysis. Interação - Revista De Ensino, Pesquisa E Extensão **20**(1), 266–281 (2019). https://doi.org/10.33836/interacao.v20i1.191
47. Oliver, M.: Technological determinism in educational technology research: some alternative ways of thinking about the relationship between learning and technology. J. Comput. Assist. Learn. **27**, 373–384 (2011). https://doi.org/10.1111/j.1365-2729.2011.00406.x
48. Pyyry, N.: Geographies of hanging out: playing, dwelling and thinking with the city. In: Sacré, H., De Visscher, S. (eds.) Learning the City. SE, pp. 19–33. Springer, Cham (2017). https://doi.org/10.1007/978-3-319-46230-1_2

49. Reed, B.: Phenomenography as a way to research the understanding by students of technical concepts. In: Núcleo de Pesquisa em Tecnologia da Arquitetura e Urbanismo (NUTAU): Technological Innovation and Sustainability, São Paulo, Brazil, pp. 1–11 (2006)
50. Sandberg, J.: Are phenomenographic results reliable? High. Educ. Res. Dev. **16**(2), 203–212 (1997). https://doi.org/10.1080/0729436970160207
51. Sandberg, J.: Understanding human competence at work: an interpretative approach. Acad. Manag. J. **43**(1), 9–25 (2000). http://www.jstor.org/stable/1556383
52. Sjöström, B., Dahlgren, L.O.: Applying phenomenography in nursing research. J. Adv. Nurs. **40**(3), 339–345 (2002). https://doi.org/10.1046/j.1365-2648.2002.02375.x
53. Souleles, N., Savva, S., Watters, H., Annesley, A., Bull, B.: A phenomenographic investigation on the use of iPads among undergraduate art and design students. Br. J. Edu. Technol. **46**(1), 131–141 (2014). https://doi.org/10.1111/bjet.1213
54. Steuer, J.: Defining virtual reality: dimensions determining telepresence. J. Commun. **42**(4), 73–93 (1992). https://doi.org/10.1111/j.1460-2466.1992.tb00812.x
55. Streitz, N.A.: From human–computer interaction to human–environment interaction: ambient intelligence and the disappearing computer. In: Stephanidis, C., Pieper, M. (eds.) UI4ALL 2006. LNCS, vol. 4397, pp. 3–13. Springer, Heidelberg (2007). https://doi.org/10.1007/978-3-540-71025-7_1
56. Thompson, T.L.: Who's taming who? Tensions between people and technologies in cyberspace communities. In: Dirckinck-Holmfeld, L., Hodgson, V., McConnell, D. (eds.) Exploring the Theory, Pedagogy and Practice of Networked Learning, pp. 157–172, Springer, New York (2012). https://doi.org/10.1007/978-1-4614-0496-5_9
57. Traxler, J.: Context reconsidered. In: Traxler, J., Kukulska-Hulme, A. (eds.) Mobile Learning: The Next Generation, pp. 190–207. Routledge, London (2015). https://doi.org/10.4324/9780203076095
58. Trigwell, K.: A phenomenographic interview on phenomenography. In: Bowden, J.A., Walsh, E. (eds.) Phenomenography, pp. 62–82. RMIT University Press, Melbourne (2000)
59. Van Dijk, J.: The Network Society, Social Aspects of New Media, 2nd edn. Sage Publications, London (2005)
60. Van Kerkhoven, M., Bakker, P.: The hyperlocal in practice. Digit. Journal. **2**(3), 296–309 (2014). https://doi.org/10.1080/21670811.2014.900236
61. Williamson, B.: Smarter learning software: education and the big data imaginary. Big Data - Social Data, 10 Dec, University of Warwick, UK (2015). https://dspace.stir.ac.uk/bitstream/1893/22743/1/Smarter_learning_software_education_and.pdf
62. Yates, C., Partridge, H., Bruce, C.: Exploring information experiences through phenomenography. Libr. Inf. Res. **36**(112), 96–119 (2012). https://doi.org/10.29173/lirg496
63. Zerubavel, E.: Hidden in Plain Sight: The Social Structure of Irrelevance. Oxford University Press, Oxford (2015). https://doi.org/10.1093/acprof:oso/9780199366606.001.0001

Digitizing Intangible Cultural Heritage in China: A Pedagogical Model for Innovation and Entrepreneurship Among New Media Art Students

YunQiao Su[1,2], Sze Seau Jill Lee[2] (iD), BeiLe Su[3], and LiLi Zhang[3(✉)]

[1] Shandong College of Arts and Design, No. 1255, College Road, Changqing District, Jinan, China
[2] UCSI University (Kuala Lumpur), 1, Jalan Puncak Menara Gading, Taman Connaught, 56000 Cheras, Kuala Lumpur, Malaysia
`leess@ucsiuniversity.edu.my`
[3] School of Art, Shandong Jianzhu University, No. 1000, Fengming Road, Licheng District, Jinan 250101, Shandong, China
`281309090@qq.com`

Abstract. Applying digital technologies to preserve cultural heritage is hardly a new concept. In 1990s, with the launch of the Memory of the World project by UNESCO, scholars all over the world began to pay attention to the digital protection of cultural heritage, both tangible and intangible [1]. Through the Memory of the World research network that could be forged globally, UNESCO aims for concerted efforts in mediating, safeguarding, and even promoting cultural heritage by new means of information communicating technologies [2]. Nonetheless the efforts, although commendable, have been more focused on the digital documentation instead of promotion of cultural heritage. Concurrently, as China attaches great importance to "entrepreneurship and entrepreneurship" education, college students' innovation and entrepreneurship education has become an important field of research in China. This study defines intangible cultural heritage, explains digitization of intangible cultural heritage, points out the limitations of the efforts on digital preservation, overviews entrepreneurship education for college students in China, and proposes a pedagogical model targeted at new media art in higher education which seeks to propagate the efforts to digitally preserve and promote intangible cultural heritage under the values of innovation and entrepreneurship.

Keywords: Innovation and entrepreneurship · Digital preservation · Intangible cultural heritage · New media art

1 Defining Intangible Cultural Heritage

Since the Second World War, UNESCO has supported a series of world heritage initiatives, starting with tangible heritage, both immovable and movable, and expanding to natural heritage, and most recently to intangible heritage [3]. Although there are three separate heritage lists, there is increasing awareness of the arbitrariness of the categories and their interrelatedness. Tangible heritage is defined as 'a monument, group of buildings or site of historical, aesthetic, archaeological, scientific, ethnological or anthropological value' and includes such treasures as Angkor Wat, a vast temple complex surrounding the village of Siem Reap in Cambodia; Robbin Island in Cape Town, where Nelson Mandela was incarcerated for most of the 26 years of his imprisonment; Teotihuacan, the ancient pyramid city outside Mexico City; and the Wieliczka Salt Mine, not far from Cracow, which has been mined since the thirteenth century.

Natural heritage is defined as 'outstanding physical, biological, and geological features; habitats of threatened plants or animal species and areas of value on scientific or aesthetic grounds or from the point of view of conservation' and includes such sites as the Red Sea, Mount Kenya National Park, the Grand Canyon and, more recently, Brazil's Central Amazon Conservation Complex [4]. Natural heritage initially referred to places with special characteristics, beauty, or some other value, but untouched by human presence, that is, as wilderness, but most places on the natural heritage list – and in the world – have been shaped or affected in some way by people, an understanding that has changed the way UNESCO thinks about natural heritage. At the same time, natural heritage, conceptualized in terms of ecology, environment, and a systemic approach to a living entity, provides a model for thinking about intangible heritage as a totality, rather than as an inventory, and for calculating the intangible value of a living system, be it natural or cultural.

Over several decades of trying to define intangible heritage, previously and sometimes still called folklore, there has been an important shift in the concept of intangible heritage to include not only the masterpieces, but also the masters. The earlier folklore model supported scholars and institutions to document and preserve a record of disappearing traditions. The most recent model seeks to sustain a living, if endangered, tradition by supporting the conditions necessary for cultural reproduction. This means according value to the 'carriers' and 'transmitters' of traditions, as well as to their habitus and habitat. Whereas like tangible heritage, intangible heritage is culture, like natural heritage, it is alive. The task, then, is to sustain the whole system as a living entity and not just to collect 'intangible artefacts'.

UNESCO's efforts to establish an instrument for the protection of what is now called intangible heritage dates from 1952. The focus on legal concepts, such as intellectual property, copyright, trademark and patent, as the basis for protecting what was then called folklore, failed. Folklore by definition is not the unique creation of an individual; it exists in versions and variants rather than in a single, original, and authoritative form; it is generally created in performance and transmitted orally, by custom or example, rather than in tangible form (writing, notating, drawing, photographs, recordings) [5].

During the 1980s, legal issues were distinguished from preservation measures and in 1989 the UNESCO General Conference adopted the Recommendation on the Safeguarding of Traditional Culture and Folklore [6]. Dated 16 May 2001, the Report on the Preliminary Study on the Advisability of Regulating Internationally, through a New Standard-setting Instrument, the Protection of Traditional Culture and Folklore significantly shifted the terms of the 1989 document. First, rather than emphasize the role of professional folklorists and folklore institutions to document and preserve the records of endangered traditions, it focused on sustaining the traditions themselves by supporting the practitioners. This entailed a shift from artefacts (tales, songs, customs) to people (performers, artisans, healers), their knowledge and skills. Inspired by approaches to natural heritage as living systems and by the Japanese concept of Living National Treasure, which was given legal status in 1950, the 2001 document recognized the importance of enlarging the scope of intangible heritage and the measures to protect it. The continuity of intangible heritage would require attention not just to artefacts, but above all to persons, as well as to their entire habitus and habitat, understood as their life space and social world.

Accordingly, UNESCO defined intangible heritage as: All forms of traditional and popular or folk culture, i.e. collective works originating in a given community and based on tradition. These creations are transmitted orally or by gesture, and are modified over a period of time through a process of collective recreation. They include oral traditions, customs, languages, music, dance, rituals, festivities, traditional medicine and pharmacopoeia, the culinary arts and all kinds of special skills connected with the material aspects of culture, such as tools and the habitat [7].

And, at the March 2001 meeting in Turin, the definition further specified: Peoples' learned processes along with the knowledge, skills and creativity that inform and are developed by them, the products they create and the resources, spaces and other aspects of social and natural context necessary to their sustainability; these processes provide living communities with a sense of continuity with previous generations and are important to cultural identity, as well as to the safeguarding of cultural diversity and creativity of humanity [8].

This holistic and conceptual approach to the definition of intangible heritage is accompanied by a definition in the form of an inventory, a legacy of earlier efforts at defining oral tradition and folklore: The totality of tradition-based creations of a cultural community, expressed by a group or individuals and recognized as reflecting the expectations of a community in so far as they reflect its cultural and social identity; its standards and values are transmitted orally, by imitation or by other means. Its forms are, among others, language, literature, music, dance, games, mythology, rituals, customs, handicrafts, architecture and other arts [9].

With 30 cultural sites, 9 natural sites, and 4 mixed sites inscribed on the World Heritage List as of 2012, China is a treasure of cultural heritage [10]. In fact, the Chinese government has publicly announced the implemented measures to integrate intangible cultural heritage items into the modern life while developing the nation's economic and social well-being [11, 12]. The categories of intangible cultural heritage have been updated to 11 categories, including folklore, traditional music, dance, opera, sports, arts, crafts, medicine and diet. The efforts to sustain intangible cultural heritage have also been supported by academic research, given that China is one of the high-yield countries recognized for research on intangible cultural heritage [13]. Concurrent with its efforts to sustain intangible cultural heritage are the efforts to boost mass entrepreneurship and innovation under the 14th Five-Year Plan period 2021–2025 [14]. Higher education institutions were identified as the talent training epicentre to transform education for mass entrepreneurship and innovation.

2 Digitizing Intangible Cultural Heritage

Intangible cultural heritage is the most stable cultural DNA of a nation, as well as the symbolic symbol that distinguishes one nation from another [15]. With China's attention to intangible cultural heritage and the introduction of a series of policies, China's protection and inheritance of intangible cultural heritage has achieved fruitful results. With the rapid development of information technology and digital media technology, the dissemination of intangible cultural heritage must progress with the times. The interactive, convenient and immersive characteristics of digital media can provide more choices for the expression of intangible cultural heritage information. For example, digital technologies such as virtual reality and holographic projection are used to provide audiences with vivid scenes of intangible cultural heritage, so as to enhance their perception of the real intangible cultural heritage environment and enrich their sense of experience and immersion. Therefore, it is necessary to understand the new development direction of intangible cultural heritage communication from multiple aspects, such as digital communication mode, digital communication display and digital communication media. Only by integrating the communication of intangible cultural heritage into the new digital media communication system can the accurate communication of intangible cultural heritage be realized and be promoted.

2.1 Digital Communication Mode

As a kind of intangible cultural heritage existing as a living culture, its dissemination must reflect regionalism and immediacy, that is, the dissemination of intangible cultural heritage cannot be separated from the original natural environment, ecological environment and social environment, and can be synchronized with the live display of intangible cultural heritage. The biggest advantage of digital communication is that it can make full use of information technology and digital technology to change the one-way mode of point-to-point or point-to-point communication of oral communication, text communication, printing communication and even the earlier electronic communication into multi-to-many, multi-face communication and face-to-face communication. As a result, passive audience become active producers, users and consumers. At present, there is limited research on digital communication modes of intangible cultural heritage. The existing research in this area could be further understood through these four categories:

Mass Media. This digital communication mode can make full use of the influence of mass media such as traditional newspapers, radio and television, realize the transformation and upgrading of communication services with the help of the network platform, and contribute to the reform of the communication mode of intangible cultural heritage. For example, the integration of TV and Internet technology can realize the trend of networking, intelligence and large-screen dissemination of intangible cultural heritage, and meet the needs of the audience in the family living room.

Digital Archives. Digital archives as a digital communication mode refers to the digitization of intangible cultural heritage resources by the intangible cultural heritage protection unit, the construction of its thematic database, and the audience through the Internet to promote the dissemination and circulation of intangible cultural heritage information. At present, the digital library and digital museum are the most typical examples of digital archives, such as America's first virtual library "American Memory", which combines the use of voice, text, images and video data to digitize America's intangible cultural heritage, and establish the corresponding database project for the audience to read online and download.

Internet Dissemination. The interactive advantages of the Internet are utilized to disseminate intangible cultural heritage activities in real time so that the audience can feel the live intangible cultural heritage in real time. Audiences can share their cognition of the cultural space of intangible cultural heritage. However, the internet as a digital communication mode lacks such a shared context and cultural background, which greatly reduces its communication effect.

Immersive Media. 3D technology, virtual reality and augmented reality technology have the potential to draw the audience into the scene and enable them to be immersed in the context of intangible cultural heritage through interaction. Some scholars believe that the immersive protection and communication of intangible cultural heritage will become the mainstream of online media [16]. At present, the digital communication modes of intangible cultural heritage cultural heritage mainly consist of mass media, digital archives and the Internet. The sophisticated requirements of technology and capital by the immersive media as a digital communication mode have resulted it in being only a supplement to the first three modes.

2.2   Digital Communication Display

The various types of intangible cultural heritage could be divided into 11 categories, including including folklore, traditional music, dance, opera, sports, arts, crafts, medicine and diet [17]. It needs to be pointed out that all these categories of intangible cultural heritage have diversified contents and diversified forms of expression. Hence, to ensure the effective digital dissemination of these categories of intangible cultural heritage, it is necessary to first understand and master the characteristics of the different categories, and adopt different display methods according to different conditions. Peng et al. (2006) proposed that digital display of intangible cultural heritage should be based on the representation and characteristics of different types of intangible cultural heritage, classify and store information through various digital technologies, and realize digital display by various new media technologies [16]. Huang et al. (2012) proposed that intangible cultural heritage has various types and complex contents, with corresponding display methods that can be divided into traditional information display type, mechanical control display type, interactive touch screen display type, sensor-based display type, virtual reality display type, etc. [18]. Shan (2012) believes that traditional performance is a highly integrated intangible cultural heritage culture integrating music, dynamics, stories and other audio-visual elements. It transcends regional boundaries through digital audio and video, completes standardization and restoration, and realizes cultural sharing [19].

According to the characteristics of intangible cultural heritage, the selection and collocation of different digital display methods can achieve the optimal allocation of communication resources and real digitalization transmission. At present, under the new technical support system, digital communication and display methods have become rich and diverse, instead of being limited to traditional graphic printing and screen display, as shown in Table 1. On the basis of traditional information display, digital communication of intangible cultural heritage is realized with the help of various technologies, such as logistics network, 4G mobile network and virtual reality.

Table 1. Digital communication display mode

display	Related technologies and advantages and disadvantages	
Traditional information form display	The intangible cultural Heritage resources such as text, picture, audio and video and 3D model are displayed item by item in the way of traditional text and text and screen display. This kind of presentation Low cost, low technical requirements.	
Mechanical control type display	Through the mechanical device to simulate the intangible cultural heritage activity process, combined with a variety of display equipment, to achieve the intangible cultural heritage information visualization. This kind of display has a strong sense of experience, but relatively high maintenance costs.	
Interactive touch screen display	Users browse intangible cultural heritage information through touch operation. Reasonable interaction can improve the efficiency of information acquisition and enhance users' sense of immersion. The development cost of this exhibition is low, and it is mostly used in museums and other public cultural service places.	
Sensor based new Media interaction mode	Through gyroscope, sound field, magnetic field and other sensor technology, in view of the user interaction feedback information, after processing computing technology to respond. In recent years, it has been widely used and the technology is relatively mature.	
Based on virtual reality Sensory experience mode	Through computer technology to generate realistic three-dimensional vision, hearing, touch, smell and other sensory world, restore intangible cultural heritage information of a strong sense of reality. This display method has high requirements on hardware and site.	

2.3   Digital Communication Media

Rich and diversified digital media enable intangible cultural heritage to have more and richer forms of expression. This section will discuss four types of digital communication media which have been involved in digitizing intangible cultural heritage.

The Internet. This is one of the earliest and most popular traditional media in China. Jia et al. (2012) mentioned that digital intangible heritage resources can be presented through pictures, videos, music and other video forms by browsing online intangible heritage resources based on personal computer terminals [20], such as "China Intangible Heritage Network", "Chinese Traditional Villages captured" and the website of the International Intangible Heritage Expo Park. In addition, Wang (2014) proposed that the application of VR virtual display technology enables intangible cultural heritage to be simulated on the computer network platform, thus greatly enhancing the audience's sense of involvement and experience in the display media [21].

Intelligent Devices. Smart mobile products, such as smart watches and mobile phones, are subtly influencing the way of life and entertainment of human beings, and this kind of smart products also have a wider audience. The Palace Museum has launched a number of mobile apps that make it easy for the public to see the cultural relics in its collection. At the same time, more interactive experience is integrated into the application, which can improve the breadth and speed of the dissemination of intangible cultural heritage to a certain extent.

Social Networks. As the most popular and popular social tool in the Internet era, social network has the advantages of fast propagation and popularity, and has also become an important channel for the exhibition and dissemination of intangible cultural heritage. Multimodal features of social networks such as WeChat and QQ complement the original oral, paper, stage, image of traditional media. The strength of this digital communication media is that the audience who access intangible cultural heritage through social networks can choose the cultural information of intangible cultural heritage according to their needs, and re-organize and create it.

Public Cultural Platform. Museums, art galleries, cultural centers and other public cultural platforms do not only display intangible cultural heritage through traditional media, but also provide a good public platform for the dissemination and display of intangible cultural heritage through digital construction [22]. Taking museums as an example, digital display forms can be added to display exhibits and interactive devices such as holographic projection and 3D can enhance the sense of participation of audiences. At the same time, audiences will use internet devices to enable information transmission and sharing. For example, in The Dongba Cultural Non-body Examination Museum in Lijiang, Yunnan, virtual try-on of ethnic costumes can be realized through photo collection, and composite photos of "try-on" can be transmitted to the audience. The simple cultural interaction experience leaves the audience with a deeper impression on the local culture and effectively communicates the regional non-material culture.

2.4   Limitations of Digitization of Intangible Cultural Heritage

At present, research on digitization of intangible cultural heritage needs to explore more theoretical developments and methodical improvements to ensure the continual transmission of the digital communication of intangible cultural heritage. For instance, there should be explorations of the integration of different types of media, implementation of all-media communication projects, and digital transmission between different media. We should look forward to research that involves deep integration of broadcasting and the construction of a media communication platform adapted to "Internet+" [23].

In addition, there is also the problem of narrow research perspectives. There are more studies at the micro-specific level, but less studies at the macro-global level and systematic multi-perspective analysis. Digital communication of intangible cultural heritage is not only a technical issue, but also a complex cultural issue which involves complex subjects. The existing digital communication mode is unable to show the vitality of intangible cultural heritage.

The digital dissemination of intangible cultural heritage should be carried out in a dynamic or active way, independent of material carriers and with its own characteristics in communication channels and modes. Digital communication must fully consider the characteristics of the live communication of intangible cultural heritage to make digital communication more effective. In the past, the simple communication mode of video or picture plus text explanation can no longer meet the requirements of the communication of intangible cultural heritage. At the same time, different categories of intangible cultural heritage should have different forms of digital communication. For example, the material carrier for folk literature which mainly relies on oral creation and transmission should be different from folk art and other intangible cultural heritage items. However, the existing communication mode is in the form of "one size fits all", which lacks the diversity and diversification of communication mode.

In 2006, 2008, 2011, 2014 and 2021, The State Council published five batches of the list of state-level intangible cultural heritage projects, totaling 1,557 state-level representative intangible cultural heritage projects. In addition, each province, city, district (county) has corresponding representative intangible cultural heritage projects. As of 2021, Hubei province has a total of 352 representative intangible cultural heritage projects at the provincial level, and there are many representative intangible cultural heritage projects listed in the project list of all levels in China [17]. The digital transmission modes based on the mass media and digital libraries usually focus on big projects that hold the promise of extensive audiences and social recognition, such as the Spring Festival, Lantern Festival, Dragon Boat Festival, Mid-Autumn festival, the Peking Opera; and intangible items such as calligraphy and acupuncture. However, the proportion of representative intangible cultural heritage projects transmitted by mainstream media is very small, and most intangible cultural heritage projects are escaped the attention of mass media. However, it is precisely these intangible cultural heritage in a weak position, due to lack of social attention which are in danger of being lost or dying out. Internet communication mode can better promote the dissemination of intangible cultural heritage in disadvantaged status, but there are only few studies in this area.

Different contents of the communication of intangible cultural heritage determine that the corresponding media must be selected. In particular, with the development of big data, virtual reality, artificial intelligence and other emerging technologies, technology-driven communication has begun to leap from the mass media era to the intellectual media era. The intellectual media era does not only involve application of new technologies but will affect the entire communication ecology and pattern. At present, the research on the communication of intellectual media is in its infancy, with few research achievements. Therefore, devising strategies to capitalize on emerging technologies and their relationship with the media and applying the technologies of intellectual media to the communication of intangible cultural heritage will be a significant challenge to be overcome.

In recent years, although the film and television communication of intangible cultural heritage has developed rapidly, its themes are concentrated on myths and legends. Mythological novels such as Journey to the West and Saga of The Gods have several well-known characters who have attained the status of Image Intellectual Property such as Sun Wukong, Nezha and Jiang Ziya. Adaptation based on this theme can save a lot of publicity costs and produce relatively small risks, so it has become the main source of topic selection of film and television animation for all ages. From Princess Iron Fan to Uproar in Heaven, and from Monkey King: Monkey King: Hero is Back to The Journey to the West, it is typical to reproduce homogenized cultural representations within the scope of traditional myths and legends. The negative implication would be the audience's aesthetic fatigue on the communication of intangible cultural heritage films and television. The issue of how to creatively integrate more diverse elements of Chinese intangible cultural heritage into film and television, so that the audience can appreciate the beauty of their intangible cultural heritage, hence requires attention.

3 Innovation and Entrepreneurship Education for College Students in China

Innovation and entrepreneurship education is an important contributor to employability and skill enhancement of college students. This section explains the practical motivation and theoretical interests that resulted in the higher education institutions in China being the apex for innovation and entrepreneurship education.

The focus of China's national strategy has been on effectively improving China's progress in innovation and entrepreneurship work. As a result, colleges and universities carry out diversified entrepreneurship education, mainly in five forms: participating in "entrepreneurship and innovation" competition, constructing entrepreneurship parks or bases, opening makerspaces, establishing entrepreneurship colleges, and setting up entrepreneurship courses [24]. Thus, driven by the national policy of entrepreneurship and innovation, the original social concept of "entrepreneurship" has been endowed with more interdisciplinary connotations, presenting "entrepreneurship education" in the educational discourse system.

With China's attention to innovation and entrepreneurship, innovation and entrepreneurship has become an important driving force of China's economic development, and also become an important goal of college students' education and teaching. In research, entrepreneurship education and innovation education have become research hotspots. Based on different disciplines, researchers have carried out in-depth studies on the model, mechanism and implication of entrepreneurship education. For the model of entrepreneurship education, it is when entrepreneurship education has developed to a certain stage and accumulated certain experience that replicable and extendable experience and practices are condensed. This study identified 4582 relevant studies with the use of these words in search: "entrepreneurship education for college students". Furthermore, "entrepreneurship education for college students" was taken as the key word and "mode" was included in the index. The resulting amount of literature was 827 related studies, accounting for 18.05% of the literature on entrepreneurship education for college students (Fig. 1).

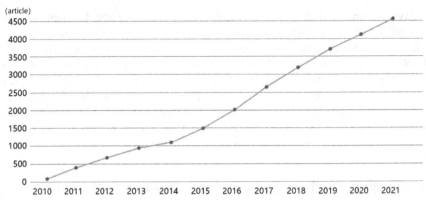

Fig. 1. Literature research trend of entrepreneurship education for college students (2010–2021)

4 Current Focus of Research on Entrepreneurship Education for College Students

The research on entrepreneurship education for college students involves various disciplines and education theory. The focus that could be inferred from the current research are school-enterprise cooperation, educational models, key components of entrepreneurship education, and dialectical approach to innovation and entrepreneurship.

4.1 School-Enterprise Cooperation

School-enterprise cooperation emphasizes the need to strengthen the cooperation between schools and enterprises in the development of entrepreneurship education for college students, and effectively enhance the entrepreneurial ability of college students through close school-enterprise cooperation and industry-university-research. This focus makes full use of the advantages of enterprises and makes up for the inherent deficiency of entrepreneurship education in schools. For example, Zhou believes that diversified cooperation can make full use of the support of enterprise policies and funds, and also resolve the disconnection between universities and enterprises [25]. At the same time, the university-enterprise cooperation could cultivate the entrepreneurial ability among college students through real experience of enterprise operation procedures and production procedures, work norms and technical processes, so as to enhance the entrepreneurial experience and ability of college students. For example, scholars Le and Lei proposed a "combat" innovation and entrepreneurship education model based on school-enterprise cooperation in view of the actual situation of students' entrepreneurship in vocational colleges [26]. Thus, institutions of higher learning should no longer remain insular ivory towers, but need to strive for joint enterprise, linking classroom of entrepreneurship education with actual operations of enterprises, thereby prompting students promote entrepreneurship in the actual business dealings.

4.2   Education Models

Originally, the word "entrepreneurship" belongs to a typical sociological concept. Since the proposal of "entrepreneurship and entrepreneurship", colleges and universities in China have carried out innovation and entrepreneurship education, in which entrepreneurship education is the ultimate purpose of innovation education, but also the most recent version of employment education in China. Therefore, Chinese colleges and universities put forward their own unique entrepreneurship education models that utilize and maximize their educational resources and niches of the colleges and universities involved. These institutions capitalize and re-design college entrepreneurship education programs for college students. For example, Liao et al. proposed the 3 + 1 entrepreneurship education model of higher vocational colleges [27], and Gao (2016) proposed the "one, two, three" model of entrepreneurship education for college students [28]. In addition, there is the "three planes" entrepreneurship education model [29]. These entrepreneurship education models rely on professional knowledge as an important basis, and integrate elements in the process of entrepreneurship education, with the aim to effectively improve the entrepreneurial ability of college students. For example, the "Trinity" entrepreneurship education model [30], the "four-in-one" entrepreneurship education model [31] and the "six-In-one" entrepreneurship education model [32].

4.3   Key Components of Entrepreneurship Education

Based on different disciplines and emphases, colleges and universities deconstruct the key components of entrepreneurship education while implementing it in their respective institutions. Some scholars believe that key components in entrepreneurship education could highlight the niche of the school to cultivate entrepreneurial talents [33]. For example, Xu and Zhang who studied entrepreneurship education for art and design majors put forward the "four holistic education" entrepreneurship education model of full staff, full process, full integration and full environment [34]. It can hence be inferred that entrepreneurship education is not accomplished overnight, but require careful focus on the process of education and teaching practice to improve the entrepreneurial ability of college students.

4.4   Dialectical Approach to Innovation and Entrepreneurship

The educational goals of innovation education and entrepreneurship education are different. In general, innovation education is an important part of entrepreneurship education which promotes college students' employability. Nonetheless, ever since the "double gen" concept was proposed, innovative education and entrepreneurship education has become a pair of "twin brothers", concurrently serving the roles of logic and purpose. Therefore, some colleges and universities integrate innovation education and entrepreneurship education into research and practice, besides forming personalized innovation and entrepreneurship education models. For example, Huazhong University of Science and Technology has put forward a new model of entrepreneurship and entrepreneurship education featuring "one body, two wings and three fulcrum", which provides a useful reference for universities to carry out innovation and entrepreneurship [35]. Hui et al. proposed the innovation and entrepreneurship education model based on entrepreneurial ecosystem theory [36]. Therefore, the current focus is on using a dialectical approach towards innovation and entrepreneurship in entrepreneurship education.

5   The 4321 Pedagogical Model as the Proposed Model

As educators in higher education institutions, the authors accept the challenge of transforming education to promote mass entrepreneurship and innovation while sustaining China's wealth of intangible cultural heritage. Past studies contributed many innovative ideas on enterprising intangible cultural heritage, such as constructing an 'experiencescape' [37] or developing a web platform [38]. Funded by a university-level grant which aims to develop talents in digitizing intangible cultural heritage, the first author intends to transform the pedagogical approach in the new media art studies of his university to nurture innovation and entrepreneurship among the students. In this paper, the authors would describe a pedagogical model named 4321 (Fig. 2) which would be explored in the design of teaching and learning of digitalization of intangible cultural heritage involving 50 degree students in new media art.

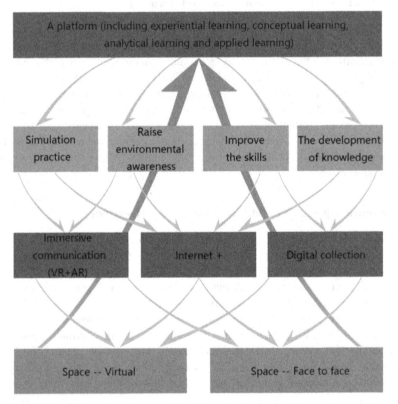

Fig. 2. The 4321 pedagogical model with knowledge application as the core focus

The 4321 pedagogical model involves three levels, four stages of learning and two spaces which would be integrated in one platform. The three levels of mastery are Digital Archive, Internet + and Immersive Communication (VR + AR). The four scaffolded stages of learning are development of knowledge, enhancement of skills, raising of environmental awareness and simulation of practice. All the teaching and learning activities would be carried out through two spaces – the face-to-face physical classroom and the virtual space. The single platform that integrates these levels of mastery, stages of learning and learning spaces would be the new media art course in the university. The theoretical framework of 4321 would be the Multiliteracies pedagogy which involve experiential learning, conceptual learning, analytical learning and applied learning [39, 40]. Four educational objectives were identified under the 4321 pedagogical model.

5.1 Re-conceptualize Educational Goals

At present, the value orientation of innovation and entrepreneurship education in colleges and universities is too utilitarian, which is not conducive to the cultivation of advanced entrepreneurial talents and the construction of a positive and healthy atmosphere of innovation and entrepreneurship education. Therefore, the overall goal of innovation and entrepreneurship education should be re-conceptualized to stimulate students' innovation consciousness, forge entrepreneurship spirit, cultivate high-quality enterprises and develop the industry iteratively. Guided by the competence-oriented entrepreneurship education concept, innovation and entrepreneurship knowledge is divided into six levels: memory, understanding, analysis, synthesis, evaluation and application, so as to clarify students' learning objectives and establish an information-symmetric teaching contract relationship with them [41].

5.2 Align Teaching Content with Educational Objectives

Innovation and entrepreneurship education in colleges and universities should re-select and design teaching content based on educational objectives, and transform the currently widely implemented curriculum-based innovation and entrepreneurship education into entrepreneurship education based on consciousness stimulation and ability cultivation. For example, innovation targeted at college students should cultivate thinking by setting up innovative thinking training courses for college students. The training should aim for team collaboration, organizational coordination, crisis management and other entrepreneurial skills. To aim at the skills of enterprise establishment and management, operation and management of entrepreneurial enterprises should be gradually changed to a more flexible content, with education ability training as the premise, and students can choose independently. Only in this way can we achieve the consistency of goals and the iterative upgrading of all links in the whole innovation and entrepreneurship education system.

5.3 Innovate Teaching Methods to Support Educational Objectives

At present, innovation and entrepreneurship education in colleges and universities adopts various teaching methods and media, which are different in class and after class. However, with the gradual refinement of educational objectives, existing teaching methods must be comprehensively innovated to support the realization of educational objectives [42]. Brainstorming, group debate, role play, and entrepreneurial teaching methods can continue, but should not be the only teaching methods. Innovation and entrepreneurship teachers need to constantly innovate teaching methods according to the change of entrepreneurship education goals. Some ideas and means of high-quality innovation and entrepreneurship education can be appropriately introduced. For example, students are required to set up online or offline micro-enterprises as a team, experience the management skills of enterprises in actual operation, and document enterprise operation in the course assessment, in order to change virtual operation into actual learning. Entrepreneurship mentors who are professional mentors should be arranged for students so that students can enjoy individualized guidance in innovation and entrepreneurship education.

5.4 Implement Graded Assessment

Innovation and entrepreneurship education in colleges and universities must be based on its educational objective system and there should be comprehensive assessment indicators and standards for six levels of memory, understanding, analysis, synthesis, evaluation and application. A fuzzy assessment system will directly lead to the failure of the whole education system. The assessment system must be rigorous enough to evaluate if students can memorize entrepreneurial knowledge, accurately understand entrepreneurial theory, internalize entrepreneurial ability and use entrepreneurial skills to some extent. Innovation entrepreneurship education evaluation system should be implemented with quantitative measures which contain detailed descriptions of the six levels of mastery which are memory, understanding, analysis, synthesis, evaluation and creation.

References

1. National library of Australia: Guidelines for the preservation of digital heritage (2003). https://unesdoc.unesco.org/ark:/48223/pf0000130071
2. UNESCO: Memory of the World and the academic world: a proposal to introduce Memory of the World studies (2011). https://unesdoc.unesco.org/ark:/48223/pf0000378497.locale=en
3. Several histories of UNESCO's heritage initiatives have been written. For a particularly thoughtful account, see Jan Turtinen, Globalising Heritage: On UNESCO, SCORE Rapportserie 12 (2000)
4. Defining our Heritage. http://www.unesco.org/whc/intro-en.htm. Accessed 15 Jan 2003
5. WIPO (the World Intellectual Property Organization) is making efforts to deal with these issues as are such organizations as the Secretariat of the Pacific Community in Noumea, New Caledonia. See their Regional Framework for the Protection of Traditional Knowledge and Expressions of Culture (2002)
6. UNESCO, Recommendation on the Safeguarding of Traditional Culture and Folklore adopted by the General Conference at its twenty-fifth session, Paris, 15 November 1989. http://www.unesco.org/culture/laws/paris/html_eng/page1.shtml/
7. UNESCO, Intangible Heritage, last updated 24 March 2003. http://www.unesco.org/culture/heritage/intangible/html_eng/index_en.shtml/. This formulation is close to the one in UNESCO's 1989 Recommendation on the Safeguarding of Traditional Culture and Folklore

8. Quoted in UNESCO, Report on the Preliminary Study on the Advisabilityof Regulating Internationally, through a New Standard-setting Instrument, the Protection of Traditional Culture and Folklore, UNESCO Executive Board, 161st Session, 161 EX/15, PARIS, 16 May 2001. Item 3.4.4 of the provisional agenda, paragraph 26. http://unesdoc.unesco.org/images/0012/001225/122585e.pdf/

9. UNESCO, Recommendation on the Safeguarding of Traditional Culture and Folklore, op. cit

10. Zhao, W.: China: managing cultural heritage and the world heritage list. In: Smith, C. (ed.) Encyclopedia of Global Archaeology. Springer, New York (2014). https://doi.org/10.1007/978-1-4419-0465-2_1967

11. The State Council of the People's Republic of China. China steps up protection of intangible cultural heritage (2021). http://english.www.gov.cn/policies/latestreleases/202108/13/content_WS6115a4b7c6d0df57f98de5f7.html

12. The State Council of the People's Republic of China. Nation expands intangible cultural heritage item list (2021). http://english.www.gov.cn/news/pressbriefings/202106/11/content_WS60c2aba4c6d0df57f98db126.html

13. Su, X.W., Li, X., Kang, Y.X.: A bibliometric analysis of research on intangible cultural heritage using CiteSpace. SAGE Open, April–June, pp. 1–18 (2019)

14. The State Council of the People's Republic of China. More actions to promote mass entrepreneurship and innovation (2021). http://english.www.gov.cn/premier/news/202106/25/content_WS60d589a4c6d0df57f98dbddd.html

15. Li, Y., Gu, J.: Scientific evaluation of intangible cultural heritage protection. J. Primitive Ethnic Cult. 9(1) (2017)

16. Peng, D., Pan, L., et al.: Digital protection – non-materialnew means of quality cultural heritage protection. Cult. Herit. (1) (2006)

17. Chinese Intangible Cultural Heritage Network. National intangible culture Heritage Representative Project List (2020). http://www.ihchina.cn/project.html. Accessed 09 Aug 2021

18. Huang, Y., Tan, G.: Number of China's intangible cultural heritage. J. Central China Normal Univ. (Humanit. Soc.) **51**(2) (2013)

19. Shan, X.: The construction of grassroots public digital cultural resources problems and thinking. Hundreds Arts **28**(S1) (2012)

20. Jia, X., Wang, J.: Digital means in our cultural heritageApplication in the field of inheritance and Innovation. Mod. Commun. **34**(2) (2012). (Chinese media University of science and technology of China)

21. Wang, C.: Cultural heritage based on 3D panoramic interactive system. J. Wuhan Univ. Technol. (Soc. Sci. Ed.) **27**(2) (2014)

22. Yang, X.Y.: The role of media in intangible cultural heritage protection. Guizhou Soc. Sci. (7) (2012)

23. Xinhua News Agency. The CPC Central Committee is concerned with formulating the national economy and societyDevelopment of the 14th Five-Year Plan and the establishment of the 2035 vision (2020). http://www.gov.cn/zhengce/2020-11/03/content_5556991.htm. Accessed 09 Aug 2021

24. Kuang, Y., Shi, W.: Analysis of "entrepreneurship and Innovation" education in vocational colleges: based on reality review and rational thinking. Educ. Res. (2), 97–99 (2017)

25. Zhou, Y.: Analysis and exploration of school-enterprise cooperation mode under the situation of innovation and entrepreneurship education reform Suo. Public Sci. (Sci. Educ.) (3), 139 (2016)

26. Le, L., Lei, S.: Research on innovation and entrepreneurship education model in higher vocational colleges. Vocat. Educ. Theory Altar (9), 31 (2019)

27. Liao, C., Zhou, Y., Liu, J.: "3+1" entrepreneurship teaching in higher vocational colleges under the background of "entrepreneurship and innovation". Educ. Career (23), 69–73 (2018)

28. Gao, Q.: Tacit knowledge and college students entrepreneurship education model analysis. Xi'an Airlines J. Chin. Acad. Sci. (2), 69 (2016)
29. Hu, Y.: Construct the "three planes" model of professional oriented entrepreneurship education in colleges and universities. Chin. Educ. (7), 79 (2012)
30. Zhou, Q., Zhao, F.: "Trinity": the construction and model of entrepreneurship education for college students its operation – experience from Ningbo University. China High. Educ. Res. (4), 84 (2009)
31. Cao, J., Zhou, H., Luo, Y.: Innovative education model for college students. Exp. Res. Explor. (8), 195–198 (2010)
32. Shi, J.: Construction of a new model of "six-in-one" entrepreneurship education for college students. China Adult Educ. (4), 54–55 (2010)
33. Gu, X., Ju, Z.: A review of entrepreneurial education model for college students in China. J. Tin Bus. Vocat. Tech. Coll. (12), 67 (2017)
34. Yang, T., Liu, Y.: A comparative study of entrepreneurship education models in Chinese and American Universities. China Cheng Hum. Educ. (9), 23–24 (2008)
35. Li, J., Yang, L.: Practice and exploration of the new mode of "entrepreneurship and innovation" education – based on central china science and technology of china universities (10), 55 (2019)
36. Hui, X., Xu, K., Luo, G.: Innovation and innovation based on entrepreneurial ecosystem theory vocational education model and practice. Innov. Entrep. Educ. (4), 70–72 (2014)
37. Chen, Z.Y., Suntikul, W., King, B.: Constructing an intangible cultural heritage experiencescape: the case of the feast of the drunken dragon (Macau). Tourism Manag. Perspect. **34** (2020). https://doi.org/10.1016/j.tmp.2020.100659
38. Dimitropoulos, K., et al.: A multimodal approach for the safeguarding and transmission of intangible cultural heritage: the case of i-Treasures. IEEE Intell. Syst. **33**(6), 3–16 (2018). https://doi.org/10.1109/MIS.2018.111144858
39. Cope, B., Kalantzis, M.: The things you do to know: an introduction to the pedagogy of multiliteracies. In: Cope, B., Kalantzis, M. (eds.) A Pedagogy of Multiliteracies: Learning By Design, pp. 1–36. Palgrave, London (2015)
40. Cope, B., Kalantzis, M.: Pedagogies for digital learning: from transpositional grammar to the literacies of education. In: Sindoni, M.G., Moschini, I. (eds.) Multimodal literacies across digital learning contexts, pp. 34–54. Routledge (2022)
41. Liu, S., Wang, Z., Guo, X.: TBL + flipped classroom and economic law teaching under bloom's classification of educational objectives – a case study of a university in Liaoning Province. Big Sch. Educ. (11), 13–17 (2018)
42. Hong, Y.: On the practical approach of college students' entrepreneurship education under the background of higher education popularization. J. Jilin Univ. Agric. Sci. Technol. **26**(6), 35–38 (2017)

Interactive Design of Assistant Education Software Application for Autistic Children

JinLiang Tian(✉)

Shandong University of Art & Design, No. 23 Qianfushandong Road, Jinan, Shandong, China
164239197@qq.com

Abstract. This paper proposes the guidance of methodology on mobile terminal platforms for the assistant education application of autistic children. With the objective of the assistant intervention treatment of autistic children, this paper designs an application to be used in the assistant education of autistic children according to the user demand of the education of families with autistic children with the contents of cognition training, behavior training, and attention training in combination with ways of game and psychological counseling. The design of application gives full play to the multimedia characteristics of game, sound, and picture of mobile platform, and provides the interactive design, color design, and page design applicable for autistic children to use in combination with the professional courses and special needs of autistic children, to explore the application and design strategy of mobile platform software in the assistant education of autistic children.

Keywords: Autistic children · Interactive design · Assistant education · Design strategy

1 Introduction: Current Situation and Demand of the Development of Autistic Children Education

1.1 Development Situation of the Assistant Education of Autistic Children

Autism is also called an autistic disorder. It is a developmental disorder caused by the disorder of nervous system. The symptoms include abnormal social competence, ability to communicate, interests, and behavior patterns. According to relevant statistics, there are about 67 million patients with autism all over the world at present. According to the data of china Autism Education and Recovery Industry Development Report III published in 2019, there are over 10 million patients with autism in China, including over 2 million children under 14 years old. Although 1811 institutions are working on the education and rehabilitation of autism, the service can only cover 200,000 to 300,000 people. According to the study, 2 to 6 years old is the golden treatment period for autistic children. With scientific intervention, autism can be obviously improved after intervention treatment and assistant rehabilitation education. Thus, it is especially important to develop a popular home rehabilitation education tool aiming at autistic children. With the development of the digital era, the combination between digital techniques and the internet, the development of new education technologies, and especially the popularization of intelligent devices, more and more assistant education applications aiming at autistic children based on mobile terminal platforms are developed. This professional application design provides new ideas and new methods for the intervention treatment and assistant education of autistic children.

1.2 Development of Application Software About the Education of Autistic Children

With the development of digital technology, more and more new technologies and intelligent devices are applied in the treatment of autism. For example, LuxAI designed a QTrobot aiming at children with autism spectrum disorder (ASD) in 2017 to assist them in study and education. At present, many institutions and companies in the world, such as the Massachusetts Institute of Technology and SoftBank Robotics, have carried out relevant research on the autism treatment assisted by intelligent robots. Mobile intelligent devices are also regarded as an important tool in the assistant rehabilitation of autism. An application software based on mobile platforms can not only make use of various media, such as picture, animation, and video but also provide an excellent experience of interactive design. Under the background of internet, it can also provide on-line courses to realize the purpose of course sharing and communication, providing good communication characteristics. It can also realize the tasks of remote teaching and home study. These characteristics and properties are applicable to be applied in the education and study of autistic children.

In recent years, although the software development of children education applications is huge in quantity, few applications are designed aiming at the use of autistic children as this kind of application is small in user scale, low in income, and difficult in design. For example, a psychologist of California Bill Thompson designed and developed two applications for autistic children after spending a lot of time and effort based on the survey of 500 handicapped children - Look2Learn and Stories2Learn. Europe and America started early in this aspect, but China is relatively late. At present, some applications are aiming at autistic children, such as "Small Raindrop", "MITA", "Wait for the Bloom", "Monster Day", and "A Sunny Day". These applications have different design focuses that some of them focus on vision and communicate by picture exchange and communication system, some of them complete some cognitive training by interactive games, and some of them complete relevant communication behaviors and achieve the purpose of communication training by voice, video and other carriers. In terms of the overall design objective, mobile platform and technical characteristics are utilized to complete some assistant learning tasks of autistic children under the tutorship of parents, and some needs for home study of autistic children can also be satisfied.

2 Preliminary Design and Planning of Assistant Education Software Application for Autistic Children

2.1 Preliminary Software Design Task: Determining Design Objectives and Tasks

Autism is a developmental disorder caused by the disorder of nervous system. The design of assistant education application of autistic children should be carried out according to the applied characteristics of mobile terminal as well as autistic children's cognitive competence, physiological and psychological features to teach the knowledge in the way of recreational interaction in combination with psychological guidance. At the beginning of the development of a piece of software, a wide preliminary survey (see Table 1) is also required, such as investigating the education appeal of families with child patients, the suggestions of professional physicians in relevant fields, and the teaching of professional education institutions, such as autism rehabilitation center. Only on the basis of the comprehensive survey data in all aspects can a piece of professional software suitable for the rehabilitation of autistic children be designed. In the preliminary design of software, the formulation of basic design objectives and tasks is an important link in software design planning.

Table 1. Summary of survey data information of "a sunny day" software project

Survey institution	Place and project of survey	Suggestions acquired from survey
Peking University Sixth Affiliated Hospital	Director of Pediatric Department, famous expert of ADD: Professor Wang Yufeng	1. Autism is a problem of brain development. Child patients have disordered sociability, ability to communicate, interests and behaviors. By cognitive training and behavior training, preliminary intervention treatment provides a good effect 2. They are more sensitive to visual stimulations than normal people, but it is more difficult to cure girls because of girls' congenital sensitive character
Beijing Association for Rehabilitation of Autism	Several experts of the Association for Rehabilitation	1. Autism is not classified by age bracket, but into two stages of high function and low function according to the performance uniformly 2. It is difficult to achieve complete rehabilitation to a certain extent, and it requires long-term persistence for the treatment and rehabilitation of autism. Scientific educational methods are required in intervention and study

(*continued*)

Table 1. (*continued*)

Survey institution	Place and project of survey	Suggestions acquired from survey
Autism education institution: Beijing Sunshine Friendship Children Rehabilitation Training Center	The responsible person of the center, expert of special education: Wei Qingyun	1. Scientific training and professional courses are very important for rehabilitation. Rehabilitation training requires long-term persistence 2. Software can be regarded as a means of assistant rehabilitation to absorb relevant training methods of professional courses
	Professional course survey and professional teacher interview	1. Child patients are sensitive to sound, and they have an extremely weak ability to associate language with real things 2. Imitation learning requires segment and repeated exercises 3. Child patients have poor attention in the study, and parents need to assist the study
Families with autistic children	Interview of several families with autistic children	1. It is expected that software can solve the problem of behavioral learning in daily life, strengthen communication, and improve function. With low studying fees, it is convenient to use for a long term 2. It is expected that the learning contents of home study can refer to the contents of professional training institutions. It is expected to periodically update the learning contents. It is expected that other parents can strengthen the exchange of experiences

Design Objective: As the intervention effect of autistic treatment is better in childhood, the software mainly regards autistic children as the target users. The design is carried out according to autistic children's characteristics of visual features, auditory characteristics, and interaction characteristics. For example, according to the research, autistic children's sensibility to visual stimulation is different from normal people's. They are easier to be intervened and affected by details. As a result, during the visual design, the design should be as simple as possible and unnecessary visual interference factors should be avoided. Autistic children are sensitive to environmental changes so that the stimulation of sudden irritant behaviors or actions should be avoided to prevent anxious emotions. The situation of child patients is classified into high function and low function. The needs of child patients at different levels should be considered during the design, and general software should be used with the help of parents and other assistants. The use of assistants should also be taken into consideration to formulate different use templates according to different needs.

Design Task: The design task of software is mainly to solve the problems of autistic children's cognition, behavior and social contact. Cognitive education and training is the important task in the intervention treatment of autism. By image, figure and words, autistic children's vision, memory, thinking and other abilities can be improved. As autistic children's brain development is abnormal, their cognitive competence is much poorer than ordinary children. It can only be realized by repeated training and reinforcement exercises. Besides, according to the research, behavior therapy provides a obvious effect for the rehabilitation and intervention of autistic children. Autistic children's cognition can be improved by professional training of behavior, and child patients' attention can be trained by interactive games to learn while playing. In combination with the teaching methods and course structure of professional courses in autism rehabilitation centers, the objective of assistant education can be completed by the ways of combined training and psychological guidance.

2.2 Planning of the Design Structure of Software

After determining the design objective and task of software, integrated planning is also necessary for the design structure of software. In order to complete the structure design of software, some surveys and relevant tests are also required. For example, should adopt physical people and things or painting images be adopted for the setting of visual style? Which one do autistic children prefer or is more acceptable to them? In the aspect of interactive behavior, what interactive actions of behavior can autistic children accept and complete? Can autistic children's interactive behaviors to sound and animation be correctly reflected? These problems can acquire relevant data by tests and surveys. For example, in the pre-design phase of the learning software of autistic children "A Sunny Day", the design team select different types of software, such as Talking Tom, SoundTchLite, and Bubble Tap, to test the use of autistic children, including the favorite types of autistic children, the interactive modes that they can participate in, and their feedback on sound, color, picture and interactive game. The reflection on some typical cases is also recorded. For example, a 4-year-old boy with autism is interested in the interactive actions in the software of Talking Tom very much. He can actively participate in the communication and kiss Tom to express his love to sound. Another 5-year-old girl with autism also knocks on the screen to interact and express initiative communication. She also shows interest in the simulated animal sounds made by the software. Most autistic children participating in the test show interest in this kind of software interaction and can complete basic interactive actions and have good learning interest cooperated by action and sound. It means that the multimedia characteristics of animation, game, and sound and the forms of screen interaction integrated into the application software are suitable for the assistant education of autistic children very much. Children can learn knowledge, acquire good experiences and relax their minds while playing.

Except for tests, a certain amount of extensive surveys can be adopted to acquire relevant data, which is also necessary. The design team can formulate questionnaires aiming at the need for software development. For example, in the software design of "A Sunny Day", the design team formulate a questionnaire consisting of 8 questions aiming at the specific problems of software design. This questionnaire mainly focuses on the problems that the children face at present, the expectations of parents for course and software, and the children's interest points. After the survey on over 100 parents of autistic children, the survey data are organized (Fig. 1), to determine the basic contents and orientation of software design. For example, according to the parents' needs for home study, the contents formulated should focus on the study of daily behaviors at home. According to the characteristics of communication mode, the mode of game interaction should be selected and used to learn knowledge in the interaction and achieve the learning objective in the recreation.

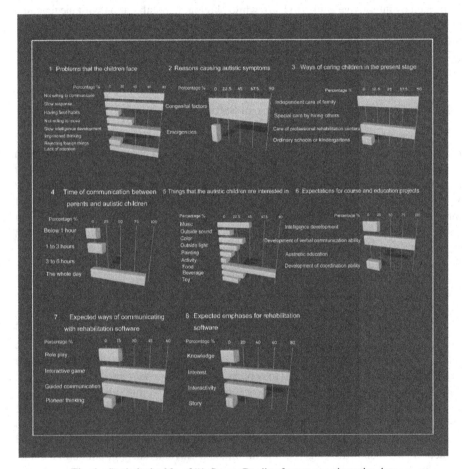

Fig. 1. Statistical table of "A Sunny Day" software questionnaire data

3 Design of Assistant Education Application for Autistic Children—Take the Design of "A Sunny Day" as an Example

3.1 Software System Structural Design and Function Module Design

Compared with the design of ordinary applications, the design of assistant education applications for autistic children has many specific characteristics. At first, the design of software should not blindly pursue to be large and comprehensive. If the software can solve specific problems, it is a successful design. For example, taking the design of the iPad application "A Sunny Day" as an example, The design objective is to solve the basic behavior cognition for autistic children, train the attention and expand the imagination based on cognitive learning by interactive game and other ways to complete the objective of assistant education in combination with psychological guidance.

The system structural design of software selects the scenes of life, including home and school, with the background of the scenes of life in a day according to the time axis of normal work and rest in the time sequence of morning, noon and night. In this background, different function modules are integrated to teach the knowledge. For example, three contents of getting up, tooth brushing, and eating breakfast are arranged in the home scene in the morning. These three modules are daily behavioral learning integrated with cognitive training. In the school scene at noon, two interactive game modules are designed. The first game is a game of seeking food by rotating the animal's eyes. For example, by rotating the eyeball of a rabbit, the autistic children can choose the correct indication direction and select the target food. The design not only trains the attention by interactive design but also learns the favorite food of animals by cognitive training. The second game is a game of tangram. The design purpose is to train the children's ability to recognize and judge different shapes on the one hand and training their thinking ability by combination exercises on the other hand. They learn knowledge in the recreation by interactive games. The third scene is home at night, and the learning content of the module is taking a bath and sleeping. The return of this module is not only knowledge learning but also the cognition of the law of life.

Software system structural design and function module design are inseparable combinations. Function module is the core and foundation of study. And system design is based on the design of function module. System structural design better integrates the function modules that are scattered before. For example, in this software, the development sequence of a day is the main axis of software design. Everyone experiences the process from sunrise to sunset. This law of life makes every study module nature. The introduction of three scenes also provides the function of master navigation. By slightly sliding the design of a rotating dynamic impeller, the selection of three master scenes can be realized. If one wants to enter a module of a certain scene to study, it only requires clicking the gate. By the overall design of this process, the hierarchy is clearer and the goal directness of study is more definite. As the software aims at the use of autistic children, the process should be as standards as possible, and the difficulty in operation and selection should be reduced as much as possible. The design of a clear function flow chart (Fig. 2) is an important link.

188   J. Tian

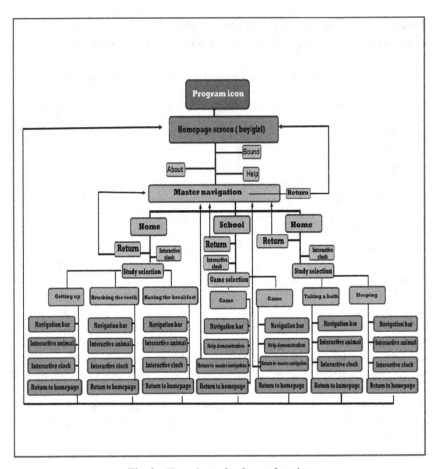

Fig. 2. Flow chart of software function

3.2 Visual Design and Interactive Design

The software "A Sunny Day" is developed aiming at the iPad platform. The reason for choosing this platform other than the platform of mobile phone use is that the comparatively big screen size of iPad provides a clear vision so that it is more convenient in detail interaction, so as to better complete the design tasks of the software.

After the software solves the problem of flow and framework design, attention should be paid to visual design and interactive design in the next step. Visual design includes interface design (Fig. 3), icon design (Fig. 4), homepage design (Fig. 5) and other aspects. It is required to consider the particularity of autistic children's use in many design details. For example, in the aspect of color design, on the one hand, efforts should be made to select bright and pure colors with a high lightness that autistic children like; on the other hand, in the aspect of color matching design, it is not recommended to be complicated, and the disordered color matching should be avoided to divert the attention. In the aspect of interactive design, on the one hand, interactive actions should be simple and easy to

Fig. 3. Interface design

operate; on the other hand, the importance of order should be emphasized according to the study of autistic children, and the buttons should be designed in the irreversible sequence of straight development in the aspect of learning steps. In the design of learning sequence on the navigation bar, the study can only proceed in the correct sequence. Only after an action is correctly done can the next action proceeds. This design is a teaching method commonly used in the teaching of autism rehabilitation centers. The purpose is to reinforce autistic children's cognition of steps. Moreover, in the study of an action, the process steps are more detailed than normal people to be suitable for the cognitive level of autistic children. It is also required to design control buttons for parents in the software interface, such as return, repeated practice, and review. The interactive design of some details should also be paid attention to. For example, on the learning page, in order to attract the learning interest of the children, a pet image is designed at the page corner, such as dog and giraffe. By clicking these animals, animal sound and animation effects are provided to reinforce the children's learning interests and attraction.

Fig. 4. Icon design

Except for visual and interactive design, the cooperation of multimedia effects, such as sound and animation, is also important. For example, at the home screen after opening the application, users will hear children's hearty laughter. In this friendly laughter, users select the role. After entering the learning page, after simulated sound and basic sound effects, there will be animation and the sound of encouragement after the completion of every behavior, to provide the children with a sense of achievement by the sound.

In addition to the special design aiming at autistic children, some detail problems should also be taken into consideration, such as whether relatively older parents can successfully use the software, the problem of collecting training data generated by the software, whether the software opens social functions, and whether the software is an open free version and a paid version.

Fig. 5. Page design

3.3 Software Test and Return Visit

After the software design, some relevant use tests and return visits are required. The shortcomings of the software and users' demands can be learned by return visits and tests. For example, the software "A Sunny Day" acquires many improvement suggestions and information in the user return visit:

[a] The learning contents are few at present and can be richer, and it is expected to introduce more professional courses to the software.
[b] The effect of screen teaching is not as direct as the teaching by physical articles, and the effect of real video demonstration can be added except for picture teaching.
[c] It is expected that the software can make use of the internet platform to develop more interactive content, share course experiences, and establish communication patterns. All of these can be realized in software upgrading.

4 Conclusions

Under the rapid development of internet digital era at present, the progress of technology is more and more applied in the education field, and the application software based on mobile terminal platforms is necessary for the assistant study of autistic children's education, and the education of families with autism. By the interactive functions and multimedia features of intelligent devices, the children can learn knowledge while playing and relax their minds in a happy mood. It is helpful for the cognition and behavioral intervention of autistic children. Assistant education applications for autistic children should be designed according to the characteristics of autistic children. It is foreseeable that assistant teaching based on intelligent devices and mobile platforms will be more and more widely applied in the assistant education of autistic children.

References

1. Lu, M., Zhang, W.: Current situation of application and inspiration of iPad in the education of autistic patients in the US. e-Educ. Res. **8**, 122–128 (2017)
2. Wucailu Child Behavior Modification Center: Report on Chinese Autistic Children's Development and Current Situation: China Autism Education and Recovery Industry Development Report. Beijing Normal University Publishing House, Beijing (2015)
3. Zhou, Y., Song, F.: Cognitive training APP for autistic children based on applied behavior analysis. Packag. Eng. **04**, 132–139 (2018)

A Virtual Reality Scaffolding Prototype for College Students Self-directed Learning in STEAM

Jun Xu[1,2]([✉]), Jinlei Weng[1], Ye Xu[1], and Yuling Xin[1]

[1] Nanjing Vocational College of Information Technology, Nanjing, People's Republic of China
xujun@njcit.cn
[2] School of Education, Universiti Teknologi Malaysia, Johor Bahru, Malaysia

Abstract. Self-directed learning (SDL) is an effective method to model the core technology for STEAM college students. However, STEAM includes immersion technologies and many fields, and learning usually crosses semesters, which is difficult for students to construct personal skill models. The VR scaffold developed based on SDL theory, hints, and expert modeling visualization help students construct their core technical models. The prototype is editable and sets up tasks and levels in a gamified way, and finally shows the learning results.

Keywords: VR Scaffold · Self-directed Learning

1 Introduction

STEAM has extended from K-12 education to higher education. In addition to engineering technology, it also includes business, design, etc. STEAM has appeared discipline integration specialty in higher education. Innovation, integration, and production have become prominent characteristics (Innella and Rodgers 2017). In the context of integration and intersection, STEAM includes wide and complex learning content, and the learning activities are separated into multiple semesters.

Self-directed learning (SDL) is an autonomous learning model with students' self-driving and self-management as the core. It usually completes learning activities with the help of peers or instructors. In the learning process, students independently evaluate their learning needs, find their learning materials, formulate learning plans, select and implement learning methods and strategies, and reflect and evaluate their learning outcomes. There are four general characters in SDL models. Learners tend to self-realization and learning responsibility; learners are the main managers and monitors of the learning process; learners at different stages have different levels of autonomous learning; the subject of learning is the learner.

Self-management and monitoring are not only important features of self-directed learning but also the key link for learners to complete self-learning. For a long time, the difficulty of self-management and self-monitoring lies in the lack of visualization and unclear key nodes.

The Virtual Reality (VR) scaffolding prototype developed according to the SDL theory visualizes the hints and expert technology model, which help students independently complete the modeling of core technology learning according to the STEAM

N. A. Streitz and S. Konomi (Eds.): HCII 2022, LNCS 13326, pp. 193–204, 2022.
https://doi.org/10.1007/978-3-031-05431-0_14

syllabus while learning (Andrea Bravo and Cash 2021). The prototype sets the tasks and levels of the syllabus gamification so that learners can model their learning in the open open-source environment and finally display the learning results.

2 Background

2.1 Related Work

The popularity of VR has opened up opportunities for more educators to understand its educational advantages. Although VR environments with avatar personifications have been used quite effectively when designing games for recreation and education (Squire and Jenkins 2003), the education research on more open-ended, higher education-focused applications is less developed. Younger individuals, based on their prior virtual experiences, will be more motivated to participate in virtual settings because of the remote video teaching. A VR environment is merely the background for what can be a rich, interactive experience. McManimon (Mok et al. 2001) purports how virtual environments, when used with constructive principles, can support pedagogically sound activities, such as situated learning, role-playing, cooperative/collaborative learning, problem-based learning, and creative learning. From the perspective of constructivism, self-directed learning is the unification of internal processes and external process.

With the development of modern information technology, the research on self-directed learning has paid more and more attention to the application of information technology. The concept of a self-learning circle under network conditions with online self-learning is closely related to cognition, control, commitment, and content (Yen 2005). A self-directed learning model was developed using online education (Badilova 2018). And right now, VR/AR is being treated as a tool for self-directed Learning (Gregor Rozinaj et al. 2018) focuses on game-based virtual reality in education. As an example, a game-based VR application describing the functionality of the "Firewall" application is discussed.

2.2 Foundations for VR Scaffolding

Between the real level of development and the potential level of development, there exists a zone of proximal development. This zone can be regarded as an area where scaffolds are needed to promote learning.

There are three properties of the scaffold: 1) The scaffold is a temporary support for the learner to ensure the success of a learning activity; 2) The scaffold is extensible and can be offered through interactions between the learner and the learning environment. 3) The scaffold should be removed in time after the learner can accomplish the learning task independently.

While a single scaffolding strategy is not enough for a wide variety of learners, here are six scaffolding strategies to mix and match. The six strategies are, 1) Show and tell, 2) Tap into prior knowledge, 3) Give time to talk, 4) Pre-teach vocabulary, 5) Use visual AIDS, 6) Pause, ask questions, pause, review.

As mentioned in point 5 above, visual AIDS help students visually represent their ideas, organize information, and grasp concepts such as sequencing and cause and effect.

The application of virtual reality in education is a leap forward in the development of educational technology. It creates an environment of "self-directed learning", replacing the traditional learning mode of "teaching to promote learning" with a new learning mode in modelch learners acquire knowledge and skills through the interaction between themselves and the information environment. In a sense, VR scaffolding can play the role of visual teaching AIDS well. In this research, VR scaffolding is used to help students construct their core technical models. To this end, the interactive 3D content production tool Creator is introductory to visualize the draft.

2.3   SDL Elements for Immerse Technology College Student

Many studies provide evidence that learners need to immerse themselves in authentic learning environments and gain expertise through participation.

Immersive technologies can greatly help educators implement pedagogical approaches that are aligned with the situated-constructive learning theories. Well-designed simulations and games provide immersive environments with appropriate tools, content, feedback, and scaffolds.

Educational games and simulations can also provide pedagogical contexts. For example, SimCity, is one of the best-known and most commercially successful simulation games and has established the genre of city builder games. Its use as a planning tool has been discussed from the first release (Arnold 2019). The use of SimCity for planning can also be expanded to specific planning disciplines such as water infrastructure, urban planning, Geographical Information systems. The VR scaffolding prototype in this paper helps students build their technology prototype across disciplines and semesters through gamification.

Learning from the success computer gaming achieves with the young generations, the principles of gamification can be applied to educational applications, too, to boost engagement and enhance the learning process. Moreover, an educational application can be easily included in novel learning paradigms, like self-directed learning.

Self-directed learning means allowing students to manage their own in the educational process, maybe be successfully applied to all levels of education. For self-directed learning, the following benefits may be listed, 1) Increased interest in learning through student's active participation, 2) Raised awareness of learning styles and which learning styles work best, 3) Obtaining additional, workplace-required skills, such as problem-solving, planning and decision making, 4) Boost appreciation of learning, 5) Improve motivation, satisfaction, and academic achievement.

Several limitations may be identified for self-directed learning that has to be challenged, 1) Shift and limitation of educational focus from learning towards preparing and passing the examination, 2) Heavy teacher workload, requiring individual approach teach student, 3) Difficulty of adjusting the learning modules or creating new ones.

The VR scaffolding constructed by immersive technologies represented by virtual reality can avoid limitations 2 and 3 to a certain extent. VR scaffolding help college students build technology prototypes that belong to them. Everyone's archetypes are different, but the way they are constructed leads to similar patterns that can lighten the workload of educators. The creator is the visual programming software. Its feature is that scenes are easy to delete and add. Therefore, it is not difficult to adjust the learning module corresponding to the scene.

3   From Program Syllabus to Students Skills Models

3.1   Higher Education in STEAM

STEAM education originated in the United States and has gone through the three stages of STS, STEM, and STEAM. Its fundamental purpose is to enhance college students' ability to integrate scientific disciplines, provide comprehensive talents for scientific and technological undertakings.

Innovation, integration, and make are the three philosophical views of STEAM courses. The important meaning of making lies in the integration of knowledge and practice. Through STEAM learning, students can connect the knowledge they have learned in and out of class with the real world, making it easier to find STEAM-related careers and opportunities (Zaher and Hussain 2020). The STEAM curriculum is conducive to cultivating artistic design, creative abilities, problem-solving, flexible thinking, and courage to assume responsibility in the process of artistic creation.

STEAM is interdisciplinary and interesting, experiential, contextual, collaborative, artistic, empirical, and technological enhancement. Recently, it has been extended from K-12 education to higher education, which adds computer science, computational thinking, investigation and research, creation and innovation, global communication, collaboration, and other emerging knowledge (Belland et al. 2017). This is aimed at maximizing the benefits of STEAM courses and striving to pursue the individual, society, and the whole of mankind a happy attempt has a distinct utilitarian color.

In China, STEAM education research started late, and related research did not appear until 2008. In 2018, the "China STEAM Education 2029 Innovation Action Plan" was launched. Focusing on STEAM education, different researchers have researched the aspects of the online teaching model, the establishment of teaching platforms, online courses, the development of learning projects, and the online teachers' training.

3.2   From STEAM Program Syllabub to Students Skills Models

The professional curriculum system constructs curriculum modules according to the educational goals and the student's graduation requirements. The curriculum modules are set according to the difficulty of knowledge and skills, and the students' understanding and mastering as well. They are open in different semesters. Taking immersion technology as an example, the teaching goal is to to the digital creative industry and train developers who both have the abilities to apply information technology and engage in the design and development of virtual reality, augmented reality, and mixed reality. From the curriculum aspect, it includes four modules: virtual reality programming, graphics and image technologies, digital video technologies, and project design. Table 1 shows the courses included in each of the four modules, such as (Table 1).

In VR programming module, it contents two U3D programming courses and one VR project course. In Interactive Design course, it gives a general and common interaction introduce and practice using software and hardware. In the graphic & image technology module, students learn to create 2D and 3D computer graphics which might be used in a VR environment. The third module, digital video technology includes the two parts, basic digital video technology, and visual programming. There have three courses in the

Table 1 Curriculum module.

Course module	VR programming	Graphic & ImaTechnology	Digital video technology	Project design
1	Basic U3D programming	Basic graphic	Technology	Creativity design
2	U3D 3D programming	Information graphic	Programming	Maker project
3	VR project	3D model & Animation		Senior project
4	Interactive design			

project design module, creative design, maker project, and senior project. All of these three are integrated and project-based.

According to the level of technical difficulties and the process of immersive project development, the courses in the four modules are separated into 5 semesters. Four colors represent the four modules above (Fig. 1).

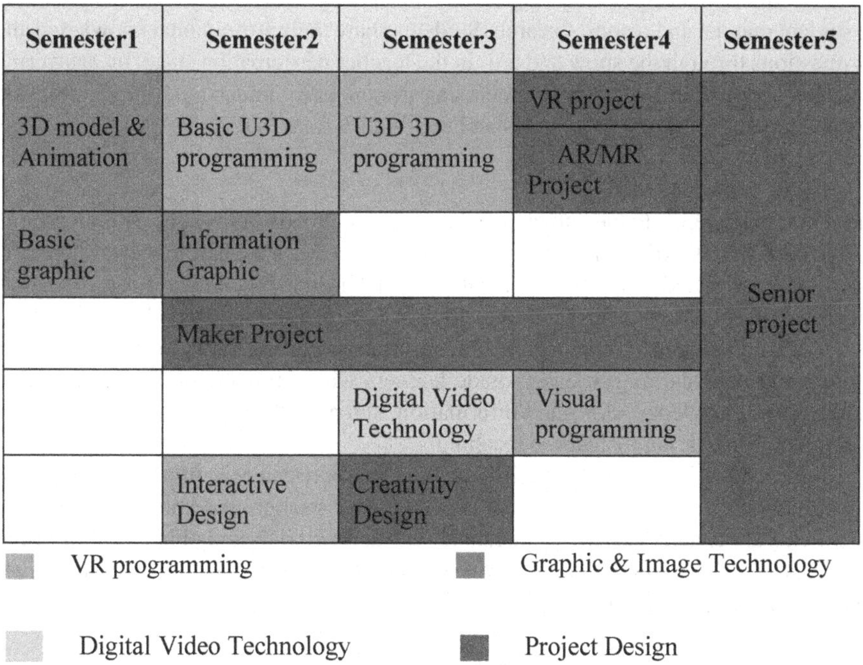

Semester1	Semester2	Semester3	Semester4	Semester5
3D model & Animation	Basic U3D programming	U3D 3D programming	VR project	Senior project
			AR/MR Project	
Basic graphic	Information Graphic			
	Maker Project			
		Digital Video Technology	Visual programming	
	Interactive Design	Creativity Design		

VR programming   Graphic & Image Technology

Digital Video Technology   Project Design

Fig. 1. Core courses in fours modules

4 VR Scaffolding Prototype Development

4.1 Five Steps of Scaffolding

According to the scaffolding instructional design and the notion of the zone of proximal development (ZPD) theory, instructors construct a conceptual framework that could interact between a 'more knowledgeable other' and an apprentice. The main function of scaffolding is training learners to be self- during the learning process and helping them exceed their previous abilities.

Three strategies could support learners learning progression, questions, prompts, and feedback (Mamun, et al. 2020). POE (predict, observe, explain) strategy has been considered a successful pedagogical model in both physical and virtual learning environments. In instructional design, the scaffolding was constructed between student-content, student-teacher, and student-student interaction.

Modeling for students is directed learners' key in scaffolding. In this paper, VR scaffolding was developed in 4 steps, show and tell among instructors and students, activate prior knowledge, transfer new technologies into personal learning outcomes and quizzes, share, and review.

1) Show and tell among instructors and students
In scaffolding education, learners are first required to understand the main modules of the core courses in the university stage and connect them with society and life by reading the student manual and resource search. Students share their professional knowledge and ask questions through the show and tell. In the teacher participation stage, by answering questions and asking questions, learners can more clearly understand the relationship between the above four skill modules and the final learning outcomes.

2) Activate prior knowledge
Prior knowledge refers to the knowledge that learners already know before new learning. It is the knowledge, skills, and literacy that learners already have before the new learning activities. It is related to learners' educational background, social and life experience. Prior knowledge is very important. It is the basis of new knowledge. Activating prior knowledge helps students understand the connection and relations between previous learning and new learning. It can provide learners with a framework for better understanding new knowledge, skills and information, and provide instructors with formative assessment information to adapt to teaching.

This process helps students establish a connection between new information and what they already know. Students who already know some background knowledge know in many fields are usually easier to understand relevant materials and obtain new information. They usually predict what they will encounter in learning and connect these new ideas with their existing knowledge.

3) Transfer new technologies into personal learning outcomes and quiz
In this research, learners have understated the four technologies modules in this period, we integrated gamification into prototype development. Gamification refers to the use of game elements in a non-game environment to increase the interaction between people

and computers and effectively solve problems. Gamifithe cation of the learning process can be considered as the use of game fragments to motivate learners, which involves the use of game-based mechanisms, aesthetics, and game thinking to attract learners, stimulate action, promote learning and solve problems. Gamification is an integral part of scaffolding because its main goal is to improve user efficiency and understanding through interesting and pleasant learning, it can ensure the effectiveness of its usage in a learning environment.

When the learners set game stages, they matched technologies they had learned and game elements based on learning outcomes. The most commonly used elements of the game were badges and points systems. The learning environment can also support these and allow the teacher to select appropriate scaffolding learning tools based on the game-like elements in the game to promote certain desired behaviors.

Based on students' preferences, a gamification prototype was developed. Gamified archetypes have five attributes. The first attribute is called "stage" and it is assigned based on elements from the basic courses. The second attribute is called "level." This attribute has four elements for each concept or sub-concept, including a concept layer, an explanation layer that explains how to use the concept, and an exercise layer that provides more examples for each concept to enhance students' understanding. The third property is the timing system. The fourth attribute called "display" calculates the total score for all the questions. Based on the total points accumulated, each student at the presentation step will receive a badge based on the total points and ranking to be displayed on the leaderboard. The final attribute called "report" shows the overall learning progress report for each student and describes whether the student will continue to the next level, while also showing the student's progress in the form of a graphical graph.

In this paper, the VR scaffolding prototype has three stages and contented five key skills that immerse technology students need to learn.

4) Share and review
Share and revies an effective way to check whether students understand new technologies. Usually, questions are prepared in advance to ensure that students are open-minded. Students discuss what they have learned, what they have found, or what problems they have mentioned. Students can actively participate. This paper creates a VR scaffolding prototype, which supports students sharing their prototype source documents in learning groups. Students could review their learning in and after learning.

4.2 Tools and Implementation

In this paper, researchers use a VR software, Creator to develop a scaffolding for immerse technology college students learning. Creator a codeless virtual reality editor that can integrate multiple elements such as 2D/3Dpictures, panoramic pictures, videos, 3D models, and sounds. It supports publishing on multiple hardware platforms, for example, VR glasses, mobile phones, and computers. This research transferred four curriculum modules into a VR scaffolding prototype with gamification elements. Take a student project of A college, for example, students created a virtual reality garden based on their campus environment. In Chinese culture, because schools are places to cultivate people, they are often metaphorically compared to gardens, Teachers are likened to gardeners, and students are generally likened to flowers. In the VR garden, students were likened to a sunflower, they set three stages for every two semesters. In each stage, they developed 3 to 5 quizzes according to the courses they learned and the courses' outcomes. After the lunch the program and answer correctly, they got water, sunlight, and nutrient, and the sunflower would grow up.

Students constructed a flowchart at first. A flowchart is used to show the operation process to achieve a certain goal, the sequence of user steps required visually. It also needs to connect the relationships between the various stages. The student's project, included the main three stages, "if...else" conditions, key skills students need to masted in stages (Fig. 2).

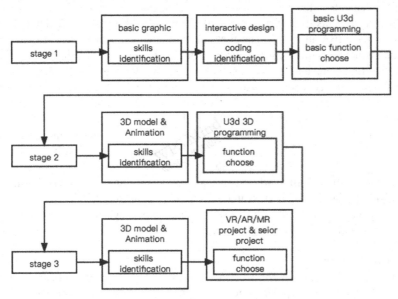

Fig. 2. Flowchart 1

In stage one, students separated graphic & image technology modules courses, basic graphic and 3D models into a quiz, which were skills identification (Fig. 3), tools in software identification (Fig. 4), functions chosen in some programming (Fig. 5). Students will award "soil" when they answered all questions correctly (Fig. 6). Stage two corresponds to students' 2rd-year learning. The type of quizzes is more diverse, which includes analyzing students' assignments and identifying tools and skills, functions choose and operate choose. All these quizzes contain digital video technology, VR programming, and project design modules courses (Fig. 7). Stage three are contained all project-based courses, for example, VR/AR/MR project, senior project. Skills identification and function choice are the main types of quizzes.

Fig. 3. Quiz1 in stage one

Fig. 4. Quiz2 in stage one

Fig. 5. Quiz3 in stage one

Fig. 6. Pic 5. Award "soil"

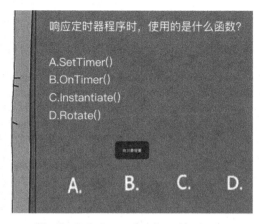

Fig. 7. Quiz in a project-based course

5 Discussion

In this study, we answered the research question of how to build VR scaffolding based on technical modeling for college students in STEAM. We interview technical learners and prototype developers at the same time. The interviewee is a second-year student in a VR major. She developed a game with three levels by learning the study manual and the three-semester courses she has studied. The interviewee reflected on her past learning experience. She was engaged in the various interactive cases and had a strong willingness to participate, she also expressed a strong willingness to learn AR technology courses next semester.

So far, we have not started experimental research with a sufficient number of learners' samples, the changes in self-monitoring and management abilities in the self-directed learning elements have not been obtained yet.

6 Conclusion and Future Directions

This study set out to combine scaffolding strategies and a self-built VR prototype, aiming at the difficulty of constructing a personal technical model for college students in STEAM. The paper took the virtual reality program as an example, sorted it out, and constructed a technology framework based on the curriculum syllabubs. The study proposed the five-step scaffolding development method in the prototype development, set hints and expert mode in the gamified prototype, set game levels according to the technical framework and rules. The hardware and software tools included pictures, video editing equipment, and rich media editors.

In the later stage, learners will use the VR scaffolding prototype to model their learning process and results according to the technology framework, and carry out teaching experiments, interviews, and works analyses.

Acknowledgement. Sponsor by: Teaching Innovation Team Project of NJCIT (2020–2022); Joint studio of Chinese and foreign Experts Project (2021).

References

Andrea Bravo, A.M.M., Cash, P.J.: Watch that Seam! Designing Hybrid Presentations with Data Visualisation in Augmented Reality (2021)

Arnold, U., et al.: SimCity in infrastructure management education. Educ. Sci. **9**(3), 209 (2019)

Belland, B.R., et al.: Synthesizing results from empirical research on computer-based scaffolding in STEM education: a meta-analysis. Rev. Educ. Res. **87**(2), 309–344 (2017)

Gregor Rozinaj, M.V., Vargic, R., Minárik, I., Polakovič, A.: Augmented virtual reality as a tool of self-directed learning. In: 2014 IEEE 12th International Conference on Emerging eLearning Technologies and Applications (ICETA) (2018)

Innella, G., Rodgers, P.A.: Making sense: harnessing communication through prototyping. Des. J. **20**(sup1), S1154–S1166 (2017)

Mamun, M.A.A., et al.: Instructional design of scaffolded online learning modules for self-directed and inquiry-based learning environments. Comput. Educ. **144**, 103695 (2020)

Miriam Badilova, G.R.: Virtual-reality-in-on-line-education. In: 12th International Workshop on Multimedia Information and Communication Technologies (2018)

Mok, M.C., Cheong Cheng, Y.: A theory of self-learning in a networked human and IT environment: implications for education reforms. Int. J. Educ. Manag. **15**(4), 172–186 (2001)

Yen, S.-H., et al.: Scaffolding-for-activity-supervision-and-self-regulation-in-virtual-university. Tamkang. J. Sci. Eng. **8**, 133–146 (2005)

Zaher, A.A., Hussain, G.A.: STEAM-based active learning approach to selected topics in electrical/computer engineering. In: 2020 IEEE Global Engineering Education Conference (EDUCON), pp. 1752–1757 (2020)

MusicCollage: A Music Composition Tool for Children Based on Synesthesia and a Genetic Algorithm

Ge Yan[1], Cheng Yao[2(✉)], Chao Zhang[1], Jiadi Wang[1], Yuqi Hu[3], and Fangtian Ying[4]

[1] College of Software Technology, Zhejiang University, Hangzhou, China
{yange,zhangchaodesign,wjd1024}@zju.edu.cn
[2] College of Computer Science and Technology, Zhejiang University, Hangzhou, China
yaoch@zju.edu.cn
[3] International School of Design, Zhejiang University, Ningbo, China
yuqihu@nit.zju.edu.cn
[4] College of Design, Hubei University of Technology, Wuhan, Hubei, China

Abstract. Creating music can be challenging for children aged 4–6. Making the creation procedure more interesting has been proved to stimulate and build children's interests in music. Based on the design concept of synesthesia from vision to hearing, we propose an application by which children aged 4–6 can create collages by matching different images of scenes and animals. The information contained in the created collages is then used as input parameters for generating music so as to create melodies corresponding to the collages. To evaluate our approach, we conducted a quantitative and qualitative user study with children (n = 6) by using our initial prototype. We concluded that the proposed application helps cultivate children's willingness to create melodies, and helps children better perceive and understand music by combining scenes and animal images in the collages.

Keywords: Synesthesia · Music creation · Children · Collage · Genetic algorithm

1 Introduction

The benefits of a quality music education are immense. Interaction with music is important for the development of young children. Exposure to music from childhood onward can help children speak more clearly, develop a larger vocabulary, and strengthen their social and emotional skills [1]. Musical skills can also give people, both children and adults, joy during their lives. There are also indications that musical development helps children with their overall development [2]. This is why an effort must be made to try to stimulate children's interest in music composition.

Music creation requires a certain knowledge of music theory as a background, which is a great challenge for children. However, schools and parents lack the appropriate music education for children. Music education in many public school jurisdictions has been downgraded to insignificant or non-existent because of the expense [3]. In addition,

N. A. Streitz and S. Konomi (Eds.): HCII 2022, LNCS 13326, pp. 205–216, 2022.
https://doi.org/10.1007/978-3-031-05431-0_15

children are less likely to be encouraged in this direction if their parents did not benefit from a quality music education. For these reasons, we established a design principle to simplify music-making to make it easier for children to participate in music creation and enjoyment.

There have been previous studies on designing children's music creation tools. LEGO Bricks [4] was found to provide a physical and social interaction environment for young children. Amal Tidjani [5] designed MuSme, a tangible skin suit that uses different parts of the body as metaphors for different musical instruments. The interactive software designed by Yin Ling [6] takes synesthesia into account, which refers to the establishment of the correspondence of color and shape (e.g., circle, line, and square) to a music scale and note, but this refers to a color or shape corresponding to a single note or scale, without the correspondence of the whole picture. It is difficult to complete a melody by only relying on a combination of notes for children.

With the help of synesthesia, children can better perceive music. In addition, the technology of artificial intelligence (AI) lowers the threshold of creation, making the process easier [7]. According to this idea, we developed a web application based on Brower/Server (B/S) architecture. Children can use the application by accessing a browser. Children can create a complete picture by selecting different scenes, matching different kinds of animals, and adjusting the placement of those animals. The information in the collage will then be used as input parameters of the music generation algorithm to ultimately create unique melodies based on a genetic algorithm.

Before using the application, one of the researchers gave the children a brief introduction to it and a demonstration of the process. Six children aged 4–6 completed at least one collage with this application in 20 min. After confirming that the collage did not need to be modified, the corresponding melody could be played. At the end of the experiment, we asked the children to submit the questionnaires and describe their feelings about using the application. Finally, we talked to parents who had observed the whole experiment and recorded their thoughts.

The main contributions of this paper are:

- We designed a synesthesia-based strategy by matching different scenes and animals to cultivate the interest of 4–6-year-old children in creating music and improve their perception of music.
- We developed a web application based on B/S Architecture, whereby children can create their own pictures and corresponding unique music by selecting different scenes and animals and adjusting the placement of animals.
- Using quantitative and qualitative methods, we conducted user studies to verify the effectiveness of using this application to cultivate children's interest in music creation and improve their ability to perceive music.

2   Related Work

2.1   Children's Music Education and Creation

Musical education has a positive impact on children's intelligence, creativity, and memory [8, 9]. Many studies on musical education for children have been conducted to help them grow and develop. Ian McKinnon [3] outlined the development of an interactive software program called "Children's Music Journey" to deliver affordable and pedagogically rigorous music education to children everywhere, and as a result, improve attitudes toward learning and promote better behavior in school. Leyi Ouyang's research [10] proved that tangible designs have great potential in engaging young children in early music learning concepts, such as rhythm, pitch, dynamics, and expression; they provide an environment for young children to interact physically and socially, which in turn arouses their curiosity and sense of fantasy. Steve Altieri [11] produced an interactive tool called "keyboard" for students and gives them an opportunity to "play around with music." Yin Ling [6] designed an interactive visual music education software that integrates scales, intervals, and harmonies. The product enables children to increase their musical knowledge and develop their musical perception and understanding. These rich forms of interaction stimulate children's interest and make music easily accessible to them.

The creative process enables children to better understand and learn about music. Children composing music without a threshold can make them appreciate the joy of music more. TempoString [12] is an easy-to-use tool that assists children with music creation. It provides a fun and novel platform by allowing children to "draw" music on a canvas. Amal Tidjani [5] proposed MuSme, a tangible skin suit that reimagines a user's limbs and organs as metaphoric representations of different instruments. Jane Rigler [13] designed Cre8tor, an interactive music composition system controlled by motion sensors that allows children to create music while playing. Uwe Oestermeier [4] presented a multi-touch tabletop application that utilizes LEGO bricks as physical representations for musical notes to create a novel digital learning environment for musical composition principles. PlaceAndPlay [14] presented a new design of a digital music authoring tool for children. It incorporates multimodal interaction techniques, including voice-based synthesis of instruments and sound effects, to assist younger users who do not play musical instruments or do not have knowledge of sound effects. The above research demonstrated the wonderful integration between children and music creation, and it inspired us to design a platform for children that is fun, accessible, and allows them to create music while playing.

2.2 Synesthesia of Sound and Image

People's senses are closely interconnected, and visual and auditory experiences are often associated with each other. Many researchers have conducted interesting research on the synesthesia of sound and image. Current research has indicated that the application of synesthesia can effectively improve the user experience. Michael Voong's research [15] indicated that there is a reasonable degree of consistency between users' associations of color and music, and that an indirect descriptor can aid in the recall of music via mood. Siyu Jin [16] designed an interactive work where users select music and images as the main interactive contents, and the parameters of the music are used as the dynamic expression of human emotions. The new pixel generation process of the image is regarded as the result of emotions affecting humans. Vegas [17] explored the interactive potential through live performances and the space for aesthetic expression by synthesizing the audio and the visuals. This project related to the genre of visual music and abstraction in the arts and created a synesthetic experience for the audience. Dimitris Kritikos [18] developed a deterministic process to produce a melody after processing a painting, mimicking the production of notes from colors in the field of view of persons experiencing synesthesia.

Motivated by synesthesia design, we imagined that correlating colors and sounds would enable children to create images in a form that intuitively generates music of the same emotion.

2.3 AI Music Creation

AI has great potential in the field of music creation, made possible by advances in machine learning and algorithms that allow people without expertise to lower the threshold of creation and be inspired with the assistance of AI [7]. Emma Frid [19] presented a user interface paradigm that allows users to input a song to an AI engine and then interactively regenerate and mix AI-generated music. This solution makes music generation easily and understandable. Ryan Louie [20] found that AI-steering tools not only enabled users to better express musical intent, but they also had an important effect on users' creative ownership and self-efficacy vis-a-vis AI. Cong Ning [21] designed a musical tabletop application that enables both novice and musically trained users to compose and play music in a creative and intuitive way. This tangible musical interface supports finger operations and aims to lower the barriers to composing music in order to enrich the music-playing experience. These studies demonstrated the power of AI in the field of music creation. We hope that with the assistance of AI, the creative process for children will become easier, and the content they create will be richer.

3 MusicCollage

3.1 User Flow

The whole process of interacting with MusicCollage is divided into the following steps. First, children choose their favorite scenes, which is important, as it establishes the style of the whole melody. Then, children can choose the animals they want to appear in the collage and can drag the animal images in the selector to the positions. During this process, the positions of the images can be adjusted. To delete an animal that was dragged onto the screen last time, children simply need to click the undo button on the screen. Children can also click the reset button if they want to remove all of the animals. After that, they can continue adding animals. Finally, after confirming the scene and animals, children can play the melody created with the picture information as the input. Both the collages and the generated melodies will be saved on the server (Fig. 1).

3.2 System Design

MusicCollage consists of two main parts: one is a picture generation module, and the other is a music generation module.

Picture generation module: The homepage of the application contains a scene selector, an animal selector, and a canvas (Fig. 2). By clicking the start button in the center of

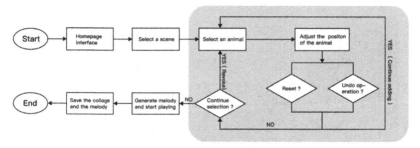

Fig. 1. Workflow of MusicCollage

the canvas, the child can begin the journey of creating the collage. Afterward, children can start using a scene selector and an animal selector. The background of the canvas is temporarily set to the first background of the scene selector by default. Children can drag the images of the scene selector horizontally to view various scenes. The scene selector can be dragged horizontally to view various scenes. After clicking on the desired scene, the background of the canvas will be replaced by the selected scene. The animal selector allows children to view animal images by dragging them vertically. After choosing the animal, children can click on and drag the desired animal into the screen. The scene selector contains eight scenes, and different scenes have different picture styles. Similarly, the animal selector includes 17 animals, including elephants, hippos, raccoons, monkeys, and rabbits. As shown in Fig. 3, children can click the reset button or undo button to complete the removal of all of the animals or the last one, respectively. If the child is satisfied with the collage, they can enjoy the music after clicking the play button.

Fig. 2. The homepage interface includes the (a) canvas, (b) scene selector, (c) animal selector, and (d) start button.

Fig. 3. The user interface includes the (a) undo button, (b) reset button, and (c) play button.

Music generation module: We considered the following two goals: 1. Ensure consistency and correlation between the information in the picture and the input parameters in the music generation algorithm. Consistency refers to the exact same picture, and the corresponding algorithm input parameters should also be consistent. Correlation means that the correspondence between the picture information and input parameters should be reasonable and in line with people's understanding and cognition. 2. We should focus on cultivating children's interest in creating music so that the melody created by children is unique. Specifically, even identical drawings with exactly the same input parameters should not produce exactly the same music. For these reasons, we chose to use an open-source genetic-algorithm-based music generation algorithm [22]. It contains a total of 10 input parameters (Table 1).

Table 1. Input parameter of the algorithm

Name	Description
Number of bars	Length of the generated melody in bars
Notes per bar	Number of notes inside of a bar
Number of steps	Number of pitches per note
Introduce pauses	Should the algorithm introduce pauses between notes or do you want a constant stream of notes?
Key	Key of the scale the melody should fit in
Scale	Type of scale the melody should fit in
Scale root	Pitch of the scale (ex.: 4 means C4 is the root note of a scale in C)
Population size	Number of melodies per generation to rate and recombine
Number of mutations	Max number of mutations that should be possible per child generated
Mutation probability	Probability that a mutation will occur

3.3 Synesthesia in Design

We used the total number of animals as the parameter Number of bars. Then, we used the distance between the leftmost horizontal axis coordinate and the rightmost horizontal axis coordinate divided by the value of the total number of animals to map the parameter Notes per bar. Specifically, the more animals there are, or the smaller the distance between the animals in the left-most and right-most positions, the smaller the parameter. Next, we used the mean value of the vertical axis coordinate center to map the parameter Number of steps. As for the parameter Key, we represented it by the rounded average value of the corresponding value of animals (Table 2). For example, when the average value of all of the animals is 9.6, the input parameter Key of the algorithm will be Gb. How these numbers correspond depends on whether the animal is more likely to be perceived as deep and big or cheerful and flexible. Parameter Scale is one of the following: major, minorM, Dorian, Phrygian, Lydian, mixolydian, major blues, and minorBlues. Each type of input corresponds to a scene (Fig. 4). As for the parameter Introduce pauses, we chose the default parameter true as suggested by the algorithm because it is more in line with the rules of music creation. We also chose the default parameter 4 when coming to the parameter Scale Root. Finally, when it came to the input parameters of the genetic algorithm itself, including Population Size, Number of mutations, and Mutation probability, we still selected the default parameter after trying several input parameters.

Table 2. Value of parameter key and animal

Value	Key	Animal	Value	Key	Animal
1	C	elephant	10	Gb	sheep
2	C#	hippopotamus	11	G	fox
3	Db	crocodile	12	G#	dog
4	D	bear	13	Ab	raccoon
5	D#	lion	14	A	hedgehog
6	Eb	tiger	15	A#	monkey
7	E	panda	16	Bb	rabbit
8	F	giraffe	17	B	mouse
9	F#	donkey			

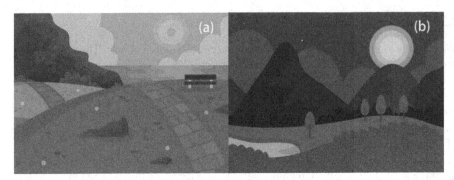

Fig. 4. (a) The scene that corresponds to "major;" (b) the scene that corresponds to "minorBlues."

4 Evaluation

4.1 Participants

We recruited six children to participate in our experiment. They ranged in age from 4 to 6 years (M = 5.0, SD = 0.58). Three were boys, and three were girls. Six parents were also invited to observe our experiment.

4.2 Procedure

Before the experiment, a letter was sent to the children's parents informing them of the study and asking for their consent.

Children were given a 10-min introduction to the application's functions and general structure, followed by a five-minute demonstration of how the system works, including how to build pictures and how to play music.

They were then given 20 min to create their own favorite drawing using the scene selector and animal selector. They could change scenes at will, add or remove animals, and adjust the placement of animals. After the final confirmation of the picture, the music was played (Fig. 5). In the whole process, children could create more than one picture, resulting in more than one piece of music.

After the experiment, the children were asked to fill out a questionnaire for a quantitative study. Each child was then asked to describe how they felt about using the application. We also conducted semi-structured interviews of about 10 min each with parents who had observed the process.

Each child participating in the experiment and each parent interviewed received a gift worth $10 for participating. In addition, the researchers gave the children pictures and music generated by the server.

4.3 Measurements

The questionnaire for children consisted of the four questions that follow. We used a Likert scale and asked the children to rate each question on a scale of one to five. Five means strongly agree while one means strongly disagree.

Q1: Do you think it is fun to write melodies this way?
Q2: Would you like to use this application often to create melodies?
Q3: Is the feeling you get from the pictures similar to the feeling you get from the melodies?
Q4: Can you use the application to create the melody you want to hear?
The questions asked during the semi-structured interviews were as follows:

- Do you think our system helps children understand music?
- What do you think can be improved about our application?
- Would you be willing to let your child use it for a long time?

Fig. 5. Children interacting with MusicCollage in the experiment.

5 Result

5.1 Quantitative Analysis

Q1 and Q2 from the questionnaire are related to cultivating children's interest in music creation, and Q3 and Q4 are related to enhancing children's musical perception. Through the feedback of the questionnaire, we found that children still showed high interest in using this application. Moreover, the children showed a high degree of agreement that different music could be created through the application.

In the end, we obtained a moderate score on the question of whether the application could create the music children wanted. This may have stemmed from the fact that some children do not fully understand synesthesia from sight to hearing. Another reason is that there is room for improvement and iteration in the algorithms that generate music (Fig. 6).

Answers

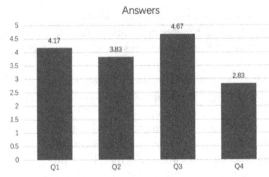

Fig. 6. Average of the answers children gave for the following questions after interacting with MusicCollage: Q1: Do you think it is fun to write melodies this way? Q2: Would you like to use this application often to create melodies? Q3: Is the feeling you get from the pictures similar to the feeling you get from the melodies? Q4: Can you use the application to create the melody you want to hear? (measured by Likert scale on a scale of one to five and five means strongly agree while one means strongly disagree)

5.2 Qualitative Analysis

Children generally believed that the application was interesting. Four children tried to create music many times during the experiment, and C2 even created it 12 times. C1, C2, C3, and C5 told us that they liked the pictures they created and were also satisfied with the music they created. It is worth mentioning that C5 told us that he would like his kindergarten teachers to experience the application.

In the interview with parents, P1 mentioned that her child was obviously excited when using the application. P2 told us that he thought the application was interesting, and felt the effect of the generated music was better than he expected. P3 asked whether children could be allowed to freely doodle on the picture instead of simply choosing the picture. What attracted our attention was that P4 was unwilling to let his child use this application for a long time because he did not want his child to touch the electronic screen, believing it might affect the child's eyesight. P5 proposed trying to use it herself and finally tried to create three pieces of music, and expressed satisfaction with two of them.

We made an innovative attempt to design an engaging application for children to create music by drawing pictures based on the design concept of synesthesia. Most of the children showed great interest in using the application. On the whole, children were satisfied with the pictures and music they had created, and some children showed a strong interest in the application and repeatedly created music. In our communication with the parents, we found that the parents as a whole also thought highly of the application. Some parents pointed out that they liked the design method based on synesthesia and could fully understand it, but they were worried that some children could not fully understand the change from picture style to music style. The most amazing thing for us was that one parent proposed to try using the application themselves. After creating pictures and music, she expressed that it was a good experience.

6 Limitations and Future Work

There are still some areas that can be improved in the application. For example, the types of elements can be more diversified rather than limited to scenes and animals, and children can be allowed to doodle to a certain extent on the picture so as to accommodate children's tendency to doodle. Some parents worried that this application would affect their children's vision, and we hope that this problem can be solved.

We will continue our research in the future. First, we will compare more open-source music generation algorithms. At the same time, we will try to improve the algorithm by including chords, remixes, and other effects to perfect the sound. In addition, we will try to add some new elements in the application, such as clouds or trees, to enrich the content of the picture and enable the whole picture to contain more information. Also, the application could provide more input parameters for the generation algorithm. We also plan to add different instruments so that children can hear the effects of their favorite instruments, which will make the system more lively and interesting. Finally, we plan to complete a combination of physical methods, such as replacing the scene selector and picture selector in our system with canvas and hard cards, to present a similar effect; this will avoid eye injury caused by electronic screens to children.

7 Conclusion

In summary, we designed and created a music creation application for children aged 4–6 that generates music through drawing; it is conducive to cultivating children's interest in music creation and enhancing their musical perception. In contrast to the previous systems, we aimed to stimulate children's interest in actively making music. A fun format was designed to make it easier for children to create and understand music.

Overall, this study is considered to allow children to experience the joy of music creation while drawing, and provide children with a visual and auditory experience at the same time. We designed and developed MusicCollage to bring the experience of music composition to children and improve their enthusiasm for music creation.

Acknowledgments. This research was funded by the Engineering Research Center of Computer Aided Product Innovation Design, Ministry of Education, Fundamental Research Funds for the Central Universities, National Natural Science Foundation of China (Grant No. 52075478), and National Social Science Foundation of China (Grant No. 21AZD056).

References

1. Ostrov, J.M., Gentile, D.A., Mullins, A.D.: Evaluating the effect of educational media exposure on aggression in early childhood. J. Appl. Dev. Psychol. **34**(1), 38–44 (2013)
2. Taylor, H.: Music with the Under-Fours by Susan Young. Routledge Falmer, London and New York (2003). (139 p. £ 14.99, paperback. Br. J. Music Educ. **21**(1), 131 (2004))
3. McKinnon, I.: Children's music journey: the development of an interactive software solution for early childhood music education. Comput. Entertain. **3**(4), 1–10 (2005)

216   G. Yan et al.

4. Oestermeier, U., et al.: LEGO music: learning composition with bricks. In: Proceedings of the 14th International Conference on Interaction Design and Children, pp. 283–286. Association for Computing Machinery, Boston, Massachusetts (2015)
5. Tidjani, A., Cho, E., Lee, P.: MuSme: a tangible skin suit for music creation. In: Proceedings of the TEI 2016: Tenth International Conference on Tangible, Embedded, and Embodied Interaction, pp. 743–748. Association for Computing Machinery, Eindhoven, Netherlands (2016)
6. Ling, Y.: Interactive visual music education software for children. In: Proceedings of the 20th International Academic Mindtrek Conference, pp. 453–456. Association for Computing Machinery, Tampere, Finland (2016)
7. Moruzzi, C.: Creative AI: music composition programs as an extension of the composer's mind. In: Müller, V.C. (ed.) PT-AI 2017. SAPERE, vol. 44, pp. 69–72. Springer, Cham (2018). https://doi.org/10.1007/978-3-319-96448-5_8
8. Brown, L.L.: The benefits of music education. PBS KIDS for Parents (2012)
9. Jaschke, A.C., et al.: Music education and its effect on intellectual abilities in children: a systematic review. Rev. Neurosci. 24(6), 665–675 (2013)
10. Ouyang, L., et al.: Designing tangible interactions with children for pre-school music education. In: 32nd Australian Conference on Human-Computer Interaction, pp. 687–691. Association for Computing Machinery Sydney, NSW, Australia (2020)
11. Altieri, S., et al.: Music education technology for older elementary school aged children: playing around with mini Amadeus Jr. J. Comput. Sci. Coll. 20(5), 102–103 (2005)
12. He, L., et al.: TempoString: a tangible tool for children's music creation. In: Proceedings of the 2012 ACM Conference on Ubiquitous Computing, pp. 643–644. Association for Computing Machinery, Pittsburgh, Pennsylvania (2012)
13. Rigler, J., Seldess, Z.: The music creator: an interactive system for musical exploration and education. In: Proceedings of the 7th International Conference on New Interfaces for Musical Expression, pp. 415–416. Association for Computing Machinery, New York (2007)
14. Akiyama, Y., Oore, S.: Place and play: a digital tool for children to create and record music. In: Proceedings of the SIGCHI Conference on Human Factors in Computing Systems, pp. 735–738. Association for Computing Machinery, Florence, Italy (2008)
15. Voong, M., Beale, R.: Music organisation using colour synaesthesia. In: CHI 2007 Extended Abstracts on Human Factors in Computing Systems, pp. 1869–1874. Association for Computing Machinery San Jose, CA, USA (2007)
16. Jin, S., Qin, J., Li, W.: Draw portraits by music: a music based image style transformation. In: Proceedings of the 28th ACM International Conference on Multimedia, pp. 4399–4400. Association for Computing Machinery, Seattle, WA, USA (2020)
17. Šimbelis, V.V., Lundström, A.: Synthesis in the audiovisual. In: Proceedings of the CHI 2016 Conference Extended Abstracts on Human Factors in Computing Systems, pp. 301–304. Association for Computing Machinery, San Jose, California, USA (2016)
18. Kritikos, D., Karpouzis, K.: From pixels to notes: a computational implementation of synaesthesia for cultural artefacts. arXiv preprint: arXiv:2101.12038 (2021)
19. Frid, E., Gomes, C., Jin, Z.: Music creation by example. In: Proceedings of the 2020 CHI 2020 Conference on Human Factors in Computing Systems, pp. 1–13. Association for Computing Machinery, Honolulu, HI, USA (2020)
20. Louie, R., et al.: Novice-AI music co-creation via AI-steering tools for deep generative models. In: Proceedings of the CHI 2020 Conference on Human Factors in Computing Systems, pp. 1–13. Association for Computing Machinery, Honolulu, HI, USA (2020)
21. Ning, C., Zhou, S.: The music pattern: a creative tabletop music creation platform. Comput. Entertain. 8(2), 13 (2011)
22. Kunigk, D.: Generate-music (2020). https://github.com/kiecodes/generate-music

A System Design of Virtual Reality Enabled Chinese Ancient Books for Enhancing Reading Promotion and Culture Dissemination

Ning Zhang[1] , Anlun Wan[1,2(✉)] , Jingwen Huang[2] , and Peipei Cao[2]

[1] Research Center for Digital Publishing and Digital Humanities of Beijing Normal University, Zhuhai 519087, China
AnlunWan08065@bnu.edu.cn

[2] School of Journalism and Communication of Beijing Normal University, Beijing 100875, China

Abstract. Chinese ancient books (CABs) possess precious values in the aspects of Chinese literature, cultural relics, history, and arts. However, ordinary modern Chinese readers have language and cultural barriers to understanding CABs, which leads to the reader group of CABs being limited in the Chinese literature and historical research field. To enhance CABs reading promotion and Chinese culture dissemination, this paper aims to explore the method of using cultural tourism resources to illustrate CABs text in a virtual reality (VR) environment. It specifically illustrates text elements and narrative storylines contained in CABs to reduce readers' difficulties in CABs' reading comprehension, improve their reading interest, achieve the purpose of CABs reading promotion from a minority group to mass readers. This paper systematically analyzes the relevant VR cultural heritage applications and develops a VR CAB prototype based on one case. It contributes a VR CAB design method and verifies the feasibility and value of the VR CAB prototype by using illustration resources from LAMs and cultural tourism fields.

Keywords: Virtual reality · Chinese ancient book · Reading promotion · Cultural heritage · LAMs

1 Introduction

1.1 VR CABs

Chinses ancient books (CABs), which contained excellent traditional Chinese culture, have recorded more than 5,000 years of glorious Chinese history. However, ordinary modern Chinese readers have a series of barriers to understanding CABs contents, because they lack essential CABs access rights, retrieval skills, Chinese ancient language skills, professional historical knowledge, period social context knowledge, reading motivation, and so on [1]. This restricts the reader group of CABs in Chinese literature and history researchers who have rich professional knowledge [2]. Therefore, researchers

© The Author(s), under exclusive license to Springer Nature Switzerland AG 2022
N. A. Streitz and S. Konomi (Eds.): HCII 2022, LNCS 13326, pp. 217–231, 2022.
https://doi.org/10.1007/978-3-031-05431-0_16

working in libraries, research institutes, government and culture centers in China are engaged in finding solutions to help ordinary modern readers to access and read CABs, such as developing full-text retrieval supported CABs online database, translating CABs language from ancient Chinese to simplified Chinese, designing creative culture products with CABs features, organizing and running CABs related lectures and reading activities, designing digital applications based on particular CABs contents or themes[3]. These approaches have achieved great positive effects in enhancing CABs reading promotions and traditional Chinese culture dissemination.

Virtual Reality (VR) technology-enabled CABs design and application is one of the digital applications for CAB reading promotion. It is because VR provided a computer-generated world that expands the human senses, changes the product shape and service mode [4]. A higher-level immersive VR system with features such as haptic feedback, head-mounted display with full real-time motion capture, high-resolution and wide field of view, can simulate a high immersive illusion for readers of being in the virtual world [5]. In the culture field, VR enables users to experience historical-cultural sites and relic collections in an immersive way beyond the time and space constraints, and perceive historical-cultural deposits through VR representation and scene interaction [6]. This unique advantage in enhancing readers' experiences of perception and presence is highly recommended and used in cultural heritage areas [7].

VR CABs design adopts text elements illustration approach with the rich type of multimedia resources, such as detailed text, picture, audio, video, 3D model and VR sense. Readers under the interactive and immersive VR environment can interact with these types of illustration resources, for instance, walking in VR senses, zooming in pictures, rotating 3D models, and so on [8]. This design approach turns abstractive CAB contents into intuitive entities, which help reduce readers' cognitive load and improve their reading motivation [3]. Therefore, VR CABs design serves useful functions in resolving CABs reading barriers of readers by providing intuitive content, fun and memorable reading experience. This puts forward higher requirements for CABs content mining, sorting, design, production, and presentation.

1.2 Research Aims and Questions

Research Aim. Driven by CABs reading promotion needs and together with the advantages of VR CABs in resolving CAB reading barriers as mentioned above, this research attempts to explore the use of cultural and tourism resources to illustrate CABs text elements under VR environment, especially public cultural collection resources represented by libraries, museums and archives (LAMs) and cultural tourism resources represented by tangible and intangible cultural heritage. Besides, it tries to use text, picture, voice, video, 3D model, VR scenes to represent abstract text in intuitive entities, so that readers can travel and study at the same time under a VR environment, which could improve the readability and interest of CABs. The final research aim is to make CAB an easy and interesting reading for ordinary modern readers.

Research Questions. Corresponding to the aforementioned research aims, the key research question (RQ) of this paper is:

RQ-How to design VR Cabs by using text elements illustration approach to enhance the reading promotion and culture dissemination of Cabs?

2 VR Cultural Tourism Projects

2.1 VR Enabled Cultural Tourism Resources Integration

Most of cultural and tourism resources exist in the form of LAMs collections, local tangible cultural heritage (such as cultural relics, buildings, sites...), and intangible cultural heritage (such as folk literature, music, dance, folk art, acrobatics, manual skills, customs...) [9]. These local cultural and tourism resources have played an important role in regional development since ancient times and also served an internal role in education, celebration, politics, religion as regional and ethnic communication mediums [10].

The integration of cultural tourism resources has become a new approach to culture promotion in China. VR-enabled cultural resources integration can be concluded in three approaches: 1) VR-enabled LAMs collections; 2) VR-enabled cultural tourism resources; 3) VR-enabled LAMs collections combined with cultural tourism resources.

2.2 VR Enabled Cultural Tourism Research and Applications

VR-enabled cultural tourism research and applications have been increasing in recent years. The related research and practice cover the range from VR museum guide system [11], VR reading [12], and VR tourism [13] to cultural relics display [14], cultural heritage experience design [6], and cultural tourism information modeling under VR environment [15].

VR cultural tourism applications have adopted integrated resources in a variety of ways. Studies on the application of VR to experience cultural tourism have been relatively developed. Lund and Scribner studied the application of VR to the collection and preservation of archival resources [16]. Agnello and others studied VR-enabled historical architecture applications by taking the Cathedral of Palermo as an example, it creates 3D models and VR scenes in the application based on historical collections, archives, and image resources [17]. Gonizzi and others studied VR exhibits in the Archaeological Museum in Milan by providing interactive VR scenes for users to better understand exhibit information [18]. Hernandez and others designed and developed a VR system prototype named The Empty Museum to explain how users walk, explore and learn cultural site information in a VR environment [19]. The representative VR-enabled applications by using LAMs collections and cultural tourism resources are listed in Table 1.

The applications developed in the aforementioned three approaches for VR-enabled cultural tourism resource integration can bring users with immersive, interactive, intuitive, and memorable learning experiences in a VR environment. It requires in-depth sorting, organizing, and intuitive representation of cultural tourism resources in the design process of VR applications.

Table 1. VR enabled LAMs collections and cultural tourism experiences.

Category	Application project	Descriptions
VR+LAMs collections	VR *Riverside Scene at Qingming Festival* [20]	Users in the VR environment can enter in museum's ancient painting named *Riverside Scene at Qingming Festival*, to experience street scenes and cultural customs in the Northern Song Dynasty of China
	VR *British Museum* [21]	This application adopts 3D models of museum exhibits, high-resolution images, and audio explanations
	The *VR Museum of Fine Art* [21]	This application is not a real museum. It enables users to access the statue of David, the Mona Lisa, the Terracotta Army, and so on. Users can close see the incredibly detailed texture of the collections
	VR project of *Shizi Qu and the Three-Character Classic* [22]	Users in VR environment can travel back to the life of 700 years ago in ancient China, to experience period historical scenes, objects, and environment. It supports users to learn Chinese culture and historical stories under the guidance of virtual characters
	VR project of *Remembering Pearl Harbor* [23]	TIME magazine has teamed up with HTC and AMD to create a VR application named *Remembering Pearl Harbor*. Its contents are based on archival information from the National World War II Museum and the Library of Congress
	VR project of *Nanhai No.1 Ancient Ship* [24]	This application adopts integrated archival and cultural relics in LAMs, to reveal the secret history of *Nanhai No.1 Ancient Ship* and show the grand situation of the maritime Silk Road to users in a VR environment
VR+cultural tourism resources	VR *Dragon Kiln* [25]	This application restores the dragon kiln in 1:1 proportion according to its real site in a VR environment. It allows users to walk in the cave, learn intangible kiln firing culture, experience the kiln structure in the Song Dynasty of China
	Armenian Church [26]	According to the 3D model of the church and also combined with the research material, Hiverlab sets interaction functions to allow users to walk in the church, using the controller click the hyperlink, opening the treasure trove of information about the church history. It also built a delay function, allowing users to back the time, observing the images of the church in different historical periods

(*continued*)

Table 1. (*continued*)

Category	Application project	Descriptions
VR+LAMs collections + cultural tourism resources	VR Pompeii [27, 28]	Based on historical documents and archaeological collections, the VR Pompeii development team used digital animation and VR/AR technology to recreate the ancient city of Pompeii of Italy that disappeared for 2000 years. VR Pompeii constructs virtual ancient building scenes and 3D animation, which allows tourists to experience the historical context behind the ruins
	VR project of *Roman Reborn* [29]	Based on historical references and cultural sites dating back to 320 A.D., this application modeled more than 7,000 ancient buildings and historical sites in a VR environment. It allows users to explore ancient architectural scenes in Roman time by wearing VR headsets

3   VR Enabled CABs Design

3.1   VR CABs Design and Development Processes

This research adopts the approach of VR-enabled LAMs collections combined with cultural tourism resources for the design of VR CABs text element illustration. It is a process of information system analysis, design, development, test, and application, which follows five key stages as shown in Fig. 1.

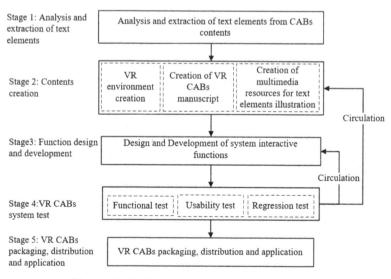

Fig. 1. VR CABs design and development processes

Stage 1: Analysis and Extraction of Text Elements. CABs contents are combining "points" and "lines", it refers to text elements (such as keywords or knowledge entities) and narrative storylines respectively. This step should firstly choose a representative case for instantiation, then according to the CABs text information to extract text elements and narrative storylines with thematic analysis method. Findings of the analysis themes may involve objects, cultural customs, ancient institutions, ancient places, historical figures, ancient laws and regulations, and so on, which are mainly used to reveal complex text elements that have great differences between ancient and modern knowledge. The narrative storylines may involve multiple narrative plots, reflecting the narrative content's coherence, logic, and integrity.

After this step researchers move to the comprehensive illustration of text elements and narrative storyline with multimedia resources that need to be created in stage 2 The specific ways for text illustration will be further explained in Sect. 3.2.

Stage 2: Contents Creation. VR CABs content creation comprehensively adopts a variety of multimedia resources. It includes 1) VR environment creation, referring to the design and creation of library location, architecture, and architectural interior furniture; 2) VR CABs creation, specifically including CABs design and interaction; 3) illustration content creation, requiring the organization and creation of texts, pictures, videos, audio, 3D models and VR scenes used for text elements and narrative storylines. The required multimedia resources are mainly collected from LAMs collections and cultural tourism resources.

Stage 3: Function Design and Development. The design and development of interactive functions of VR CABs provide users with multi-sensory experiences to obtain cultural tourism information. These functions specifically include 1) functions for users to interact with the environment, such as walking in the environment, interacting with virtual objects by using VR controllers, picking up and putting down objects, rotating 3D models; 2) functions for users to interact with VR CABs, such as using VR controller to turn pages, clicking on the menu of multimedia resources, picking up and putting down objects, rotating 3D objects, clicking to select VR scenes, switching and wandering to different VR scenes, obtaining audio and visual information of all resources in VR environment.

Stage 4: VR CABs System Test. Stage 4: VR CABs system test. The test of VR CABs aims to ensure a high-quality user experience. It includes functional testing, usability testing, and regression testing. The functional test mainly tests whether the functions of VR CABs are available, including turning on/off pages, clicking keywords and paragraphs, playing audio and video, rotating 3D models, switching VR scenes, and so on. A usability test is about whether VR CABs operation is reasonable and easy to understand. Regression testing is after system design modification of the first two rounds of testing and testing again before system release.

Stage 5:   VR CABs Packaging, Distribution, and Application.

3.2   Text Illustration of VR CABs

VR CABs content creation covers two parts: 1) manuscript; 2) and text illustration. The manuscript contains the original manuscript and the manuscript in classical Chinese. The text illustration contents include illustrations for text elements and narrative storylines respectively. To facilitate users to understand complex text contents, annotation is a common method to reveal content in VR applications [30]. Users who experienced VR contents are more likely to associate their cognitive experience with text elements information and narrative storyline contents, which have a positive effect on the improvement of reading ability and motivation of CABs [31]. Readers have many barriers to understanding CABs written in ancient Chinese. It is more conducive to knowledge discovery to illustrate text elements or narrative storylines. VR CABs design uses thematic analysis to extract text elements and narrative storylines from the selected case study (further explained in Sect. 3.3). They are illustrated with multimedia resources from the cultural tourism field, to weaken readers' CABs reading barriers.

Illustration of Text Elements.   In this research, the text elements extracted from CABs text are keywords in a narrow sense. The CABs reading barriers are weakened by illustrating one keyword after another. The design of the text element illustration is shown in Fig. 2.

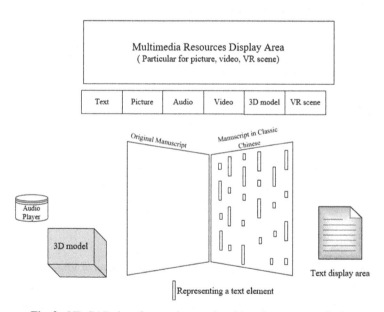

Fig. 2. VR CABs interface settings and multimedia resources display

It contains a VR CABs component and multimedia resources display area. The opened VR CAB is in the central position with a scanned copy of the original manuscript on its right page and the manuscript in classical Chinese corresponding to the original manuscript on its left page. The right page allows readers to click the text element box to refer to the detailed illustrations. Above VR CABs, it is the menu for clicking text, picture, audio, video, 3D model, and VR scene, which is used to navigate the selection of illustration contents. The display area of pictures and videos is above the menu. The display area for the audio player and 3D model is placed on the left side of VR CABs, while its right side is for the illustration text display. Readers can click the VR scene in the menu bar to enter the independent VR scene interface. When readers click any text elements, the illustrative multimedia resources of cultural tourism for corresponding text elements will appear next to the menu. Readers click different multimedia resources according to their personal preference, corresponding resources appearing in the certain display area for readers to visit and study.

Illustration of Narrative Storylines. Understanding historical texts require texts with high coherence and readers having good logical reasoning skills. Incoherent text writing requires higher requirements for readers on cognitive skills, and only readers with good knowledge preparation can complete reasoning tasks in a specific historical context [32]. Narrative discourse often has a strong logical order, usually following time, events, and plots, which enables readers to read coherently and easily [33]. Narrative storylines grounded on narrative attractions help readers understand the narrative contents of linearization. Therefore, this research adopts a narrative storyline as an illustration tool for revealing the behind period culture, logic, and future details of a biographical case study, to weak CABs reading barriers in linear logic.

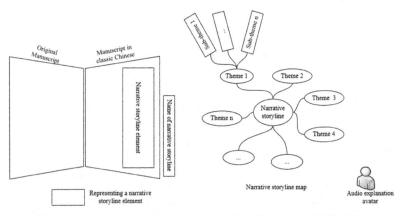

Fig. 3. Concept diagram of narrative storyline illustration of VR CABs

The design of the narrative storyline illustration is shown in Fig. 3. The story text box on the page of the manuscript in classic Chinese represents different narrative storylines. The story title box is displayed on the right-bottom corner of the CABs, which directly links each story text on the book page. When readers touch the story title box with virtual fingers, the story text box will be highlighted with color. Meanwhile, the narrative storyline map will appear on the above of CABs. Narrative storyline illustration uses story map navigation and also a virtual character with an audio explanation. The story map has three levels. The first level (the middle ellipse) is the title of the story, the second level (the ellipse linking the middle ellipse) is the story themes, and the third level (the text box) is the detailed description of the story. When readers touch the story title box, the whole story map appears and the virtual characters automatically broadcast the audio content related to the whole story. Readers can click on the secondary ellipse to select the sub-themes referring to specific story details.

3.3 Case Study Analysis

This research takes the Biography of Concubine Yang in Old Tang Book (旧唐书.玄宗杨贵妃) as a case study. It recorded the Concubine Yang's life experiences with emperor Tang Xuanzong in Tang Dynasty. The biography contains the following text element themes extracted in the thematic analysis method, such as objects, cultural customs, ancient institutions, ancient places, historical people, ancient laws, and regulations [2]. The narrative storyline themes of the biography are including 1) emperor Tang Xunzong falling in love with the wife of his son; 2) Concubine Yang become Emperor Tang Xunazong's favourite woman among all concubines; 3) scourge and corruption from Yang's family members; 4) emperor and national officers misleading the country to the war; 5) rebellion of An Lushan and Shi Siming [2].

3.4 Collection and Utilization of Illustration Resource

The illustrations for both text elements and narrative storylines of CABs require the usage of texts, pictures, audio, video, 3D models, and VR scenes in a VR environment, the collection and utilization approaches are shown in Table 2.

Table 2. Collections and cultural tourism resources used for VR CABs illustration

Multimedia resources	Illustration objectives	Sources
Text	All text elements	The majority of the text illustration is from Old Tang Book, New Tang Book, the Chinese National Knowledge Infrastructure, and cultural tourism websites
Picture	All text elements	Pictures are mostly from 28 museums, mainly Shaanxi History Museum, Henan Museum, National Museum of China, Luoyang Museum, Zhengzhou Museum, Dunhuang Academy, Xi'an Museum, and so on
Audio/Video	All text elements	Audios and videos are mostly collected from cultural programs such as Archives of National Treasure, Lecture Room, National Treasure, CCTV documentary, Classic Legend, and so on

(*continued*)

Table 2. (*continued*)

Multimedia resources	Illustration objectives	Sources
3D model	Particularly for the tangible artifacts, cultural customs, ancient organization, historical people	Three approaches are used to collect 3D models: 1) 3D scanning technology adopted to scan museum relics to generate 3D models; 2) 3D models collected from online museum exhibitions; 3) purchasing open-source 3D models on commercial websites
VR scene	Particularly for artifacts and cultural customs	Researchers purchased open-source VR scene models online, such as the imperial palace, melting and casting process, textile process, and so on

3.5 VR CAB Prototype

The application of VR CABs developed in this research requires relevant supporting devices, such as computers, HTC Vive headsets, controllers, and base stations. Figure 4 is the VR CAB prototype showing the interface with text elements and narrative storyline illustrations.

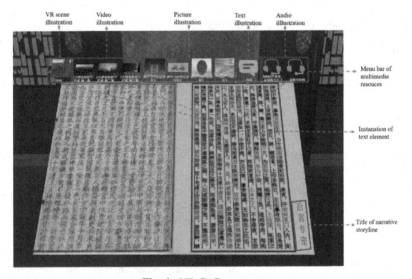

Fig. 4. VR CAB prototype

Prototype of Text Elements Illustration. Illustrations for one single text element can involve many kinds of LAMs and cultural tourism resources. the related instantiations for a different type of text elements are as below:

Instantiation of Illustration for Historical People. Taking Concubine Yang as an instantiation, it adopts library texts, exhibition pictures of museums, ancient paintings, 3D models, historical audio/video interpretations gathered from cultural websites shown in Fig. 5.

Instantiation of Illustration for Tangible Cultural Heritage. Taking ancient organization and architecture such as the imperial palace as an example, it can be illustrated and displayed in Fig. 6. It uses an immersive VR scene enabling readers to understand historical knowledge during traveling experience inside the palace. It also integrates the common multimedia illustration resources for other themes of text elements, such as texts, images, videos, and audio.

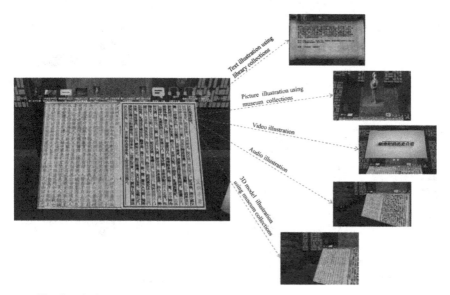

Fig. 5. The instantiation for historical people illustration with LAMs collections

Instantiation of Illustration for Intangible Cultural Heritage. VR scene can also be used to illustrate intangible cultural heritage, which can make the invisible cultural elements visible and intuitive to experience. For instance, it is difficult for modern readers to understand melting and casting processes in ancient China, while VR sense can bring them to the ancient environment to observe the whole processes from close range, and allow them to interact with the ancient worker for further explanation as shown in Fig. 7. In this circumstance, the abstractive intangible cultural heritage can be vividly presented to readers [34]. Similar to other text elements' illustration, more multimedia resources (such as texts, pictures, audio, and videos) also can be adopted to illustrate intangible cultural heritage if these resources are available and relative.

Prototype of Narrative Storyline Illustration. The prototype of the VR CAB narrative storyline illustration is shown in Fig. 8. It takes the narrative storyline theme "Rebellion of An Lushan and Shi Siming" from the case study as an example.

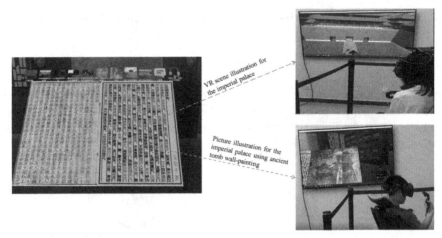

Fig. 6. The instantiation of imperial palace illustration using VR scene and cultural tourism resources

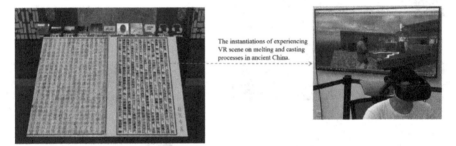

Fig. 7. The instantiation of illustration for Chinese ancient melting and casting processes by using VR scene

Readers access the illustration information by clicking the title of the narrative storyline (Rebellion of An Lushan and Shi Siming) at the right bottom corner of the VR CAB interface, and then the three-level narrative storyline map appears on the above of VR CABs to navigate readers to follow the logical storyline of the manuscript. Readers click the different levels of the map if they are interested in a certain sub-theme. Meanwhile, the audio explanation of the narrative will be performed in the theme sequence on the map from the beginning. Readers click on any sub-themes, the audio explanations will move to the associated sub-theme part.

The design and development of the VR CAB prototype verify that the text illustrations in the integrated multimedia resources from LAMs and cultural tourism fields can effectively reveal and demonstrate the meanings of CAB text elements. It shows that VR as a communication medium has advantages in providing readers with immersive, intuitive, and pleasant experiences about tangible and intangible cultural resources.

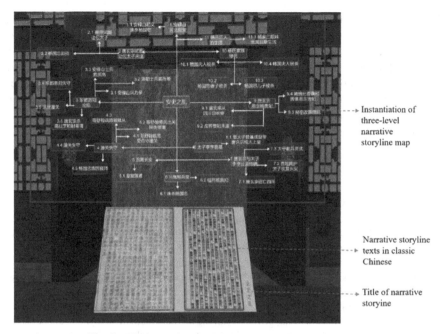

Fig. 8. The instantiation of narrative storyline illustration

4   Conclusions

The VR CAB prototype presented in this research verifies the feasibility of using LAMs collections combined with cultural tourism resources for the illustration of text elements and narrative storylines in a VR environment. It is useful and meaningful for CAB reading promotion and Chinese culture dissemination pleasantly and intuitively.

It firstly significantly enhances readers' experiences in reading CABs. This is because of the immersive and interactive nature of VR technology that provides readers with a virtual learning scene and enables them to interact with cultural resources in an immersive environment. Visually visible LAMs and cultural tourism resources, especially readers wandering in historical and cultural sites and closely observing intangible cultural scenes, improve readers' experience of whole learning processes.

CABs reading in VR environments has become more interesting. This kind of interest stems from the attraction of VR technology to readers because VR media has not been popularized yet. Hence, most readers are still psychologically exciting about VR applications. It is naturally full of fun for readers to study cultural knowledge recorded in CABs and travel to cultural sites at the same time. This "reading by traveling" approach is entertaining for readers.

The content of VR CABs is richer and more intuitive with the support illustrations by using multimedia resources. It provides illustration resources across the fields of LAMs, intangible/ tangible cultural heritage, and so on. it improves the richness and diversity of content and provides users with an integrated and deep cultural experience. This makes CABs reading is easier to understand. The abstract and difficult text is illustrated with diversified cultural tourism resources, and readers do not need to imagine corresponding cultural elements according to the text. It is to a certain extent solved the difficulty of readers' lack of historical background knowledge and ancient Chinese language skills.

VR CABs enrich the ways for CABs publishing and cultural dissemination. Compared with the traditional CABs promotion that mostly spread in the form of expert lectures, databases, and books written in simplified Chinese, VR CABs enable readers to read while they are traveling in a VR environment. It is a new design approach for CAB publishing and cultural dissemination.

References

1. Zhang, N., Nunes, M., Li, J.: An investigation of the use of VR books to resolve difficulties with access and reading of Chinese ancient books. In: Proceedings of the International Conferences on e-Health 2018, ICT, Society, and Human Beings 2018 and Web-Based Communities and Social Media 2018, pp. 131–140. Madrid, Spain (2018)
2. Zhang, N., Nunes, M.B., Li, J.: Extending thematic analysis to facilitate the understanding of Chinese ancient books. In: ECRM 2020 20th European Conference on Research Methodology for Business and Management Studies: ECRM 2020, pp. 319–331. Academic Conferences and Publishing Limited, Reading, UK (2020)
3. Zhang, N., Nunes, M., Li, J., Zhang, W.: Designing a virtual reality Chinese ancient book system for reading and culture promotion: theoretical model development and implementation. Libr. Inf. Serv. **65**(13), 12–24 (2021)
4. Banfi, F., Bolognesi, C.M.: Virtual reality for cultural heritage: new levels of computer-generated simulation of a UNESCO World Heritage Site. In: Bolognesi, C., Villa, D. (eds.) From Building Information Modelling to Mixed Reality, pp. 47–64. Springer, Cham (2021). https://doi.org/10.1007/978-3-030-49278-6_4
5. Schwind, V., et al.: Using presence questionnaires in virtual reality. In: Proceedings of the 2019 CHI Conference on Human Factors in Computing Systems, pp. 1–12. ACM, New York, USA (2019)
6. Häkkilä, J., et al.: Visiting a virtual graveyard: designing virtual reality cultural heritage experiences. In: Proceedings of the 18th International Conference on Mobile and Ubiquitous Multimedia, pp. 1–4. ACM, Pisa, Italy (2019)
7. Drossis, G., Birliraki, C., Stephanidis, C.: Interaction with immersive cultural heritage environments using virtual reality technologies. In: Stephanidis, C. (ed.) HCI 2018. CCIS, vol. 852, pp. 177–183. Springer, Cham (2018). https://doi.org/10.1007/978-3-319-92285-0_25
8. Hudson, S., Matson-Barkat, S., Pallamin, N., Jegou, G.: With or without you? Interaction and immersion in a virtual reality experience. J. Bus. Res. **100**(C), 459–468 (2019)
9. Ho, P., McKercher, B.: Managing heritage resources as tourism products. Asia Pacific J. Tour. Res. **9**(3), 255–266 (2004)
10. Coccossis, H.: Cultural heritage, local resources, and sustainable tourism. Int. J. Serv. Technol. Manage. **10**(1), 8–14 (2008)
11. Ferracani, A., Faustino, M., Giannini, G., Landucci, L., Del, B.: Natural experiences in museums through virtual reality and voice commands. In: Proceedings of the 25th ACM International Conference on Multimedia, pp. 1233–1234. Mountain View, CA, USA (2017)
12. Pianzola, F., Bálint, K., Weller, J.: Virtual reality as a tool for promoting reading via enhanced narrative absorption and empathy. Sci. Study Liter. **9**(2), 163–194 (2019)
13. Balogun, V., Thompson, A., Sarumi, O.: A 3D virtual reality system for virtual tourism. Pacific J. Sci. Technol. **11**(2), 601–609 (2010)

14. Tao, Y.: A VR/AR-based display system for arts and crafts museum. In: Proceedings on 2020 International Conference on Cyber-Enabled Distributed Computing and Knowledge Discovery (CyberC), pp. 124–129. IEEE, Chongqing, China (2020)
15. Lee, J., Kim, J., Ahn, J., Woo, W.: Context-aware risk management for architectural heritage using historic building information modeling and virtual reality. J. Cult. Herit. **38**, 242–252 (2019)
16. Lund, B., Scribner, S.: Developing virtual reality experiences for archival collections: case study of the May Massee collection at Emporia State University. Am. Arch. **82**(2), 470–483 (2019)
17. Agnello, F., Avella, F., Agnello, S.: Virtual reality for historical architecture. In: Proceedings on International Archives of the Photogrammetry, Remote Sensing and Spatial Information Sciences, pp.9–16. Bergamo, Italy (2019)
18. Gonizzi, B., Caruso, G., Micoli, L., Covarrubias, R., Guidi, G.: 3D visualization of cultural heritage artifacts with virtual reality devices. In: 25th International CIPA Symposium 2015, pp. 165–172. Copernicus Gesellschaft MBH (2015)
19. Hernández, L., et al.: Physically walking in digital spaces—a virtual reality installation for exploration of historical heritage. Int. J. Archit. Comput. **5**(3), 487–506 (2007)
20. Leiphone. https://www.leiphone.com/category/arvr/mRppIEO7hoDjESA3.html. Accessed 10 Nov 2021
21. VirtualiTeach. https://www.virtualiteach.com/post/2017/08/20/10-amazing-virtual-museum-tours. Accessed 11 Nov 2021
22. Szzs360. http://www.szzs360.com/news/2019/11/2019_7_zs66787.htm. Accessed 11 Nov 2021
23. Pico. https://news.nweon.com/24417. Accessed 13 Nov 2021
24. Sohu. https://www.chinavrway.com/subpage/vrmuchuan.html. Accessed 17 Nov 2021
25. Sohu. http://www.sohu.com/a/330862909_442943. Accessed 17 Nov 2021
26. CNBC. https://www.cnbc.com/2016/12/07/hiverlab-creating-a-virtual-heritage-of-the-worlds-most-historic-sites.html. Accessed 18 Nov 2021
27. Retro Futuro. https://pompeii.refutur.com/en/. Accessed 18 Nov 2021
28. VIVE ARTS. https://arts.vive.com/us/articles/projects/culture-heritage/Pompeii/. Accessed 18 Nov 2021
29. Roman Reborn. https://romereborn.org/. Accessed 18 Nov 2021
30. Georgia Tech Library. https://smartech.gatech.edu/handle/1853/3649. Accessed 9 Nov 2021
31. Paquette, K., Laverick, D., Sibert, S.: Virtual reality experiences as an instructional strategy for promoting comprehension. Read. Improv. **57**(4), 173–179 (2020)
32. McNamara, D., Kintsch, W.: Learning from texts: effects of prior knowledge and text coherence. Discourse Process. **22**(3), 247–288 (1996)
33. Greninger, D.: Another look at storyline marking in Sherpa narrative. Himalayan Linguist. **10**(1), 77–99 (2011)
34. Hayes, A., Johnson, K.: Cultural embodiment in virtual reality education and training: a reflection on representation of diversity. In: Chang, M., et al. (eds.) Foundations and Trends in Smart Learning. LNET, pp. 93–96. Springer, Singapore (2019). https://doi.org/10.1007/978-981-13-6908-7_13

Distributed, Ambient, and Pervasive Well-Being and Healthcare

Digital Wellbeing and "Meaningless" Interactions with Mobile Devices

Michael Gilbert[1]([✉]) and Mark Zachry[2]

[1] Google, New York, NY 10011, USA
mdgilbert@google.com
[2] University of Washington, Seattle, WA 98195, USA
zachry@uw.edu

Abstract. Much of the research on digital wellbeing (DWB) in HCI focuses on increasing happiness, reducing distraction, or achieving goals. Distinct from this is a conceptualization of DWB sensitive to another commonly observed type of interaction with technology: the interstitial, the mundane, or the "meaningless." We examine DWB with a mixed methods approach – a series of three separate but related Experience Sampling Method studies (ESM) paired with user interviews and diary studies. Through both quantitative and interpretive analyses, we clarify the distinction between what is identifiable – in terms of what is observable, measurable, or significant – and what is, from a human perspective, important. Extending from our analysis, we define and operationalize meaningless interactions with technology, highlighting how those interactions can contribute to self-empathy and contentment. Ultimately, we suggest a framing for DWB sensitive to these observations to support design for people in their lived experiences.

Keywords: Digital wellbeing · Experience sampling method · Habit · Mindfulness · Meaningless

1 Introduction

The HCI community has become increasingly interested in designing for happiness, designing for positive outcomes, or designing in a manner that allows people to minimize or avoid behaviors that are disruptive, undesirable, or unhealthy. These designs include interventions to mediate social media addiction, address gaming addiction, or facilitate smoking cessation, among many other possible examples. Such design ambitions to either make real the aspirational or make immaterial the undesirable, by emphasizing the special, may overlook the everyday and mundane. As we discover in this study, many of our daily interactions with technology have very little to do with the aspirational, or even the intentional. As we find, a non-trivial portion of our interactions with technology are not wholly "meaningful," with many having more to do with distraction than consumption; more to do with nothing than with something.

But what counts as a meaningless, or meaningful, interaction? Barring an existing established definition of the meaningless in prior HCI literature, we might broadly define it very simply as: an interaction that is not, in itself, meaningful to the interactor. In this sense we intentionally follow Ellen Langer's example in defining mindfulness as simply the opposite of mindlessness [22]. This definition will be unpacked and refined in the sections that follow.

1.1 Defining the Meaningless

We will clarify this working definition by drawing a clear contrast between our definition of the *meaningless* and prior conceptualizations of the *habitual*. [31] define *habit* as "automatic behavior triggered by situational cues, such as places, people, and preceding actions," drawing their definition from recent theory in cognitive psychology [27, 28]. They further clarify that habit in the context of smartphone use is the outcome of two interrelated things: automatized behaviors relating to prior use, and the contextual cues that trigger those cues. [31] further clarify that their framing of habit should not be conflated with frequency of behavior, suggesting that while habitual behaviors are a subset of frequent behaviors they additionally must be consistently associated with an explicit or implicit cue.

From a psychological perspective, Ouellette and Wood [30] provide perhaps a more expansive overview of *habit*. They define it as "tendencies to repeat responses given a stable supporting context." These routine responses given supporting contexts result in increasing automaticity of actions, decreasing the cognitive processing required for those actions and allowing them to occur in parallel with other actions. [30] further introduce *intention* into their conceptualization of habit, stating that intentions are "formed from salient beliefs about the outcomes of an act," and "reflect attitude toward the behavior, defined as the favorability of the consequences of an act and the importance of these effects." The relationship between intention and habit formation is dynamic. Similar to skill acquisition, habit formation typically begins with intentional action. Through repetition in stable contexts, intentions may eventually operate autonomously with little conscious guidance.

An example they provide is talking on the phone. For many adults for whom answering the phone is not a novelty, the act can be almost entirely involuntary. There is little consideration around how to hold the phone, how to lift it to one's ear, or what greeting might be uttered in what tone of voice when answering. Through repeated behavior each of those individual actions, originally each with their own intentions, may be enacted with a more general goal in mind: answering the phone after it rings.

We can now move towards a clearer definition of the *meaningless* through contrast to the concepts above. Where habit may be indicated by repeated behavior enacted in stable contexts, we suggest that meaningless actions, while frequently repeated, may occur outside of those stable contexts. As we highlight in the analysis and discussion below, some actions that occur commonly frequently do so without a consistent cause. From our data, causes provided for these types of interactions include "wasting time," "I don't know," or the rather poetic, "I was at home. We had just finished watching a movie. I can't really think of why I looked at Instagram."

Similarly, where intention may be indicated by "salient beliefs about the outcome of an act," [30], we suggest that the meaningless may be identified in both unintentional and intentional acts. Examples of the former may be seen in the quotes above, instances where actions appear absent of any clear intent. An example of the latter may include, this quote from a participant reflecting on a challenge in the prior week.

"... Basically, it seems that, if I focus on one thing and manage to catch up, I will have fallen behind on something else in the meantime. In general during these times when I feel really busy technology functions as an outlet/distraction for me. Normally, if I was less busy I may go on a trip over the weekend. When I'm feeling very busy and like I don't have the time to get everything done I may turn to my computer/cell phone to take breaks from being productive, instead of the outdoors for example."

In this instance, we see an individual for whom technology offers a respite from the other challenges of their day. The context of this reflection is not stable. The challenges that inspire those interactions with their devices will likely vary given the predictable complexities of contemporary life. But there is an intention behind the desire to interact with technology described above – the explicit salient belief that the outcome of that interaction may provide some solace from the stresses they describe.

Ultimately, we suggest that meaningless actions can be frequently repeated, but their repetition is not their defining factor. Unlike habitual actions, they do not require a stable context. And while intention may be a necessary antecedent for habit formation, meaningless actions may or may not involve intention. Conversely, while habitual actions may be expressed in static ways (e.g., how you answer the phone), expression of the meaningless can be more varied.

At this point, we have defined the meaningless in terms of how it is related to but distinct from prior conceptualizations of habit and intention. We will build on this definition of the meaningless through the analysis and discussion sections of this paper. But first, with this working definition in place, we can more clearly introduce the challenges of *studying* the meaningless.

1.2 Studying the Meaningless

As should now be clear, studying meaningless interactions is inherently challenging. Given our working definition above, the attribution of meaning to any individual interaction must be sensitive to the intentions of the interactor. Accordingly, we suggest that identification of the meaningless through behavioral signals alone may not be feasible. While app logging and location tracking do allow for complex and nuanced models of individual behavior to be constructed, those models will be lacking the internal perspective of the actors necessary to distinguish between the meaningful and meaningless.

Qualitative methods like semi-structured interviews can facilitate a more generative understanding and evaluation of recent activities. However, given that the *meaningless* is a complex concept, interviews alone may not be sufficient. For instance, interview participants can be prone to overestimate the salience of their most common activities given their prevalence, which would directly impact our ability to identify the types of phenomenon described above (e.g., availability biases, in [38]). Ethnographic observation may also provide a clearer perspective on participants' interactions with technology.

However, to the extent that what is meaningful is a reflection of an internal state, both its identification through observation and its interpretation could be problematic. For example, our data shows that in many instances identical activities at different times can have dramatically different meanings to the interactor. What mediates those meanings is frequently the participants' internal state – their current emotion, or their intention behind the activity. Such factors are almost impossibly difficult to ascertain solely from the perspective of an outside observer.

To manage this challenge, we took a mixed methods approach. By combining qualitative interviews with multiple diary studies, we aimed to anchor participants in the immediate while still gauging the impactful. By combining open-ended ESM queries with a more "targeted" ESM (described below) we aimed to identify and qualify the most trivial or transient aspects of our interactions with technology, while seeking to reduce the risk that the "trivial" would be interpreted as ignorable.

1.3 Contribution

Through a targeted identification and analysis of the meaningless, this study aims to build on how we, as a community, examine the nature of our interactions with technology. In the sections that follow, we aim to (1) describe the method we adopted through which a broader perspective of the lived experience can be recorded and analyzed, (2) identify the salient characteristics of that lived experience, sensitive to both meaningful and meaningless moments, and (3) suggest how those characteristics may allow us to expand our understanding of what it means to design for Digital Wellbeing. And we close with the introduction of four themes, suggesting they represent the total set of possible interventions for Digital Wellbeing. In turn, each of the sections above aim to describe how to *measure*, how to *understand* and *interpret*, and how to *design for* Digital Wellbeing.

2 Related Work

While there has been an increase of focus on Digital Wellbeing (DWB), there is still no clearly accepted definition of DWB. In this section, we will introduce some of that work, offer a brief synthesis of prior conceptualizations of DWB across both industry and academia, and provide a working definition of DWB for the purpose of this paper. The section will conclude with a description of how sensitivity to the meaningless provides a lens through which DWB can be more effectively understood and practiced.

2.1 Part 1: DWB and Industry

We start with DWB & Industry because that is arguably where "Digital Wellbeing" was first introduced. According to [32], the "first rumblings" of digital wellness began at Google in 2012. This was when Tristan Harris, at the time a product manager working on the Inbox email app, noticed that the notifications from his device would consistently distract him from the "real world." The outcome of this epiphany was a 144 page slide presentation titled "Call to Minimize Distraction & Respect Users' Attention." As the title suggests, this early effort framed DWB primarily through the lens of minimizing unwanted distractions or reducing unwanted use of mobile devices. Similarly, Google's current hub for DWB [11] describes DWB primarily through the suite of tools they provide to foster wellbeing, with many of those tools focused on encouraging reflection, reducing distraction, or unplugging from digital technology when needed. Along those same lines, Apple has also released a suite of DWB features for the latest versions of iOS, again promoting functionality to monitor screen time, set time limits for app use, or reducing distractions, among others [25].

There is a common thread in how each of the above aims to frame and promote DWB. By suggesting that DWB can be supported by product interventions that aim to reduce interactions with mobile devices or increase intentionality around those interactions, these approaches suggest that (1) left unchecked, mobile devices can have a negative impact on DWB. And (2), mobile devices may also be the solution to the negative impact they have the capacity to have. We suggest that this approach to DWB represents a relevant starting point to frame DWB more broadly in the sections that follow.

2.2 Part 2: DWB and Academia

While issues around wellbeing and digital health have been studied for a long time, "Digital Wellbeing" specifically as a target of study is relatively undefined. In fact, as recently as 2019 a CHI workshop was still aiming to provide a clear definition for DWB [6], asking among other questions: "What do we consider digital wellbeing to be and is there a shared understanding of it?".

Also in CHI 2019, work by [26] define DWB in a manner similar to [11], through the lens of increasing reflection and reducing overuse. In particular, they focus on the problems of unwanted distraction and technology addiction. Accordingly, the rubric they propose for evaluating successful DWB applications is primarily focused on supporting behavior change and the formation of habits to promote self-regulation.

2.3 Part 3: Designing for the Positive

Distinct from DWB, a line of prior research investigates how technology can support positive human experiences. Notably, this includes work on Positive Design [7], on Positive Technology [24], work on Experience Design [10, 15, 17], and work on Positive Computing [5, 33]. This also includes recent methodological innovations, such as designing for social innovation [24], designing for human capabilities [29], or design for socially constructive behavior [37], with a slightly more expansive overview on design for well-being available in [20].

These approaches have a shared aspiration for designs that create, foster, or support "desirable" experiences with positive outcomes. Taking the first two from above, for example – Positive Design aims to increase people's subjective wellbeing and, along with it, their own appreciation of their lives; its intention is to allow people to flourish [8]. Positive Technology, similarly, aims to "manipulate the quality of experience with the goal of increasing wellness, and generating strengths and resilience in individuals, organizations, and societies" [34]. And while Positive Design aims to frame a design process to optimize subjective wellbeing by focusing on pleasure, personal significance, and virtue, Positive Technology aims to promote personal wellbeing by focusing on design's impact on affective quality, engagement/actualization, and connectedness of experience – that is, by focusing on hedonic, eudaimonic, and social/interpersonal dimensions of personal experience. Both of these approaches cite their theoretical lineage extending primarily from Positive Psychology, notably [35].

2.4   Part 4: Synthesizing Conceptualizations of DWB

What these conceptualizations of DWB across both industry and academia have in common is a framing of DWB fundamentally as a solution to a specific problem. Commonly, that problem is related to overuse, distraction, or addiction to technology. Given that perspective, the conversation around DWB is typically focused on identifying strategies to mitigate the problems of overuse, distraction, or addiction. While we agree that problems of overuse or addiction are unquestionably worthy of study, we suggest that a broader framing of DWB may facilitate more productive conversations from both the design and research perspectives. We argue that this broader perspective may allow us to shift the conversation from DWB as a set of interventions meant to remedy digital psychopathology, to instead, DWB as a holistic approach to foster human wellbeing through interactions with digital devices.

Drawing once again from industry, [14] provides a definition of DWB along these lines, suggesting that DWB is "a state of satisfaction that people achieve when digital technology supports individual wellbeing, incorporating the consideration of user needs that extend beyond a single product experience." Similarly, once again from academia, recent work by Abeele [1] proposes a definition of DWB that is sensitive to the balance between the need for autonomy and the need for support:

> "Digital wellbeing is a subjective individual experience of optimal balance between the benefits and drawbacks obtained from mobile connectivity. This experiential state is comprised of affective and cognitive appraisals of the integration of digital connectivity into ordinary life. People achieve digital wellbeing when experiencing maximal controlled pleasure and functional support, together with minimal loss of control and functional impairment."

Abeele introduces this as the "mobile connectivity paradox," stating "while ubiquitous connectivity can support autonomy, it can also challenge that very experience." She continues, "Autonomy is challenged when mobile technologies exert direct control over thoughts and behaviors by directing attention away from people's primary activities." While this framing of DWB is more holistic than those above, precisely how we frame autonomy has implications for how we might describe an "optimal" balance between human and technology. For instance, if we accept that autonomy is challenged when attention is directed away from primary activities, the DWB strategies above of reducing distractions and limiting screen time would appear to be productive interventions.

Conversely, if we suggest instead that autonomy is challenged when intention, as defined in the Introduction, is directed away from primary activities, then more precise interventions may be more productive.

Once again citing [6], "The frames we adopt are important because they shape the problem space in which particular solutions can emerge." By participating in the discussion around the framing of DWB, we hope to shape the space in which we, as researchers and designers, can make a productive contribution to how people interact with their mobile devices.

2.5   Closing: DWB and the Meaningless

We conclude this section by once again drawing attention to the meaningless. We suggest that the absence of explicit attention paid to this topic in current literature is not due to its lack of importance, but is at least in part a result of the framing of DWB that has been adopted to this point. Support of the meaningless, as defined in this paper, is a subset of a productive pursuit of DWB. Sensitivity to the meaningless is one potential path towards resolving some of the tensions behind Abeele's "mobile connectivity paradox," supporting autonomy while still allowing for self-regulation. And finally, explicit support of the meaningless may highlight design interventions that acknowledge a more holistic view of our lived experiences, and improve our abilities to amplify rather than constrain productive aspects of those lived experiences, regardless of how trivial or mundane they may otherwise appear.

3   Methods

This study was the result of an industry/academia partnership between Google and the Human Centered Design & Engineering department (HCDE) at the University of Washington. This partnership took the form of a *directed research group*, an opportunity for graduate and undergraduate students to receive course credit for contributing to ongoing research. The primary goal of this research group was to examine the nature of our interactions with our mobile devices – identifying and differentiating between the salient and the non, between the habitual and the reflective, and eventually, between the meaningful and the meaningless.

The study involved 13 participants, with primary data collection taking place over 10 weeks. Participants were 23% male, 77% female, and included both students from the HCDE BS (45%) and MS (65%) program. All participant involvement in group projects was completed with informed consent; all course materials were constructed with approval from both the university and industry partner; all data collection was fully voluntary, and could be redacted at any time; and permission was given for all data collected to be used by any research group member for any purpose in the future (e.g., to publish or for profit).

During this period, the research group completed three separate rounds of study, each involving Experience Sampling Method (ESM) data collection [7], mobile device application logging, semi-structured interviews, and diary studies. Afterwards, we completed two separate analyses – a quantitative analysis primarily focusing on ESM data, and an interpretative analysis, focusing primarily on the interview and diary study data. We present each of those analyses in the sections that follow.

3.1 Quantitative Analysis of ESM Data

Round 1 of the study answered the question of why participants used their phone at multiple device activation "on" events during a week. Round 2 of the study focused on specific aspects of behavior, shifting from asking about in-the-moment behavior in the abstract (e.g., "why'd you open your phone?") to asking the more targeted question: "when you opened your mobile device recently and used these specific apps, what were you really doing?" In the third round of the study, sustained app usage by participants would trigger our experience survey, asking them to relate their device usage to their activity(ies) in the real world at that moment. All ESM data were collected using the Paco mobile application [3]. For an overview of data, see Table 1.

Table 1. Overview of data collected across three rounds of study

Round	Data
Pilot: Why'd you open your phone?	302 responses, collected over 8 days
Round 1: Why'd you open your phone	275 responses, collected over 8 days
Round 2: Targeted ESM	324 responses, collected over 14 days
Round 3: Focus on the meaningful	334 responses, collected over 17 days

Round 1 – Why'd You Open Your Phone?
Participants were asked two questions during Round 1. First, "Why'd you open your phone?" And second, "After opening your phone, what was your activity related to?" For the first question, participants were provided with an open text box and allowed to indicate single or multiple objectives for opening their phone. For the second question, participants were given the option to select one or more of work, school, personal, or other. The survey prompt was triggered by unlocking or entering the home screen on participants' devices. There was a minimum of 90 min between each trigger for each participant, with no maximum on triggers per day. An overview of the characteristics identified and their prevalence among our participants' experiences in this round of the study is shown in Fig. 1.

Both plots above show counts of what the device activity was related to during the ESM probe – showing work/life context at left where *personal* activities were most prevalent, followed by *school*, *work*, then *other*. The plot at right presents the count for the objective of each reported activity, as defined through multiple coders coding the open response data. Inter-rater reliability was calculated across objectives with 88% agreement ($\alpha = 0.83$), indicating a satisfactory classification scheme given social science data [21]. Significance testing between work/life balance and *objective* identified a significant relationship – X2 (df = 9, stat = 17.347, crit = 15.507, p = 0.027). One interpretation of this result may be that there is a significant relationship between an activity's work/life context and the objective of that activity. For instance, if I'm doing something for personal reasons, I may be doing it in a particular way.

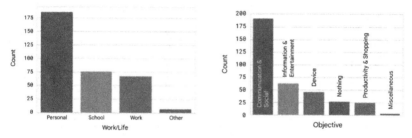

Fig. 1. Breakdown of characteristics identified in round 1 of the study.

Round 2 – Targeted ESM

In this round, we asked four primary questions with two possible follow-ups, with all questions framed by a brief representation of a prior recent activity session with their mobile device (a modification to experience sampling we designated *Targeted ESM*). The first question allowed for open text responses, prompting the participant to describe their activity when the device session pictured occurred. Second, we again asked the participant what that given device session was related to: one or more of work, school, personal, or other, with an open text follow-up when they chose other. Third, we asked if the apps in the given device session were being used for the same goal, or were part of the same activity, with a follow-up prompt asking them about the nature of that similar activity. And fourth, we asked them to rate their level of engagement during the pictured device session, presented as a continuous scale.

Participants' prompts to participate occurred randomly over a 14 day timespan throughout the day up to eight times, with a minimum 120 min between prompts and a blackout period between 11pm and 7am (i.e., no prompts during nighttime hours). An overview of the data collected for Round 2 is shown in Fig. 2.

In this round, we found a significant relationship between participants' self-reported level of engagement with a given activity and their work/life context – X2 (df = 6, stat = 28.212, crit = 12.592, p < .001). In particular, it appears that low engagement activities are more likely to be personal relative to not-personal. It is worth noting, however, that even among high engagement activities, those activities qualified as personal were still more prevalent than non-personal activities. We suggest that this finding should inspire caution in those who may otherwise equate activities done for personal reasons as somehow universally less engaging or otherwise less salient than those completed for non-personal contexts (including for instance, for work or "productive" contexts).

Round 3 – Focus on the Meaningful

In this round, the ESM prompt was triggered when a participant unlocked their device and used any non-system app for at least 20 s (e.g., not including the home screen or a default menu). This round introduced one additional question to those above: "Thinking about what you were doing on your mobile device just now and the real-world activity that it may be related to, how meaningful is that activity?" This trigger would occur no more than once every two hours, with a blackout period at night.

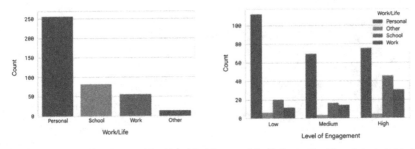

Fig. 2. Breakdown of characteristics identified in round 2 of the study. The plot at right shows the relationship between the Work/Life context and the self-reported **engagement** level of device interaction

We found a significant relationship between participants' self-reported level of meaning and their work/life context. This finding remained true, testing for all work/life contexts included in our study – e.g., work, personal, school, and "other;" X2 (df = 6, stat = 25.719, crit = 12.592, p < .001) – as well as simply distinguishing between personal and non-personal work/life contexts – X2 (df = 6, stat = 24.758, crit = 5.991, p < .001). In particular, experiences that were qualified as "personal" appear to have been far more likely to also have been qualified as having a lower level of *meaning*, in general (see Fig. 3 for an illustration of this).

We suggest two insights from this observation. First, similar to the level of engagement in round 2 we would caution drawing the conclusion that personal activities are universally less meaningful than non-personal activities. They are more prevalent, but among more highly meaningful interactions, personal activities are still comparable with non-personal. And second, further examination of the data identified the cross-section of interactions that were highly meaningful and personal, but where the objective was "Nothing." It's in this cross-section that we suggest our examination of what is meaningless – as defined above – may fruitfully turn.

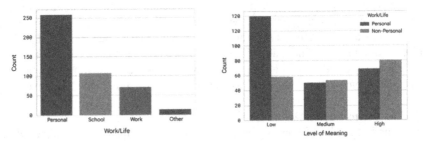

Fig. 3. Breakdown of characteristics identified in round 3 of the study. The plot at right shows the relationship between the Work/Life context and self-reported estimates of how **meaningful** an interaction was.

The "Nothing" Objective

Throughout the duration of the studies above, one thing that became apparent early on was that many of our daily interactions with our mobile devices may not be described as highly useful, by most definitions of that term. Specifically, a fair amount of what participants did on their mobile devices was not just towards undefined objectives (i.e., the "Nothing" objective in our coding scheme), but was also enacted with little to no intent or motivation (i.e., the "Low" engagement level).

Consider the following examples in response to the question "Why'd you open your phone?": "Not sure," (P09); "killing time before class. I don't know," (P06); or "In elevator so opened Instagram," (P16).

Something that a purely logging perspective may identify as directed activity on a mobile application here will be identified through the intent of what brought the participant to the device in the first place – for instance, to avoid something else. In that capacity, the specific objective may be less meaningful than the activity that inspired the interaction (e.g., distraction, avoidance).

A closing question for this section of the analysis is: consider what a meaningful or beneficial intervention would be in a context where there is no real intent behind an interaction, but also no real desire to artificially increase intent. What might an intervention sensitive to the needs of the user be in that case? What might that intervention look like in the cases below, for instance – again, each providing an answer to the question, "Why'd you open your phone?" (emphasis on the last ours): "distracting myself from homework. in my room. I should go for a walk instead. I'm tired" (P06); "**I don't know. sometimes I just open my phone,**" (P16).

3.2 Interpretative Analysis of Interview and Diary Data

The quantitative analysis above focused on ESM data collected during three separate studies, ultimately highlighting the role that the "Nothing" objective played in many interactions with our mobile devices. That analysis allowed us to identify the existence and the shape of the meaningless. The interpretive analysis described below focused on the diary study and semi-structured interview data, allowing us to refine our understanding of the meaningless, situating it among a broader set of interactions with technology, and suggesting possible directions for design interventions.

We would like to introduce two considerations prior to continuing. First, this data was collected over 10 weeks. Throughout the time data was being collected, we were engaging in a set of practices aimed to allow us to more effectively reflect on and engage directly with our interactions with technology. Accordingly, the themes we introduce below were identified in the context of that engagement.

And second, while methods like Interpretative Phenomenological Analysis (IPA) may suggest a single set of unstructured interviews as typical for data collection suitable for interpretative analysis [36], our data is more disparate. We argue that the depth we were able to achieve with our participants given the extended duration of data collection and the direct and targeted engagement with those participants over that duration make our data suitable for interpretative analysis.

Ultimately, this analysis resulted in the identification of three states that most of our participants went through. We additionally identify two human-centric themes of our participants' experiences, and two technology-centric themes describing prior DWB interventions. Together, we suggest these themes collectively describe the complete set of DWB interventions, allowing us to more effectively organize and design for wellbeing in the future.

Three States Identified

Each of the three states identified occur chronologically. Per the first consideration above, the context in which these states were encountered involved ongoing experience sampling, consistent reflection, and exercises intentionally aimed at unpacking our interactions with our mobile devices in a manner likely exceeding what most people typically engage in. Accordingly, in replicating these states – in particular states 2 or 3 – we would encourage a similar level of engagement and reflection.

State 1: [Misalignment] Misalignment Between Real and Perceived Use

This state happens early on, prior to reflection and engagement. This is commonly our default position. Both the existence and extent of misalignment can most easily be identified by providing an accurate representation of device use to the individual. That representation can take many forms. For instance, some of the experiments at [12] allow researchers to measure screen time, track app usage, or count the number of times a mobile device is unlocked on a daily basis. In our case, this misalignment was identified through the use of Paco [3], the mobile app that we used to both trigger our ESM queries as well as for app logging and visualization of daily activities.

We observed three common causes behind this misalignment. First, individuals might be misaligned about the specific type of technologies they use, and their frequency. This was most commonly expressed as surprise at the amount of time people spent on their mobile devices or the number of times they unlock their phones in a day, although we also observed surprise at the opposite – how little someone used their device. Second, misalignment may be about duration or frequency of use of a specific product. In our data this was frequently expressed at surprise around the use of social media apps (e.g., Facebook) or communication apps (e.g., WhatsApp). And third, misalignment may be about the existence or frequency of a context. In our data this could include regret at spending the entire weekend doing homework, or surprise at how often group conversations and coordination were occurring on the mobile device.

State 2: [Awareness] Adjustment of Perceived Use

Where the misalignment in state 1 may be our default position, state 2 is the position people switch to once that misalignment has been identified. This does not imply a change of behavior. At this point, "awareness" is simply an indicator that, for the behavior under observation, one's perception of that behavior is accurate. Continuing from the examples above, state 2 is the outcome of surprise or regret upon realizing that one has been misaligned.

Once state 2 had been reached, group members were generally more able to articulate clearer opinions about their technology use as indicated in our data by both the clarity around recollections of past use and, importantly, the justifications given for that use. This ability to accurately assess one's own experiences was a key component leading to state 3 – articulating value judgments around one's current interactions with mobile devices, to more intentionally shape one's future interactions.

State 3: [Correction] Modify Behaviors; Modify Ideals
Once group members were able to accurately reflect on their interactions with their mobile devices (state 1), and once they were able to establish a set of values around those behaviors (state 2), state 3 marks the point at which they enacted change to realize those values. In some instances this is a behavioral shift, entailing modifying use of technology closer towards an ideal – closer to what was commonly the perceived use prior to state 2. In other cases, this is a perceptual shift, involving modifying individual conceptions of what constitutes ideal interactions towards the current use. Once state 3 had been reached, group members were generally more able to suggest ideas for possible design interventions. During reflection, we would commonly see iteration between state 2 and state 3, between awareness and action.

To clarify the progression through these three states we provide two brief examples. Variations on this first progression may be familiar to many who have engaged in similar types of self-logging exercises.

The first example involves *modifying behavior*, with each number representing a state described above: (1) I thought I was on Facebook for 30 min yesterday, but realized it was 3 h; (2) I was surprised I spent that much time on Facebook – 3 h is too long!; (3) I started being more aware of my time on Facebook, aiming to keep it under an hour.

The second example involves *modifying ideals*, with each number representing a state described above: (1) I realized I was watching quite a bit of television, probably more than I'd like to admit; (2) I also realized that television brought me some joy – it was an experience I looked forward to; (3) I started checking out a projector from school for movie nights to better embrace the experience.

Two Human-Centric Themes of Experience
Through this analysis we identified two primary themes of participants' experiences. These two themes were identified in the recurring cycle between Awareness and Correction, states 2 and 3. The first occurs primarily during the shift of real and perceived interactions towards an individual ideal. The second occurs as the ideal shifts towards the real and perceived. These themes are human-centric, highlighting the opportunities in which individual experiences rather than technology can be mediated to more effectively support wellbeing.

Theme 1: Modifying Behavior to Support a Perceived Ideal
As outlined in the first example above, this theme involves modifying *behavior* to more closely align with an *ideal*. We commonly observed that when participants were made aware of their own activity and that activity was misaligned with participants' conception of themselves, they would modify their behavior to close that gap. An illustration of this in the first example above – once that individual realized unmistakably how much time they spent on social media, they enacted change to move their activity back into closer alignment with their ideals.

In practice, presence of this theme among our participants might be indicated by actions like using an app less, uninstalling an app, turning off notifications, rearranging app icons on the home screen, or hiding the launcher for apps. This experience does not always involve interactions with the device, however. Simply making a deliberate effort to modify the nature of one's interactions with a mobile device may be all that's required to realize that change. Given this, operationalizations of this theme may be difficult outside the context of the types of reflection practices this group was engaged in. Outcomes of this theme may include a greater perceived value of the remaining time spent with technology, an increased feeling of self-control, or autonomy.

Consider the following from one of our interviews, in which a participant was reflecting on what they want versus what they do not want from technology and remembered this moment from their childhood:

"When I was 10, I snapped my CD-ROM of Roller Coaster Tycoon, so I wouldn't get addicted to it. It was so fun, I played it for six hours straight, I realized on my own, and then I snapped it in half. Cause I was like, this is not healthy for me!" (P06, interview).

In this example, there is a clear assertion of values being made. They felt they played a game too much, and they were concerned about becoming addicted to it. Once they realized their actions were not aligned with their ideals (state 2, above), they acted in accordance with their values to correct that misalignment (state 3, theme 1). This type of environmental mediation to support behavior change was fairly common across our data. Consider one more example:

"The addition to Paco and the reflections, have definitely changed the way I use my devices. Since day one I changed a little my behavior, mainly related to games. I used to waste time on games, for any waiting time that I had I used to play. I think the difference on me changing from day 1, to other changes that happen later on the experiment was that I was already aware of that behavior before starting logging anything..." (P11, diary entry).

There are two points to call out from this. First, this participant provides an example of the occasional *intentional* disconnect between ideal and real interactions. They acknowledge knowing about the time they previously spent on games, as well as admitting that time was "wasted." And second, the intervention of the study was introducing *Awareness* (state 2), after which the participant changed their behavior to be in closer alignment with how they value their own time (state 3, theme 1). This shift in behavior was a common response to the clear realization that one's activities did not align with one's ideals.

Theme 2: Modifying a Perceived Ideal to Support Behavior
In contrast with theme 1 above, this theme involves modifying *ideals* to more closely align with *behavior*. Where theme 1 above was relatively common and fairly straightforward to identify, this theme posed slightly greater challenges. Specifically, identifying and attributing a change in perception resulting from an increase in awareness is methodologically difficult in most contexts. Our ability to do so is primarily the result of the nature of our study – repeated iteration between Awareness and Correction, states 2 and

3. This repetition allowed us to probe specific facets of observed behavior, identifying the values our participants attributed to those behaviors. And it allowed us to ask how, if at all, those values might be impacted by this iterative reflection.

In practice, presence of this theme might be indicated by signals like making an explicitly stated decision *not* to change a behavior, clearly establishing a new value, or clearly modifying an established value. And while these signals may be methodologically challenging to capture, conceptually they are still relatively simple. For instance, consider the following three examples of how ongoing and iterative reflection may impact my state of being: (1) I may change how I understand myself; (2) I may change how I feel about myself; or (3) I may change how I feel about my actions. We intentionally share these examples in the first person singular to clearly make the point: though these signals may be difficult to identify, they are not inherently complex. In some instances, the results of these shifts might be quite mundane. But we suggest they are an important facet of experience to consider in our broader framing of DWB.

Consider an example from one of our participants in which they were reflecting on a triumph from the prior week involving shifting their thinking from "defeating" to "supporting" language:

"… I practiced being aware of switching my defeating language to supporting language and it really made a positive difference for me. It reduced the pressure I put on myself in the context of school. I even caught myself doing work after 10pm, which is rare for me! I think because I knew I 'wanted' to do that work. It's the same work, just my context for thinking about it changed, which changed my attitude and made me feel happy. My biggest triumphs are usually when I change my thinking habits. It means a lot to me," (P06, diary entry).

The triumph in this example is not specifically the shift in language, from defeating to supporting. As the participant explicitly states, the triumph is in the shift in thinking habits themselves; it is the impact that shift has on how they experience their activities. The work that was previously a source of stress and pressure was recast as something they "wanted" to do.

Or consider the example we gave in the Introduction, which featured one participant reflecting on a recent frustration juggling multiple demands with limited time:

"… Basically, it seems that, if I focus on one thing and manage to catch up, I will have fallen behind on something else in the meantime. In general during these times when I feel really busy technology functions as an outlet/distraction for me. Normally, if I was less busy I may go on a trip over the weekend. When I'm feeling very busy and like I don't have the time to get everything done I may turn to my computer/cell phone to take breaks from being productive, instead of the outdoors for example." (P09, diary entry).

This is again likely a familiar experience to many – too many demands on time and attention, given too little time and finite attention. For this participant, the turn to their mobile device was not to facilitate the completion of those competing demands; it was intentionally a distraction from them. The shift that is being made explicit here is the decision that the mobile device can be a welcome source of distraction. The language the participant uses, that they turn to their device to "take breaks from being productive" indicates both acknowledgement and acceptance that the device interactions they're describing may not contribute to their productivity.

Two Technology-Centric Themes of Experience
The emphasis above has been on articulating the human-centric themes identified through an interpretive analysis of this data, highlighting where the *meaningless* may reside within this framing. Additional technology-centric themes were also identified, indicated through both our analysis as well as reviews of prior work on DWB. As these themes largely describe established interventions, we introduce them here only briefly, to provide a clearer perspective of the broader DWB landscape.

Theme 3: Technology to Inhibit a Negative
This theme includes many current DWB interventions. In the past, these have involved apps that count the number of times you unlock your phone, the amount of time you spend in each app, or apps that block or limit specific types of interactions or interactions at specific times. In general, many of these interventions aim to reduce use or increase reflection around use. We hope that the analysis and discussion throughout this paper clarifies how other approaches may also be fruitful, aiming to more holistically support individual wellbeing while also allowing for a future in which technology may become ubiquitous.

Theme 4: Technology to Facilitate Change
This theme includes interventions designed to support intentional behavior change. This would include products that facilitate weight loss, smoking cessation, mindfulness, exercise tracking, or, broadly speaking, goal setting.

All considered, these four combined themes might be described thusly: (1) I change what I do, (2) I change what I think, (3) Technology inhibits an action, or (4) Technology supports a behavior. We suggest that these four themes are complementary, and that the demarcation between human-centric and technology-centric themes may provide a useful lens to evaluate the interventions we design. We propose that this perspective will be useful as we consider not just what technology to build, but how that technology may impact the people who use it, sensitive to both the meaningful and, of course, the meaningless.

We conclude this section with a brief summary and synthesis of both the quantitative and qualitative analyses described above, reduced to five observations. First, as our ESM data shows, it is possible to have an objective of "nothing" in our interactions with technology. That objective has been identified and differentiated between habitual or strictly intentional versus unintentional behavior. Second, the "nothing" objective can represent valid experiences. When participants were prompted about specific actions in our Targeted ESM experiment, those behaviors that may otherwise have been overlooked or ignored could be identified as a valuable part of their lives.

Focusing on the interpretative analysis – third, we suggest that it is possible to identify value in even meaningless interactions, as defined in the Introduction. We suggest that this value in particular may be realized in how those interactions allow each of us individually to reflect on, amplify, or mediate our ideals (e.g., theme 2). Fourth, once that value is identified, it can indicate possible interventions that may be more sensitive to the holistic nature of our interactions with technology, to support wellbeing while allowing for ubiquity. And, finally, given the framing of DWB we provide above, we suggest that these human-centric interventions can complement prior DWB efforts.

4 Discussion

Consider the design provocation: How might we effectively understand what is most meaningful in our daily interactions with technology? We hope what has become apparent through the investigation above is that the *meaningless* may be among those phenomena that are not undesirable from a human perspective. We hope to suggest that beyond *habitual* interactions, and distinct from *intentional* versus *unintentional* interactions, there exist a set of behaviors that may on the surface appear less salient, but when it comes to our everyday lived experiences are quite rich. These are the "meaningless" experiences we aimed to understand. Put simply, we suggest that design that supports these experiences will be design that supports DWB more holistically.

While prior work has cemented DWB as a perspective capable of driving design practice, much of that work emphasizes what is visible, observable, or intentional. Positive Design emphasizes and amplifies those aspects and capacities of designed experiences that foster flourishing [8]. Positive Technology emphasizes affective quality, engagement and actualization, and the connectedness of experiences [34]. From an experience perspective, Experience Design [10, 15, 17] emphasizes the construction of patterns or abstract representations of desirable interactions. For instance, in [17], the authors state that "this pattern strips down the idiosyncratic and attempts to extract the structure of a 'good' shared consumption." However, by virtue of an emphasis on the identification, abstraction, and amplification of the "good" in experiences, it is possible that the arbitrary or mundane (e.g., the invisible or meaningless) may be overlooked.

More broadly, from the perspective of the analysis or measurement of experience, Forlizzi and Battarbee provide a broad overview of prior theoretical approaches to understanding experience [13]. They break down those prior approaches into product centered (e.g., [2, 19]), user centered (e.g., [16, 18], or interaction centered (e.g., [9, 39]) models of qualifying experience.

Our approach aims to offer a means to more effectively examine those moments of daily life. In this manner, we draw slightly more from prior work on explorations of boredom, e.g., Lomas's examination of the value of boredom through introspective phenomenology [23], or Bell's examination of the value of boredom [4]. Rather than boredom, though, we suggest a focus on the meaningless. Beyond designing for intention, for behavior change, or for goals, we suggest designing for DWB should be sensitive to our ability to just, *be*. Through our identification and exploration of the meaningless and the themes above, we hope to provide a path for others to create impactful interventions, sensitive to those moments.

5 Conclusion

Ultimately, we hope that the study and discussion above serve to reframe the conversation around DWB. Rather than using technology to "manipulate the quality of an experience" [34], we ask that you consider a technology for DWB that aims to understand and amplify our experiences. Consider a technology for DWB that encourages reflection and refinement of our intentions, rather than seeking to mediate our behaviors directly – a shift from Theme 4 to Theme 2, as defined above.

While we acknowledge that the growth of technology may be exponential or nearly so, the capacity for humans to reasonably incorporate the expanding role of technology into their lives may not be on the same pace. Accordingly, we suggest a moment of reflection from the designers and developers of those technologies to ensure that the activities they intend to foster, to nurture, support, constrain, or remove, are aligned with human needs. We suggest that the themes and methods outlined above are a step in that direction, and call for the continued refinement and examination of research methods to support a broader conceptualization of DWB, inclusive of all those parts of our existence and experience that we may quietly cherish. Finally, we suggest that future work needs to be done that is sensitive to those *meaningless* experiences that may resist easy observation and categorization, or risk optimizing only for those things which are easily observable or categorized.

Acknowledgements. We'd like to thank the members of the Human Centered Design & Engineering Picture 2 Practice Research Group at the University of Washington, whose participation and active engagement was instrumental to our ability to complete the work above.

References

1. Abeele, M.: Digital Wellbeing as a Dynamic Construct, Communication Theory, qtaa024 (2020). https://doi.org/10.1093/ct/qtaa024
2. Alben, L.: Quality of experience: defining the criteria for effective interaction design. Interactions **3**(3), 11–15 (1996)
3. Baxter, K.K., Avrekh, A., Evans, B.: Using experience sampling methodology to collect deep data about your users. In: Proceedings of the 33rd Annual ACM Conference Extended Abstracts on Human Factors in Computing Systems, pp. 2489–2490. ACM (2015)
4. Bell, G.: The value of boredom. Paper presented at the TEDxSydney Conference (2011)
5. Calvo, R.A., Peters, D.: Positive Computing: Technology for Wellbeing and Human Potential. MIT Press (2014)
6. Cecchinato, M., et al.: Designing for digital well-being: a research and practice agenda. In: CHI 2019 Extended Abstracts (2019). https://doi.org/10.1145/3373362
7. Csikszentmihalyi, M., LeFevre, J.: Optimal experience in work and leisure. J. Pers. Soc. Psychol. **56**(5), 815 (1989)
8. Desmet, P.M.A., Pohlmeyer, A.E.: Positive design: An introduction to design for subjective well-being. Int. J. Des. **7**(3), 5–19 (2013)
9. Dewey, J.: Art as Experience. Penguin (2005)
10. Diefenbach, S., Gerber, N., Hassenzahl, M.: The 'Hedonic' in human-computer interaction – history, contributions, and future research directions. In: DIS 2014 – Proceedings of the 2014 ACM Designing Interactive Systems Conference (2014)

11. Digital Wellbeing. Retrieved from 11 Feb 2021. https://wellbeing.google/
12. Digital Wellbeing Experiments. Retrieved from 11 Feb 2021. https://experiments.withgoogle. com/collection/digitalwellbeing
13. Forlizzi, J., Battarbee, K.: Understanding experience in interactive systems. DIS2004 - Designing Interactive Systems: Across the Spectrum, pp. 261–268 (2004). https://doi.org/ 10.1145/1013115.1013152
14. Gilbert, M.: What "Digital Wellbeing" Means to Material Design (2020). Retrieved from 11 Feb 2021. https://material.io/blog/digital-wellbeing-design-systems
15. Hassenzahl, M.: Experience design: Technology for all the right reasons. Syn. Lect. Hum.-Center. Inf. 3(1), 1–95 (2010)
16. Hassenzahl, M.: The thing and I: understanding the relationship between user and product. In: Blythe, M., Monk, A. (eds.) Funology 2. HIS, pp. 301–313. Springer, Cham (2018). https:// doi.org/10.1007/978-3-319-68213-6_19
17. Hassenzahl, M., Eckoldt, K., Diefenbach, S., Laschke, M., Lenz, E., Kim, J.: Designing moments of meaning and pleasure. Experience design and happiness. Int. J. Des. 7(3), 21–31 (2013)
18. Hudspith, S.: Utility, ceremony, and appeal: a framework for considering whole product function and user experience. DRS News (electronic version), V2 N, 11 (1997)
19. Jääskö, V., Mattelmäki, T.: Observing and probing. In: Proceedings of the 2003 International Conference on Designing Pleasurable Products and Interfaces, pp. 126–131 (2003)
20. Keinonen, T., Vaajakallio, K., Honkonen, J.: Designing for wellbeing (2013). https://aaltodoc. aalto.fi:443/handle/123456789/11818
21. Krippendorff, K.: Reliability in content analysis. Hum. Commun. Res. 30(3), 411–433 (2004)
22. Langer, E.J.: Mindfulness. Addison-Wesley/Addison Wesley Longman (1989)
23. Lomas, T.: A meditation on boredom: Re-appraising its value through introspective phenomenology. Qual. Res. Psychol. 14(1), 1–22 (2017)
24. Manzini, E.: Design research for sustainable social innovation. In: Design Research Now, pp. 233–245. Birkhäuser Basel (2007)
25. Paul, M.: Apple launches iOS 12 with suite of digital wellbeing features (2018). Retrieved 11 Feb 2021. https://digitalwellbeing.org/apple-launches-ios-12-with-suite-of-digital-wellbe ing-features/
26. Monge Roffarello, A., De Russis, L.: The race towards digital wellbeing: issues and opportunities. In: Conference on Human Factors in Computing Systems - Proceedings, pp. 1–14 (2019). https://doi.org/10.1145/3290605.3300616
27. Morsella, E., Bargh, J.A., Gollwitzer, P.M. (eds.): Oxford Handbook of Human Action. Oxford University Press, Oxford (2008)
28. Wood, W., Neal, D.T.: A new look at habits and the habit-goal interface. Psychol. Rev. 114(4), 843–863 (2007)
29. Oosterlaken, I.: Taking a Capability Approach to Technology and its Design: A Philosophical Exploration. (Unpublished doctoral dissertation). Delft University of Technology, Delft, The Netherlands (2013)
30. Ouellette, J.A., Wood, W.: Habit and intention in everyday life: the multiple processes by which past behavior predicts future behavior. Psychol. Bull. 124(1), 124–154 (1998). https:// doi.org/10.1037/0033-2909.124.1.54
31. Oulasvirta, A., Rattenbury, T., Ma, L., Raita, E.: Habits make smartphone use more pervasive. Pers. Ubiquit. Comput. 16(1), 105–114 (2012). https://doi.org/10.1007/s00779-011-0412-2
32. Pardes, A.: Google and the rise of 'digital well-being' (2018). Retrieved from 11 Feb 2021. https://www.wired.com/story/google-and-the-rise-of-digital-wellbeing
33. Peters, D., Calvo, R.A., Ryan, R.M.: Designing for motivation, engagement and wellbeing in digital experience. Front. Psychol. 9(MAY), 1–15 (2018). https://doi.org/10.3389/fpsyg. 2018.00797

34. Riva, G., Baños, R.M., Botella, C., Wiederhold, B.K., Gaggioli, A.: Positive technology: using interactive technologies to promote positive functioning. Cyberpsychol. Behav. Soc. Netw. **15**(2), 69–77 (2012). https://doi.org/10.1089/cyber.2011.0139

35. Seligman, M.E.P., Csikszentmihalyi, M.: Positive psychology: an introduction. Am. Psychol. **55**(1), 5–14 (2000). https://doi.org/10.1037/0003-066X.55.1.5

36. Smith, P.J.A., Larkin, M., Flowers, P.: Interpretative Phenomenological Analysis: Theory, Method and Research. SAGE Publications, United Kingdom (2009)

37. Tromp, N.: Social Design - How Products and Services Can Help Us Act in Ways that Benefit Society (Unpublished doctoral dissertation). Delft University of Technology, Delft, The Netherlands (2013)

38. Tversky, A., Kahneman, D.: Judgment under uncertainty: heuristics and biases. Science **185**(4157), 1124–1131 (1974)

39. Wright, P., McCarthy, J., Meekison, L.: Making sense of experience. In: Blythe, M., Monk, A. (eds.) Funology 2. HIS, pp. 315–330. Springer, Cham (2018). https://doi.org/10.1007/978-3-319-68213-6_20

PERACTIV: Personalized Activity Monitoring - Ask My Hands

Vishnu Kakaraparthi(✉)🆔, Troy McDaniel🆔, Hemanth Venkateswara🆔, and Morris Goldberg🆔

Arizona State University, Tempe, USA
{vkakarap,troy.mcdaniel,hemanthv}@asu.edu, masmmlesbaux@me.com

Abstract. Medication adherence is a major problem in the healthcare industry: it has a major impact on an individual's health and is a major expense on the healthcare system. We note that much of human activity involves using our hands, often in conjunction with objects. Camera-based wearables for tracking human activities have sparked a lot of attention in the past few years. These technologies have the potential to track human behavior anytime, any place. This paper proposes a paradigm for medication adherence employing innovative wrist-worn camera technology. We discuss how the device was built, various experiments to demonstrate feasibility and how the device could be deployed to detect the micro-activities involved in pill taking so as to ensure medication adherence.

Keywords: Wearables · Wrist-worn camera · Micro-activty detection · Medication adherence · Pill taking

1 Introduction

Human activity recognition has been an active field for more than a decade. Recent advancements in machine learning and deep learning have spurred an explosion in human activity recognition wearable technologies [45]. Wearables have been used in both consumer-facing and non-consumer-facing applications for human activity recognition such as pose estimation, health monitoring, entertainment, fall detection, etc. [2,22]. Capturing human motion provides insights into activities that are being performed.

Humans use their hands to perform a majority of actions and often involve their hands to manipulate different objects and environments. We utilize our hands at a subconscious level, so we don't deliberately reflect on or regulate the movement of our hands. Thus, observing the movement of the wrist, palm, and fingers, and how they manipulate objects in the immediate environment can

Supported by National Science Foundation under Grant No. 1828010, Greater Phoenix Economic Council (GPEC), The Global Sport Institute at Arizona State University (GSI), and Arizona State University.

N. A. Streitz and S. Konomi (Eds.): HCII 2022, LNCS 13326, pp. 255–272, 2022.
https://doi.org/10.1007/978-3-031-05431-0_18

provide information to decipher human activity. In this paper, we introduce a new paradigm for monitoring the movements of palms and fingers, and explore the activity of pill taking in the setting of medication adherence.

Although pill taking is an important daily activity, it has been estimated that only 25% to 50% of patients correctly and consistently take their medications. In the U.S., in the order of 125,000 people die annually from non-adherence to medical prescription [50]. It is estimated that failure to take medicines as prescribed costs the healthcare system about $100–$300 billion annually [44]. Aids such as pillboxes marked with the days of the week do help; however, they leave responsibilities to the patient and do not address forgetfulness, incorrect ingestion, dropped or misplaced medication. This paper introduces a method to monitor medication adherence for pills using a wrist-worn camera device.

We structure this paper as follows. Section 2 reviews various exocentric and egocentric camera technologies for human activity recognition and the relevant research in the field of wrist-worn technologies. In Sect. 3, we detail a wrist-worn camera-based wearable technology for human activity understanding and its potential applications. The activity of pill taking and the proposed approach are discussed in Sect. 4. Section 5 provides our conclusions and suggestions for future work.

2   Related Work

2.1   Human Activity Understanding

There has been an increased interest in understanding human behavior using exocentric and egocentric sensors in the recent decade. Conventionally, activity monitoring is done with inertial sensors, such as accelerometers, gyroscopes, magnetometers, etc. These sensors in wearable smart wristbands and smartphones provide a means to keep track of people's daily and fitness activities by auto-logging different activities such as sitting, standing, lying down, climbing floors, cycling, running, swimming, walking, jogging, or the like. Although these inertial sensors can observe simple activities of daily living, they do not measure all aspects of motion that are important to understanding the behavior of humans. For example, traditional human activity monitoring systems may use accelerometers solely to capture movement and posture changes. Still, they do not account for body orientation changes, environmental information, and nearby objects, which substantially impact the body motion; also, inertial sensors are subjected to erroneous data. Substantial integration drift due to the errors such as time-variant sensor biases and measurement noise [30].

Understanding the finer details of human motion in certain activities such as manipulating objects, daily living activities, and sports could improve human activity recognition. The need to deeply understand human behavior has prompted the move to camera-based technologies and traditional vision-based approaches. Human action recognition using temporal images was first introduced in Yamato et al. [46]. The primary goal is to analyze a video to identify the actions taking place. Traditional approaches to action recognition rely on object detection, pose detection, dense trajectories, or structural information. In the last ten years, significant progress has been made in deep learning-based computer vision approaches for monitoring the physical and physiological aspects of human activities to better understand tasks we perform. Camera-based technologies can be broken down into two classes, *exocentric* and *egocentric*, characterized by their viewpoints. In exocentric, viewpoints (third-person view) of both the subject and the actions are captured. In egocentric, (first-person view) the camera is placed on the subject with only parts of their anatomy being visible [1].

An extensively studied example of the exocentric class is "fall detection" for seniors wherein different camera-based devices such as Microsoft Kinect [4, 37, 48], RGB [17, 49], 3D cameras [23, 38], and thermal cameras [36] have been investigated. A second example is the use of motion sensing input devices such as the Microsoft Kinect, Playstation II Eyetoy, and Nintendo Wii in applications such as VirtualGym [19], and other Exergames [10, 35, 47] to motivate physical activity among seniors and promote a non-sedentary lifestyle.

Egocentric or body-mounted video cameras come in different flavors and support the monitoring of varying activity. Head-mounted cameras have been proposed for finding missing objects [41], and when mounted on glasses, for hand segmentation [3]. Body-mounted cameras have been used for lifelogging [7], for location detection [13], for gait analysis when worn on shoes, obstacle detection, and context recognition [20].

We are particularly interested in exploiting wrist-mounted cameras which focus on the fingers and hands. We use our hands, in particular, to touch, displace, hold onto and manipulate objects as we perform different activities. Our hands are continuously moving; therefore, monitoring the hand movements and interactions of the hand with other objects in the environment is vital for understanding how different actions are performed.

Hand Pose estimation is the process of predicting the position of the hand and different joints in a 3D space and has become an important area of study with the emergence of Virtual Reality, Mixed Reality, and Augmented Reality [6].

Digits [14] is a wrist-worn sensor that uses an Infrared line projector and Infrared camera to understand the 3D pose of the hand with the help of kinematic models in eyes-free interaction with mobile devices and gaming. Finger occlusions and rapid motions still pose significant challenges to the accuracy of such methods [11].

The first mention of a wrist-worn camera technology to identify gestures was in [43], where a video camera was worn on the ventral side of the wrist to observe discrete changes in movements of three fingers from a rest position. Other researchers have implemented similar wrist-worn cameras for keystroke detection [39], and activity detection [26]. WristCam [43] uses a video camera worn on the ventral side that is used to observe discrete changes in movements of three fingers from a rest position to identify seven variations of the finger gestures and one rest position. Keystroke detection was performed using a very similar setup by

[18]. WristSense [26] is a wrist-worn device equipped with an accelerometer, microphones, and a camera. The sensor data is sent to a Bluetooth-enabled smartphone. Traceband [16] uses a wist-worn camera with proximity sensors to find missing items. The camera captures frames for 5 s at up to 10 frames per second. This paper aims to solve the problem of locating daily used objects in both young and the elderly due to absentmindedness or perceptual issues.

3   Wrist-Camera Technology

We propose PERACTIV - **Per**sonalized **Activ**ity Monitoring, a wrist-worn lightweight, low-cost, scalable, unobtrusive, and easy-to-use wearable technology that tracks the movements of the hand and fingers and generates a video stream of the activities performed and the immediate environment. In the simplest embodiment, this wearable device comprises a printed circuit board, camera, housing, and wrist cuff as seen in Fig. 1.

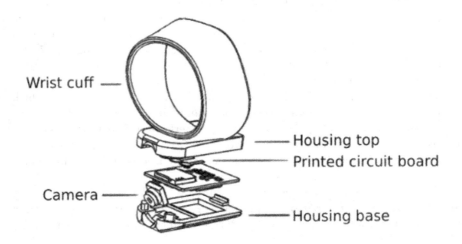

Fig. 1. PERACTIV device.

Figure 2 depicts the wrist-mounted vision-based device with a camera aimed at the user's hand and fingers (hand-centric view) to capture the user's nuanced interactions with their surroundings. The ventral side of the wrist is an ideal location for this wearable camera because it provides a detailed view of the palm and fingers, which we use for fine interactions with different objects. This location effectively captures the panoramic views of the locale along with the fingers and palm. Wrist-mounted cameras provide the ability to more consistently observe movements of the hand and its interactions while not having to detect and track the hands [9].

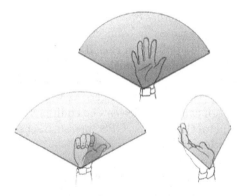

Fig. 2. Illustration of the wrist-worn device's placement and the field of views from different viewpoints.

3.1 Design

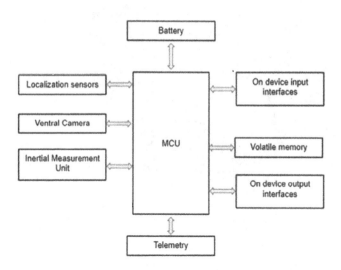

Fig. 3. Structural components of the PERACTIV device.

The structural components of the wrist-worn device are comprised of a micro-controller unit, various sensory modules such as the camera, IMU, etc., along with other essential components such as a battery, memory, on-board storage, expandable storage, and telemetry in terms of WiFi and Bluetooth adapters. This can be seen the Fig. 3. The current iteration of the device is built using a Raspberry Pi Zero W kit, a Raspberry Pi Camera Module, an MPU-9250, and a battery.

The micro-controller unit handles on-device user interactions through the on-board input and output interfaces. It connects to all the sensory modules and communicates with a mobile application executable by a mobile phone or other mobile devices through the telemetry unit.

The device tracks the movements of the wrist, hands, and fingers while also producing a video feed of the hand and fingers as well as their immediate surroundings. The wrist-worn camera device can be equipped with Near-Field Communication (NFC), Bluetooth beacons, GPS, pressure sensors, and many other sensors to increase functionality and use cases.

The final product, as illustrated in Fig. 4 would be part of a smartwatch which includes a miniature camera on the ventral side embedded into the wrist strap. This smart device can be used to monitor and track the environment and the movements of the palm and fingers during object interactions.

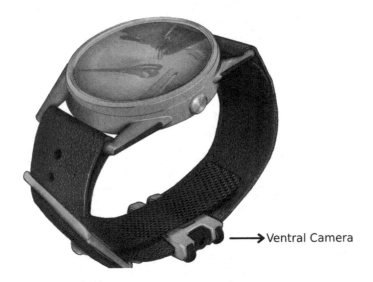

Ventral Camera

Fig. 4. PERACTIV device as a Smartwatch.

3.2 Experiments

Different experiments and literature have supported and helped our design process immensely. We developed multiple prototypes for testing the most simple and useful configuration of the device, as seen in Fig. 5. These experiments have helped to identify the possible placement of the camera on the wrist, the angle, and the type of camera used.

Fig. 5. An array of PERACTIV prototypes.

Ventral and Dorsal Placement of Wrist Ccamera: The goal of this experiment is to find the best possible placement of the camera on the wrist that is completely unobtrusive, and does not interfere in any way with the movements of the hands and fingers but also gives a clear view of the interactions of the hands within the environment. From this experiment, we learned that cameras placed on the ventral and dorsal sides of the wrist, as seen in Fig. 6, are the two best locations.

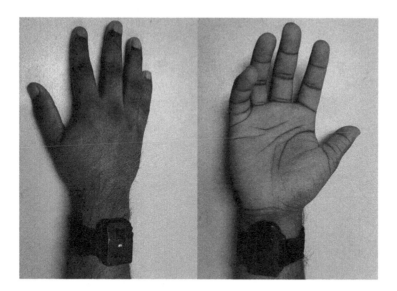

Fig. 6. Camera placed on both Ventral (left) and Dorsal (right) side of the wrist.

The immediate surroundings are captured by one video camera on the dorsal side of the wrist, while the fingers, hand, and object of interest are captured by the second video camera on the ventral side of the wrist. For most cases, the ventral side of the wrist is an ideal location for a wearable camera because it provides a thorough view of the palm and fingers, which we employ for fine object contact.

Understanding Different Motions of the Wrist: The wrist's normal functional range of motion has to be tested with the device. The range of motions from the wrist for wrist flexion to extension are between 38° and 40°; wrist radial and ulnar deviation is between 28° and 38°; and forearm pronation and supination is between 13° and 53° [31].

These movements in Fig. 7 were verified with different participants. The participants identified no discomfort in the actions performed, and the device was able to capture the motion performed.

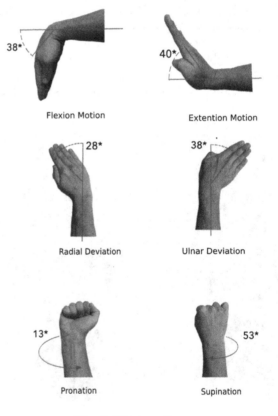

Fig. 7. Wrist motions.

Understanding Interactions with Different Kinds of Objects: Hands are often in motion; however, we are only interested in a subset of these motions that are relevant to the action of interest. Reaching towards an object is a basic motion that all people perform. Typically, depending on the object of interest, an individual makes these motions in a stereotypical manner; for example, little objects such as pills are pinched between the thumb and index, whereas large objects such as a set of keys utilize both the palms and fingers as seen in Fig. 8.

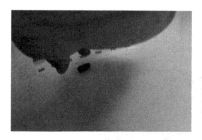

Fig. 8. The hand approaching a tiny object (left) and approaching a large object (right).

The fingers take varied positions when the hand contacts, grasps, displaces, or manipulates an object. The pattern of hand position and motion is determined by the object, and it varies from person to person. We tested the device with participants holding different objects to understand the various grasps as mentioned in [5]: Cylindrical grasp, Tip grasp, Hook or Snap grasp, Palmar grasp, Spherical and Lateral grasp.

Along with exploring the different grasps, we wanted to understand the activities performed. This study was then extended to investigate grips in sports. Interviews were conducted with Power Lifting, Weight Lifting, Rock Climbing, Boxing, Golf, and Lacrosse athletes and sports professionals. This provided us with a comprehensive insight into different holds and grips in sports. Especially in rock climbing, there exist different types of grips for each type of rock. These include the jug, sloper, undercut, crimp, and pinch. Capturing and identifying these grips is a difficult task, but the device is capable of capturing grasps from simple everyday tasks.

Understanding Occlusion by Palm and Visibility of Fingers: A silhouette study was performed to understand the occlusion caused by the Thenar and Hypothenar eminences of the hand. The results from this study, as seen in Fig. 9, helped us understand that sometimes the view of the fingers is occluded by the eminences. Following this study, we also moved the camera away from the wrist and pointed it towards the thumb and index finger to improve visibility and reduce occlusion.

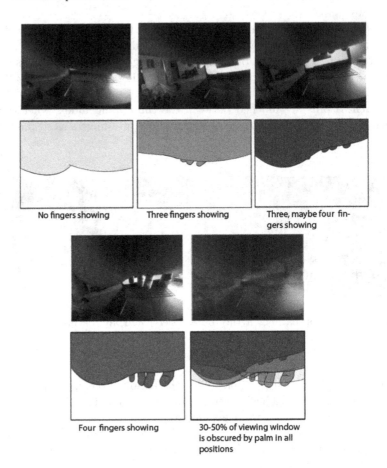

Fig. 9. Visibility of the fingers while approaching objects under obstruction from thenar and hypothenar eminences.

3.3   Applications

Based on all our experiments and interviews, we have identified various applications for this device. The wide array of sensors on the device can be used with various applications such as tracking everyday objects, health and fitness tracking, elderly care, aids for the vision-impaired, gesture-based interfaces, sports, education, and Virtual Reality, Mixed Reality, and Augmented Reality gaming. The device can leverage modern machine learning and deep learning techniques for objects, locales, and activities identification. The technology has significant potential to lead to a new class of products and associated services centered on monitoring human activity associated with the hand. A wide array of additional sensors such as NFC readers can be added to the device to improve the functionality in various applications.

In Elderly Care, which is the focus of this paper, the system could be trained and customized using show and tell techniques to track personal items such as pills, keys, glasses, credit cards, etc. This can also be extended as a stand-alone device for individuals to track daily objects and monitor day-to-day activities. With voice or playback on a display device, an interactive Q&A system can then respond helpfully to a variety of user questions such as, "Where did I leave my glasses?" and "Did I take my medication this morning?". This can also be expanded to missing object detection and pill detection for medication adherence, as seen in Figs. 10 and 11, respectively.

Fig. 10. Missing object identification and localization.

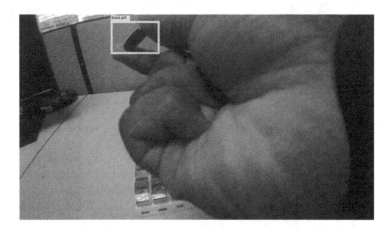

Fig. 11. Pill detection.

4 Pill Taking Activity

As previously discussed, failure to take prescribed medications is anticipated to cost the healthcare system between $100 and $300 billion each year [44]. Many studies have been performed to try and reduce the medication non-adherence issue. Some studies involve drug therapy education alone; however, the efficacy and effectiveness of education alone on a long-term basis is poor [12]. Automated pill dispensing systems such as Philips Lifeline Medication Dispenser [25], Hero [21], Pria [34], MedaCube [28], e-Pill MedSmart Voice [29] are programmable devices used to dispense the right pills, determine the right pill amount and at the right time. However, these are quite costly, difficult to use, immobile [15], and often prone to mechanical failures [42]. They also do not ensure the pill has been ingested. The medication can be dropped or misplaced after it has been dispensed. Using the PERACTIV device, we investigated the activity of pill-taking to better understand the process, its hurdles, pain points, and worries individuals have with pill taking. To interpret human action involving hands and objects, we must simultaneously monitor the hand and its surroundings.

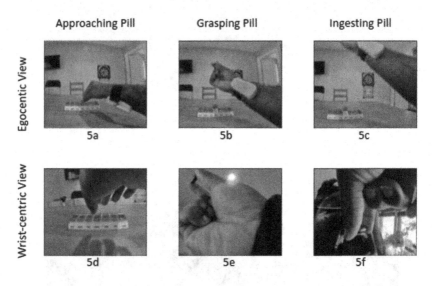

Fig. 12. Comparing egocentric and wrist-centric view for pill taking.

Research in computer vision for predicting and detecting human activities has been carried out using exocentric views (cameras placed within the environment) [27] or egocentric views (cameras placed on the body) [33]. This device provides a new paradigm with wrist-centric views. We use the videos of patients taking medication using a wrist-worn camera put on the dominant hand. The dataset is comprised of videos with successful and unsuccessful attempts for the activity of pill taking.

As seen in Fig. 12, the wrist-centric placement enables a clearer view of the movement of the fingers (i.e., opening, closing, manipulating) and their interactions with the medication as compared to an egocentric view. The pill is always visible and can be tracked until it reaches the mouth. This ensures detection of weather the medication has been successfully ingested, and also, the reason why the medication may not be ingested.

The occlusion of objects due to the user's hands and fingers makes object detection a difficult task in various contexts and environments despite advances in object detection algorithms and techniques using the wrist-mounted camera technology [32]. In many cases, we see that the fingers may completely or partially enclose the object, causing complete object occlusion or providing only partial views of an object. In Fig. 13, we can see the pill is completely occluded by the fingers. A fine-grained pill-taking analysis is a challenging task since people have different styles and ways of taking medication, different pillboxes, different medications, and also, different situations such as standing, sitting, indoors, and outdoors with different lighting.

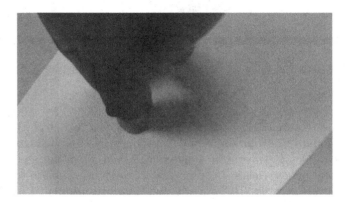

Fig. 13. Finger occlusion.

Our approach is based on insights into how individuals grasp objects. The visual system's task is to find and identify the object and then guide the hand in its approach to the object subconsciously. From a behavioral point of view, i.e., as it appears to the outside observer, the hand moves autonomously without any mental effort towards the object and changes its pose as it approaches the object. When it is within touching distance, the fingers and the hand have assume a pose, ready to grasp the object, where fine control depends upon one's sense of touch. We propose a model involving the identification of finer activities, in which the movement and actions are broken down into manageable granular actions, which we call micro-activities.

In the case of pill-taking, one possible decomposition is: (i) moving towards a pill, (ii) grasping the pill, (iii) moving with the pill in hand and, finally, (iv) releasing the pill into the open mouth. If these micro-activities are identified with

268   V. Kakaraparthi et al.

high confidence levels, then we may conclude that the individual has successfully completed the process of taking the pill. An example of successful completion of the pill-taking activity is shown in Fig. 14.

This approach will not only help to identify success or failure in taking medication, but will also identify the fault or reason for failing in the activity of pill taking. These may include situations where the pillbox may contain incorrect pills, the individual might drop a pill, the individual might interrupt the process to take food or a drink, etc.

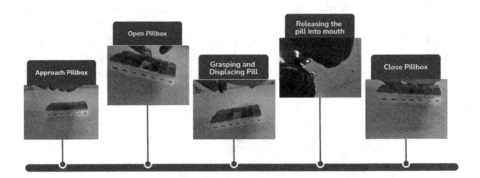

Fig. 14. Micro-activities involved in taking medication captured by the PERACTIV device.

We propose to apply deep neural network models to detect these micro-activities. Standard Convolution Neural Networks (CNN) treat frames independently by extracting features from single images and might miss temporal and Spatio-temporal dependencies. Deep neural networks using spatio-temporal filtering approaches such as 3DCNNs [40] and TwoStream-Inflated 3DCNNs [8] capture temporal information and can be trained to detect micro-activities. We propose to develop a probabilistic inference model that can string together the detected micro-activities to infer the success or failure of pill taking.

The micro-activities, as seen in Fig. 14, can have different lengths, spatial and temporal dependencies, and object interactions. In the instance of pill-taking, these may be the use of different pills and pillboxes, different styles of taking a pill, e.g., use of the fingers to pickup the pill or use of the palm, on the other hand, to place the pill, pill taking while sitting or standing, and in different environments such as indoors or outdoors. A common neural network model will to incapable of detecting micro-activities of all the users. We intend to train a base model with data from all the users and apply transfer learning to adapt a base model to the data of each user to create a customized pill activity recognition system for every user.

5   Conclusion

Medical adherence is very complicated; through our interviews and background research, we have identified the different ways and settings that medication can be administered. Medication may be administered orally as liquids, pills, tablets, or chewable tablets, by injection into a vein, sprayed into the nose, applied to the skin, and many more. To add to the complexity, the medication can be taken while standing or sitting, using various pillboxes, in different locations and lighting conditions, and the arm, hand and fingers movements vary significantly from person to person.

The fine-grained pill-taking analysis is a challenging task. Based on our findings, we plan to collect and publish a wrist-worn camera dataset for the activity of pill taking involving various scenarios and styles, examine how we can enhance the activity of pill taking by augmenting the data through adding additional variations to the data, and work on identifying algorithms for this data.

The proposed research aims to help individuals with varying cognitive deficits living alone or in nursing homes. The results of this research will also enhance our understanding of both the utility and impact of intelligent, wrist-centric wrist wearables on senior activities of daily living, quality of life, and independence.

Acknowledgements. This paper was supported by funding from National Science Foundation under Grant No. 1828010, Greater Phoenix Economic Council (GPEC), The Global Sport Institute at Arizona State University (GSI), and Arizona State University.

The authors thank partner facility, Mirabella, at ASU for helping in recruiting participants for interviews. The authors also thank Joshua Chang for his help in sketching Figs. 1, 2, 4, 9 and Abhik Chowdhury for his help in developing the device.

References

1. Almasi, M., Riera, J, Boza, S.: Undestanding human motions from ego-camera videos. https://doi.org/10.13140/RG.2.2.31884.54409
2. Attal, F., Mohammed, S., Dedabrishvili, M., Chamroukhi, F., Oukhellou, L., Amirat, Y.: Physical human activity recognition using wearable sensors. Sensors. **15**(12), 31314–31338 (2015)
3. Bambach, S., Lee, S., Crandall, D., Yu, C.: Lending a hand: detecting hands and recognizing activities in complex egocentric interactions. In: 2015 IEEE International Conference on Computer Vision (ICCV) (2015)
4. Barabas, J., Bednar, T., Vychlopen, M.: Kinect-based platform for movement monitoring and fall-detection of elderly people. In: 2019 12th International Conference on Measurement (2019)
5. Baritz, M., Cotoros, D., Singer, C.: Thermographic analysis of hand structure when subjected to controlled effort. In: 2013 E-Health and Bioengineering Conference. EHB 2013, pp. 1–4 (2013)
6. Barsoum, E.: Articulated hand pose estimation review. arXiv preprint arXiv:1604.06195 (2016)
7. Blum, M., Pentland, A., Troster, G.: InSense: interest-based life logging. IEEE Multim. **13**(4), 40–48 (2006)

8. Carreira, J., Zisserman, A.: Quo Vadis, Action Recognition? A New Model and the Kinetics Dataset, pp. 4724–4733 (2017). https://doi.org/10.1109/CVPR.2017.502
9. Chan, C.-S., Chen, S.-Z., Xie, P.-X., Chang, C.-C., Sun, M.: Recognition from hand cameras: a revisit with deep learning. In: Leibe, B., Matas, J., Sebe, N., Welling, M. (eds.) ECCV 2016. LNCS, vol. 9908, pp. 505–521. Springer, Cham (2016). https://doi.org/10.1007/978-3-319-46493-0_31
10. Chao, Y., Scherer, Y., Montgomery, C.: Effects of using Nintendo Wii^{TM} Exergames in older adults. J. Aging Health **27**(3), 379–402 (2014)
11. Chatzis, T., Stergioulas, A., Konstantinidis, D., Dimitropoulos, K., Daras, P.: A comprehensive study on deep learning-based 3D hand pose estimation methods. Appl. Sci.. **10**(19), 6850 (2020)
12. Clark, N.P.: Role of the anticoagulant monitoring service in 2018: beyond warfarin. Hematol. Am. Soc. Hematol. Educ. Program. **2018**(1), 348–352 (2018)
13. Clarkson, B., Mase, K., Pentland, A.: Recognizing user's context from wearable sensors: baseline system. J. Neurol. Sci. **248** (1999)
14. Kim, D., et al.: Digits: freehand 3D interactions anywhere using a wrist-worn glove-less sensor. In: Proceedings of the 25th annual ACM symposium on User Interface Software and Technology, pp. 167–176. Association for Computing Machinery, New York (2012)
15. Doshi, V., et al.: An IoT based smart medicine box. Int. J. Adv.Res. Ideas Innov. Technol. **5**(1), 205–207 (2019)
16. Tavakolizadeh, F., Gu, J., Saket, B.: Traceband: locating missing items by visual remembrance. In: Proceedings of the Adjunct Publication of the 27th Annual ACM Symposium on User Interface Software and Technology (UIST 2014 Adjunct), pp. 109–110. Association for Computing Machinery, New York (2014)
17. Feng, W., Liu, R., Zhu, M.: Fall detection for elderly person care in a vision-based home surveillance environment using a monocular camera. Signal Image Video Process. **8**(6), 1129–1138 (2014). https://doi.org/10.1007/s11760-014-0645-4
18. Ahmad, F., Musilek, P.: A keystroke and pointer control input interface for wearable computers. In: Fourth Annual IEEE International Conference on Pervasive Computing and Communications (PERCOM 2006), pp. 10–11 (2006)
19. Fernandez-Cervantes, V., Neubauer, N., Hunter, B., Stroulia, E., Liu, L.: VirtualGym: a kinect-based system for seniors exercising at home. Entertain. Comput. **27**, 60–72 (2018)
20. Fitzpatrick, P., Kemp, C.: Shoes as a platform for vision. In: Proceedings Seventh IEEE International Symposium on Wearable Computers, 2003. (n.d.)
21. Automatic Pill Dispenser - How the Hero Dispenser Works!. https://herohealth.com/our-product/. Accessed 24 Feb 2022
22. Khusainov, R., et al.: Real-time human ambulation, activity, and physiological monitoring: taxonomy of issues, techniques, applications, challenges and limitations. Sensors **13**(10), pp. 12852–12902 (2013)
23. Kim, S., Ko, M., Lee, K., Kim, M., Kim, K.: 3D fall detection for single camera surveillance systems on the street. In: 2018 IEEE Sensors Applications Symposium (SAS) (2008)
24. Lee, J., Lee, J., Lim, I., Kim, Y., Hyun-Namgung, Lee, J.: Kinect-based monitoring system to prevent seniors who live alone from solitary death. In: Computational Science and Its Applications, UCCSA 2014. ICCSA 2014. LNCS, vol. 8582, pp. 709–719. Springer, Cham (2014). https://doi.org/10.1007/978-3-319-09147-1_51
25. Medication Dispensing Service: Philips Lifeline. https://www.lifeline.philips.com/business/medicationdispensing. Accessed 24 Feb 2022

26. Maekawa, T., Kishino, Y., Yanagisawa, Y., Sakurai, Y.: WristSense: wrist-worn sensor device with camera for daily activity recognition. In: 2012 IEEE International Conference on Pervasive Computing and Communications Workshops (2012)
27. Muhamada, A.W., Mohammed, A.A.: Review on recent computer vision methods for human action recognition. Adv. Distrib. Comput. Artif. Intell. J **10**(4), 361–379 (2022)
28. Pharmadva MedaCube™. MedaCube. https://www.medacube.com/. Accessed 24 Feb 2022
29. e-Pill MedSmart Voice. https://www.epill.com/medsmart-voice.html. Accessed 24 Feb 2022
30. El-Sheimy, N., Hou, H., Niu, X.: Analysis and modeling of inertial sensors using Allan variance. IEEE Trans. Instrum. Measur. **57**(1), 140–149 (2008)
31. Nelson, D.L., Mitchell, M.A., Groszewski, P.G., Pennick, S.L., Manske, P.R.: Wrist Range of motion in activities of daily living. In: Schuind, F., An, K.N., Cooney, W.P., Garcia-Elias, M. (eds.) Advances in the Biomechanics of the Hand and Wrist, pp. 329–334. Springer, Boston (1994). https://doi.org/10.1007/978-1-4757-9107-5
32. Nguyen, T., Nebel, J., Florez-Revuelta, F.: Recognition of activities of daily living with egocentric vision: a review. Sensors **16**(1), 72 (2016)
33. Núñez-Marcos, A., Azkune, G., Arganda-Carreras, I.: Egocentric vision-based action recognition: a survey. Neurocomputing **472**, 175–197 (2022)
34. How to Use Your Auto Pill Dispenser: Medication Management: Pria. Pria. https://www.okpria.com/How-it-works. Accessed 24 Feb 2022
35. Rusu, L., Mocanu, I.G., Jecan, S., Sitar, D.S.: Monitoring adaptive exergame for seniors. J. Inf. Syst. Oper. Manag. **10**, 336–343 (2016)
36. Kido, S., Miyasaka, T., Tanaka, T., Shimizu, T., Saga, T.: Fall detection in toilet rooms using thermal imaging sensors. In: IEEE/SICE International Symposium on System Integration (SII) 2009, pp. 83–88 (2009)
37. Stone, E., Skubic, M.: Evaluation of an inexpensive depth camera for in-home gait assessment. J. Ambi. Intell. Smart Environ. **3**(4), 349–361 (2011)
38. Stone, E., Skubic, M.: Evaluation of an inexpensive depth camera for passive in-home fall risk assessment. In: Proceedings of the 5th International ICST Conference on Pervasive Computing Technologies for Healthcare (2011)
39. Tavakolizadeh, F., Gu, J., Saket, B.: Traceband. In: Proceedings of the Adjunct Publication of the 27th Annual ACM Symposium on User Interface Software and Technology – UIST 2014 Adjunct (2014)
40. Tran, D., Bourdev, L., Fergus, R., Torresani, L., Paluri, M.: Learning Spatiotemporal Features with 3D Convolutional Networks. In: Conference: 2015 IEEE International Conference on Computer Vision (ICCV), pp. 4489–4497 (2015)
41. Ueoka, T., Kawamura, T., Kono, Y., Kidode, M.: I'm Here!: a Wearable object remembrance support system. In: Proceedings of 5th International Symposium on the Human-Computer Interaction with Mobile Devices and Services, Mobile HCI 2003, Udine, Italy, 8–11 September 2003, pp. 422–427 (2003). https://doi.org/10.1007/978-3-540-45233-1_40
42. Van Onzenoort, H.A., Verberk, W.J., Kroon, A.A., et al.: Electronic monitoring of adherence, treatment of hypertension, and blood pressure control. Am. J. Hypertens. **25**, 54e59 (2012)
43. Vardy, A., Robinson, J., Cheng, L.T.: The WristCam as input device. Digest of papers. In: Third International Symposium on Wearable Computers (n.d.)
44. Watanabe, J., McInnis, T., Hirsch, J.: Cost of prescription drug-related morbidity and Mortality. Ann. Pharmacother **52**(9), 829–837 (2018)

45. Wu, D., Sharma, N., Blumenstein, M.: Recent advances in video-based human action recognition using deep learning: a review. In: 2017 International Joint Conference on Neural Networks (IJCNN). IEEE (2017)

46. Yamato, J., Ohya, J., Ishii, K.: Recognizing human action in time-sequential images using hidden Markov model. In: Proceedings/CVPR, IEEE Computer Society Conference on Computer Vision and Pattern Recognition. IEEE Computer Society Conference on Computer Vision and Pattern Recognition J76-D-II, pp. 379–385 (1992). https://doi.org/10.1109/CVPR.1992.223161

47. Yang, C., Chen Hsieh, J., Chen, Y., Yang, S., Lin, H.: Effects of Kinect exergames on balance training among community older adults. Medicine **99**(28), e21228 (2020)

48. Yang, L., Ren, Y., Zhang, W.: 3D depth image analysis for indoor fall detection of elderly people. Digit. Commun. Netw. **2**(1), 24–34 (2016)

49. Zhang, C., Tian, Y., Capezuti, E.: Privacy preserving automatic fall detection for elderly using RGBD cameras. In: Miesenberger, K., Karshmer, A., Penaz, P., Zagler, W. (eds.) ICCHP 2012. LNCS, vol. 7382, pp. 625–633. Springer, Heidelberg (2012). https://doi.org/10.1007/978-3-642-31522-0_95

50. Zullig, L., Deschodt, M., Liska, J., Bosworth, H., De Geest, S.: Moving from the trial to the real world: improving medication adherence using insights of implementation science. Ann. Rev. Pharmacol. Toxicol. **59**(1), 423–445 (2019)

An Exercise-Promoting System for Exercising While Doing Desk Work

Mizuki Kobayashi[1], Airi Tsuji[2], and Kaori Fujinami[2(✉)]

[1] Graduate School of Bio-Functions and Systems Sciences, Tokyo University of Agriculture and Technology, 2-24-16 Naka-cho, Koganei, Tokyo 184-8588, Japan
[2] Division of Advanced Information Technology and Computer Science, Tokyo University of Agriculture and Technology, 2-24-16 Naka-cho, Koganei, Tokyo 184-8588, Japan
fujinami@cc.tuat.ac.jp

Abstract. Recently, the importance of exercise has been attracting attention. Exercise has positive effects on the body and mind. However, many people do not get enough exercise, and this trend has not improved over the years. One fundamental challenge why people do not have more opportunities to exercise is that they are too busy with work and household chores. Therefore, to develop an exercise habit, it is necessary to incorporate "exercising" into daily life, which can be done while working or doing housework. In this paper, through the design of a system to promote "doing exercise while working at a desk," we propose both suggestion and feedback methods that conform to working at a desk and enable users to continue to exercise. As future work, we would like to improve the accuracy of the state judgment and the notification timing of the feedback method, thereby adapting the system to various work situations.

Keywords: Internet of Things (IoT) · Exercise promotion · Sensing chair · Sitting posture recognition · Dynamic time warping (DTW)

1 Introduction

Recently, the importance of exercise has been gaining attention. Exercise has been proven to have a positive effect on the body and mental state, as it prevents diseases, such as heart disease, diabetes, and cancer, maintains a healthy weight, and delays the onset of dementia. However, from a survey by the World Health Organization in 2006, more than 1.4 billion people in the world do not get enough exercise, and this trend is continuing [1]. With the COVID-19 pandemic, people are constrained to less frequently go out, and the tendency toward physical inactivity has increased.

There are many possible solutions to the lack of exercise. Training at a gym can be done safely under the guidance of a trainer with expertise, but it can be expensive. Additionally, since users must consciously make time to go to the gym, maintaining their motivation is an issue. Self-directed training can be done without the high cost, however, it meets the concern of increased risk of injury due to incorrect methods or excessive load. Also, as with training at a gym, maintaining motivation is an issue. Furthermore, there is training using electrical muscle stimulation (EMS) equipment, which uses electricity to stimulate muscles. It is used for training in rehabilitation, and is effective in sports training [2]. The EMS belt, introduced recently, can send stimulation to muscles just by wearing it, even while performing other tasks. Therefore, it can solve the problem of maintaining motivation, which is an issue in the abovementioned two training methods. However, its repeated use in the same part of the body causes muscle fatigue with the risk of damaging the muscles without the user noticing. Additionally, when used together with medical electrical devices, such as pacemakers and artificial heart lungs, it may malfunction and result in significant physical damage [3].

In a public opinion survey on the status of sports activities conducted by the Japan Sports Agency in 2020 [4], the most common reason for the decrease in exercise and sports was "busy work schedules and household chores." Therefore, to make exercise a habit, incorporating exercises that can be performed while working or doing household chores into daily life is necessary. In this paper, we will discuss "exercise while working" that meets this requirement. It has the advantage of being incorporated into daily activities even for people without time for exercise and anyone can perform it at an appropriate intensity with a low risk of injury. For example, the regularity and intensity of exercise are important when exercising for weight loss; Bouchard et al. found that years of regular exercise at least five times a week and up to 50% intensity can normalize body weight in many cases, but high-intensity exercise does not necessarily increase weight loss. Moreover, it does not necessarily increase the effectiveness of weight loss; rather, it may have negative effects, such as increased exercise-induced injuries and decreased motivation [5]. Additionally, people with no exercise habit tend to exercise at a higher intensity when they set their exercise intensity [6].

To maintain an exercise habit, it is important to decrease negative factors and increase positive factors, i.e., exercise intensity without pain and positive exercise experiences. Additionally, introducing a benign cycle consisting of the following six parts into daily life contributes to the continuity of exercise: 1) pleasant mood, 2) mental well-being, 3) physiological effects, 4) long life span, 5) motivation to exercise, and 6) moderate exercise [7]. It is important to suggest exercises of appropriate intensity and provide feedback to users so they can recognize the exercise they have done and maintain their motivation to realize this virtuous cycle model. Therefore, it is necessary to have a system that suggests exercises to be performed, recognizes the exercises performed, and provides feedback. However, no research has been found on a system that proposes exercises that do not interfere with the main task, recognizes the exercises, and provides feedback.

In this paper, we present a system that proposes and recognizes the most appropriate exercise for a work situation and provides feedback on the exercise while performing other tasks. Here, this system suggests and recognizes the most appropriate exercise for the work situation and provides feedback on the exercise performed. We limit the work situation to desk work and compare the appropriate suggestion methods to promote exercise and clarify the effective notification method and presentation contents. The paper is organized as follows. In the next section, we introduce previous studies related to this research and show the position of this research. Section 3 describes the design and implementation of a system that promotes exercise while working at a desk. Section 4 shows the basic system performance evaluation, followed by the user evaluation in Sect. 5. Section 6 presents and discusses the results obtained from the evaluation experiments. Finally, Sect. 7 describes the issues and prospects of this study.

2 Related Work

2.1 Exercise Promotion System

Consolvo et al. [8] investigated the effectiveness of presenting information on an underutilized cell phone background screen to increase awareness of exercise in daily life. They implemented a system in which a cell phone is equipped with sensors to automatically estimate activities, and when users record their goals, the wallpaper of the cell phone displays a picture of the activities achieved. Results from this study showed that the abstract display of users' activities on the background screen increased the their awareness and influenced their behavior.

In a study that developed and evaluated two systems to promote physical activity, Klasnja et al. [9] described the lessons learned. One of the systems encourages users to increase the number of steps they take each day by rewards for achieving goals, and the ability to share the number of steps with peers. The other is a system that uses a sensor attached to the waist and a cell phone application to record physical activities. These studies showed the possibility of developing a system that effectively motivates behavior by supporting sustained goals for maintaining health, encouraging various healthy behaviors, and promoting social support.

These studies evaluate users' motivation to exercise; however, it is considered that people who do not exercise do not know what training to engage in. Therefore, a system that promotes exercise should propose specific exercise contents and recognize them.

2.2 Dual-Task Encouragement

A method for memorizing English words using aerobic exercise was proposed by Yuasa et al. [10]. Because of the same number of days for memorizing English words while exercising with a stepper and sitting in a chair, respectively, no difference in performance was observed in the test after one day. However, after three days and one week, the performance of learning while exercising improved more than that of learning while sitting in a chair. Shimizu et al. [11] proposed an exercise system that replaces computer key-strokes with body movements. The proposed system was designed to encourage users to perform physical activities equivalent to walking while working, and to compensate for the lack of physical activities in their daily life by physical movements during desk work. By assigning keys to body movements that carry a load equivalent to that of walking, it becomes possible to perform the exercise naturally. Based on these previous studies, we develop a system to promote exercise while working at a desk. Additionally, unlike in these previous studies, we investigate a proposed method to enable the continuation of exercise using the developed system.

2.3   Physical Training Recognition

Shen et al. [12] proposed a smartwatch-based automatic tracking system for aerobic exercise and weightlifting. The system tracks both aerobic exercise and weightlifting and can recognize the training event and repetition without the user inputting the event to be performed while achieving a fit and repeatability rate of over 90%. There are other studies on exercise recognition systems using smartwatches and other devices [13–15]. For many of these systems, the results show that they recognize the training actions with high accuracy. However, these systems cannot increase the exercise time because they assume the user has originally set the training time. Therefore, a system that can recognize a training performed without the user consciously setting aside time is necessary.

2.4   Chair-Based Activity Recognition

Griffiths et al. [16] investigated the frequency of sitting, posture, and chair type used as a sensing device. They found that 55% of their test subjects sat for more than 9 h a day, and 20% of them sat for more than 14 h a day. Also, it was found that the chairs were fixed to some extent and used only by the subjects. Additionally, most of the subjects used backrests and armrests. Apart from this study, many other studies on postural recognition using chairs have been reported [17–19]. These studies show that the weight distribution while seated can be analyzed and postural classification with high accuracy can be performed. However, most studies are limited to the recognition of seated posture, and few studies on recognizing exercises performed while seated have been recorded, so there is room for further research.

3   Prototype System Implementation

3.1   Overview

The system suggests abdominal exercises that can be done while sitting in a chair. Here, the exercise proposed is a knee-pull-up abdominal exercise [20]. This exercise is effective for the abdominal and lumbar muscles and improves posture and prevents stiff shoulders and back pain. Therefore, it is the best exercise to do while working at a desk. The method for performing this exercise is as follows:

1. Sit down on a chair, while making a space between the chair and desk, and put both feet together.
2. Slightly round your back, pull your chin back, put your strength into your stomach, and pull your legs toward your chest while not leaning on the backrest. If it is difficult to pull both legs up, you can do it with one leg.

If the user performs the suggested exercise, the system evaluates the exercise and sends feedback to motivate him/her to use the system in the future. This system is constructed using three requirements for a system that promotes exercise while working at a desk: 1) Sensing by a device used during desk work, 2) Provide users with suggestions and feedback to maintain their motivation to exercise while working, and 3) Recognition of detailed exercise posture. Figure 1 illustrates the major system components, consisting of a sensor-augmented chair and information display.

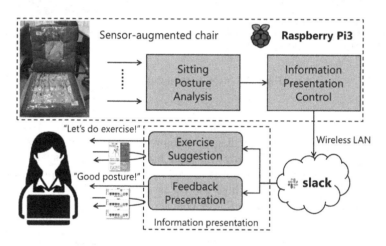

Fig. 1. Prototype system architecture.

3.2   Hardware Set-up of Sensor-Augmented Chair

The sensor-augmented chair contributes to analyzing the sitting posture to determine the timing of suggesting exercises, evaluating the form of exercise, and sending feedback from the evaluation. On the seat of the chair, pressure sensors were installed in a grid of $28\,cm^2$ with 7 cm intervals, and on the back of the chair, pressure sensors were installed at the vertices of $15\,cm^2$. All the pressure sensors are connected to a Raspberry Pi3 (RP3) to acquire data. RP3 is connected to the network using a wireless LAN. A box is placed at the rear of the chair to hold RP3, a circuit to connect pressure sensors to RP3, and a mobile battery. In this way, the connection cables do not interfere with the experiment, and the exercise can be performed naturally. The chair device we created is shown in Fig. 2.

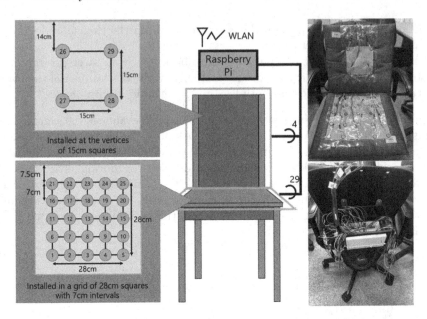

Fig. 2. Sensor-augmented chair

Figure 3 shows the values of each of the 29 pressure sensors in two states by heatmaps. The left and right diagrams show the pressure distributions when both legs pulled up and when only the right leg is pulled up, respectively. The difference between the two diagrams is caused by the fact that the point touching the sensor differs depending on how the leg is pulled up. When only the right leg is raised, sensors 4 and 5 (see Fig. 2) contact the leg, and the diagram on the

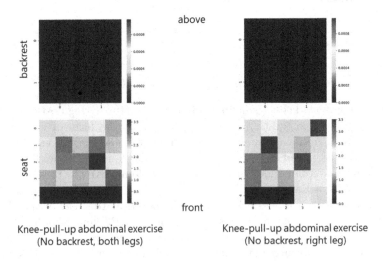

Knee-pull-up abdominal exercise   Knee-pull-up abdominal exercise
(No backrest, both legs)   (No backrest, right leg)

Fig. 3. Left: Sensor value when both legs are pulled up. Right: Sensor value when only the right leg is pulled up.

right of Fig. 3 shows sensors 4 and 5 responding. In this way, the user's posture can be grasped by obtaining the pressure distribution from multiple sensors.

3.3   Sitting Posture Analysis

We acquired the values of the pressure sensors installed on the chair using a sampling frequency 10 Hz. The system processed the collected pressure sensor values to recognize the user's state according to the flow in Fig. 4. It is necessary to specify the segment to recognize the user state because the data collected from the pressure sensors are variable in length. For this purpose, we segmented the collected data. The segmentation was performed by finding an interval between large changes, i.e., peaks. A peak is found by calculating variance in the sliding window using a fixed-length.

Fig. 4. Processing flow of user state classification

Figures 5 and 6 show a data processing flow for calculating moving variance and the notion of segmentation using the peaks obtained by moving variance values, respectively. In the windowing process, the pressure sensor data were divided into fixed-length windows of 0.5 s (5 samples) with 50% overlap. The pressure sensor data in sensor $k \in [1, 29]$ and window index i (i-th window) is defined as $w_{k,i}$ (Fig. 5(a)). Then, the variance was calculated using the fact that the value of each sensor changes significantly when the user state transitions. The variance of the pressure sensor data in each window $v_{k,i}$ is expressed by the following Eq. (2), where $var(\cdot)$ is a function of calculating the variance of a set

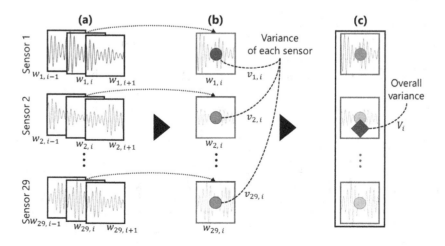

Fig. 5. Peak detection preparation

of data given as an argument (Fig. 5(b)). An overall variance V_i is calculated using the variance of each sensor by Eq. (2) (Fig. 5(c)).

$$v_{k,i} = var(w_{k,i}) \tag{1}$$

$$V_i = var(v_{1,i}, v_{2,i}, ..., v_{29,i}) \tag{2}$$

Overall variance exceeding a certain threshold value is a peak. The interval between two successive peaks is a segment, denoted as S_j in Fig. 6. The window indices representing the beginning and end of a segment S_j were determined and used to obtain the sensor data for user state recognition. Additionally, the threshold value was determined using the intensity of the user's movement.

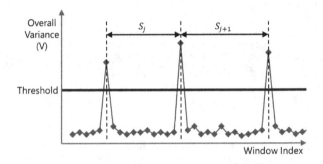

Fig. 6. Notion of data segmentation

The system classified the segment into the following nine states, which is illustrated in Fig. 7.

State 0: Leaving the seat
State 1: Seated (With backrest)
State 2: Seated (No backrest)
State 3: Knee-pull-up abdominal exercise (No backrest, both legs)
State 4: Knee-pull-up abdominal exercise (No backrest, right leg)
State 5: Knee-pull-up abdominal exercise (No backrest, left leg)
State 6: Knee-pull-up abdominal exercise (With backrest, both legs)
State 7: Knee-pull-up abdominal exercise (With backrest, right leg)
State 8: Knee-pull-up abdominal exercise (With backrest, left leg)

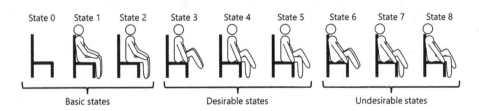

Fig. 7. User state to be classified

The seated states of the user including leaving the seat are recognized as the basic states (State 0, 1, and 2). It is desirable to raise both legs without using a backrest when performing the knee-pull-up abdominal exercise (State 3). Considering the possibility of feeling that the load is too large, the user can raise only one leg (States 4 and 5). The movement of raising both legs while using the backrest (State 6) may cause excessive load on the lower back, and the movements of raising one leg while using the backrest (States 7 and 8) cause a much smaller load, so these three states are considered undesirable postures.

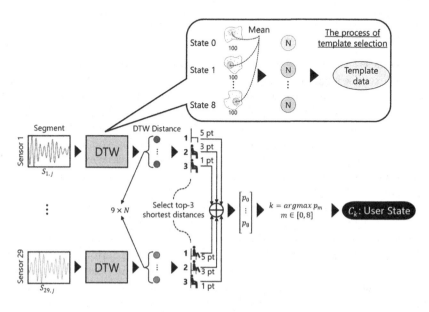

Fig. 8. Overview of state recognition

Figure 8 shows a schematic of the processing of the user state recognition from the segment data. We applied dynamic time warping (DTW) to recognize the nine states. DTW allowed us to measure the similarity between two data segments with different lengths. To calculate the DTW distance and determine the user's state, data representing the posture of each state, called the template, were required as references. The template data were collected 10 times in advance while maintaining each posture for 10 s and then divided into 1-s segments, making 100 segments for each state. Additionally, we further extracted a specific number (N) of 100 segments for each state in order of importance to improve the processing speed of DTW. The importance of the template data is measured by the DTW distance between the average of 100 segments in a state and the data of each sample. The shorter distance, the more important, i.e., the closer to an average waveform. The number of template data extracted (N) is determined based on the result of performance evaluation in Sect. 4. Here, a database of templates was created for each subject in the evaluation.

The DTW distances between the template and test data were calculated for each sensor, from which $9 \times N$ distances were obtained. Then, the top three classes with the shortest DTW distances were given points according to their ranks, where 5 points, 3 points, and 1 point are given to the first, second, and third rank, respectively. The points from each sensor are accumulated to obtain an array of 9 elements, in which each element corresponds to a class ($p_{m \in [0,8]}$), and the class (C_k) with the highest point (p_k) is determined as the user's state. After the user state is determined, the content of the message to be posted to Slack is decided using the user state.

3.4   Presented Information

Here, two message types are presented to the user: exercise suggestion and feedback. The exercise suggestions are sent to users to encourage them to do exercises that they can perform while at their desks. Alternatively, the feedback message is presented to the user when the system detects the completion of the proposed exercise, including words of exertion such as "Good job," or a simple evaluation such as "Be careful of your posture when performing this exercise." Users receive these messages as notifications, i.e., push-based messages, from the Slack application. Additionally, the detailed messages are presented to the users upon their requests, i.e., pull-based, where the method and goal of the exercise are presented with text and images in the Slack by clicking the notification.

Figure 9(a) shows the exercise suggestion consisting of 1) the method of knee-pull-up abdominal exercise, 2) effects of the exercise on lower abdominal muscles, and 3) goals of the exercise that hold the posture for 8 s and perform 6 sets in total. The detailed feedback includes the results of the analysis (exercise time, etc.). Figure 9(b) shows the time spent holding the posture and frequency of exercise as three bar graphs. "Both" shows the result when both legs are raised, "Right" shows the result when only the right leg is raised, and "Left" shows the result when only the left leg is raised. An icon with the most recent result is also displayed.

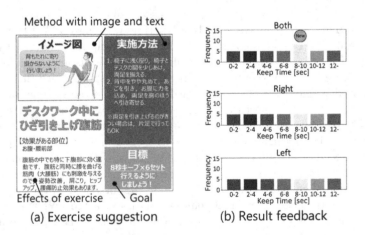

Fig. 9. Detailed information: (a) exercise suggestion and (b) result feedback

4 Basic Performance Evaluation

4.1 Method

To evaluate the accuracy of this system in determining the states, test data were collected from 10 university students (six males and four females). To clarify the relationship between the number of template data to be extracted (described in Sect. 3.3) and the accuracy of the state judgment, we increased the number of template data to be extracted when calculating the DTW distances by 10, and compared the F-measure. Additionally, since the time required for state determination affects the usability of the system, the time required for a single state determination was also compared.

We considered a macro F-measure as a recognition performance indicator. A macro F-measure is obtained by averaging the F-measure of each class. An F-measure is a harmonic mean of precision and recall given by Eq. (3), and precision and recall are defined by Eqs. (4) and (5), respectively. Note that the definitions of true positive (TP), false negative (FN), false positive (FP), and true negative (TN) are summarized in Table 1.

Table 1. Data category

	Predicted Positive	Predicted Negative
Actual Positive	True Positive (TP)	False Negative (FN)
Actual Negative	False Positive (FP)	True Negative (TN)

$$F - measure = \frac{2 \cdot Recall \cdot Precision}{Recall + Precision} \tag{3}$$

$$Precision = \frac{TP}{TP + FP} \tag{4}$$

$$Recall = \frac{TP}{TP + FN} \tag{5}$$

4.2 Result

Figure 10 shows the results of the F-measure for the number of template data and time required for each state to be determined. From Fig. 10, the F-measure is highest when the number of template data is 90. However, the time required for the 90-template data is about three times more than that required for the 30-template data, which has the second-highest value. Therefore, in the following experiment, we used 30 template data for each state, i.e., $N = 30$, which maintains relatively high recognition performance and requires less time. Figure 11 shows the confusion matrix of the state recognition under this condition, which is the sum of the confusion matrices obtained for each test consisting of the data and templates from the same person. Table 2 shows the F-measure for each class calculated under the same conditions. There are many misclassifications regarding the use of the backrest and the raising of the legs, as shown in Fig. 11. In particular, the misclassification of the posture with one leg raised (States 4 and 5) is high, suggesting its similarity to the other states. Additionally, Table 2 shows that the classification accuracy for the no-backrest state is lower than that for the backrest-using state.

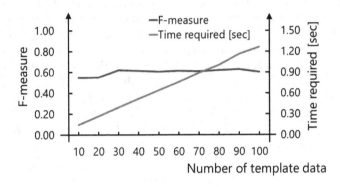

Fig. 10. Graph of F-measure and time required for the number of template data

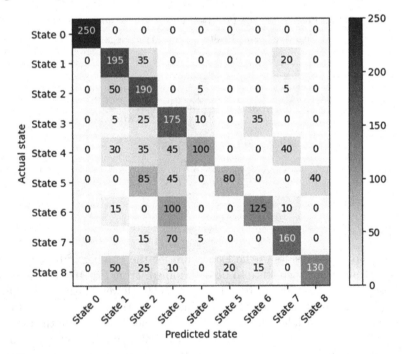

Fig. 11. Confusion matrix $(N = 30)$

Table 2. F-measure for each class ($N = 30$)

	State 0	State 1	State 2	State 3	State 4	State 5	State 6	State 7	State 8
F-measure	1.000	0.655	0.576	0.504	0.541	0.457	0.588	0.660	0.619

5 User Evaluation

We performed an experiment to investigate an effective exercise suggestion and feedback to motivate people to exercise.

5.1 Method

For this experiment, eleven university students (seven males and four females) participated. We specified video watching as the main task, in which subjects viewed lecture videos. Other candidate tasks that we considered were text input and presentation. However, we concluded that watching a video was the most passive, and performing the exercise might not or had very little impact on performing the main task. Detection of video watching is a future agenda.

When subjects receive a message suggesting an exercise while watching a video or a notification of feedback, they were allowed to pause the video and view the screen of the Slack application. Three conditions were provided regarding the timing of exercise suggestion: 1) only at the beginning of the desk work (BEG), 2) when the participant sits on the chair and a probability of 0.5 of exercise suggestion (PRB), and 3) every time the participant sits on the chair (EVY). Additionally, participants performed activities without the system as a baseline (BLN), in which they referred to a printed instruction of Fig. 9(a), and no feedback was given.

After the experiment, participants answered questions regarding the ease of the suggested exercise and their preference to do the exercise again for the four experimental conditions. Also, the clarity and necessity of the elements of exercise suggestion and result feedback, and those of their initial exercise suggestions, were investigated. A five-point Likert scale was used, in which the rating above 3.0 indicates that the subjects were affirmative on the specific questionnaire item.

5.2 Result

Table 3 shows the average ratings on the timing of exercise suggestion, in which the intervention of the system (BEG, PRB, and EVY) got higher scores than the baseline approach (BLN), and exercise suggestion with a probability of 0.5 (PRB) was considered the best option. This implies that an appropriate frequency should exist in proposing exercise.

The clarity and necessity of message elements for exercise suggestion and result feedback are shown in Tables 4 and 5, respectively. In either case, push-based messages were considered necessary (above 3.0), but least clear, which we consider reasonable because they are triggers to obtain detailed information, and carry a minimum amount of information. In the information pulled by users in exercise suggestion, goal presentation was rated the clearest and necessary, followed by the image-based explanation of the exercise method. This is because the textual expression took longer to understand than the image-based expression. In Table 5, the evaluation of the clarity of the graphs showing the user information was high, suggesting that feedback by graphs was easily accepted by subjects in terms of clarity and necessity.

Table 3. Rating on the timing of exercise suggestion.

	BEG	PRB	EVY	BLN
Ease of doing (1: difficult – 5: easy)	3.5	4.0	3.0	2.9
Preference to do again (1: dislike – 5: like)	3.1	3.8	2.5	2.1

Table 4. Clarity and necessity of the elements of exercise suggestion.

	Push-based message	Information pulled by users			
		Image	Text	Effects	Goal
Clarity	3.8	4.6	4.0	3.9	4.8
Necessity	4.5	3.9	3.5	3.4	4.0

Table 5. Clarity and necessity of the elements of result feedback.

	Push-based message	Information pulled by users
Clarity	3.3	4.0
Necessity	4.1	4.2

Opinion from Participants

O_1: "BLN did not inspire me to exercise because it did not notify me on the screen I was looking at."

O_2: "BEG only notifies me at the beginning, so I need not do the exercise."

O_3: "PRB was less annoying than EVY and did not cause me to forget to exercise."

O_4: "EVY gave me too many notifications, so I could not concentrate on the task, and the notifications did not feel meaningful anymore."

O_5: "I want a short video of the exercise being done."

O_6: "The results of the exercise postural assessment are difficult to understand."

6   Discussion

6.1   Contents of Presentation

From Tables 4 and 5, the evaluation of the necessity of the exercise was low for text and effects. This is attributed to the fact that these elements require more text than the others and can be substituted with images. One solution to this problem is to present videos (O_5). This would make it possible to explain how to perform the exercise and what part of the body is effective to increase clarity. Additionally, although the push notification reminds users to perform the exercise, certain users found its contents difficult to understand (O_6). Therefore, the content of the notification needs reconsideration.

Furthermore, the short duration of the experiment and participants' bias may affect the necessary contents presented. In this experiment, we asked participants to use each proposed method for 30 min, respectively, and evaluated the results. Since this system is designed for people who do not exercise regularly, it may not be effective for people who exercise regularly to continue exercising by the appropriate presentation contents revealed in this experiment. To solve this problem, it is necessary to extend this system to support multiple types of exercise to meet the needs of various users.

6.2   Timing of Notification

From the results of the experiments described in Sect. 5.2, the appropriate amount of notification can effectively encourage subjects to perform the exercise (O_1, O_2, O_3). PRB was evaluated more favorably than BEG and EVY because the notifications were more appropriate. For BLN, the evaluation was low because the exercise depended on the participants' own will. Additionally, too much notification reduced the effectiveness of the notification (O_4). It is important to provide notifications at a frequency that does not cause discomfort to users.

6.3   Trust in Suggestion

Two issues should be addressed to improve the reliability of the proposed system. First is the large number of misrecognition. From Fig. 11, several cases were reported where the knee-pull-up abdominal exercise (with backrest, both legs) (State 6) were misrecognized as knee-pull-up abdominal exercise (no backrest, both legs) (State3), and knee-pull-up abdominal exercise (no backrest, left leg) (State 5) was misrecognized as seated (no backrest) (States 2 or 3). To investigate the cause of the misrecognition of states 2 and 5, Fig. 12 shows the pressure distributions of states 2 and 5 being similar except for the right side in front of the seat surface. This difference is equivalent to the difference in the values of four sensors (sensors 4, 5, 9, and 10), and is likely to cause misrecognition. Therefore, to recognize detailed motion posture, increasing the sensors installed in locations where errors are likely to occur and analyzing the pressure distribution in detail is necessary. Furthermore, our system used the DTW distance to recognize the state. However, the F-measure was 0.622 ($N = 30$), which is insufficient. In the future, we will create a machine learning model by calculating various features from the pressure sensors in addition to the DTW distance, to reduce misrecognition and improve the speed of state recognition.

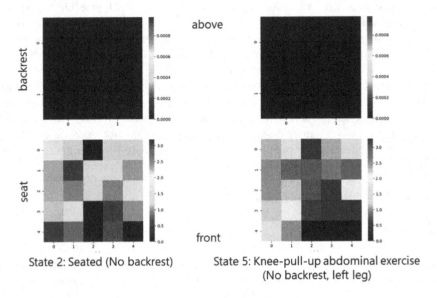

State 2: Seated (No backrest)   State 5: Knee-pull-up abdominal exercise
(No backrest, left leg)

Fig. 12. Pressure distribution (State 2: left) and (State 5: right)

The second issue is the delay in the timing of the feedback notification. In this system, feedback after the exercise plays an important role in promoting exercising. We conducted a questionnaire survey on the speed of the notification timing of our system and the acceptable delay feedback time. Most participants agreed that the notification time from the system was too long. The reason for such complaints may be attributed to the exercises often being repeated before receiving feedback. The segment data of the user evaluation was longer than the data used in the basic performance evaluation, and it took longer to calculate the DTW distance, so the system took more than 30 s to recognize the state. As for the acceptable delay of feedback, half of the participants suggested no more than 10 s and refuted a delay of 30 s or more. Therefore, we concluded that the delayed feedback after exercise decreased the motivation due to the distrust of the system. Thus, the system should be redesigned to consider the feedback presentation speed after the exercise, such as constantly updating the segment data for recognizing the state to the latest one.

7 Conclusion

In this paper, we proposed a system to promote exercise during desk work. We investigated the use of a sensor-augmented chair to recognize sitting postures and abdominal exercises. Furthermore, Slack was leveraged as messaging infrastructure. We conducted a comparative experiment of several methods that enabled the continuation of exercise and investigated the ease of performing the exercise and desire to continue the exercise. As a result, the following findings were obtained.

- On the notification method and timing:
  - Exercise should be proposed with consideration of the appropriate content and frequency.
  - The appropriate amount of notification can effectively encourage the user to perform the exercise.
  - The number of times the user follows the notification depends on the user's motivation to exercise.
- On the content of notifications:
  - Push notifications are effective in promoting exercise while working, but the content of notifications must be considered.
  - A straightforward explanation is effective in promoting exercise.
  - It is effective to send notifications when concentration drops or when a certain period has passed since the exercise was performed.
  - The clarity of notifications can be increased by effectively using diagrams and reducing the written content.
  - It is effective to show the part of the body to focus on during exercise using a diagram, so that the user can quickly understand briefly which part of the body was used.

There are still issues, such as the content of push notifications, accuracy of state determination, and delay of feedback notifications. In addition to solving these issues, we are currently reconfiguring the system architecture to adapt the system to various everyday situations.

References

1. Guthold, R., Stevens, G.A., Riley, L.M., Bull, F.C.: Worldwide trends in insufficient physical activity from 2001 to 2016: a pooled analysis of 358 population-based surveys with 1–9 million participants. Lancet Glob. Health 6(10), e1077–e1086 (2018). https://doi.org/10.1016/S2214-109X(18)30357-7
2. Maffiuletti, N.A., Cometti, G., Amiridis, I.G., Martin, A., Pousson, M.L., Chatard, J.C.: The effects of electromyostimulation training and basketball practice on muscle strength and jumping ability. Int. J. Sports Med. 21(6), 437–443 (2000). https://doi.org/10.1055/s-2000-3837, https://www.thieme-connect.de/products/ejournals/abstract/10.1055/s-2000-3837

3. The Japan Home-health Apparatus Industrial Association.: voluntary standards for the safety of ems equipment for home use. https://www.hapi.or. jp/documentation/information/ems_20201009r.pdf. Accessed 11 Jan 2022. (In Japanese)

4. Japan Sports Agency.: Public opinion poll on the status of sports implementation, etc., https://www.mext.go.jp/sports/content/20200507-spt_kensport01-000007034_1.pdf. Accessed 11 Jan 2022. (In Japanese)

5. Bouchard, C., Deprks, J.P., Trernbluy, A.: Exercise and obesity. Coron. Artery Dis. **11**(2), 111–116 (2000). https://doi.org/10.1097/00019501-200003000-00004

6. Dishman, R.K., Farquhar, R.P., Cureton, K.J.: Responses to preferred intensities of exertion in men differing in activity levels. Med. Sci. Sports Exerc. **26**(6), 783–790 (1994). https://doi.org/10.1249/00005768-199406000-00019, http://journals. lww.com/00005768-199406000-00019

7. Nabetani, T., Tokunaga, M.: A new approach to exercise adherence. Health Sci. **23**, 103–116 (2001)

8. Consolvo, S., et al.: Flowers or a robot army?: encouraging awareness and activity with personal, mobile displays. In: UbiComp 2008 - Proceedings of the 10th International Conference on Ubiquitous Computing, pp. 54–63 (2008). https://doi.org/ 10.1145/1409635.1409644

9. Klasnja, P., Consolvo, S., McDonald, D.W., Landay, J.A., Pratt, W.: Using mobile and personal sensing technologies to support health behavior change in everyday life: lessons learned. In: AMIA 2009 Symposium Proceedings, pp. 338–342 (2009). https://www.ncbi.nlm.nih.gov/pmc/articles/PMC2815473/

10. Yuasa, S., Kise, K.: Confirmation of the effect of aerobic exercise on English vocabulary memorization. IPSJ SIG Technical Report 2020-HCI-1(10), pp. 1–5 (2020)

11. Shimizu, Y., Ohnishi, A., Terada, T., Tsukamoto, M.: DeskWalk: an exercise system by replacing key inputs with body movements. In: Proceedings of the 18th International Conference on Advances in Mobile Computing and Multimedia, pp. 202–209 (2020)

12. Shen, C., Ho, B.J., Srivastava, M.: MiLift: efficient Smartwatch-Based Workout Tracking Using Automatic Segmentation. IEEE Trans. Mob. Comput. **17**(7), 1609–1622 (2018). https://doi.org/10.1109/TMC.2017.2775641

13. Guo, X., Liu, J., Chen, Y.: When your wearables become your fitness mate. Smart Health **16**, 100114 (2020). https://doi.org/10.1016/j.smhl.2020.100114

14. Morris, D., Saponas, T.S., Guillory, A., Kelner, I.: Recofit: using a wearable sensor to find, recognize, and count repetitive exercises. In: Proceedings of the SIGCHI Conference on Human Factors in Computing Systems, pp. 3225–3234. CHI 2014, ACM (2014). https://doi.org/10.1145/2556288.2557116

15. Hao, T., Xing, G., Zhou, G.: RunBuddy: a smartphone system for running rhythm monitoring. UbiComp **2015**, 133–144 (2015). https://doi.org/10.1145/2750858. 2804293, https://dl.acm.org/doi/pdf/10.1145/2750858.2804293

16. Griffiths, E., Saponas, T.S., Brush, A.J.B.: Health chair: implicitly sensing heart and respiratory rate. In: Proceedings of the 2014 ACM International Joint Conference on Pervasive and Ubiquitous Computing - UbiComp 2014 Adjunct, pp. 661–671 (2014). https://doi.org/10.1145/2632048.2632099, http://dl.acm.org/citation. cfm?doid=2632048.2632099

17. Tan, H.Z., Slivovsky, L.A., Pentland, A.: A sensing chair using pressure distribution sensors. IEEE/ASME Trans. Mechatron. **6**(3), 261–268 (2001). https://doi.org/10. 1109/3516.951364, http://ieeexplore.ieee.org/document/951364/

18. Roh, J., Park, H.j., Lee, K., Hyeong, J., Kim, S., Lee, B.: Sitting posture monitoring system based on a low-cost load cell using machine learning. Sensors **18**(2), 208 (2018). https://doi.org/10.3390/s18010208, http://www.mdpi.com/1424-8220/18/1/208

19. Ren, X., Yu, B., Lu, Y., Chen, Y., Pu, P.: HealthSit: designing posture-based interaction to promote exercise during fitness breaks. Int. J. Hum. Comput. Interact. **35**(10), 870–885 (2019). https://doi.org/10.1080/10447318.2018.1506641

20. Nagano, S.: Get rid of your busy schedule and get some exercise! One-minute exercise diet, PHP Institute (2003). (in Japanese)

Persuasive Design for Healthy Eating: A Scoping Review

Xinyue Liu[1], Xipei Ren[1(✉)], and Sibo Pan[2]

[1] School of Design and Arts, Beijing Institute of Technology, Beijing, China
x.ren@bit.edu.cn
[2] Department of Industrial Design, Eindhoven University of Technology, Eindhoven, Netherlands

Abstract. In this scoping review, we aimed to summarize and analyze the latest research developments of persuasive design for healthy eating behavior and explore future design opportunities. This paper initially collected 1231 papers from 2011 to 2021 in three different databases: the Association for Computing Machinery (ACM) digital library, IEEE Xplore and SpringerLink databases. Based on a selection process, 28 papers that mainly focused on addressing dietary health by persuasive designs were eventually included in final analysis. These 28 papers were sorted by three characteristics: research specifications, methodologies, and design rationales. Our data analyses revealed that the reviewed papers primarily utilized persuasive technologies for eating behaviors monitoring, recording, and healthy eating suggestion. Moreover, six types of design applications were commonly implemented, including mobile applications, persuasive messages, digital products and service systems, wearable devices, chatbots/assistants, and public devices. Our review showed that persuasive design, as a generic approach for promoting healthy eating, lacked research investigations on personalized solutions for particular user groups such as office workers and teenagers. Future works could explore persuasive design strategies by applying the research factors of user experience and examining the efficacy of persuasive technology tools to effectively promote healthy eating behaviors for various user groups in different contexts.

Keywords: Persuasive design · Healthy eating · Health-promoting technology · Review

1 Introduction

According to Fogg [1], persuasive technology can be regarded as an interactive system that achieves the goal of changing people's behavior and attitudes based on the principles of psychological theories and computing engineering. It is also known as "behavior design", which refers to shaping user behaviors through persuasion and social influence in design, rather than through coercive methods [33]. Persuasive technology was deemed as a beneficial approach to solve health problems, while the rapid development of ICTs made it widely applied in various fields [2].

© The Author(s), under exclusive license to Springer Nature Switzerland AG 2022
N. A. Streitz and S. Konomi (Eds.): HCII 2022, LNCS 13326, pp. 292–303, 2022.
https://doi.org/10.1007/978-3-031-05431-0_20

Given the fact that persuasion is meant to change people's behavior, it is widely used to achieve public goals and support self-management, such as improving people's awareness of sustainability, lowering the risk of developing chronic diseases, and enhancing work efficiency [32]. In this light, persuasive design has been increasingly developed to encourage behavior changes on a wide range of human vitality, including physical activity [10, 11, 34], oral health [35], mental health [36, 37], and diet [3–31], etc.

In this paper, we reviewed recent design research that employed persuasive technologies to solve eating problems or promote healthy eating behaviors. The scoping review summarized research from 2011 to 2021 on persuasive design for the purpose of healthy eating. Rather than focusing on the outcomes of designs and technologies, this review aims to provide an overview of the design considerations for healthy eating and the development processes of these design proposals. Based on this scoping review, we hope to discover the research gap in the persuasive design for promoting healthy eating and identify design opportunities accordingly. In particular, our research questions are threefold:

- How have persuasive designs been applied to the research domain of healthy eating?
- How have persuasive strategies been employed to intervene users' behaviors related to diets?
- What are the design opportunities of future health-promoting tools that can support healthy eating practices?

2   Methods

2.1   Search and Selection

The scoping review was conducted according to the following procedure: 1) identifying research questions, 2) searching for related papers, 3) selecting papers, 4) drawing data charts, 5) sorting, summarizing and reporting results. The full papers published in related conferences and journals were searched mainly in two databases, namely Association for Computing Machinery (ACM) Digital Library. In addition, IEEE Xplore and Springer-Link databases were used as supplementary sources. Based on our research questions, the search keywords were identified as: health* AND (eat* OR diet) AND (persuade OR persuasive OR persuasion) AND design. The publication date of the article is limited to the period from 2010 to 2021.

After receiving 1231 papers based on our searching criteria, we screened those papers with the following steps. To start, we excluded copies of the same research papers and experimental studies derived from the same study in different groups or cultural contexts, based on the title and abstract of the searched papers. 773 related papers were obtained for the next step of paper screening. Then, we reviewed the full text of the papers due to the following criteria for the final paper selection:

- Objective: Healthy eating must be the main application objective. We excluded articles that target health management purposes such as exercise, sleep and rest, or research on diet as an influencing factor on emotions and well-being of special groups.

- Theoretical grounds: We excluded papers that did not apply persuasion design theory, or persuasion techniques were only applied to study economics behavior and other related literature.
- Methods: Articles that did not conduct empirical studies and did not design and develop technical solutions were excluded.

After the screening process as described above, a total of 28 papers were finally selected for this scoping review.

2.2 Paper Coding

The selected papers were focusing on user studies and technology evaluations, the 28 selected papers were coded (shown in Table 1), sorted by three types of characters: research specifications, methodologies, and design practice.

Table 1. Paper coding

Primary	Secondary	Coding status
Research specifications	Target user	People with health problems such as alcoholism; older people, children, office workers, younger people such as diabetics and university students, without differentiating between user types
	Intervention area	Promotion of healthy eating choices and nutritional mix, control of snacking and emotional eating, aid in diet monitoring and recording, aid in the eating process, management of other health indicators in an integrated manner
Methodologies		User-centered approach, theory-based approach, context-driven approach, technology-driven approach
Design rationales	Type of application	Mobile applications, information, smart products and complex product systems, wearable devices, chatbots or virtual assistants
	Design evaluation	Qualitative, quantitative, mixed method

3 Results

3.1 Research Specifications

In order to examine the specific application objectives of the persuasive design in the selected papers, the application objectives were divided into two dimensions: 1) the

Table 2. Target users in the included technologies and designs

Target users	Included papers
Patients	[3–7, 16]
Older adults	[17, 18]
Children	[10–13, 15, 16]
Office workers	[19, 22]
Teenagers	[23]
No specification of users	[8, 9, 19–21, 24–28]

target user, and the branch of the healthy eating problem in which they are located, and the distribution of the study objectives are shown in Tables 2 and Table 3.

Target Users. *Patients.* As shown in Table 2, healthy diet management for patients with diabetes and obesity is an important application research field of persuasive design. Using persuasive designs can help patients with the process of self-regulation [3–7, 16], reduce the burden on processing information [3, 5, 7], improve the efficiency of dietary supervision [3, 4, 6], and increase their motivation for healthy living [3–7, 16]. For example, strategies such as transforming weight management goals into game challenges [3–5, 16] can encourage users with diabetes mellitus to learn nutritional knowledge and make healthy diet choices. Smart technologies with self-monitoring mechanisms [4, 6] can automatically track the diet status of users with metabolic syndrome (i.e., eating speed, food ratio control, and calorie and sodium intake management), and can do the same for people with emotional eating problems. Additionally, metaphoric designs [5] could help patients with difficulties in processing information easily understand the relevant information.

Older Adults. Persuasive design has been applied to support healthy eating for older adults in several recent research projects [17, 18]. The benefits of persuasive design could be helping the older adults know the nutrients of their body needs in time and to offering suitable dietary guidance for them. For example, the elderly could use the tablet application of persuasive communication [17] and the smart foodbox [18] to record dietary intake, get reminders and suggestions of protein intake and prevent malnutrition.

Children. Persuasive design has been widely used to form children's healthy eating habits and prevent childhood obesity symptoms. For children, persuasive design could teach them healthy eating knowledge, motivate them to change their behaviors and develop healthy habits. For example, a mobile game called MACO [11] was designed to educate children to eat healthy foods and engage in physical exercises. The designed verbal and bodily features of the social robots [12] could motivate children to increase vitamin intake. A gamified chatbot was developed [13] to help children obtain personalized healthy eating recommendations. There are also tools designed as aids to parents in educating children, such as the digital enhanced food [14] and the smart tableware products [15], which could encourage children to eat healthy food in a joyful eating process.

Office Workers. There have been office-based health management systems using wearable devices and mobile applications. Such systems were created for diet tracking and promoting exercise in the workplace scenarios [22].

Teenagers. For teenagers, a persuasive toolkit [23] composed by an awareness video and a text messaging campaign could prompt healthy food choices, through elevating awareness about the importance of proper dieting during adolescence.

Table 3. Intervention areas of the paper included in the analysis

Intervention areas	Included papers
Healthy food choices and nutritional combinations	[4, 5, 11, 12, 13, 14, 18, 23, 24, 25, 27, 28, 30]
Snacking and emotional eating	[6–9]
Diet supervision and documentation	[3, 10, 18–23]
Eating process	[4, 14, 29, 30]

Intervention Areas. *Healthy Food Choices and Nutritional Combinations.* As shown in Table 3, persuasive design has been widely used for a healthy food choice of nutritional eating in different settings. For example, an information system was designed to enable reflection about nutrition by showing the collective food consumption patterns of a family [28]. Similarly, a personalized shopping assistant could provide guidance to users on healthy food product purchases [26]. A gamified online shopping service could promote the reflection on nutritional choices [25]. It has been explored the embodiment of music in the food information interfaces could influence users' meal choices for health promotion [29]. There are also controls for the intake of a specific nutritional element. For instance, *Nutritionavatar* [27] is an intention for low-sodium dieting, which was designed to supporting people gain awareness of high blood pressure risk.

Snacking and Emotional Eating. For emotional eating issues, persuasive design aims to intervene users' behavior with a light burden. For example, through a just-in-time intervention system with playful notifications and visual reports, users were encouraged to moderate emotions and control themselves to avoid unhealthy eating conditions [6]. For excessive drinking, [7] investigated an empathic virtual agent that can send messages with emoticons to improve the interventional efficiency. To address unhealthy snacking, [8] has provided empirical evidence that tailored persuasive text messages may have effects on influencing users to reduce snacking. Additionally, heuristic information design has been proved to be effective in prompting users to choose lower-calorie healthy snacks [9].

Diet Supervision and Documentation. To support diet managements, design studies have increasingly employed persuasive strategies in recent years. For example, a sensor network [10] has been designed and implemented to automatically detect eating and exercise of obese children under clinical treatment. In collective settings, through sharing eating records with each other in a social network [19–21], users were motivated to achieve healthy eating goals with this type of social support.

Eating Process. Among papers published in recent years, several persuasive designs for optimizing the eating process have been proposed to support eating speed and food portion control. For instance, *Foodworks* [14] was designed to digitally augment a plate of food and provide rewards upon the completion of a meal, encouraging children to eat vegetables. *Eat2pic* [30] uses a pair of chopsticks with sensor modules to collect food data for generating visual pictures during eating process to motivate users to slow their eating pace down for a balanced diet. Similarly, *Eco-meal* [4] based on a smart tray and a smartphone application was designed for eating speed and food portion control, as well as managing calorie/sodium intakes.

3.2 Methodologies

According to the description of characteristics, 28 included papers adopted 4 different design approaches, namely *user-centered approach, theory-based approach, context-driven approach*, and *technology-driven approach* (see Table 4).

Table 4. Design approaches mentioned in the included papers

Approches	Included papers
User-centered approach	[3–7, 9–18, 20–23, 26, 27]
Theory-based approach	[7, 8, 10, 22, 25–27, 29, 30]
Context-driven approach	[3, 8, 19, 20, 24]
Technology-driven approach	[4, 8, 10, 14, 20, 28, 30]

On the one hand, twenty-one included papers used a user-centered approach. Specifically, six papers [4, 6, 10, 13, 14, 20] combined with a technology-driven approach to make intervention of food choice and eating process in specific groups such as children with obesity problem and people with emotional eating problems. Six papers [7, 8, 10, 13, 22, 26] combined with theory-based approach during the whole process, which focus on the result of related framework experiment. For example, [7] used a virtual counselor to deliver Brief Motivational Interventions for behavior change for avoiding excessive drinking. Other papers [5, 9, 12, 15, 17, 18, 21, 23] developed mobile software and multimedia such as game and video based on the user-centered approach to achieve behavior change.

Table 5. Distribution of papers for different design types

Types	Included papers	Picture examples
Digital apps	[3, 5, 6, 11, 16, 21, 22, 24, 25, 26, 27]	Food record and avatar intervention UI [27]
Social media	[8, 9, 23]	Text messages [23]
Smart products service systems	[4, 14, 15, 18, 28, 30]	prototype design [15] EcoMeal prototype [4]
Wearable devices	[6, 10]	Sensor placement outline [6]
Conversational agents	[7, 12, 13]	paper sheet for children [12] The CiboPoli Conversational UI [13]

(continued)

Table 5. (*continued*)

Types	Included papers	Picture examples
Public services	[19, 20, 29]	 [29] [19]

On the other hand, for the rest eight included papers, four papers [8, 25, 29, 30] adopted theoretical models to guide to present related application example and testing which mainly used a theory-based approach. Three included papers [8, 28, 30] take the technology-driven approach to increase the effects of persuasive technologies. Five included papers [3, 8, 19, 20, 24] applied the context-driven approach that focuses on e.g., daily mealtime [19] and snacking [8], etc.

3.3 Design Rationale

Type of Application. As shown in Table 5, the included persuasive designs of all the reviewed papers could be classified into six different types of applications, including digital apps, social media, smart product service systems, wearable devices, conversational agents, and public services. Specifically, the majority of persuasive designs were mobile apps that designed to change users' attitudes and behaviors via data visualizations and motivational elements. For example, gamification of shopping platform was designed in [25] to influence food choice. Additionally, several studies combined smart products and wearable devices with mobile apps for promoting healthy eating behaviors [4, 14, 15, 18, 28, 30]. e.g., *Healthy Cradle* [15] realizes a smart tableware with an associated mobile app to improve the experience of the eating process.

Design Evaluation. As shown in Table 6, eight included papers present qualitative results as the design evaluation and nine had quantitative data analysis from the user survey or data from the persuasive design application. Six included papers applied mixed method to show both quantitative and qualitative results to verify their designs. Nevertheless, studies from two papers did not evaluate their design outcomes.

Table 6. Design evaluations mentioned in the included papers

Approches	Included papers
Qualitative	[3–5, 11, 21, 23, 25, 28]
Quantitative	[6, 8–10, 12, 16, 17, 24, 26]
Mixed method	[7, 13, 18, 19, 22, 27]
Not evaluated	[29, 30]

4 Discussion and Conclusions

This scoping review is set out to summarize and analyze the latest research developments of persuasive design for healthy eating behavior promotion. Through a literature search from three databases across a span of ten years, we selected and analyzed 28 selected papers published between 2011 and 2021. This scoping review provided a holistic view of paper characteristics, including their research specifications, methodologies, type of design applications and evaluations. The narrative analysis revealed the following two gaps in current research direction.

Firstly, we found that persuasive design, as a generic approach for promoting healthy eating, lacked personalized applications for specific user type and focused scenes. Personalization is of great importance in intervening unhealthy behaviors, especially on the food choices and nutritional combinations. Only recording personal eating patterns and exercise data can lead to improved nutrition and diet recommendations. E.g., Nutritionavatar [27] is a future-self avatar-based sodium reduction intervention; Lubbe et al. [18] have a proposal of personalized suggestions for older adults based on their protein intake. In addition, for snacking and emotional eating, detection of related data (i.e., emotion curve, snack time) could help reflections and self-management in a personalized way. Moreover, technologies (i.e., wearable sensors, chatbots, smart tableware) play an essential role in personalized persuasion. Thus, it is crucial to utilize user experience design that incorporates a variety of design approaches like user-centered design and data-driven innovation.

Secondly, from our review we learned that the major user groups in persuasive designs for healthy eating are patients and children. In contrast, relatively few studies were designed for teenagers (1/28), office workers (2/28), and older adults (2/28). However, it has been increasingly suggested to investigate technologies for encouraging these different user groups to reduce their unhealthy diet. As revealed by [17, 22, 23], healthy eating promotion is essential to address the increase of suboptimal health problems among vulnerable people like teenagers, older adults, and workers with heavy mental workload. Therefore, design researchers of future design studies could dedicate efforts to persuasive designs of healthy eating promotion for special user groups such as teenagers, office workers, and older adults.

In addition, most of the selected papers have created complete designs to promote healthy eating but did not pay attention to their feasibility to be easily adopted in the real-life setup. There is a growing tendency of persuasive design in avoiding complexity to incentivize users through easy tasks. As a support for this principle, Reinhardt et al.

[9] proved that simple heuristic information design is effective in prompting users to choose lower-calorie healthy snacks.

Based on this scoping review, we suggest future studies to explore the user experience factors for categorizing user according to the application contexts to achieve the personalized persuasion. Meanwhile, future work should also focus on simple forms of persuasive design application to promote healthy eating behavior in different contexts by expanding research on factors affecting user experience, experimenting with new technologies and materials, exploring innovative solutions to specific problems.

Acknowledgements. This work was supported by Beijing Institute of Technology Research Fund Program for Young Scholars.

References

1. Fogg, B.J.: Persuasive technology: using computers to change what we think and do. Ubiquity. **2002**(December), 2 (2002)
2. 周洁. 基于劝导技术的自我健康管理策略研究.浙江大学 (2014)
3. Marcus, A.: The health machine: mobile UX design that combines information design with persuasion design. In: Marcus, A. (ed.) DUXU 2011. LNCS, vol. 6770, pp. 598–607. Springer, Heidelberg (2011). https://doi.org/10.1007/978-3-642-21708-1_67
4. Kim, J., Park, J., Lee, U.: EcoMeal: a smart tray for promoting healthy dietary habits. In: Proceedings of the 34th Annual CHI Conference on Human Factors in Computing Systems, CHI EA 2016, 7–12 May 2016, San Jose, CA, United states, Association for Computing Machinery (2016)
5. Lazar, J., et al.: Co-design process of a smart phone app to help people with down syndrome manage their nutritional habits. J. Usabil. Stud. **13**(2), 73–93 (2018)
6. Carroll, E.A., et al.: Food and mood: just-in-time support for emotional eating. In: Proceedings of the 2013 5th Human Association Conference on Affective Computing and Intelligent Interaction, ACII 2013, 2–5 September 2013, Geneva, Switzerland, IEEE Computer Society (2013)
7. Lisetti, C., et al.: I can help you change! An empathic virtual agent delivers behavior change health interventions. ACM Trans. Manage. Inf. Syst. **4**(4), 1–28 (2013)
8. Kaptein, M., et al.: Adaptive persuasive systems: a study of tailored persuasive text messages to reduce snacking. ACM Trans. Interact. Intell. Syst. **2**(2), 1–25 (2012)
9. Reinhardt, D., Hurtienne, J.: Only one item left? Heuristic information trumps calorie count when supporting healthy snacking under low self-control. In: Proceedings of the 2019 CHI Conference on Human Factors in Computing Systems, CHI 2019, 4–9 May 2019, Glasgow, United Kingdom. Association for Computing Machinery (2019)
10. Zaragozá, I., et al.: Ubiquitous monitoring and assessment of childhood obesity. Personal Ubiquit. Comput. **17**(6), 1147–1157 (2013)
11. Almonani, E., et al.: Mobile game approach to prevent childhood obesity using persuasive technology. In: Proceedings of the 2014 International Conference on Computer and Information Sciences, ICCOINS 2014, 3–5 June 2014, Kuala Lumpur, Malaysia, 2014. Institute of Electrical and Electronics Engineers Inc. (2014)
12. Baroni, I., et al.: Designing motivational robot: how robots might motivate children to eat fruits and vegetables. In: Proceedings of the 23rd IEEE International Symposium on Robot and Human Interactive Communication, IEEE RO-MAN 2014, 25–29 August 2014, Edinburgh, United Kingdom, Institute of Electrical and Electronics Engineers Inc. (2014)

13. Fadhil, A., Villafiorita, A.: An adaptive learning with gamification and conversational UIs: the rise of CiboPoliBot. In: Proceedings of the 25th ACM International Conference on User Modeling, Adaptation, and Personalization, UMAP 2017, 9–12 July 2017, Bratislava, Slovakia, 2017, Association for Computing Machinery (2017)
14. Ganesh, S., et al.: FoodWorks: tackling fussy eating by digitally augmenting children's meals. In: Proceedings of the 8th Nordic Conference on Human-Computer Interaction, NordiCHI 2014, 26–30 October 2014, Helsinki, Finland. Association for Computing Machinery (2014)
15. Joi, Y.R., et al.: Interactive and connected tableware for promoting children's vegetable-eating and family interaction. In: Proceedings of the 15th International Conference on Interaction Design and Children, IDC 2016, 21–24 June 2016, Manchester, United Kingdom, 2016. Association for Computing Machinery (2016)
16. Alsaleh, N., Alnanih, R.: Gamification-based behavioral change in children with diabetes mellitus. In: Proceedings of the 11th International Conference on Ambient Systems, Networks and Technologies, ANT 2020/3rd International Conference on Emerging Data and Industry 40, EDI40 2020/Affiliated Workshops, 6–9 April 2020, Warsaw, Poland, Elsevier B.V (2020)
17. Van der Lubbe, L.M., Klein, M.C.A.: Designing a system with persuasive communication to improve diet compliance for elderly users. In: Proceedings of the 13th EAI International Conference on Pervasive Computing Technologies for Healthcare, PervasiveHealth 2019, 20–23 May 2019, Trento, Italy, 2019. ICST (2019)
18. Lubbe, L.V.D., et al.: Experiences with using persuasive technology in a diet trial for older adults. In: The 14th PErvasive Technologies Related to Assistive Environments Conference. Corfu, Greece, pp. 244–251. Association for Computing Machinery (2021). https://doi.org/10.1145/3453892.3458686
19. Chang, K.S.-P., Danis, C.M., Farrell, R.G.: Lunch line: using public displays and mobile devices to encourage healthy eating in an organization. In: Proceedings of the 2014 ACM International Joint Conference on Pervasive and Ubiquitous Computing, UbiComp 2014, 13–17 September 2014, Seattle, United States. Association for Computing Machinery (2014)
20. Parker, A.G.: Reflection-through-performance: personal implications of documenting health behaviors for the collective. Personal Ubiquit. Comput. 18(7), 1737–1752 (2014)
21. Pereira, C.V., et al.: We4Fit: a game with a purpose for behavior change. In: Proceedings of the 2014 18th IEEE International Conference on Computer Supported Cooperative Work in Design, CSCWD 2014, 21–23 May 2014, Hsinchu, Taiwan. IEEE Computer Society (2014)
22. Maimone, R., et al.: PerKApp: a general purpose persuasion architecture for healthy lifestyles. J. Biomed. Inform. 82, 70–87 (2018)
23. Altammami, O., Chatterjee, S.: Utilizing persuasive technology package to elevate dietary awareness. In: Proceedings of the 21st Americas Conference on Information Systems, AMCIS 2015, 13–15 August 2015, Fajardo, Puertorico, Americas Conference on Information Systems (2015)
24. Orji, R., Vassileva, J., Mandryk, R.L.: LunchTime: a slow-casual game for long-term dietary behavior change. Pers. Ubiquit. Comput. 17(6), 1211–1221 (2013)

25. Adaji, I., Vassileva, J.: A gamified system for influencing healthy e-commerce shopping habits. In: Proceedings of the 25th ACM International Conference on User Modeling, Adaptation, and Personalization, UMAP 2017, 9–12 July 2017, Bratislava, Slovakia. Association for Computing Machinery (2017)

26. Siawsolit, C., Seepun, S., Choi, J., Do, A., Kao, Y.: Personalized assistant for health-conscious grocery shoppers. In: de Vries, P.W., Oinas-Kukkonen, H., Siemons, L., de BeerlageJong, N., van Gemert-Pijnen, L. (eds.) PERSUASIVE 2017. LNCS, vol. 10171, pp. 95–106. Springer, Cham (2017). https://doi.org/10.1007/978-3-319-55134-0_8

27. Fuchs, K., et al.: Nutritionavatar: designing a future-self avatar for promotion of balanced, low-sodium diet intention. In: Proceedings of the 13th Biannual Conference of the Italian SIGCHI Chapter Designing the Next Interaction, Italy 2019, 23–25 September 2019, Padua, Italy ICST (2019)

28. Reitberger, W., Spreicer, W., Fitzpatrick, G.: Situated and mobile displays for reflection on shopping and nutritional choices. Personal Ubiquit. Comput. **18**(7), 1721–1735 (2014)

29. Espinoza, G.E.T., Baranauskas, M.C.C.: Motivation, persuasion and healthy eating: a case study on a socially-aware persuasive system design. In: Proceedings of the 19th Brazilian Symposium on Human Factors in Computing Systems, IHC 2020, 26–30 October 2020, Virtual, Online, Brazil. Association for Computing Machinery, Inc. (2020)

30. Nakaoka, R., et al.: eat2pic: food-tech design as a healthy nudge with smart chopsticks and canvas. In: Proceedings of the 2021 IEEE International Conference on Pervasive Computing and Communications Workshops and other Affiliated Events (PerCom Workshops), 22–26 March 2021 (2021)

31. Nakamura, Y.: IoT nudge: IoT data-driven nudging for health behavior change. In: Proceedings of the 2021 ACM International Joint Conference on Pervasive and Ubiquitous Computing and the 2021 ACM International Symposium on Wearable Computers, UbiComp/ISWC 2021, 21–25 September, 2021, Virtual, United States, 2021. Association for Computing Machinery, Inc. (2021)

32. 张珏. 劝导设计及其在健康行为导向型产品中的应用研究. 江南大学 (2014)

33. Fogg, B.J.: Creating persuasive technologies: an eight-step design process. In: Proceedings of the Proceedings of the 4th International Conference on Persuasive Technology (2009)

34. Ladwa, S., Grønli, T.-M., Ghinea, G.: Towards encouraging a healthier lifestyle and increased physical activity – an app incorporating persuasive design principles. In: Kurosu, M. (ed.) HCI 2018. LNCS, vol. 10902, pp. 158–172. Springer, Cham (2018). https://doi.org/10.1007/978-3-319-91244-8_13

35. Ojo, A., et al.: OH-BUDDY: mobile phone texting based intervention for diabetes and oral health management. In: Proceedings of the 48th Annual Hawaii International Conference on System Sciences, HICSS 2015, 5–8 January 2015, Kauai, HI, United states, IEEE Computer Society (2015)

36. Nkwo, M.: Designing mobile persuasive technology to promote mental healthcare in developing African nations. In: Proceedings of the 16th International Web for All Conference, San Francisco, CA, USA; Association for Computing Machinery (2019). Article 27. https://doi.org/10.1145/3315002.3332433

37. Masthoff, J.: Towards utter well-being: personalization for guardian angels. In: Proceedings of the 27th ACM Conference on User Modeling, Adaptation and Personalization. Association for Computing Machinery, 3 (2019)

Towards Social Companions in Augmented Reality: Vision and Challenges

Anton Nijholt[✉]

Faculty EEMCS, Human Media Interaction, University of Twente, PO Box 217,
7500 AE Enschede, The Netherlands
a.nijholt@utwente.nl

Abstract. In future omnipresent Augmented Reality (AR), virtual creatures (humans and pets) will play an important role, not so much as task-oriented individuals, but as friends and companions with whom we can walk and chat when we want to. A companion can also suggest physical activity, motivate healthy eating behavior, or help in reminding taking medication. We survey existing approaches to introduce virtual humans and pets in AR. We indicate shortcomings and mention research approaches to deal with them. We conclude with a few observations on some aspects of AR-specific situational awareness of (multisensorial) virtual humans and pets that must reflect in their behavior to be believable.

Keywords: Augmented reality · Social companions · Virtual humans · Ever-present augmented reality · Multisensorial situational awareness

1 Ever-present Augmented Reality and Social Companions

In the next decade, we expect to see the development of optical and sensor technology that enables everyday Augmented Reality (AR) use. It allows you to be continuously present in an AR world during your daily real-world activities. Ronald T. Azuma predicts that smart glasses will supplant the smartphone for accessing digital information [1] and will become a ubiquitous consumer AR display. Also in Facebook's ARIA project, all-day usage of AR with smart glasses is foreseen [2]. Such glasses should be light and comfortable to wear, they should be multipurpose, personalized, context-aware, and proactive. They should allow natural multimodal interaction (speech, touch, gaze, and gestures), have artificial intelligence (AI), and be integrated into the Internet of Things (IoT) [3]. AR users should be able to share environments and experiences. Moreover, senses other than sight, that is, hearing, touch, smell, and taste are nowadays being addressed to aid in expanding human capabilities and sensory experiences [4, 5].

Ever-present AR calls for research into real-world scenarios in which users are active in urban environments, for example, going shopping, looking for a quiet terrace, taking a walk in the park, or taking children to school. In short, mobile activities and experiences and social interactions, usually involve some social interaction [6]. In addition to other human AR users, whether they appear in reality or as an avatar in the virtual layer that is superimposed on reality, virtual algorithm-controlled agents can be present in a user's AR world as well. The focus in this paper is on the latter type of virtual agents, in particular virtual humans, also known as embodied interactive agents or intelligent virtual agents.

These interactive virtual humans have been investigated in the context of two- and three-dimensional environments where they play the role of a (virtual) shopping assistant, trainer, educator, or adviser [7]. It is common for them to have some knowledge of their task, but otherwise, they are isolated from the physical environment in which they operate. In more recent mobile applications, they can of course know of time and place, but not or hardly of events that take place in their direct environment, especially real-world events that are not task-related. In an AR world, virtual humans need to be aware of virtual and real events.

Social companions have been introduced as interactive 2D and 3D virtual embodied agents or robotic agents with verbal and nonverbal communication skills. They have social and task-oriented knowledge that allows them to have a (spoken) dialogue-like interaction with their users. The assumption is that virtual or robotic companions can provide social support to older adults [8], keeping them socially engaged, improving social and mental health, for example, by reducing loneliness.

More generally, and also for other audiences, a companion can act in a motivating way to promote healthy eating behavior, physical activity, and health self-care. It is no surprise that there are many examples of virtual embodied agents that are designed to play the role of exercise, fitness, train, or health coach. What about a coach in aid of smoking cessation [9]? Or have a virtual embodied agent that takes the role of a patient for nurse training [10]? But these are monitor- or smartphone-based [11] applications and do not take the visually perceived real world into account.

Virtual pets and companion animals can play a similar role, for example in helping to prevent and manage obesity [12]. In [13] a social companion is introduced to improve assisted living. It is embedded in a sensor-rich smart home environment and has been given an anthropomorphic version inside a humanoid robot. A next step could be having such a companion implemented as an assistant in an AR home environment or having it as a mobile AR agent. AR social companions that share the same physical space with their owners can accompany them when they go for a walk or shopping, visit friends, or attend public events. They receive information from the user and his AR device and sensors integrated into the environment. Social intelligence and situational awareness [14] are properties that need to be considered in the design of social companions in AR. Our expectations about the social behavior and the social intelligence of an AR companion are partly determined by its designed appearance.

This paper aims to draw attention to the possibility to introduce social companions in AR. In this paper, we survey some preliminary observations on introducing social companions in AR. To do so we survey the (very) modest attempts to introduce virtual humans in AR environments, discuss some general properties, both from the point of view of virtual humans and AR, and give some examples of (task-oriented) virtual assistants that have been introduced in AR. Where possible, these points of view are complemented with observations on how these virtual humans and assistants can be given a role as social companions. In [15] a more globally oriented companion paper can be found.

2   Virtual Characters: Embodiment, Cognition, and Emotion

A virtual human in AR can be a social companion, collaborator, trainer, educator, shopping assistant, or character in an entertainment or game application. Cartoon characters and virtual pets can also play some of these roles. Here we give an example of an early occurrence of a human-like agent in an AR entertainment application that is ready to play a game with its human partner. "Checkers" [16] is an augmented reality interaction between a real and a virtual human playing the checkers game. The human plays checkers using a real checkerboard and real pieces. Board and pieces are tracked with a camera, the camera position and orientation can change, and the position of the virtual player is updated relative to the board. The decisions of the virtual player which moves to make are generated by a checkers program. Virtual board, virtual pieces, virtual player, and its animations (grasping the pieces), are superposed to the real images taken by the camera. These real images include the human player making the moves on the checkerboard. The mixed scene is displayed on a large monitor that provides the real player with visual feedback. That is, the player sees the virtual opponent integrated into the image the camera has recorded of themselves, a kind of (magic) mirror-AR (see Fig. 1). An audience can also see the mixed scene on the monitor.

Fig. 1. Playing checkers, Computer Graphics Lab (LIG), Lausanne, 2000 [16].

This example gives some indication of what kind of applications we can think of if we do not limit ourselves to the usual assistant-like virtual humans. The example comes from a graphically oriented research environment. The emphasis is on the integration of the virtual and the real world. In general, with virtual humans in an AR environment, we expect more autonomous action and interaction from the virtual humans if they have to play a role as companions, educators, or assistants. Moreover, although this example satisfies the AR definition originally posited by Azuma [17] we need to look at virtual human applications in optical and video see-through AR too. First, however, some more notes on virtual human research are needed.

2.1 Virtual Humans: Cognition and Emotion

Instead of virtual humans in AR, we can talk about AR-embodied agents. By using the word "agent" we make clearer that we not only aim at the embodied appearance of the virtual human and its behavior but also the modeling of a cognitive and affective state (the agent's 'brain' and 'emotion') with its beliefs about the world, its desires, its intentions, and its reasoning from which behavior is actuated. Real sensors in the real world and "virtual software sensors" in the virtual layer of the augmented world provide the agent's "brain" with input. Hence, through its sensors, the AR agent perceives information from its environment (both real and virtual), and it reacts with its perceptible bodily behavior and by the control of its social or task environment. Agent research aims at making these agents autonomous, reactive, proactive, and assigning to them some social abilities [18]. This provides an agent with a mental and emotional state, a disposition to act.

Initial research on virtual humans in virtual - and later years in augmented - reality has been graphics-driven. Virtual humans require animations for body movements, gestures, and facial expressions. Agent research, on the other hand, aims at modeling an agent's mental state, not necessarily looking at embodiment. Intelligent virtual agents' research in the human-computer interaction community aims at providing embodied virtual agents with interaction capabilities requiring the modeling of facial expressions, gaze behavior, and gestures during interactions, sometimes done by using emotion models but usually without having such behavior generated from an integrated model of knowing about the world, intelligence, and affect. In later years we see these virtual humans appear in educational, entertainment, and health applications where they are expected to engage in a (natural language) dialogue with their human users. Much of this research began with the seminal book "Embodied Conversational Agents" [19] by Justine Cassell et al. and has been presented in the last decades at the yearly international conferences on Intelligent Virtual Agents (IVA) that are held since 1999. See [20] for a survey of this research and [Burden] for a recent book on virtual humans.

In [21] an overview is given of the research topics, areas of artificial intelligence, and examples of research approaches to achieve a human-level performance of virtual agents. We mention perception, planning, representation of beliefs and intentions, communication ability, and social and emotional reasoning. Many sub-issues can be distinguished. Dialogue requires speech recognition, natural language understanding and generation, and nonverbal communication (gaze, facial expressions, gestures). Emotion modeling requires interaction between coping (dealing with emotions by acting on the world or changing beliefs) and appraisal (assessing the world and how it relates to the agent's goals). Beliefs require knowledge of the past and the current world. Intentions and acts have to be guided by a task model and a task reasoner.

2.2 A Social Companion in (Mirror-based) Augmented Reality

Clearly, not for any virtual agent application comprehensive modeling of human-like cognitive, affective, and social interaction behavior is necessary. In our daily life, we interact socially not only with fellow humans and our family members but also with our pets: dogs, cats, marmots, or goldfish. Our virtual interaction partners have different roles with corresponding intelligence and social skills. For a virtual shop assistant, we can aim at 'shop-assistant-level' behavior, for a virtual butler we aim at 'butler-level' behavior, and for a virtual dog at 'dog-level' behavior.

An example, in many ways, of an agent approach to a virtual character in an AR-like environment is the ALIVE project [22]. A camera image of the user is composited in the virtual world and sees herself projected in this world on a large screen. This "Magic Mirror" or Mirror-AR approach allows the user to interact, using speech and gestures, with a virtual character in the virtual world. Both characters and the user are part of an agent architecture. The virtual character is an embodied autonomous agent with an internal state in which needs, and motivations are modeled. The agent tries to satisfy its needs in the environment and chooses its behaviors accordingly. Its virtual sensors are its 'synthetic vision'. They make the character aware of the objects and events in the environment and trigger the desired animations to deal with them. In [23] the character that is chosen in ALIVE is an interactive virtually animated dog called Silas T. Dog. A study was made of dog behavior to have Silas behave realistically, including realistic interactions with the user of the system. Rather than an assistant in augmented reality, Silas is a companion with a motivational state and intentionality that shows in his behavior. Silas has his own agenda, including playing with the user. He responds to the gestures and postures of the user and can invite the user to play if his motivation to play has not been satisfied for some time.

3   Virtual Characters in Augmented Reality

There is still a long way to go from the current first steps to introducing virtual humans in augmented reality to virtual humans or pets serving as believable companions. Embodied conversational agents and intelligent virtual agents have been the topic of research since the 1990s. It seems clear that many of the results of this research can be used seamlessly for the virtual agents we intend to introduce in AR environments. Think of speech, language, non-verbal aspects of interaction, emotion modeling, interaction modeling (the 'understanding' of the conversational partner), and animation. It seems clear that many of the results of this research can be used seamlessly for the virtual agents we intend to introduce in AR environments.

However, for many AR applications, we expect more from a virtual human in AR than reasonably maintaining a conversation or other language-oriented interaction. They can act as an opponent in a game, participate in an interactive play, demonstrate fitness exercises, or be a walking companion with whom you share experiences on the walk. Social companions have additional tasks, such as providing social support and wellness coaching, promoting walking behavior and physical exercise, and helping to change unhealthy behavior [8]. But preferably these tasks need to be integrated with a user's daily activities. So, they must be aware of the behavior of the user, the real-world objects that are and appear in the user's environment, and when the user's augmented world has virtual objects in addition to the virtual human, the virtual human needs to be aware of these virtual objects or even understand how to deal with them.

On a smartphone or smart glasses, virtual humans acting as social companions can continuously accompany a user. That is, not just as a talking head on a wearable device, but as a full-bodied virtual human that can be as much physically involved in activities as its human user. Different from virtual humans that have been introduced in artificial 2D and 3D environments, our AR virtual humans have to perform in the real world. They are included in a virtual layer that is imposed on the real world and they have become part of an augmented reality in which they are displayed on a head-worn display, a handheld, a static display, or in spatial AR. And, more importantly, AR technology enables them to perceive both the real world and whatever is present in the virtual layer, whether it addresses their virtual sight, hearing, touch, taste, or smell senses, assuming these senses have been implemented and assigned to them.

Virtual embodied creatures have been implemented in AR. We see them appear as virtual assistants, as virtual pet animals, as virtual trainers, or as virtual opponents in a game. Implementations address research questions on the effects of anthropomorphic and behavioral realism on aspects of user experience such as attractiveness, engagement, and presence. However, rather than acting as a social companion, the agents in this research are meant to provide training and education, or just add speech or text information to what a user perceives in a domestic or urban environment. Just as AR devices allow human users access to augmented sensors and augmented reality, virtual humans can be given access to real-world information, including veritable humans, through the sensors of the AR device and possibly wearables that are coupled to the AR device.

The many sensors in an AR device make it possible to gather all kinds of information about the user and his environment. That information can be made available to an AR assistant who can integrate it with existing knowledge and use it in AR tasks to be performed, perhaps without the user being aware of it. In this way, the AR device is made part of the ubiquitous computing (Ubicomp) world, it provides an intuitive and intelligent interface to a digital world aligned with physical reality [24]. In [25] the possibility of autonomous behavior of virtual AR humans is emphasized. They can draw their perceptions from the state of both the virtual and the real world and they can affect both the virtual and the real world in a ubiquitous computing setting. In their framework, they have implemented demo applications of intelligent AR agents for repair and maintenance on handheld computers.

Equipped with these observations we can have a closer look at the few examples of virtual creatures that have been introduced in AR worlds. What do these creatures know about the user and the user's real environment? What is present in the virtual layer in which they are included and what do they know about it? Can they initiate changes in the real world without the intervention of their user? This is a young field of research and we see that many of the virtual humans introduced have the goal of examining how users experience and value such agents. Co-presence (does the user feel that they are co-located with the virtual human), social presence (does the user feel they are socially connected to the virtual human), and behavioral realism (does the virtual human behave as a veritable human in the physical world) are keywords in this research.

3.1 The Development of Task-Oriented Virtual Humans in Augmented Reality

Virtual humans have been introduced as interactive 2D and 3D embodied agents in 2D and 3D interactive environments. Often, they appear as embodied agents that can be engaged in chats, question and answering, and conversation. These virtual humans are communication oriented. They use keyboard input or speech and are embedded in natural language dialogue systems. Modeling nonverbal interaction has become part of this embodied agent research. In virtual and augmented reality environments these human-like embodied agents need to know about real and virtual objects, they should be able to show their knowledge about the world they live in and should be able to communicate such knowledge while using verbally and nonverbally appropriate interaction behavior, including, when necessary, the expression of emotions.

A virtual human toolkit that allows designers to build virtual humans using available technologies for audio-visual sensing, speech recognition, natural language processing, nonverbal behavior generation and realization, text-to-speech generation, and rendering has been made available to the research community [26]. In later years the toolkit has been extended to support the design of embodied agents ("ubiquitous virtual humans") that have to perform in virtual and augmented reality environments [27].

There are not many examples of virtual humans, humanoids, or virtual pet animals that have been introduced in AR environments. As mentioned above, when this was done, the motivation was often to look at how certain behavior of virtual people affected the presence experience, rather than to see how users could find pleasure, comfort, and support in the presence of such an agent.

Our focus is on mobile optical see-through AR to have our social companions share our world during our daily activities. For completeness, we mention some other AR possibilities for virtual creatures to appear in our daily environment. We already mentioned the checkers playing partner who plays the game with a human opponent [16] and the Silas dog [22, 23], as an example of an autonomous character that can respond to human gestures and commands. Both the checkers player and the dog act in a mirror-AR application, aware of their user, the dog handler, and the human opponent, but otherwise fully isolated from the surrounding real world and without other virtual objects in the virtual layer they inhabit. In [28] we have "urbanimals" in a projection-based AR application that are familiar with the physical public space in which they perform and that interact with passers-by in the real world. Video see-through AR examples of virtual creatures exist as well. Well-known is the Pokémon Go example of handheld AR but there are also commercial video see-through examples on billboards and bus shelters [29] that can be experienced without having to wear a headset. But also, no possibilities to influence the AR experience in any other way than observing it or happily faking interaction with it [30, 31].

3.2   Virtual Humans and Animals in Augmented Reality: A Survey

In what follows we only consider virtual creatures that inhabit a virtual layer superimposed on reality and displayed on a head-worn optical see-through AR device. And, of course, we assume that today's rather bulky headsets will be succeeded by smart glasses that can be worn continuously in a non-obtrusive way without having to sacrifice sensors or rather, on the contrary, even having more smartness integrated into the eyewear. This also means that we do not consider the virtual humans in the Façade project [32], a conversation-oriented project that was ported from an existing desktop application to a video see-through AR application. These virtual humans had no knowledge of the real world in which they were projected, only of their mutual conversation and interaction with a veritable human being.

Welbo [33], on the other hand, can be mentioned as the first interactive humanoid in optical see-through AR with knowledge of both the real world (a physical living room with furniture) and virtual object (furniture). Welbo knows about the position and orientation of the user and it can move the virtual objects in the physical space until the user is satisfied with the result. We can say that Welbo has both virtual and real perceptions. It knows what is virtual and what is real, and it aligns the virtual with the real.

MARA [34] is a virtual human in an outdoor application of AR. She is present in an optical see-through HMD and she guides a visitor through a university campus, presenting and explaining the real campus buildings that are visible to the visitor. The AR device's sensors allow her to know about the position and the orientation of the user, therefore she can walk towards the user, turn to the user, and follow the user while walking around the campus. However, virtual objects are not part of MARA's world.

We have to wait more than ten years before we see another few modest attempts to introduce virtual humans into AR environments. Interestingly, one of the attempts is by a commercial HMD producer (Magic Leap). Their AR assistant Mica is a virtual embodied agent that Mica has some knowledge of the real world. Her movements consider her orientation towards the user and she can maintain eye contact with the user [35]. In demonstrations[1] and on webpages[2] she can perform tasks that include virtual objects, she can interact with the user, and she has been given a personality (see Fig. 2).

Fig. 2. AR assistant Mica in a Magic Leap demonstration, 2019 [35].

A virtual job interviewer in AR is introduced in [36]. This desktop application allows young adults with Autism Spectrum Disorder (ASD) to practice job interviews. The interviewer is designed to look seated on a real chair behind a table (the real-world objects). Apart from the interviewer virtual objects do not play a role in the application. The interviewer has verbal and nonverbal interaction with the interviewer, who wears a Magic Leap HMD. The nonverbal aspect consists of the interviewer maintaining eye contact with the user. The application allows collecting statistics about head orientation,

---

[1] https://www.youtube.com/watch?v=-PzeWxtOGzQ.
[2] https://www.magicleap.com/en-us/news/op-ed/i-am-mica.

eye gaze, and blink rate which can be useful to improve a user's performance during job interviews and to train the job interviewer. There is no need for the interviewer or user to move around and to know more about the AR environment than the static interview setting with the interviewer and user sitting opposite each other, a 'seated AR application. Also ported to AR from a VR application is the Jefferson agent, named after Thomas Jefferson, the third president of the United States [36]. Users can walk around and interact with Jefferson displayed on their phone or tablet and embedded in the real world, but again, with limited use of current AR technology such as navigation and alignment of real and virtual objects.

One of the agents introduced in [37] is Jake, an embodied agent that assists a user in solving a hidden object puzzle on a touchscreen, using dialogue and mutual gaze. The user is wearing an AR headset (Microsoft HoloLens) and Jake is displayed at a size comparable to a physically present human sitting across from you at a table. Apart from the puzzle and the user, the agent is not aware of the real world and apart from the agent, there are no other virtual objects in this AR world. A rather simple, from an AR point of view, is a virtual coach for balance training for older adults [38], requiring an (optical see-through) AR HMD. This personal coach demonstrates exercises in the user's familiar environment and the user can see the exercises from different distances and perspectives by moving in the AR world. The chosen position and movements of the coach do not conflict with other real or virtual objects, thus avoiding occlusion problems. No additional virtual objects are present and interaction is minimal (see Fig. 3).

Fig. 3. Virtual coach for home-based balance training, 2020 [38].

In [39] a companion dog is made visible in optical see-through AR with a HoloLens device and experiments were set up to study the effects of accompanying the virtual dog on proxemics and locomotion behavior of the dog handler and a passer-by. However, the different dog behaviors were remotely controlled by an experimenter, so its knowledge of the physical environment (mainly the proximity of human participants) was simulated. Its behavior included falling over when knocked over by a distracted passer-by and some auditory feedback such as panting, whining, and barking. Significant differences were shown in walking behavior when walking with the AR dog as compared to walking alone. So, while there is no implementation of a companion aware of its AR environment, the study can be seen as a step that provides information on what to take into account to realize natural walking behavior with a social companion in AR. Some interesting design questions follow (see also [40]). Should anyone other than the owner be aware of the virtual dog's presence? Can virtual dogs from different owners communicate with each other? How responsive do they need to be to events in their environment? We will come back to this in a next subsection. Some informal observations about what a long-term companion should be can be found in [41].

Finally, an example of a virtual pet animal that shows natural behavior in a physical apartment (living room, bedroom, and kitchen) is presented in [42]. Objects in the apartment are annotated with cat behavior. Typical objects are a food bowl, a couch, a bed, a table et cetera. Idling, scratching, eating, resting, and soiling are distinguished behaviors. The geometry of a scene is obtained with the spatial mapping technique of a HoloLens, an object detection algorithm provides the scene semantics, and paths can be computed for the cat to walk from one object location to the other and perform generated sequences of behavior. There is no interaction between the cat and its owner and apart from the cat, there are no virtual objects in the AR environment.

Some other examples of virtual beings in AR that assist real people can be given, but often the aim is to investigate, usually in a Wizard of Oz (WoZ)[3] setting, how aspects of appearance and behavior influence presence-related issues. As noted earlier in [25], it makes sense to distinguish between AR interface agents that rely on explicit user input for their conversational actions and AR beings that can show some autonomous behavior, have also own interests, and can act in parallel with the user in a dynamically changing AR world.

3.3 Augmenting Virtual Humans

Task-oriented agents can help us because they have knowledge and capabilities that we do not (yet) have. They provide information, advise, provide training, and demonstrate. They have built-in knowledge or know how to query the environment in a way that we as users of AR do not have at our disposal. There is, of course, no problem in equipping the agents with senses and resulting skills and experiences that differ from those of human beings or that can be regarded as augmentations of known human senses and abilities. We can speak of non-human senses, skills, and experiences.

In a previous section, we already met Silas T. Dog and its dog-level behavior and intelligence. Silas could show sensitivity to sounds and smells that are imperceptible to his human handlers. More generally, with appropriate sensors in AR devices and the real-world environment, we can equip a virtual character with infrared viewing, thermal perception, smell perception, or hearing sound beyond the human spectrum and design applications that make use of these perceptual qualities. With AR we can design fairytale and magical environments superimposed on the real world for entertainment applications in which virtual magicians, elves, and trolls make use of AI and sensor technology that provide them with non-human senses and capabilities and show them to the human

---

[3] In a Wizard of Oz experiment subjects believe that they interact with a computer system when in reality the interaction is mainly done with an invisible experimenter. In this way it can be examined how people will act in a setting that has not yet been realized with a computer.

AR users of such environments. In AR cartoon-physics can be superimposed on the real world as well. It requires a different implementation than follows from Newton's laws of physics. For example, physics-defying Roadrunner can pass through a solid wall painted to resemble a tunnel entrance, Wile E. Coyote cannot. In a suitable AR environment, these non-human capabilities are nevertheless plausible impossibilities.

A virtual human in an AR world can use all the technology that we can make available to an AR device. That technology gives the virtual human senses, perceptions, capabilities, and experiences that can be shared with the human users of an AR environment. These are experiences that are not normally experienced by real people, but that can be accepted as being natural and belonging to a social companion just as the display of non-human sensory experiences of dogs are accepted by their owners. As an example, in [43] AR technology makes it possible to make visible objects that are out of the user's view or occluded by other objects. This information can be communicated by their social companion to help the elderly navigate safely in their home or nursing home environment or outside.

How far should we go in assigning virtual senses to virtual characters? Should our social companion be aware of how the perceptions made by our interoceptive senses also determine our visible behavior? Should our virtual social companion himself also refer to matters pertaining to his behavior or, more specifically, his bodily functions? Do we want our social companion to know about feeling hungry and should it be able to express its feeling of being hungry, consciously, or unconsciously? A social AR companion can obtain information about their user's health status from the user's wearables and comment on it in a friendly manner. Multisensorial awareness and display of multisensorial awareness, whether the perception is by interoceptive or exteroceptive human sensors, are issues that have hardly received attention in virtual human research until now.

3.4 Multisensorial Awareness for Social Companions in Augmented Reality

Social companions that are fed by sensors in the user's AR device and sensors in the environment can communicate their knowledge and experiences to their human partners in a human-like way. Sensors in the physical space can provide information that is related to the position of the virtual human rather than to the position of their user. This information can be transmitted to the user as coming from the virtual human. Environmental conditions for the virtual human can be different from those of the user. A virtual human can ask or suggest the user to turn on the light or to move a real object in their proximity so that they can perform a task more plausibly. As mentioned in [44], it can do so without revealing its functional deficiency. In that paper, a distinction is made between a virtual human's basic sensing that focuses on situationally and socially appropriate verbal and nonverbal interactions with its user and peripheral sensing that is more related to contextual plausibility such as sensing room temperature to empathize with the feelings of its user.

A social companion does not necessarily have to show general human intelligence. It can show limited task and social intelligence and nevertheless be accepted as a useful and appreciated companion. Does it have to show multisensorial awareness? Should it behave naturally when confronted with sudden unexpected changes in its environment? The social companion can be given some control of the real world that is of interest to its user. However, despite its sensorial input, its human-like appearance, its knowledge about its owner, and its AI knowledge about the world, it is 'just' a virtual creature superimposed on the real world. In AR, neither the user nor his social companion controls the real world. What is happening in the real world cannot be predicted but showing awareness of real-world events and reacting to them will make a social companion more acceptable. An AR agent needs to be aware of changes in its environment, even if they are not caused by its human owner. To remain believable, it must be aware of events happening in the real world, such as a loud noise, a sudden change of weather, or, more extreme, an earthquake. It should be aware of changes in scent, know about pleasant and unpleasant odors, touches, visuals, flavors, and sounds. This multisensorial awareness must show itself in their body language and behavior. When it starts to rain in the real world, our social companion should be aware of it and should advise the use of an umbrella and, moreover, its virtual representation should become wet when it goes out into the rain without a virtual umbrella. More generally, an AR companion needs to show awareness of the multisensorial characteristics of real objects and events and needs to be able to decide about appropriate reactions. And, finally, it should know that it is virtual and like a human or humorous robot, it should be able to make jokes about its poor behavior.

In various WoZ experiments a start has been made to investigate such issues. In [45] a virtual human that appears to be physically challenged shows awareness of real objects and asks for help from a human wearing an AR device to avoid implausible collisions with real objects. A possible extension is to give a virtual human simulated control of physical objects with actuation mechanisms that enable movement in the real world. In a collision avoidance task [46], a HoloLens user experiences visually synchronized vibrations felt through the floor and caused by a virtual human's walking or jumping. Higher perceived physicality and social presence are reported. Neither the user nor his social companion needs to be actively engaged in a stimuli event that should show their sense of social presence in an AR environment.

Does a companion notice that the light in a room has been turned on or that someone is passing by on the other side of the street? A virtual companion should notice a red pedestrian light and transfer this information in a human-like way to its human partner. If we walk a virtual dog, should it respond to a real dog barking and start exploring the environment using its dog's senses? In [47] many more of these examples of relationships between the virtual and the real are presented and discussed, such as a virtual bird imitating songs of real birds in the augmented reality world or a virtual pet that gets scared away by unexpected sounds. The human participant can notice this awareness behavior and any subsequent adjustments of the virtual character's behavior or embodiment where applicable. Most of these examples require a multimodal approach to augmented reality and involve crossmodal effects. In [48] a literature overview of research that addresses both AR and multimodality can be found. In the case of virtual humans, we should look at multisensorial stimuli and crossmodal effects on their behavior.

Experiments that aim at investigating the influence of awareness behavior on social presence have been designed. In [49] the "wobbly table" experiment is described. The human participant is seated at a real table that is visually extended into a virtual world displayed on a large screen. A virtual human is seated at the virtual end of the table.

If one of them leans on the table, whether virtual or real, the table will tilt slightly, synchronously in the real and in the virtual world toward the other end. The virtual agent shows awareness of the table movement at its end. From this WoZ experiment, it was concluded that this awareness caused an increase in the human participant's sense of presence and social presence. In follow-up studies, it was investigated how the introduction of (artificial) wind and its effect on virtual and human participants affected a human's sense of being present in the AR world.

Studies like these address seemingly subtle behaviors of a virtual human in social situations. However, these responses to real-world stimuli, such as the startle response in the case of hearing breaking glass, having its shadow moved, or awareness of a change in weather, are probably more important for creating a social bond between the AR companion and the user than having the AR companion as a perfect question-answering system.

4 Conclusions

We surveyed how in previous years virtual humans were introduced in augmented reality environments. In particular, we looked at virtual creatures (humans and animals) that were introduced to provide assistance or entertainment to their human partners or owners, with the aim to discuss the possibility to have such AR creatures play a role of a social companion. Virtual humans have been introduced as health and fitness coaches in desktop and smartphone versions [11]. Agents for assisted living have been given both virtual and humanoid robot appearances [13]. In this paper, we surveyed virtual humans from the point of view of having them implemented in augmented reality where they, as social companions, need to be aware of changes in the real and the virtual world that is displayed to their human partner.

In AR, virtual humans are virtual objects that simulate human senses (and beyond) and that are superimposed on the real world in an optical or video see-through way for the user. For social companions that accompany users in their daily activities, we need to choose optical see-through as made possible by head-mounted devices, smart glasses, or, in the future, smart lenses. Recent research in smart glasses and lenses [6] makes it possible to consider ever-present augmented reality and all-day smart glasses or lenses to communicate with our social companions. Many problems remain. If we want our companion to move in the real world we need to tackle occlusion problems, part of the real world will be occluded by the virtual companion, part of the virtual companion will occlude objects in the real world scene. The environments in which the social companion has to perform need to be modeled, on the fly, or in advance, to provide the companion with information about real and virtual objects and not have it appear as a semi-transparent ghost floating in front of the real scene.

Rather than solving these problems, which we consider to be a task for the AR research community, in this paper, we aimed at making them more explicit, putting them in context, and transforming these problems into challenges. While doing so, we follow AR pioneer Ronald T. Azuma [1] who predicted in 2019 that AR, in particular optical see-through glasses, will be the dominant platform and interface, supplanting the smartphone, for accessing digital information. Light-weight, non-obtrusive, and optical see-through glasses are seen as "… the best chance of achieving the long-term vision of ubiquitous consumer AR displays."

References

1. Azuma, R.T.: The road to ubiquitous consumer augmented reality systems. Hum. Behav. Emerg. Technol. **1**, 26–32 (2019)
2. Abrash, M.: Project ARIA. In: Facebook Connect Keynote: Oculus Quest 2, Project Aria and More! 1.33.20-1.47.50 (2020). https://www.youtube.com/watch?v=woXmJMw2lTM
3. Grubert, J., Langlotz, T., Zollmann, S., Regenbrecht, H.: Towards pervasive augmented reality: context-awareness in augmented reality. IEEE Trans. Vis. Comput. Graph. **23**(6), 1706–1724 (2017)
4. Schraffenberger, H., van der Heide, E.: Multimodal augmented reality: the norm rather than the exception. In: Proceedings of the 2016 Workshop on Multimodal Virtual and Augmented Reality (MVAR 2016), pp. 1–6. ACM, New York, NY, USA (2016)
5. Kerruish, E.: Arranging sensations: smell and taste in augmented and virtual reality. Sens. Soc. **14**(1), 31–45 (2019)
6. Nijholt, A.: Social augmented reality interactions. In: Proceedings 10th International IEEE Conference on Informatics, Electronics and Vision (ICIEV 2021), pp. 1–8. IEEE, New York (2021)
7. Burden, D., Savin-Baden, M.: Virtual Humans: Today and Tomorrow. Taylor & Francis/CRC Press, Boca Raton (2019)
8. Vardoulakis, L.P., Ring, L., Barry, B., Sidner, C.L., Bickmore, T.: Designing relational agents as long term social companions for older adults. In: Nakano, Y., Neff, M., Paiva, A., Walker, M. (eds.) IVA 2012. LNCS (LNAI), vol. 7502, pp. 289–302. Springer, Heidelberg (2012). https://doi.org/10.1007/978-3-642-33197-8_30
9. Grolleman, J., van Dijk, B., Nijholt, A., van Emst, A.: Break the habit! Designing an e-therapy intervention using a virtual coach in aid of smoking cessation. In: IJsselsteijn, W.A., de Kort, Y.A.W., Midden, C., Eggen, B., van den Hoven, E. (eds.) PERSUASIVE 2006. LNCS, vol. 3962, pp. 133–141. Springer, Heidelberg (2006). https://doi.org/10.1007/11755494_19
10. Hospers, M., Kroezen, E., Nijholt, A., op den Akker, R., Heylen, D.: An agent-based intelligent tutoring system for nurse education. In: Nealon, J., Moreno, A. (eds.) Applications of Software Agent Technology in the Health Care Domain, pp. 143–159. Whitestein Series in Software Agent Technologies, Birkhauser Publishing Ltd., Basel, Switzerland (2003)
11. op den Akker, H.J.A., Klaassen, R., Nijholt, A.: Virtual coaches for healthy lifestyle. In: Esposito, A., Jain, L.C. (eds.) Toward Robotic Socially Believable Behaving Systems - Volume II. ISRL, vol. 106, pp. 121–149. Springer, Cham (2016). https://doi.org/10.1007/978-3-319-31053-4_8
12. Johnsen, K., et al.: Mixed reality virtual pets to reduce childhood obesity. IEEE Trans. Visual Comput. Graphics **20**(4), 523–530 (2014)
13. Loizides, F., et al.: MyCompanion: a digital social companion for assisted living. In: Lamas, D., Loizides, F., Nacke, L., Petrie, H., Winckler, M., Zaphiris, P. (eds.) INTERACT 2019. LNCS, vol. 11749, pp. 649–653. Springer, Cham (2019). https://doi.org/10.1007/978-3-030-29390-1_55
14. Heylen, D., van Dijk, B., Nijholt, A.: Robotic rabbit companions: amusing or a nuisance? J. Multimodal User Interf. **5**, 53–59 (2012)
15. Nijholt, A.: Augmented reality humans: towards multisensorial awareness. In: Jallouli, R., Bach Tobji, M.A., Mcheick, H., Piho, G. (eds.) ICDEc 2021. LNBIP, vol. 431, pp. 237–250. Springer, Cham (2021). https://doi.org/10.1007/978-3-030-92909-1_16

16. Torre, R., Fua, P., Balcisoy, S., Ponder, M., Thalmann, D.: Interaction between real and virtual humans: playing checkers. In: Mulder, J.D., van Liere, R. (eds.) 6th Eurographics Workshop on Virtual Environments, pp. 23–32 (2000)

17. Azuma, R. T.: A survey of augmented reality. Pres. Teleoper. Virtual Environ. **6**(4), 355–385 (1997). https://doi.org/10.1162/pres.1997.6.4.355

18. Wooldridge, M., Jennings, N.: Intelligent agents: theory and practice. The Knowl. Eng. Rev. **10**(2), 115–152 (1995)

19. Cassell, J., Sullivan, J., Prevost, S., Churchill, E. (eds.): Embodied Conversational Agents. The MIT Press, Cambridge (2000)

20. Norouzi, N., et al.: A systematic survey of 15 years of user studies published in the intelligent virtual agents conference. In: Proceedings of the 18th International Conference on Intelligent Virtual Agents (IVA 2018), pp. 17–22. ACM, New York, USA (2018)

21. Swartout, W., et al.: Toward virtual humans. AI Mag. **27**(2), 96–108 (2006)

22. Maes, P., Darrell, T., Blumberg, B., Pentland, A.: The ALIVE system: full-body interaction with autonomous agents. In: Proceedings Computer Animation 1995, pp. 11–18. Geneva, Switzerland (1995)

23. Blumberg, B.M.: Old Tricks, New Dogs: Ethology and Interactive Creatures. Ph.D. Thesis, Massachusetts Institute of Technology (1997)

24. Lee, J.Y., Rhee, G.W., Dong Woo Seo, D.W., Kim, N.K.: Ubiquitous home simulation using augmented reality. In: Proceedings of the 2007 annual Conference on International Conference on Computer Engineering and Applications (CEA 2007), pp. 112–116. World Scientific and Engineering Academy and Society (WSEAS), Stevens Point, Wisconsin, USA (2007)

25. Barakonyi, I., Schmalstieg, D.: Augmented reality agents for user interface adaptation. Comput. Anim. Virtual Worlds **19**(1), 23–35 (2008)

26. Hartholt, A., et al.: All together now. In: Aylett, R., Krenn, Be., Pelachaud, C., Shimodaira, Hi. (eds.) IVA 2013. LNCS (LNAI), vol. 8108, pp. 368–381. Springer, Heidelberg (2013). https://doi.org/10.1007/978-3-642-40415-3_33

27. Hartholt, A., Fast, E., Reilly, A., Whitcup, W., Liewer, M., Mozgai, S.: Ubiquitous virtual humans: a multi-platform framework for embodied AI agents in XR. In: IEEE International Conference on Artificial Intelligence and Virtual Reality (AIVR), pp. 308–3084 (2019)

28. Dobiesz, W.S., Grajper, A.: Animating the static. case study of the project "Urbanimals". In: Herneoja, A., et al. (eds.) Proceedings of the 34th International Conference on Education and Research in Computer Aided Architectural Design in Europe (eCAADe 34), vol. 1, pp. 691–697. Oulu School of Architecture, University of Oulu, Finland, Oulu (2016)

29. Grand Visual. Unbelievable Bus Shelter. https://grandvisual.com/work/pepsi-max-bus-she lter/

30. Scholz, J., Smith, A.N.: Augmented reality: Designing immersive experiences that maximize consumer engagement. Bus. Horiz. **59**(2), 149–161 (2016)

31. Nijholt, A.: Humorous and playful social interactions in augmented reality. In: Contribuciones a la Lingüística y a la Comunicación Social. Tributo a Vitelio Ruiz Hernández, pp. 167–173. Centro de Lingüística Aplicada, Santiago de Cuba, Cuba (2021)

32. Dow, S., Mehta, M., Harmon, E., MacIntyre, B., Mateas, M.: Presence and engagement in an interactive drama. In: Proceedings of the SIGCHI Conference on Human Factors in Computing Systems, pp. 1475–1484. ACM, New York, USA (2007)

33. Anabuki, M., Kakuta, H., Yamamoto, H., Tamura, H.: Welbo: an embodied conversational agent living in mixed reality space. In: CHI 2000 Extended Abstracts on Human Factors in Computing Systems (CHI EA 2000), pp. 10–11. ACM, New York, USA (2000)

34. Schmeil, A., Broll, W.: MARA - a mobile augmented reality-based virtual assistant. In: 2007 IEEE Virtual Reality Conference, pp. 267–270. Charlotte, NC, USA (2007)

35. Bancroft, J., Bin Zafar, N., Comer, S., Kuribayashi, T., Litt, J., Miller, T.: Mica: a photoreal character for spatial computing. In: ACM SIGGRAPH 2019 Talks (SIGGRAPH 2019), Article 9, pp. 1–2. New York, Association for Computing Machinery, New York, USA (2019)
36. Hartholt, A., et al.: Virtual humans in augmented reality: a first step towards real-world embedded virtual roleplayers. In: Proceedings of the 7th International Conference on Human-Agent Interaction (HAI 2019), pp. 205–207. ACM, New York, NY, USA (2019)
37. Wang, I., Smith, J., Ruiz, J.: Exploring virtual agents for augmented reality. In: Proceedings of the 2019 CHI Conference on Human Factors in Computing Systems (CHI 2019), pp. 1–12. Association for Computing Machinery, New York, NY, USA (2019)
38. Mostajeran, F., Steinicke, F., Nunez, O.J.A., Gatsios, D., Fotiadis, D. Augmented reality for older adults: exploring acceptability of virtual coaches for home-based balance training in an aging population. In: Proceedings of the 2020 CHI Conference on Human Factors in Computing Systems, pp. 1–12. Association for Computing Machinery, New York, NY, USA, (2020)
39. Norouzi, N., et al.: Walking your virtual dog: analysis of awareness and proxemics with simulated support animals in augmented reality. In: Proceedings of the IEEE International Symposium on Mixed and Augmented Reality (ISMAR), pp. 253–264 (2019)
40. Norouzi, N., Bruder, G., Bailenson, J., Welch, G.: Investigating augmented reality animals as companions. In: IEEE International Symposium on Mixed and Augmented Reality Adjunct (ISMAR-Adjunct), pp. 400–403. Beijing, China (2019)
41. Wilks, Y.: On being a victorian companion. In: Close Engagements with Artificial Companions. Key Social, Psychological, Ethical and Design Issues, pp. 121–128. John Benjamins Publishing Company, Amsterdam, The Netherlands (2010).
42. Liang, W., Yu, X., Alghofaili, R., Lang, Y., Yu, L.-F.: Scene-aware behavior synthesis for virtual pets in mixed reality. In: CHI Conference on Human Factors in Computing Systems (CHI 2021), 12 p. ACM, New York, NY, USA (2021)
43. Gruenefeld, U., Prädel, L., Heuten, W.: Locating nearby physical objects in augmented reality. In: Proceedings of the 18th International Conference on Mobile and Ubiquitous Multimedia (MUM 2019), Article 1, pp. 1–10. ACM, New York, NY, USA (2019)
44. Kim, K., Welch, G.: Maintaining and enhancing human-surrogate presence in augmented reality. In: IEEE Symposium on Mixed and Augmented Reality Workshops, pp. 15–19 (2015)
45. Kim, K., Maloney, D., Bruder, G., Bailenson, J.N., Welch, G.F.: The effects of virtual human's spatial and behavioral coherence with physical objects on social presence in AR. Comput. Anim. Virtual Worlds **28**, e1771 (2017)
46. Lee, M., Bruder, G., Höllerer, T., Welch, G.: Effects of unaugmented periphery and vibrotactile feedback on proxemics with virtual humans in AR. IEEE Trans. Visual Comput. Graphics **24**(4), 1525–1534 (2018)
47. Schraffenberger, H.K.: Arguably Augmented Reality. Relationships Between the Virtual and the Real. Ph.D. Thesis, Leiden University (2018)
48. Kim, J.C., Laine, T.H., Åhlund, C.: Multimodal interaction systems based on internet of things and augmented reality: a systematic literature review. Appl. Sci. **11**, 1738 (2021)
49. Lee M. et al.: The wobbly table: increased social presence via subtle incidental movement of a real-virtual table. In: Proceedings of the IEEE Virtual Reality, pp. 11–17 (2016)

The Context-Aware Reasoning Health Emergency (CARE) Notification System

Mario Quinde[1]([✉]), Miguel Mendoza[1], Antonio Criollo[1], and Gerardo Castillo[2]

[1] Department of Industrial and Systems Engineering, Universidad de Piura,
Piura, Peru
mario.quinde@udep.edu.pe,
{miguel.mendoza,antonio.criollo}@alum.udep.edu.pe
[2] Departamental Area of Biomedical Sciences, Universidad de Piura, Piura, Peru
gerardo.castillo@udep.edu.pe

Abstract. Context-aware reasoning (C-AR) systems already provide users with preventive and reactive services aiding them in managing their health conditions. However, there is a gap in the services C-AR systems provide regarding the notification of health emergencies once they occur. This research aims to address this gap by proposing the Context-Aware Reasoning Emergency (CARE) notification system as a comprehensive solution allowing the personalisation of health emergency notification protocols. CARE personalised services consider several stakeholders of the occurring emergency and can adapt to their personal and health contexts. The proposal is validated following the Health IT Usability Evaluation Model and with real users with experience in dealing with health emergencies as patients and care providers. The validation results are positive and encourage further work on the subject.

Keywords: Context-awareness · Mobile health · Personalisation · Notification systems · Ambient assisted living

1 Introduction

Providing immediate support in health emergencies is crucial to saving people suffering from them and avoiding disabling consequences. Context-aware systems can provide enhanced services addressing the personalisation required to support people suffering from health deterioration affecting their conditions [2,14,17,25]. However, context-aware reasoning has not been exploited enough to provide services allowing the adequate notification of health emergencies.

Considering the user-centric definition provided in Ref. [7], context is defined as *"the information which is directly relevant to characterise a situation of interest to the stakeholders of a system"*. Context-aware Reasoning (context-awareness or C-AR) is then defined as *"the ability of a system to use contextual information in order to tailor its services so that they are more useful to the stakeholders because they directly relate to their preferences and needs"*.

© The Author(s), under exclusive license to Springer Nature Switzerland AG 2022
N. A. Streitz and S. Konomi (Eds.): HCII 2022, LNCS 13326, pp. 320–335, 2022.
https://doi.org/10.1007/978-3-031-05431-0_22

Current emergency notification systems do not follow approaches to effectively reach their information recipients and provide them with the right information as they do not consider the preferences of the people involved and interested in the occurring emergencies. Native operating systems (OS) notification solutions depend on local emergency services providers whose service quality varies depending on the country they operate. For instance, automatic calls to emergency providers located in developed countries (e.g. 911 in the US or 111 in the UK) are of higher confidence than calling to emergency providers located in undeveloped or developing countries. These notification systems are also constrained to their OS, which limits their capacity to communicate among them and their integration to intelligent systems that are made for different OS.

This research work studies the use of C-AR for the development and validation of the Context-Aware Reasoning Health Emergency (CARE) notification system, which is a comprehensive solution allowing the personalisation of the notification protocol to follow in case of a health emergency. Its features can be customised considering their users' health and personal contexts, including exhaustive information and preferences about the person suffering from the emergency and the stakeholders who are interested in their health status.

CARE allows its users to choose the people to contact in case of emergency and how to contact them. It also permits setting up the device behaviour in which it is installed when an emergency occurs, as well as the information to show and share. Its integration capability is studied from the Smart Environments Architecture [3] and the Context-aware Systems Architecture (CaSA) [6] that facilitates its communication with diverse ambient-assisted living (AAL) intelligent systems. The validation of CARE followed a user-centric approach involving real users that were affected -as patients or carers- by cardiac conditions, mental deterioration (dementia, Alzheimer), allergies, diabetes, asthma and epilepsy. The validation was based on the Health IT Usability Evaluation Model (Health-ITUEM) [9].

The remaining of the paper is divided as follows. Section 2 presents the state-of-the-art on current notification systems proposals. The methodology used in the research project is described in Sect. 3. The CARE notification system and its validation are presented in Sect. 4. Finally, Sects. 5 and 6 presents the discussion and conclusions of the research work, respectively.

2   State-of-the-Art

C-AR systems are important components in the development of user-centric systems that can be categorised under the umbrella term of Intelligent Environments (IE) [5]. C-AR allows the design and implementation of services targeting users' needs and preferences. It has been used to develop preventive and reactive features aiding people with chronic conditions in their self-management process [12,14,18]. Nevertheless, this section presents that C-AR has not been exploited enough to provide reactive notification services for emergency situations that consider the personal and health context of the people suffering from them and the people interested (stakeholders) in their health status.

Plenty of systems uses artificial intelligence techniques to detect hazardous situations and notify people whose health may be affected by them. These systems achieve their objectives reasonably well and implement preventive and reactive features aiding people with health conditions avoid risky situations and react rapidly to their early detection. Nevertheless, there is a gap regarding what these systems do once the hazard becomes real and the situation evolves into an emergency, which is an important stage to deliver appropriate healthcare to saving people's lives and avoiding disabling consequences.

The literature review included research works on systems with notification components about detecting emergencies. The search considered research works published since 2018. The selection of the proposals analysed in this section was based on a minimal maturity regarding the implementation of C-AR features that consider their medical conditions characteristics and personal preferences to drive the notification delivery. Research works only delivering simple alerts were not considered.

Most of the reviewed systems focuses on developing system detecting a emergency situations. Some of them send notifications about these detections automatically [8,11,19]. Others also allow users to notify they are suffering an emergency manually (through a mechanism similar to a panic button) [10,13,17,20,23]. The notification recipients are fixed to a specific role (e.g. medical centre carers [10], limited to a number of previously chosen persons (e.g. general practitioner or relatives [13,20,23] or chosen through artificial intelligence techniques [11]. Only one of the reviewed research work makes the detecting device to emit a sound to catch the attention from people nearby.

Regarding the information share with the emergency contacts, none of them consider the inclusion of data (similar to a Medical ID) that could help their professional and non-professional carers to provide informed care during the emergency. Some of the reviewed research works share the patient's location [10,13,17,20], but most of them provide very few information about the information included in the notification that is sent, which is usually pre-defined data (e.g. [13,20,23]. Only one proposal provides real-time information about the emergency [8]. The way the notification is delivered is mostly through mobile device notifications (e.g. [10,20]), SMS (e.g. [13,23]) and automatic calls [11,19]. One research work allow emergency carer providers send information to the hospital regarding the patient that is on the way to the medical centre [22].

Studies on users' perception towards emergency notification apps [21], factors influencing the use of emergency notification systems for a specific purpose [24], and the characteristics of emergency notification systems for a specific condition [18] were also found. Ideas from these research works were considered in the development of the proposal, considering those that enhance its C-AR features. To the best of our knowledge, ADAPT [17] is the proposal that have focused more on providing an emergency notification system that can be personalised to the medical and personal context of the patient and their stakeholders. However, the system has been developed for people affected by asthma and as a part of a bigger system that is also tailored for them, which makes their emergency notification component limited to their more narrowed context. Despite this, ADAPT still lack of a higher personalisation level regarding the information to share with the emergency stakeholders, the device behaviour when an emergency is confirmed and the Medical ID to show.

This section presents that current emergency notification proposals do not comprehensively allow to personalise their features according their users' needs and preferences. Research work has focused on developing features to detect hazardous and emergency situations (e.g. fall detection), which has been achieved at an acceptable detection confidence. However, the reviewed research works do not focus their attention to what happens when the emergency occurs, even though the detection systems effectively detects it or if it does not. Regarding the use of emergency mobile medical ID, Ref. [24] highlights that smartphone emergency medical identification applications are considerably underused, despite of their perceived benefits. Furthermore, integration with other emergency systems is another important gap that emergency notification systems should address to provide their expected benefits [21]. The reviewed emergency notification proposals are thought for the main system detecting the emergency.

Finally, is remarkable that users' preferences are not properly included in the emergency notification systems proposed by the reviewed research works. Research work on studying the inclusion of user preferences in the development of IE to provide more user-centric services has been done [7], as well as for managing and solving conflicting situations regarding their preferences [1,15, 16]. This shows a lack of attention in including and adapting users' preference management techniques to improve the emergency notification systems features and enhance their acceptance among their users.

3   Methodology

Following the User-Centric Intelligent Environment Development Process (U-CIEDP) [4], this research project involved stakeholders in the development and validation of CARE. The term stakeholders in this project refers to the people going through an emergency and those that are interested in the health status of the person suffering the emergency. The inclusion of the latter ones in the information supply chain is relevant to provide assistance in emergency situations; however, they are very dynamic depending on the person's context prone to suffering emergencies.

The methodology process is summarised in Fig. 1. The main activities done are categorised following the four-stages cycle of the U-CIEDP (Stakeholders engagement, Scoping, Main development and Prototyping). The Literature review exposed the gaps in the reviewed research works on current emergency notification systems. As part of a previous project [17], these gaps were supported by a set of interviews and questionnaires (Stakeholders engagement). These activities led to the requirements elicitation that supported the development of the personalisation module, which was the first version of CARE. This version was focused on implementing a personalised notification protocol for people affected by asthma (PaA), and it was developed as a component of the system build based on the Approach to Develop context-Aware solutions for Personalised asthma managemenT (ADAPT) [17], which was validated by PaA.

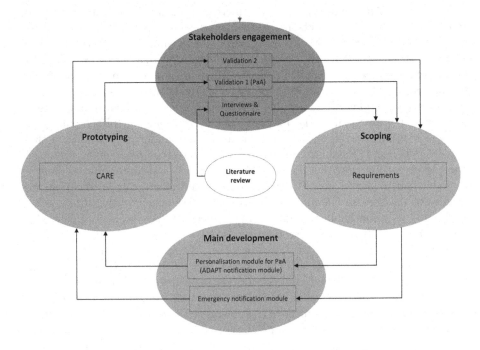

Fig. 1. Methodology

This research work reports on the second iteration of the development process. The proposal is based on the feedback received in the validation of the first version that was developed for PaA and on the updated literature review presented in Sect. 1. CARE has evolved for being used by people prone to suffer health emergency situations (not only for PaA) by implementing a more comprehensive emergency notification module that was validate with real users (patients and carers) affected by cardiac conditions (4 participants), mental deterioration (dementia, Alzheimer) (3), allergies (3), diabetes (2), asthma (4) and epilepsy (1). All the participants had experience in dealing with emergencies as patients or carers. The validation was done through individual sessions that included a demonstration of the fully functional prototype of CARE and the answer to a questionnaire with qualitative and quantitative items assessing the system. The questionnaire was based on the Health-ITUEM [9]. More information of the validation is presented in Sect. 4.2.

4   The CARE Notification System

CARE is a user-centred emergency notification system delivering services that are based on the stakeholders' personal and medical contexts of a health emergency occurrence. It was developed using Android Studio and Firebase. The following are the main features of CARE:

Feature 1 (F1) allows to configure the emergency state behaviour of the mobile devices in which CARE is installed. The user can choose whether to make the mobile device sounds like an alarm, vibrate and activate its flashlight to gather people's attention surrounding the person suffering the emergency. This behaviour must be previously personalised, and CARE gives users the option of not catching people's attention in the surrounding of the emergency. This feature was previously brought up in *Validatoin 1* (Fig. 1) by some stakeholders. Despite CARE sending notifications to the stakeholders (this feature is explained below), plenty of them, depending on the suffered condition and its severity, would like to reach for immediate help by people physically close to them because waiting for stakeholders or emergency services to arrive would be fatal.

Feature 2 (F2) refers to the personalisation of the notification protocol to trigger when an emergency occurs. This emergency notification protocol includes customising the people to contact (stakeholders), the way to contact them, and the notification they will receive when the emergency state is activated. CARE can send emails, SMS and mobile phone notifications (automatic calls are to be included in the future). These contacting options are meant to aboard two issues. The first one refers to increasing the probability of the stakeholders receiving the emergency notification. In this case, the use of several options provides contacting alternatives if some of them do not work, considering that places in which the internet connection and mobile signal are not good enough exist. This is common in countries with poor installed IT infrastructure. The second one refers to the preparedness of people with low digital literacy. In this scenario, using more user-centred ways of contacting considering their preferences increases the acceptance and effectiveness of the system. For instance, people not comfortable nor prepared to use emails and mobile phone notifications would choose more traditional contacting ways like SMS and automatic calls.

The information to send in the emergency notification to the previously chosen stakeholders can also be customised by the person prone to have an emergency. They can choose to include their current location, and the personal and medical information they would like to share with their stakeholders. The current location of the person suffering an emergency can be shared in real-time, so that their stakeholders can reach them even though the patient is on the move (e.g., on the way to a medical centre). As it is shown below, the user is always in control of the information to share and who to share it with.

Feature 3 (F3) is the configuration of the Medical ID, which can be configured, shown and shared by the person having an emergency. They can enter their medical information and choose which items of this medical information will be part of the Medical ID to show when the emergency state of the system is activated. When this happens, the Medical ID is shown on the mobile phone screen so that people aiding the person suffering an emergency can make informed decisions regarding how to help them. The Medical ID is helpful when people without access to the person's EHR aid them, considering that a person in an emergency can be unconscious or cannot communicate properly. It is also helpful for situations where there is no EHR of the person suffering from the emergency because they do not have it or their local health system does not have EHR systems effectively implemented.

4.1   CARE User Interface

CARE allows users to have the roles of patient and stakeholder. Figure 2 is the system's main screen when it is used as a patient. It shows the previously configured patient's Medical ID and the stakeholders to contact in case of emergency. The Emergency button, which is also shown on the smartphone blocked screen as a widget, activates the customised emergency state of the device and triggers the also personalised notification protocol. Figure 3 shows the screen in which users set up the behaviour of the devices when the emergency state is activated. Depending on their preferences, the devices can vibrate, sound (like a siren) and make their flashlight blink to catch the attention of their surrounding people.

Fig. 2. Main screen   **Fig. 3.** Emergency setting   **Fig. 4.** User information

Figure 4 is the screen where the patient enters their personal an medical information. The *Medical ID Information* tab allows patients to choose which personal and medical information they want to include in their Medical ID, which can be shown and sent to their stakeholders when the emergency state is activated (Fig. 5). The *Shared Information* tab (Fig. 6) permits users to define the information the stakeholders can access at any time. The first item (Location) defines whether the stakeholders will receive the patients real-time location only in case of emergency. Stakeholders to contact in case of emergency can be managed by entering and editing their names, phone number and email, and setting up how to contact each of them in case of emergency (Fig. 7). Users can confirm their stakeholders' contacting ways by entering a stakeholders identification code and checking (Check button) if the chosen contacting way to reach them works properly (verified). For this, their emergency contacts must confirm to have received a test notification. Thus, the information supply chain stakeholders will ensure the contact information entered works correctly.

Fig. 5. Medical ID setting

Fig. 6. Info to share

Fig. 7. Stakeholder setting

The screen shown in Fig. 8 appears when the emergency status is activated. The system shows the stakeholders to whom the emergency notification was sent and the contacting ways that were used to send it. It also confirms whether each notification was sent correctly or not. The medical ID is also shown on this screen in case the user chooses so. Figure 9 is the email the stakeholders receive when the emergency state is activated. It includes the patient's Medical ID and provides the option of tracking the their location, which sends the user to a map where the patient's location is shown in real-time. This notification provides the same information despite the contacting way chosen for each stakeholder. Figure 10 is the view the emergency contacts have. They have a notifications code that the patients should enter to add them as emergency contacts. Their view includes a list of the patients that have chosen them as emergency contact and provides the personal and medical information each patient chose to share with them. The *Patient* and *Stakeholder* tabs allow a user to have the roles of patient and stakeholder at the same time.

4.2   Usability Evaluation

The validation of the proposal included a demonstration of the fully functional prototype was presented to the participants (real users), who attended individual

Fig. 8. Confirmation   **Fig. 9.** Notification   **Fig. 10.** Stakeholder screen

sessions in which CARE was presented and they were able to use it. They were
then asked to answer a questionnaire that includes items quantitatively (5-Point
Likert scale) assessing the three CARE features usefulness (very useless - useless
- neutral - useful - very useful) separately. The participants were also asked to
order the three CARE features from the most useful to the least useful and to
describe what they value more of each feature, what they would improve for
each feature, and what other features they would add to CARE.

The questionnaire also have items quantitatively (5-Point Likert scale) assessing seven Health-ITUEM concepts [9]: error prevention, information needs, memorability, flexibility, learnability, performance speed and competency. Table 1
presents the scenario mapping the Health-ITUEM concepts to the questionnaire
used in the validation. Other items of the questionnaire asked the participants
to assess (using the same scale) the screen design and ease-of-use of the system.

Table 1. Scenario mapping the Health-ITUEM concepts for the evaluation

Concept	Description
Error prevention	CARE allows to prevent/undo errors or shows error messages when they occur
Information needs	CARE provides enough information to use its features Properly
Memorability	CARE allows to remember how to use its features
Flexibility	CARE allows to use its features in different ways
Learnability	It is easy to learn how to use the features of CARE
Performance speed	It is possible to use CARE efficiently
Competency	Users feel confident when they use the features of CARE

The answers to the quantitative questions regarding CARE features usefulness is summarised in Figs. 11 and 12. The first one shows that all the features were assess as useful or very useful. The second one shows that F2 was the best assessed in the comparison followed by F1. There is no much difference between F1 and F2 in the comparison; however, there is a more noticeable consensus in placing F3 as the least useful.

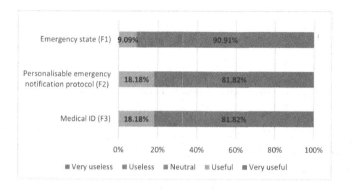

Fig. 11. CARE features absolute perceived usefulness

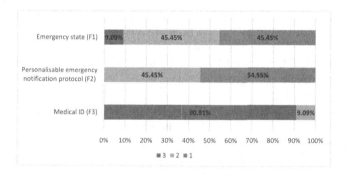

Fig. 12. CARE features compared usefulness

The answers to the questions assessing CARE based on seven Health-ITUEM concepts, its screen design and ease-of-use are summarised in Fig. 13, where the average of the participants' responses is presented using a scale from 0 (lowest) to 4 (highest). Competency is the concept with highest average assessment (4), followed by Ease-of-use, Error prevention, Flexibility, Learnability, Memorability and Performance speed (3–4). Screen design and Completeness are noticeable the concepts with the lowest assessment (≤ 3).

The answers to the open questions highlight some previously discovered needs the system addresses. F1 is considered useful to provide immediate support to

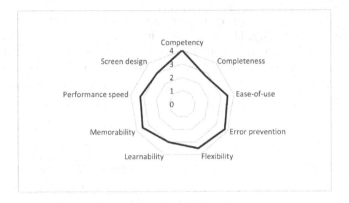

Fig. 13. CARE usability concepts evaluation

people suffering emergencies that are physically limited to catch their surrounding people attention. F2 provides carers more peace of mind in their daily activities considering they know they will be immediately alerted in case the person they take care of is in an emergency situation. One participant stated they would like to include their family general practitioner as an emergency notification recipient. However, one participant was concerned on the fact that the person they take care of do not like to ask for help and that they may do not like sending emergency notifications. Another carer affirmed they would have used it to take care of a family member who had COVID-19 because the carer could not enter to they room to check the patient during the night due to the risk of being infected. F3 was perceived as useful for care givers to make informed decisions and provide the right help.

Regarding the suggested improvements to F1, two participants suggested to replicate the emergency state behaviour on the emergency contact device. One participant would like to increase the sound of the alarm and change the alarm sound to one catching surrounding people's attention faster. The suggested improvement to F2 are: (a) using a notification sound on the emergency contact device that is noticeably different than others, (b) making the configuration easier by using, for example, QR codes, (c) sharing information about ambulances, medical insurance and preferred medical centres, (d) providing an easier way to confirm the stakeholders contacting ways for the elderly users, (e) being able to add the relationship of the stakeholder included to the information supply chain, and (f) notifying professional carers that are in the patients' surrounding.

F3 suggested improvements are summarised in (a) making the patients' names, illnesses and blood type compulsory fields to enter, (b) having a centralised repository of all users, (c) showing the Medical ID on the device blocked screen, (d) including the medicine that should be provided to the patient, the preferred medical centre, (e) improving the screen design for CARE to be more user-friendly with the elderly, and (f) being able to access a centralised medical record of the user through a QR code. One participant compared the Medical ID to the army necklace used by soldiers. Other general suggested improvements were related to making CARE easy to integrate with other ambient-assisted living systems, improving the screen design (labels font and size), including a guide (video tutorial) to set up the system, providing more ways to activate the emergency state, and showing a map with near emergency centres.

5   Discussion

This research work proposes a comprehensive user-centred emergency notification system that can be personalised to the medical and personal context of the stakeholders of an emergency situation. CARE addresses existing gaps in the development of emergency notification systems that are usually in the form of simple notification providers of previously detected emergencies. The efforts on ensuring the proper delivery of these notifications are poor, considering that care delivery in emergencies is crucial.

The human-centred approach of the system allows users (who are the patients prone to suffer from emergencies and their stakeholders) to personalise the emergency notification protocol to trigger, the emergency state of the device, and their Medical ID. This approach led to considering the specific preferences and needs of the people involved in the emergencies in the form of personalising features that can be adapted to their context. Thus, CARE considers users' specific situations due to the human-centric methodology that was followed. This approach allows using different alternatives to deliver emergency notifications (Internet, automatic calls, SMS). The stakeholders' digital literacy level, which defines their needs and preferences, is also considered through the emergency notification protocol personalisation. Moreover, the users' privacy is always at the core of CARE, which allows them to decide the features to use, the information to store and share, and the behaviour of their mobile device in case of a confirmed emergency.

The comprehensiveness of CARE and its capability to adapt to its users' needs and preferences is the main contribution of this research work. Despite that some of its features had already been proposed separately in other research works, CARE was built on the premise of combining the best of these features, enhancing them and creating a system focused on supporting stakeholders on what happens after an emergency occurs. Nevertheless, the positive results of its validation also show future work on the subject. The most noticeable one is that CARE personalising characteristics could be perceived as complicated by people with low digital literacy, so making the personalisation easier and providing guidelines to configure CARE features are essential. The suggestions for improvements presented in the usability evaluation should be considered for the development process next iteration.

The integration of CARE with AAL systems is also a short-term goal to achieve, considering that plenty of people already rely on this type of systems. However, the CARE option for being activated manually is also positively perceived for those who do not acquire AAL systems. This fact is also supported by the fact that AAL systems are not 100% accurate, so users might need to activate their emergency notification protocol and confirm that a false positive is triggered manually. Hence, the integration of CARE with the performance of other AAL systems must be thought carefully to make it independent enough.

This research work uses the Smart Environments Architecture (SEArch) [3] and the Context-aware Systems Architecture [6] as the frameworks to provide insights about the integration of CARE with other AAL systems. Figure 14 highlights the main SEArch elements that are associated with the performance of CARE, which is strongly related to the HCI component that communicates with the user (activating/confirming emergency and delivering notifications). The Preferences component (part of the users' profiles) manage the personalisation of CARE and are used to drive the Context-awareness and Reasoning elements to deploy the emergency notification protocol and the other CARE features.

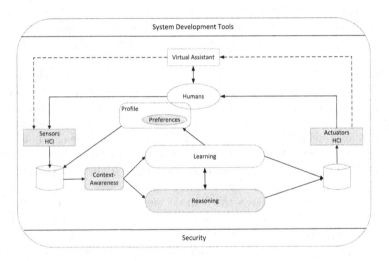

Fig. 14. CARE in the smart environments architecture

Figure 15 presents the integration of CARE with other AAL systems focusing on their independent performance. AAL systems are in constant communication with the users, and their intra and inter context-reasoning should be independent of CARE performance. The integration with CARE starts when an emergency is detected, which can be considered a high-level context provided by the AAL system to CARE. From here, this emergency detection can automatically activate the CARE emergency state or ask the user for confirmation on the potential detected emergency. When the emergency state is activated, the notification protocol is deployed considering the previously-stored preferences aiming to satisfy the emergency stakeholders needs. The third option to activate the emergency state is independent of any AAL system.

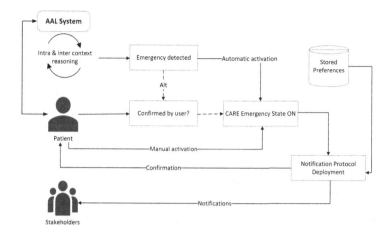

Fig. 15. CARE in the context-aware systems architecture

6   Conclusions

Research efforts on developing systems to detect hazardous situations for people with health conditions have yielded positive results. This research work presents the CARE notification system, developed for people prone to both suffer and provide assistance in health emergencies regardless of their health condition. CARE is a comprehensive and user-centred system placing users' contexts at the centre of its performance. It allows users to personalise their notification protocol to reach their emergency contacts, their device behaviour to catch the attention of people nearby, and the information to share with their stakeholders during the emergency. CARE addresses gaps in current C-AR systems providing support to people already going through an emergency, despite being warned or predicted by other systems preventive features. The system validation was done with real users with experience in emergencies, as patients or carers, due to health conditions. The validation shows positive results and encourage further work in the subject, which is also presented in the paper. The integration of CARE with other AAL systems is also analysed using two frameworks to develop C-AR systems as part of the future work in the subject.

References

1. Oguego, C.L., Augusto, J.C., Muñoz, A., Springett, M.: Using argumentation to manage users' preferences. Fut. Gener. Comput. Syst.**81**, 235–243 (2018). https://doi.org/10.1016/j.future.2017.09.040
2. Aborokbah, M.M., Al-Mutairi, S., Sangaiah, A.K., Samuel, O.W.: Adaptive context aware decision computing paradigm for intensive health care delivery in smart cities-a case analysis. Sustain. Cities Soc. **41**, 919–924 (2018). https://doi.org/10.1016/j.scs.2017.09.004

3. Augusto, J., Giménez-Manuel, J., Quinde, M., Oguego, C., Ali, M., James-Reynolds, C.: A smart environments architecture (search). Appl. Artif. Intell. **34**(2), 155–186 (2020). https://doi.org/10.1080/08839514.2020.1712778

4. Augusto, J., Kramer, D., Alegre, U., Covaci, A., Santokhee, A.: The user-centred intelligent environments development process as a guide to co-create smart technology for people with special needs. Univ. Access Inf. Soc. **17**(1), 115–130 (2017). https://doi.org/10.1007/s10209-016-0514-8

5. Augusto, J.C., Callaghan, V., Cook, D., Kameas, A., Satoh, I.: Intelligent environments: a manifesto. Human-centric Comput. Inf. Sci. **3**(1), 1–18 (2013). https://doi.org/10.1186/2192-1962-3-12

6. Augusto, J.C., Quinde, M.J., Oguego, C.L., Manuel, J.G.: Context-aware systems architecture (CaSA). Cybern. Syst. 1–27 (2021). https://doi.org/10.1080/01969722.2021.1985226

7. Augusto, J.C., Muñoz, A.: User preferences in intelligent environments. Appl. Artif. Intell. **33**(12), 1069–1091 (2019). https://doi.org/10.1080/08839514.2019.1661596

8. Bathelt-Tok, F., Gruhn, H., Glesner, S., Blankenstein, O.: Towards the development of smart and reliable health assistance networks exemplified by an apnea detection system. In: 2014 IEEE International Conference on Healthcare Informatics, pp. 226–231 (2014). https://doi.org/10.1109/ICHI.2014.39

9. Brown, W., Yen, P.Y., Rojas, M., Schnall, R.: Assessment of the health IT usability evaluation model (Health-ITUEM) for evaluating mobile health (mHealth) technology. J. Biomed. Inform. **46**(6), 1080–1087 (2013). https://doi.org/10.1016/j.jbi.2013.08.001

10. Chiou, S.Y., Liao, Z.Y.: A real-time, automated and privacy-preserving mobile emergency-medical-service network for informing the closest rescuer to rapidly support mobile-emergency-call victims. IEEE Access **6**, 35787–35800 (2018). https://doi.org/10.1109/ACCESS.2018.2847030

11. Kalinga, T., Sirithunge, C., Buddhika, A., Jayasekara, P., Perera, I.: A fall detection and emergency notification system for elderly. In: 2020 6th International Conference on Control, Automation and Robotics (ICCAR), pp. 706–712 (2020). https://doi.org/10.1109/ICCAR49639.2020.9108003

12. Manuel, J.G., Augusto, J.C., Stewart, J.: Anabel: towards empowering people living with dementia in ambient assisted living. Universal Access in the Information Society (2020). https://doi.org/10.1007/s10209-020-00760-5

13. Muangprathub, J., Sriwichian, A., Wanichsombat, A., Kajornkasirat, S., Nillaor, P., Boonjing, V.: A novel elderly tracking system using machine learning to classify signals from mobile and wearable sensors. Int. J. Environ. Res. Public Health **18**(23), 125652 (2021). https://doi.org/10.3390/ijerph182312652

14. Ogbuabor, G.O., Augusto, J.C., Moseley, R., van Wyk, A.: Context-aware system for cardiac condition monitoring and management: a survey. Behav. Inf. Technol. **2020**, 1–18 (2020). https://doi.org/10.1080/0144929X.2020.1836255

15. Oguego, C.L., Augusto, J., Springett, M., Quinde, M., James-Reynolds, C.: Using argumentation to solve conflicting situations in users' preferences in ambient assisted living. Appl. Artif. Intell. (2021). https://doi.org/10.1080/08839514.2021.1966986

16. Ospan, B., Khan, N., Augusto, J., Quinde, M., Nurgaliyev, K.: Context aware virtual assistant with case-based conflict resolution in multi-user smart home environment. In: 2018 International Conference on Computing and Network Communications (CoCoNet), pp. 36–44 (2018). https://doi.org/10.1109/CoCoNet.2018.8476898

17. Quinde, M., Augusto, J.C., Khan, N., van Wyk, A.: Adapt: approach to develop context-aware solutions for personalised asthma management. J. Biomed. Inform. **111**, 103586 (2020). https://doi.org/10.1016/j.jbi.2020.103586
18. Quinde, M., Khan, N., Augusto, J.C., van Wyk, A., Stewart, J.: Context-aware solutions for asthma condition management: a survey. Univ. Access Inf. Soc. **19**(3), 571–593, 103586 (2018). https://doi.org/10.1007/s10209-018-0641-5
19. Rahman, M.A., Ahsanuzzaman, S., Hasan, A., Rahman, I., Ahmed, T., Kadir, M.M.: Building a wheelchair controlling and fall detection system using mobile application. In: 2020 2nd International Conference on Advanced Information and Communication Technology (ICAICT), pp. 213–218 (2020). https://doi.org/10.1109/ICAICT51780.2020.9333478
20. Rai, U., Miglani, K., Saha, A., Sahoo, B., Vergin Raja Sarobin, M.: Reachout smart safety device. In: 2018 6th Edition of International Conference on Wireless Networks Embedded Systems (WECON), pp. 131–134 (2018). https://doi.org/10.1109/WECON.2018.8782071
21. Repanovici, R., Nedelcu, A.: Mobile emergency notification apps: current state, barriers and future potential. IOP Conf. Ser. Mater. Sci. Eng. **1009**(1), 012049 (2021). https://doi.org/10.1088/1757-899x/1009/1/012049
22. Sarlan, A., Xiong, F.K., Ahmad, R., Ahmad, W.F.W., Bhattacharyya, E.: Pre-hospital emergency notification system. In: 2015 International Symposium on Mathematical Sciences and Computing Research (iSMSC), pp. 168–173 (2015). https://doi.org/10.1109/ISMSC.2015.7594047
23. Tasneem Usha, R., Sazid Sejuti, F., Islam, S.: Smart monitoring service through self sufficient healthcare gadget for elderly. In: 2019 IEEE International Symposium on Smart Electronic Systems (iSES) (Formerly iNiS), pp. 276–279 (2019). https://doi.org/10.1109/iSES47678.2019.00068
24. Vella, M.A., Li, H., Reilly, P.M., Raza, S.S.: Unlocked yet untapped: the ubiquitous smartphone and utilization of emergency medical identification technology in the care of the injured patient. Surg. Open Sci. **2**(3), 122–126, 012049 (2020). https://doi.org/10.1016/j.sopen.2020.03.001
25. Yin, K., et al.: Context-aware systems for chronic disease patients: scoping review. J. Med. Internet Res. **21**(6), e10896 (2019). https://doi.org/10.2196/10896

Enhancing Self-protection: What Influences Human's Epidemic Prevention Behavior during the COVID-19 Pandemic

Liqiang Xu[✉], Yuuki Nishiyama, and Kaoru Sezaki

The University of Tokyo, Meguro City, Japan
xuliqiang@mcl.iis.u-tokyo.ac.jp, {yuukin,sezaki}@iis.u-tokyo.ac.jp

Abstract. Under the circumstance of the rapid spread of the COVID-19 pandemic, enhancing human's awareness of self-protection is one practical method to slow down the epidemic. In this study, we utilize mobile sensing to track human activity and guide human's epidemic prevention behavior by gamified feedback techniques by our developed application. Virtually, human's self-protection awareness is affected by many factors and the measures to enhance people's self-protection behavior against the epidemic COVID-19 has always been an unresolved issue. In order to search for factors that influence human's self-protection behavior, we analyzed the relationships between various human activities and the percentage complete of human's self-protection behavior and we have extracted some more general conclusions from the results. Based on our data analysis results, we also made some proposals to enhance self-protection behavior. Meanwhile, our study illustrates the effectiveness of the method that analyzes human self-protection behavior through mobile sensing. Our study also validates the effectiveness of persuasive technology on human's self-protection behavior against the COVID-19 pandemic and therefore we advocate enhancing human's self-protection awareness through external intervention and guidance by smart device.

Keywords: Self-protection behavior · Self-tracking · Mobile sensing · Infection prevention · COVID-19 · Persuasive technology.

1 Introduction

Unidentified perilous contagious diseases occur periodically and significantly impacted global public health in recent years. For example, nearly 400 million people have been infected and 5.7 million have died due to COVID-19 up to now globally [1]. Monitoring the spread of infection disease, tracking contacted people, self-isolation, and lock-down are widely used to prevent these diseases. By using these methods, some governments have achieved a certain effect in the past. Meanwhile, self-protection, like wearing a mask, washing hands, and maintaining social distance, seems one more practical solution [2] to protect people from these contagious diseases. Although some governments and public health agencies urge people to maintain self-protection, it is practically impossible to require anyone to realize long-term effective self-protection. To enhance self-protection behavior and slow down the spread of the epidemic COVID-19, external intervention may be necessary.

The number of smartphone users has reached 6.64 billion [3]. These smartphones have rich sensors that allow us to record users' daily activity [4] and provide practical information through a screen to encourage and guide users' behavior. Against the COVID-19 pandemic, the smartphone is widely used for preventing infections, such as contact-tracing [5] and daily activity tracking application [6].

However, most of them do not investigate its effects of encouraging self-protection and factors are influence self-protection behaviors. Moreover, persuasive technology and nudge are known to encourage human behaviors using external intervention; nevertheless, it has not been investigated that its effectiveness for promoting self-protection behaviors against COVID-19.

In this paper, we tackle analyzing the factors for encouraging self-protection behaviors based on the collected behavior data and the difference in incentive models. As self-protection behaviors, we track five self-protection behaviors using a self-tracking application that was previously developed, called SelfGuard [6]: a daily self-condition report, meditation for caring mental state, recording visited places with their status, periodical handwashings, and moderate exercise. These self-protection activities can be collected by human manual input such as self-report and a combination of smartphone sensors. A user study was held for two weeks with 20 participants. Using smartphone sensors, we collected self-protection and daily behavior data under three incentive models. The models were designed to provide points, as incentives, by fixed, addition, and subtraction policy. In addition, the daily behavior data contained raw sensor data such as location, daily steps, connected WiFi (see Sect. 3). Our analytics shows that mood, environment, frequency of smartphone use and daily schedule influence self-protection behaviors.

The contributions of this paper can be summarized as follows:

– To create a dataset of manually, semi-automatically, and automatically collected human behavior data to prevent contagious diseases.
– To analysis factors for encouraging human behaviors for preventing contagious diseases based on the collected data.
– To examine effects of different incentive models for encouraging prevent behaviors of contagious diseases.

The remainder of the paper is organized as follows. Section 2 referred related researches about self-tracking applications and persuasive technologies. Section 3 describes our reseach questions, collected dataset and definitions in this paper. Section 4 describes the methodology, content and results of our data analysis. Section 5 discusses our results of analysis and makes some proposals. Section 6 mentions our research limitations and future research directions. Section 7 concludes this paper.

2   Related Works

Against the COVID-19 pandemic, various types of applications for preventing the infection have been proposed. This section summarize these existing applications at Sect. 2.1. Section 2.2 shows existing methods for encouraging human behavior change using digital technologies.

2.1   Smartphone Application Against the COVID-19 Pandemic

Various applications have been proposed for the spread of infectious diseases [7]. The applications and systems includes digital contact-tracing [8–11], symptom monitoring [12, 13], and behavior recording [6].

Automatic recording, such as contact confirmation and behavioral recording using Bluetooth, GPS, and QR codes, is advantageous for long-term use because the load on the user is minimal. However, the application is not designed so that users check the application frequently, so it is unclear whether simply installing the application will promote daily preventive actions against infectious diseases (such as hand washing). On the other hand, manual operation is essential for recording physical conditions, etc. Manual recording places a high burden on the user, making it difficult to continue using the app.

Semi-automated tracking method combines automatic and manual methods, which could reduce the burden on people than manual methods and could collect various data which is difficult for automatic methods. Some strategies are designed of semi-automated tracking and recent work in real-world environments via smartphones show the effectiveness of the semi-automated method [14].

2.2   Persuasive Technology

Persuasive technology, which change attitudes or behaviors of users through persuasion and social influence, but not necessarily through coercion [15], is proved to be efficient to guide users' behavior in recent researches [16, 17]. Some previous studies used persuasive technology to find better ways to guide users by mobile devices [18], especially recently benefiting from the popularity of smartphones, the implement of Persuasive technology becomes more convenient and effective. The following four mechanisms [19] designs are listed as important items when developing applications for persuasive purposes. Rewards as incentives for users is particularly important in those mechanisms.

- **Rewards**: Rewards provide incentives to promote people's actions. There may be many actual forms of reward from spiritual inspiration to substantive items. Depending on the methods that rewards are offered, people will behave differently.
- **Goal-setting**: Users need specified explicit goals, and the goals should be plural and optional. Every goal should be confirmed at any time and the users will change their behavior in order to achieve the goals.

- **Self-monitoring**: Systems using Persuasive techniques should be able to detect the status of users completing goals and send reminders or other methods to promote user behavior.
- **Sharing**: Affected by social cognition, people always desire that their behavior is in line with the public and recognized by the society. Therefore, systems using Persuasive technology should be able to reach out to society, such as providing social networking services.

3 Research Questions

In this paper, our research questions mainly include 2 parts, analyzing factors influence human's epidemic prevention behavior during the COVID-19 pandemic(RQ1) and analyzing the consequence of our incentive mechanism(RQ2). With regard to RQ1, we collected a dataset by our previously developed self-tracking application SelfGuard [6], which includes various kinds of sensor data and manual reports so that we could compare the relationship between human activities and self-protection behavior. We designed the controlled experiments, which provide different kinds reward methods. By comparing the changes before and after adding incentive mechanism, we could solve RQ2. We define three concepts used in this paper to better understand our research questions.

3.1 Self-protection Behavior

As epidemic prevention behavior, we chose five behaviors, defined by Japan government [20] for preventing contagious diseases and living healthy in the COVID-19 pandemic. In our self-tracking application, each target behavior is used as a daily mission as shown in Table 1. The screenshots of our application are illustrated in Fig. 1. On the application, the list of missions and their achievements are shown on the top page (Fig. 1(a)). In addition, recorded users' activities are shown in timeline format as shown in Fig. 1(b).

The target behaviors are the following: (M1) daily physical and mental condition check, (M2) meditation, (M3) recording visited places and their features, (M4) moderate exercise, and (M5) periodical hand washing. Our application automatically collects M4 and M5 by a smartphone and a smartwatch. While M1 and M2 need human manual operations to report self-condition (through Fig. 1(c)) , and hold a meditation session themselves. M3 is designed for collecting visited places and its features semi-automatically. The application detects the visited places based on GPS on a smartphone automatically as shown in Fig. 1(b), and suggests the user fill the place name and features via feature input page (Fig. 1(d)). The location features include three Cs (closed, crowded, close-contact place) by five-level Likert scales, mask usage, and disinfecting hands information.

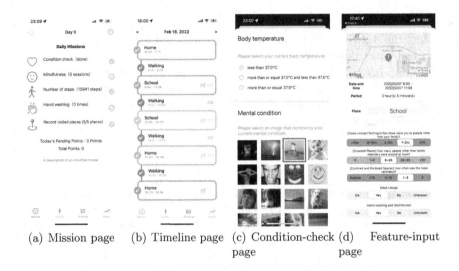

(a) Mission page   (b) Timeline page   (c) Condition-check   (d)   Feature-input
                                                 page   page

Fig. 1. Screenshots on SelfGuard

3.2 Daily Activities

As daily activity data, SelfGuard collects sensor data of smartphones 24/7 using
AWARE Framework [4] which is a build-in sensing library. Table 2 shows the
types and content of collected sensor data.

The sampling frequency of accelerometer is 5 Hz. The sensing interval for
other sensors, including location, battery, WiFi, activity recognition, pedometer,
information is 1 min. Other event-driven sensors such as screen-events, data from
HealthKit, and visited places, will be recorded when the corresponding event
occurs.

By prepossessing the collected sensor data, we could estimate human activity.
For example, mobile phone usage time could be calculated by Screen date; average heart rate could be calculated by HealthKit heart rate; displacement distance
per day could be calculated by Locations data; Battery consumption rate could
be calculated by Battery data; WiFi data could be used to help judge whether
participant is at home; the number of strenuous exercises could be inferred from
Accelerator; activity distribution could be calculated by pedometer sensor.

3.3 Control-Experiment

By email and social media, we openly recruited 21 adult participants in Tokyo
metropolitan area to conduct our experiments. Among the 67 participants
applied for our experiment, we selected 21 through comprehensive consideration of equipment and other factors. Due to one participant's data missing, we
finally collected 20 participants' data (8 female and 12 male, average age is 23.4),
including 13 undergraduate students and 7 graduate students. Each participant
used his/her own iPhone which is iOS 13 or above OS, and his/her own or rented

Table 1. Detail of each mission.

	Mission name	Record mode	Details
M1	Condition check	Manual	Temperature, mental and physical condition
M2	Mindfulness	Manual	Meditation with wearable device
M3	Stay record	Semi-automatic	Features of places
M4	Steps	Automatic	Steps taken per day
M5	Hand washing	Automatic	Times of washing hands

Table 2. Collected sensor data.

Sensor name	Frequency	Detail of the collected data
Screen	Event	Record the status of smartphone, on or off
HealthKit	Event	Record heart rate (HR) values and hand-washing events
Locations	1 min	Latitude,longitude,altitude
Battery	1 min	Battery level,health
WiFi	1 min	SSID and BSSID of every WiFi
Visited Places	Event	Characteristics of visited places like risk, density of population
Accelerator	5 Hz	Record acceleration in three directions
Activity Recognition	1 min	Inferred motion state,like Inferred motion state
Pedometer	1 min	Record steps and walk up and down stairs

Apple Watches which has watchOS 7 or later through this study. 10 participants used our rented Apple Watches. The participants install our application called SelfGuard on their smartphones which collects human-input and multiple sensor data on a smartphone data continuously.

We track every participant's activity in two weeks and provide them point as incentive, which could be exchanged as cash. In order to analyze the effects of different reward mechanisms on human behavior, we designed the controlled trials that adopt fixed points reward model for all participants in the first week and adopt three kinds of points reward models in the second week by randomly dividing participants into three groups. Table 3 shows difference between three reward models. In the first week, all participants will receive the same 100 points. But in the second week, participants' percentage complete of self-protection missions will affect their points acquisition. For participants assigned to addition model, the points they could obtain will be proportional to the number of mission completed. For participants assigned to subtraction model, given an initial value, the points will decrease proportionally for each less mission completed. Briefly, completing more self-protection missions every day will earn more points for the two incentive models.

Questionnaire is proved to be a efficient method to measure the effect of persuasive technology in previous studies [21]. Before and after the experiment, as well as during the reward model change phase, we required participants to fill out a questionnaire via Google Form as follows. The changes of the results

Incentive models of points acquisition.

Incentive model	Features
Fixed model	Provide the fixed points irrelevant to behavior
Addition model	Provide points when user fulfill a mission
Subtraction model	Reduce points if mission is not completed

of questionnaire will be able to reflect the changes of self-protection awareness before and after the experiment.

- Are you aware of ventilation to avoid a closed environment?
- Are you conscious of avoiding a crowded environment?
- Are you conscious of avoiding a close environment when eating?
- Are you care of your health status, such as temperature and physical condition?
- Are you aware of proper exercise and regular lifestyle to maintain your own health?
- Are you aware of maintaining your mental health, such as taking a break or talking to others?
- Do you allow you to explain later where you went and who you met?
- Are you aware of the health of the people around you, such as whether there are sick?
- Are you aware of frequently infection prevention such as hand washing and disinfection?
- Are you conscious of staying at home, such as avoiding unnecessary and urgent outings?

3.4   Definition

We define three concepts used in this paper.

Definition 4.1(mission percentage complete). To assess human's epidemic prevention behavior during the COVID-19 pandemic, it is necessary to define one evaluation indicator by practical behaviors. The five missions we introduced in Table 1 symbolize human's awareness and behavior of epidemic prevention to a great extent. Therefore, we assume the participant's percentage complete for each mission as our evaluation indicators of human' self-protection behavior in this study.

$$P_c = \frac{\sum_{i=0}^{n} m_i}{n} \tag{1}$$

where P_C is percentage complete of prevention behavior missions and m_i is the complete status of mission i. n is the number of missions and virtually it is 5 in this paper.

Definition 4.2(manual recording rate). In this study, we would like to know participant's willingness to manually recording the data and the frequency of submitting the report when visiting a place during the experiment could be seen as their willingness.

$$F_r = \frac{N_r}{N_v} \tag{2}$$

where F_r is the frequency of submitting the report,N_v is the number of places that user visited and N_r is the number that user visited and submit a report.

Definition 4.3(awareness raising percentage). In order to measure the magnitude of change of self-protection behavior by incentive mechanism, we introduce the awareness raising percentage.

$$P_r = \frac{P_c^a - P_c^b}{P_c^a} \tag{3}$$

where P_c^a is the mission percentage complete after adding incentive mechanism, P_c^b is the mission percentage complete before adding incentive mechanism.

4   Data Analysis

In this section, we describe the overall distribution of our data and analyze facotrs that could influence self-protective by comparing the relationshop between different kinds of human activities and mission percentage complete P_c. By analyzing the changes before and after adding incentive mechansim in three control groups, we attempt to showing the effectiveness of incentive mechanism on our dataset.

4.1   Holistic Analysis

In order to understand human's self-protective behaviors from a holistic perspective, we analyzed 20 participants' data during 2 weeks totally(320 pieces of data). Average mission percentage complete is 54.63%. Figure 2 shows overall completion of 5 missions. We find that in 93.44% cases, participants completed at least one mission. However, just in 14.44% cases, participants could complete all missions. It is indicated that although human could have a certain awareness of self-protection to some extent, they sometimes slack off and couldn't maintain it everyday. People seem less willing to submit their reports when visiting a venue and we guess that as it will consume extra time and is less convenient.

Part of our data collection experiment needs human's manual submission. To know human's intentions to submit manual records, we calculate manual recording rate F_r per day for every participant. Considering existing participants forgot to submit the report when visiting a place in the whole data, we remove the data that the number of reviewed place is zero. Figure 3 indicates that manual recording rate F_r will decrease when the number of visited places increases. It seems that human could submit most reports when the number of visited places

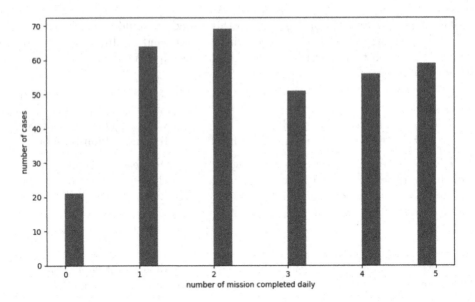

Fig. 2. The overall distribution of mission completion.

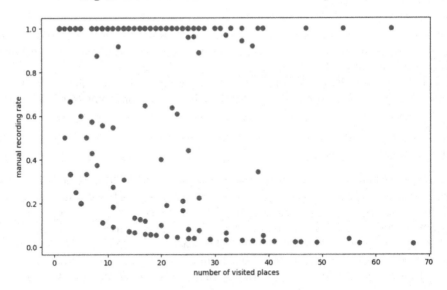

Fig. 3. Relationship between number of visited places and manual recording rate.

is not so larger, like smaller than 30. As the number of visited places increases, manual recording rate has a downward trend. This phenomenon illustrates the impact of burden which is caused by manually submitting data on people. It is indicated that the variability among 20 participants is greatly significant from Fig. 4. mission percentage complete vary greatly different in 2 weeks. On the

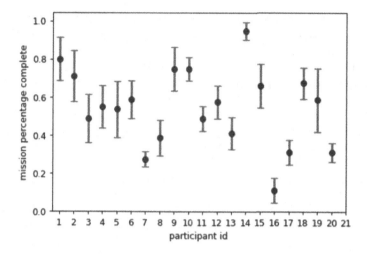

Fig. 4. Individual variation among participants

other side, some participant could maintain high P_c during the whole experiment period, but part of them always have a low P_c. Virtually, this kind of variability brings some disturbance to our experimental results.

4.2   Factors Affecting Self-protective Behavior

As is defined in Sect. 3.4, percentage complete of 5 missions could be regarded as human self-protection behavior. To know which factor and how it influence self-protective behavior, we analyzed the relationship between the human activities and mission percentage complete P_c from the collected data of each participants per day.

Smartphone use: We obtained the frequency of smartphone use by calculating the ratio of smartphone standby time to the total experimental time. By the analysis, We found that people who use smartphones more frequently have a relatively higher mission percentage complete. In cases that the frequency of mobile phones use is over 50%, the mission percentage complete P_c of is 64.78%, which is 9.51% higher than the average mission percentage of 55.27%.

Displacement distance: by latitude and longitude, we calculate the displacement distance that each participants moves per day, we found that corresponding to the data with a particularly low P_c, the displacement distance is relatively short.

Mood: mood seems to have a strong influence on human self-protection behavior. Positive emotions, including feelings of delighted, excited, glad, happy, serene promote greatly self-protective behaviors. When the mood was positive, 84.49% of the cases completed more than three missions, and 40.1% of the cases completed the five missions. However, when the emotions are negative (afraid, angry, frustrated, miserable, sad and tense), only 17.5% of the cases complete

5 missions. Especially when the emotions are afraid, angry or sad, the mission percentage complete P_c is close to 0. In the case of completing more than four missions, positive emotions accounted for 74%; in the case of completing all missions, the positive emotions accounted for 78.72%.

Frequency of taking public transport: as is mentioned in the Sect. 2, we required participants to submit a report when they visit a new place. Therefore, We can know the participant's daily poi information. Obviously, cases with the high frequency of taking the train or subways have higher mission percentage completes. It seems that these cases have occurred when people go out frequently and stay in densely populated public places, which led to their increased awareness of self-protection.

Time at home: the analysis results show that the cases that mission percentage complete of 0 are all those that the ratio of time at home to total time exceeds 50%. Combined with the previous analysis, we can find that people obviously improve their self-protection awareness when they go out and they won't have a high self-protection awareness when they are at home because they have no contact with the outside world.

Human movement pattern and regular schedule: by collected daily step counts, we analyzed the differences of human movement pattern between am and pm. As is well known, most people walk more in the afternoon every day and we verified it through data analysis. In the few cases that participant walks more in the morning, the P_c is as high as 66.20%, which is much higher than the cases that participant walks more in the afternoon (53.65%). Meanwhile, completing more than 3 missions a day is considered to have a relatively high awareness of self-protection. 55.17% cases that participant walks more in the morning completes more than 3 missions and merely 34.13% cases that participant walks more in the afternoon could completes more than 3 missions. Based on our analysis of other sensor data from these cases, people who walks more in the morning tend to have healthier schedules. Healthy sleep habits may also have positive effects on self-protective behaviors.

Environment: cases with more access to user-marked high-risk areas, which are always densely populated public places, have higher P_c.

Unfortunately, although we analyzed many other human activities, it is difficult to find qualitative relationships or conclusions for the vast majority of them based on our data.

4.3 Impact of Workload on Mission Completeness

From user perspective, ideally, all missions could be collected automatically by the application. However, it is difficult to know human' subjective feelings just by sensors, like mental state. Therefore, we require participants to submit several reports everyday. As is mentioned in Table 1, we could divide five missions into three types, manual missions, automatic missions and semi-automatic missions. In order to know the influence of workload on mission completeness, we analyze the difference of percentage complete between 5 missions in 2 weeks. Table 4 shows percentage complete of each mission. It is indicated that human prefer to complete simple and effictive mission, like washing hands. M3, stay record, requires participants to submit the report when visiting a new place, which increases most burden on participants. As a consequence, M3 has lowest percentage complete. Although M1 is manual mission, it still has a relatively high rate because participants are required to subimit just one time everyday.

4.4 Influence of Incentive Mechanism

As is mentioned in Sect. 3, we set up a controlled trial to analyze the influence of reward/incentive mechanism. In the first week, participants will earn the same points regardless of whether they complete the self-protection mission, which means that the incentive mechanism has no effect on the human behavior. In the second week, participants could earn more points for each additional mission they completed regardless of addition or subtraction incentive model, which means that the incentive mechanism could affect the human behavior.

The results indicate that awareness raising percentage P_r for all five missions is 4.28% after adding incentive mechanism. Independently, P_r of manual missions is 3.64%, P_r of semi-automatic mission is 6.06% and it is 4.025% for automatic missions.

Table 4. Percentage complete of each mission. With regard to each mission, We compare their percentage complete independently on 3 types of models in 2 weeks.

	Mission name	1st week			2nd week			Total
		G1 Fix.	G2 Fix.	G3 Fix.	G1 Add.	G2 Sub.	G3 Fix.	
M1	Condition check	80.95%	40.81%	55.1%	76.19%	65.3%	43.75%	59.06%
M2	Mindfulness	66.67%	40.82%	57.14%	69.05%	57.14%	50%	53.13%
M3	Stay record	59.52%	26.53%	44.9%	64.29%	57.14%	27.08%	43.75%
M4	Steps	83.3%	28.57%	57.14%	80.95%	53.06%	58.3%	55.63%
M5	Hand washing	69.04%	61.22%	63.26%	61.9%	71.43%	58.3%	61.56%

As shown in Table 4, the percentage complete on fixed model is declining while there is no external intervention, which means the human could not maintain high level self-protection awareness in the long-term. percentage complete for each mission could maintain a high rate and part of them increases sharply after adding incentive mechansim, including addition model and subtraction model. Obviously, incentives mechanism is beneficial for enhancing human self-protection behavior totally. Some mission percentage complete for several specific participants is reduced even after adding incentive mechanism and it could be caused by individual differences. Besides, the statistics of the questionnaire results also show that the self-protection awareness of participants has been greatly improved after we adding the incentive mechanism. Figure 5 shows change of mission percentage complete P_c as time goes.

As Fig. 6 and 7 are shown, participants' mission percentage complete varied significantly after adding incentive mechanism. The fixed model is not affected by the incentive mechanism, and P_c has a significant downward trend because people could not maintain long-term high self-protection awareness just by themselves. participants in subtraction model are clearly motivated and their self-protection behavior has been significantly enhanced. Due to randomly division of the control group and insufficient samples, participants in addition model have a relatively higher P_c, which leads to a slight increase after adding incentive mechanism.

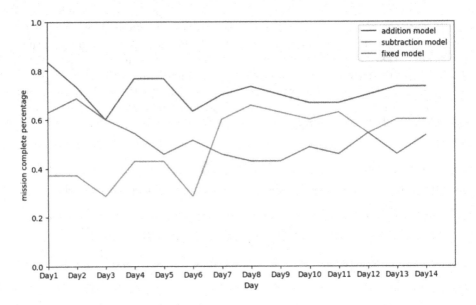

Fig. 5. Daily change of mission percentage complete.

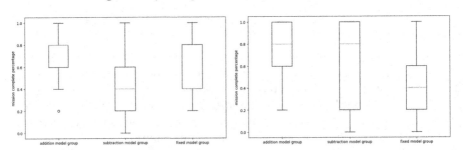

Fig. 6. Boxplot before incentive   **Fig. 7.** Boxplot after incentive

5   Discussion

By analyzing the relationship between human activities and mission percentage complete P_c, the following conclusions can be drawn:

- Positive mood is conducive to improving self-protection awareness.
- When people are in densely populated public places, they will increase their awareness of self-protection.
- People who use their smartphones more frequently and open our apps repeatedly have a stronger awareness of self-protection.
- People with regular schedule are better able to engage in self-protective behaviors.
- Frequent access to high-risk areas may increase awareness of self-protection.

According to our experimental results, human's self-protection behavior is indeed affected by external factors. Guided by our application, participant's mission percentage complete P_c reached 55.27%. Besides, according to the questionnaire before and after our experiment, it can be found that the guidance of our app is beneficial for human self-protection behavior. Therefore, it seems feasible to guide human self-protective behavior through external intervention, including providing push notifications and incentive mechanism.

As a consequence, we propose to add more guidance and incentives to induce people to strengthen their self-protective behaviors. Furthermore, people tend to strengthen self-protective behaviors when they are in a good mood or have a regular schedule according to previous analysis. Considering the influence of COVID-19, people tend to reduce their interactions with others, which could lead to depressed. It is necessary to ensure a certain level of communication with others to maintain a positive mood under the premise of ensuring a safe distance and environment. Guiding human to record and plan their schedule more reasonably to develop regular living habits may also reinforce the awareness of self-protection.

6   Limitations and Future Work

Although we have analyzed the data from various aspects, it is difficult to draw some quantitative conclusions due to the lack of data. Considering individual differences among participants, insufficient number of users will cause certain deviation and interference to the experimental analysis results. In order to obtain more accurate and comprehensive analysis results, we intend to expand the scale and period of experiments to build larger datasets in the future.

In recent years, with the increment of the number of smartphones, privacy leakage becomes an issue that cannot be neglected. More and more people pay attention to privacy issue and some organizations or governments even enforced some Data regulations to protect user privacy [22]. Therefore, We consider add some privacy protection mechanism during data collection and analysis procedure, like differential privacy [23], to protect user privacy while ensuring the accuracy of data analysis in the future.

7 Conclusion

In this paper, we investigated a method for improving self-protection behavior by gamified feedback techniques and incentives strategy. For conducting our study, we design an application for collecting self-protection related behavior by using the sensors on smartphones and smartwatches, and self-report. We investigated factors of encouraging self-protection behavior through two weeks user study with 20 participants. According to the analysis of relationship between human activity and mission percentage complete, we find that mood, environment, daily schedule and frequency of smartphone use could influence human' self-protection behavior. In addition, our results show that external interventions and incentives have an impact on human self-protection awareness.

Acknowledgement. This work was partly supported by National Institute of Information and Communications Technology (NICT), Japan.

References

1. World Health Organization (WHO): Who coronavirus (covid-19) dashboard. Accessed 1 Feb 2022
2. World Health Organization (WHO). Advice for the public: coronavirus disease (covid-19). Accessed 1 Feb 2022
3. Bankmycell: How many smartphones are in the world? Accessed 1 Feb 2022
4. Nishiyama, Y., et al.: IOS crowd-sensing won't hurt a bit!: aware framework and sustainable study guideline for IOS platform. In: International Conference on Human-Computer Interaction, pp. 223–243. Springer (2020)
5. Li, J., Guo, X.: Covid-19 contact-tracing apps: a survey on the global deployment and challenges. arXiv:2005.03599 (2020)
6. Nishiyama, Y., Yonezawa, T., Sezaki, K.: Selfguard: semi-automated activity tracking for enhancing self-protection against the covid-19 pandemic. In: Proceedings of the 18th Conference on Embedded Networked Sensor Systems, pp. 780–781 (2020)
7. Davalbhakta, S., et al.: A systematic review of smartphone applications available for corona virus disease 2019 (covid19) and the assessment of their quality using the mobile application rating scale (mars). J. Med. Syst. **44**(9) (2020)
8. Ferretti, L., et al.: Quantifying SARS-COV-2 transmission suggests epidemic control with digital contact tracing. Science **368**(6491), eabb6936 (2020)
9. Chowdhury, M.J.M., Ferdous, S., Biswas, K., Chowdhury, N., Muthukkumarasamy, V.: Covid-19 contact tracing: challenges and future directions. IEEE Access **8**, 225703–225729 (2020)
10. Ministry of Health and Welfare (Japan): Cocoa: covid-19 contact-confirming application. Accessed 1 Feb 2022
11. Ministry of Health (Singapore). Tracetogether. Accessed 1 Feb 2022
12. Menni, C., et al.: Real-time tracking of self-reported symptoms to predict potential covid-19. Nat. Med. **26**, 07 (2020)
13. Han, J., et al.: Exploring automatic covid-19 diagnosis via voice and symptoms from crowdsourced data. In: ICASSP 2021–2021 IEEE International Conference on Acoustics, Speech and Signal Processing (ICASSP), pp. 8328–8332 (2021)

14. Choe, E.K., et al. Semi-automated tracking: a balanced approach for self-monitoring applications. IEEE Perv. Comput. **16**(1), 74–84 (2017)
15. Fogg, B.J.: Persuasive technology: using computers to change what we think and do. Ubiquity **2002**, 2 (2002)
16. Oyibo, K., Orji, R., Vassileva, J.: The influence of culture in the effect of age and gender on social influence in persuasive technology. In: Adjunct Publication of the 25th Conference on user Modeling, Adaptation and Personalization, pp. 47–52 (2017)
17. Widyasari, Y.D.L., Nugroho, L.E., Permanasari, A.E.: Persuasive technology for enhanced learning behavior in higher education. Int. J. Educ. Technol. High. Educ. **16**(1), 1–16 (2019)
18. Matthews, J., Win, K.T., Oinas-Kukkonen, H., Freeman, M.: Persuasive technology in mobile applications promoting physical activity: a systematic review. J. Med. Syst. **40**(3), 1–13 (2016)
19. Munson, S.A., Consolvo, S.: Exploring goal-setting, rewards, self-monitoring, and sharing to motivate physical activity. In: 2012 6th International Conference on Pervasive Computing Technologies for Healthcare (PervasiveHealth) and Workshops, pp. 25–32. IEEE (2012)
20. Labour Ministry of Health and Japan Welfare. New lifestyle against covid-19 (2021). https://www.mhlw.go.jp/stf/seisakunitsuite/bunya/0000121431_newlifestyle.html
21. Toscos, T., Faber, A., An, S., Gandhi, M.P.: Chick clique: persuasive technology to motivate teenage girls to exercise. In: CHI 2006 extended abstracts on Human factors in Computing Systems, pp. 1873–1878 (2006)
22. EU. Regulation (EU) 2016/679 of the European parliament and of the council on the protection of natural persons with regard to the processing of personal data and on the free movement of such data, and repealing directive 95/46/ec (general data protection regulation) (2016). https://eur-lex.europa.eu/legal-content/EN/TXT
23. Dwork, C., Roth, A., et al.: The algorithmic foundations of differential privacy. Found. Trends Theor. Comput. Sci. **9**(3–4), 211–407 (2014)

Smart Creativity and Art

Design or Art? Technological Interactivity and Connectivity in Designed Objects in a Speculative Design Approach

Jiajia Chen[✉]

Nanjing University of the Arts, 15 Huju North Road., Nanjing 210013, China
chachachen@126.com

Abstract. Speculative design, as a new approach in design filed, is believed to open new ways of thinking and perception of the future. Through the creation of designed objects, this approach attempts to challenge assumptions and preconceptions about the role that products, services and systems play in everyday life. Products or services or systems can be regarded as fictions that can create stories and scenarios in a participatory and humanized way for the view of future. In this sense, speculative design is a method to discover and discuss technology's influence on everyday life. Based on the literature review of speculative design, the relationship between technology and design, as well as the longtime discussed question: difference between art and design, the author analyzes the technological interactivity and connectivity in 3 typical speculative design cases. In the end, the author points out the nature of speculative designers are new designers who are very close to artists. Two paths of speculative design are classified. As a conclusion, speculative design work are both design as well as art.

Keywords: Speculate design · Interactivity · Connectivity

1 Introduction

1.1 The Rise of Speculative Design in China

In the last two or three years, a new design approach has been heatedly discussed in China, which is speculative design. It has been regarded as a new approach representing the developing trend of design after the emergence of service design, social design, experience design and transformation design in China. Although it remains in discussion whether it is a new approach or not, it shows its specialty in inspiring people to think or rethink of the existing or ongoing design works. This kind of enlightening nature brings it considerable quantity of followers in China. It is introduced to Chinese academic world by a book called 'speculative everything: design, fiction, and social dreaming', which is translated into Chinese and published by Jiangsu Phoenix Publishing House in 2017. The translator of this book, Li Zhang, has become the pioneer of speculative design in China. With countable but influential lectures, Ms. Zhang has successfully aroused the interest of her colleagues in academic world. And in 2018, Central Academy of Fine Arts,

Parsons School of Design, The New School and Tongji University have cooperated in carrying out speculative design workshops, expanded the influence of it in China. This highly prized new approach is followed by voice of doubt: Does the development of design discipline in China really need speculative design? What's the value of it? Can it make some contributions in today's world helping to work out something that meets the challenge of the latest technologies?

1.2   The Impact of Epidemic and Possibility of Solutions on Technology

With no doubt, we all agree with one opinion that the epidemic of COVID-19 and the following mutant pathogen such as Omicron has changed our life silently: the increasing amount of plastic waste in the ocean, the wandering wild animals along the edge of the city, the increased social distance, the decreasing number of published academic papers…Naturally, as people always depend on technological developments to solve the problems, the problems caused by this epidemic is of no exception. But here comes the question: can today's technology fix these problems? Throughout the history of human development, when a kind of technology has emerged, we human beings have enough time to adapt it, explore it, apply it, refine it… We can do this process without hurry because new technology comes alone. And what about today? Today, the emerging technologies appear like a blowout, we human beings are busy or even in a hurry to learn about them. We can't finish the previous process for all the emerging technologies at the same time. Because they are updated at an exponential speed. That is to say, the future is likely to materialize itself before we human beings have insight into its basic shape and properties. Not to mention one fact that although emerging technologies are closely related to people's lives, due to the high cognitive threshold of technology, it is difficult for ordinary people to understand its impact fully.

1.3   The Redefine of the Relationship Between Designers and Technology

Designers, especially modern designers, starting from the first day in history, they are trained to apply the technology to the latest design. It is like their destiny, never be questioned. The modern design in China is greatly influenced by Bauhaus. Chinese designers, generation by generation, are trained to passively embrace a kind of technology and consider possibilities of its application. But nowadays, a different way of thinking is proposed by young generation of designers. They manage to grow up with emerging technologies, proactively identifying the fissures between needs from we human beings and social needs. They learn to identify which realities created by technology should be changed. They learn to identify which technology should be updated and be warned. And what is the most important thing: which future profiles are possible for we human beings to approach. At this point, it is easy to find out that the relationship between designers and technology has undergone a fundamental shift. They are cocreating each other. With this cocreation, the rift between technology and society can also be possibly repaired. At the same time, it offers another possibility for designers: for some designers who are not willing to just produce and solve the problem by technology, or for some designers who are not willing to produce products of desire for consumption by technology, they can have an exciting, enjoyable, and discursive journey through cocreating with technology.

2 Literature Review

2.1 Speculative Design

Speculate. In the dictionary of Oxford English, speculate means 'form a theory or conjecture about a subject without firm evidence', image subjectively. In philosophy, speculate means pure thinking, which is based on rational inquiry, introspection and microscopic exploration. Just like famous philosopher, Kant, mentions: speculation is a purely rational philosophical inference based in the absence of empirical objects. Hegel regarded himself as a typical speculative philosopher because he infers pure concepts from objects. We can see from here, speculate means think critically by using the logics and sensibility, free from the prejudice and emotions.

The Origin of Speculative Design. There are two important people to be mentioned. One is Anthony Dunne; the other is Fiona Raby. They found Dunne & Raby studio and used to teach in Royal College of Arts in UK together. Speculative design comes into being during their teaching period in RCA. In his PHD study, Dunne keenly discovered the limitations of industrial or product designers in the development of electronic products. Later, in his book, 'Hertzian Tales: Electronic Products, Aesthetic Experience and Critical Design', Dunne points out the noncommercial aspect of design, which he believes an important way to understand design itself and study the growth of the society. He mentioned in his book 'Design is not engaging with the social, cultural, and ethical implications of the technologies it makes so sexy and consumable'. Together with Raby, Dunne questioned design and technology at that time, discussing their influence on people's daily lives in their book 'Design Noir: The Secret Life of Electronic Objects'. In 2013, drawn from the B part of A/B manifesto (see Table 1), Dunne and Raby proposed 'speculative design' as a subsidiary of critical design. In the A/B manifesto, they list and compare the broad design(A), which provides only problem solution within business logic, with the parallel dimension of design(B) that they are exploring the future of design. The aim is not to present commercially-driven design proposals but to design proposals that identify and debate crucial issues that might happen in the future [1]. In their book, they also mentioned that anti-design and Italian radical design could be considered as ancestors of speculative design [1, 2]. But critical design 'use speculative design proposals to challenge narrow assumptions, preconceptions, and givens about the role products play in everyday life' [1]. According to Matt Malpass, speculative design is a form of critical design that is concerned with future proposals [2].

The Definition of Speculative Design. Dunne and Raby describe the term speculative design as 'an activity where conjecture is as good as knowledge, where futuristic and alternative scenarios convey ideas, and where the goal is to emphasize implications of mindless decisions for mankind' [1]. James Auger thinks that speculative design 'combines informed, hypothetical extrapolations of an emerging technology's development with a deep consideration of the cultural landscape into which it might be deployed, to speculate on future products, systems and services' [3]. And speculative design (1) moves away from the constraints of the commercial practice which is steered by the market; (2) uses fiction and speculates on future products, services, systems and worlds, thus reflectively examining the role and impact of new technologies on everyday life;

Table 1. A/B manifesto by Dunne and Raby.

A	B
Affirmative	Critical
Problem solving	Problem finding
Provides answers	Asks questions
Design for production	Design for debate
Design as solution	Design as medium
In the service of industry	In the service of society
Fictional functions	Functional fictions
For how the world is	For how the world could be
Change the world to suit us	Change us to suit the world
Science fiction	Social fiction
Futures	Parallel worlds
The 'real' real	The 'unreal' real
Narratives of production	Narratives of consumption
Applications	Implications
Fun	Humor
Innovation	Provocation
Concept design	Conceptual design
Consumer	Citizen
Makes us buy	Makes us think
Ergonomics	Rhetoric
User-friendliness	Ethics
Process	Authorship

(3) and initiates dialogue between experts such as scientists, engineers, designers…and users of new technologies. Speculative design emphasizes the 'philosophical inquiry into technological application' [3]; it tends to take the discussion on technology beyond the experts to a broad population of the audience. In a conclusion, Speculative design is a discursive practice, based on critical thinking and dialogue, which questions the practice of design in its modernist definition, at the same time, making speculations on future scenarios for mankind. This design approach does not deal with meeting current or future consumer needs, but with rethinking a technological future that reflects the complexity of today's world. Its task is very simple: speculate on possible futures and design an alternative present.

Speculative Design Thinking. We can see from the definition of speculative design that it coins a more comprehensive, open-minded, and critical way of thinking compared to 'design thinking' as we all know today. It speculates the role of objects/products in society as the entry point to discuss issues such as functions, styling, semantics etc. In the concept of speculative design, designers should forget about the commercial world and build their standpoint of knowledge avoiding being the representative of capitals. Designers should change their minds to provide solutions, but to find possibilities. Design itself becomes a medium for study and discussion. It allows designers to create their design works without any limitation of technology, markets… instead, designers can present their ideas in an unrealistic way, just to show their view on future scenarios. All in all, speculative design is always asking the question 'what if', it is in nature a kind of simulation for people to discover, discuss and debate. It enables us to think about the future and critique current design practice. Based on his personal design works and teaching experience in RCA, James Auger concluded six strategies to do speculative design: 1) Design for the context: the ecological approach; in this strategy, designers should think about the context of products and services in the future. 2) The uncanny: desirable discomfort. In this strategy, some sensitive, bizarre yet familiar means of visual expression will be used in order to arouse the cognitive dissonance. 3) Verisimilitude: design fiction or design fiction? This strategy leads to unrealistic results which normally are lack of details. 4) Observational comedy: rooting the speculation in the familiar. This strategy use the way a comedian usually does. The comedian is good at integrate comprehensive and complex knowledge or information into a humorous story. 5) Alternative presents: counterfactual and alternate histories. This strategy is very close to the anti-realistic approach of writing in literature. Based on history, this strategy can provide a unique thought, provoking insights and perspectives on contemporary life. 6) Domesticating technology: literally. Just like the relationship between men and their pets, this strategy indicates one possibility that through speculation, technology can be domesticated by changing its genes. All these six strategies show to us not only how to design speculations, but also the specific way of speculative design thinking.

2.2 Design vs Technology

The 20th century was an era of technological change and development for mankind. The developments from all the fields in the society have been swept by digitalization, networking, informatization and intellectualization. The highlighted moments in the history of technology development almost lit up every corner of different social forms. The evolution of technology in the history of design has a long tradition, ranging from the nature of materials to the philosophy of technology. It has profoundly influenced the construction of authority in the design field. Especially, the transformation of modern design has always been closely linked to the digitalization of technology. For example, when we talk about the futuristic design, Apple knowledge Navigator (see Fig. 1) is always to be mentioned. It is a concept proposed by John Sculley, the former Apple Computer CEO, in his book in 1987. It shows the functions of a device which can access to a large, networked database of hypertext information, and use software agents to assist in searching information. In a video, all the featured, advanced capabilities of this device has been shown. We can find the existing technology nowadays in it, such as Siri, Internet, Google search, I-pad, Folded-screen, Touch screen, Realtime 3D animation, AI assistant...It is amazing to see the embryonic form of today's technology in an old video of last century. As we discuss the relationship between design and technology, we should firstly review the philosophy of modern technology. It is believed that modern technology has gone through three transitions: the first empirical turn with a social orientation, the second empirical turn with an engineering orientation, and the third one is 'thinglyturn' [4]. Technology, as a pervasive and dominant phenomenon, must be integrated with design in order to be used by people. And design is believed to be the connection with users. To some extent, design connects technology and people/users. Before, the philosophy of modern technology rethink of its social impact only through writings. Nowadays, with design stepping inside, the modern technology can be closely observed through designed objects. It is the turn from macro to micro level. Speculative design creates designed objects of daily life, visualizing the technology which fits the future scenarios, to absorb the attention and provoke reflective thinking. As James Auger said, speculative design is a good way to expand the scope of the discussion on technology from experts to the public. A case in point is the 'Bad News Bot' (see Fig. 2) shown at the 2016 London Design Festival by studio PSK. Robots are taking over jobs previously done by humans, it might be the monotonous, mechanically precise, simple tasks that we lose to them first—but what of the most uncomfortable ones; jobs, that are not rewarding, tasks that we do not enjoy. Who likes to tell their employees that the company has decided to let them go? It is the original intention of the design of 'Bad News Bot'. It can deliver potentially disheartening or uncomfortable news. Installed in an office, the bot informs employees about dropping share values, failing project aims, exploding expenditures, it fires employees and cancels the office Christmas party. It's programmed and designed to know what humans might need when they receive bad news and to provide consolation with its machine charms to soften the blow. In the design festival, the public were invited to experience receiving bad news from a machine. And the exhibit used physical metrics, such as heart rate, to adjust how the bad news was delivered – tailoring messages through change of tone, attempting to deliver even the most personal messages in the most efficient yet empathetic way. It brings the following questions to the public and encourage them to think about—how changes in AEI may affect our relationships with machines, and what tasks may or may not one day be done by them.

Fig. 1. Apple knowledge navigator 1987

Fig. 2. Bad news bot designed by studio PSK

2.3 Design or Art? A Clichéd Question

Design has been primarily regarded as a problem-solving practice according to the modernist perspective. It usually aims to provide solutions in an economic or social or cultural point of view. In this sense, design is hand in hand with industries to meet the users' needs or at least address client's needs. Different from modern design, modern art has presented a rich and diversified synthesis, reflecting to a certain extent the endogenous logic of the resonant interaction between art concepts and the aesthetic transformation of social styling. As we date back to the history of Art and Design, we find several stages that Art and Design is similar to each other. For example, visual arts and visual design are like each other in 1950s. This kind of similarity starts to push Art and Design to find the boundary from each other. In 1960s, Design has been defined and emphasized its scientific standpoint. And because of this, later, Design has become the center for cross-disciplinary cooperation. The core value of this cooperation is the interactions happened during the process. In no surprise, some designers use methods and tools from other disciplines to realize their design works. In the meanwhile, other designers still depend on traditional artistic way to present their design works. Sometimes it is difficult to tell whether an object is a designed on or art piece. It becomes even more difficult to tell whether a piece of speculative design work from modern or contemporary art piece. For example, Spanish designers El Ultimo Grito used to exhibit a collection of blown-glass architectural models at the Aram Gallery in London in 2010. This collection is called 'Imaginary Architectures' (see Fig. 3, 4), the objects are created to feature tubes, funnels and steps, each representing a different building typology, including a hotel, car park and theatre. From the first sight, you can not tell it is a piece of design work. It looks much more like an art piece. In the shape of glass, city buildings and industrial architectures are conceptualized in a series of fictitious spaces, from city skyscrapers to cinemas and chemical plants to mine shafts. These imaginary architectures are spatial expressions, re-scaled 'vehicles' which contain familiar elements of known spaces, prompting us to question what are they representing, and which is their purpose, and invite us to imagine what it would be like to navigate and inhabit their interiors. Their typological characteristics suggest them as model of industrialized architecture, and this leads our enquiry into the physical language of the systems. As spectators, we find ourselves extracting meaning and second-guessing the implied logic of these pareidolic illusions. It provokes people to think. This kind of way of making things is usually observed in Art. So from here, we can boldly infer that speculative design, as one of the design forms, uses simplest visual language, unrealistic aesthetics and abstract metaphors to indicate the questions to think, to change the way people think about it, and what's more important, leading to the atmosphere that conducive to think.

Fig. 3. 'Imaginary Architectures' by El Ultimo Grito: apartments (left), hotels (right). 2010

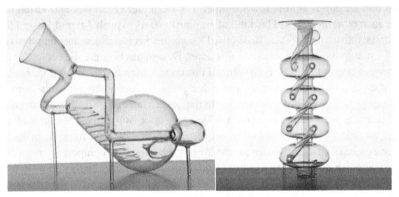

Fig. 4. 'Imaginary Architectures' by El Ultimo Grito: Theatre (left), Parking Side (right) 2010

3   Case Study

3.1   Technological Dreams Series: Robots, 2007

In order to explore speculative design practice, Dunne and Raby finished one project called 'technological dreams series: Robots'. They designed four robots to induce the complex and emotional relationship between home robots and human beings. They thought one day in the future, we will have robots to do everything for us. Especially nowadays, robots are destined to play a significant role in our daily lives. Do we look on them as super functional smart machines? Or another form of life? Or as technological cohabitants? What is the interactivity between robots and human beings? And what is the connectivity among them? Is it the new interdependencies that different types of robots of different levels of intelligence have? Robots, as designed objects, can generate what kind of relationship between human beings and them.

Robot 1. It is a very independent one. It always lives in its own world, working on its own work. You don't need to figure out the complex functions of it. You just need to know whether it finish his work or not. Or does it finish well. It could, for instance, be running the computers that manage our home. It has one quirk; it needs to avoid strong electromagnetic fields as these might cause it to malfunction. Every time a TV or radio is switched on, or a mobile phone is activated it moves itself to the electromagnetically quietest part of the room. As it is ring shaped, the owner could, if they liked, place their chair in its center, or stand there and enjoy the fact that this is a good space to be in.

Robot 2. It is not designed for specific tasks. It is like a baby who has many possibilities since it can grow up. So, people can give it or train it to do jobs based on its capabilities. For instance, robot 2 is quite nervous and coward at a certain stage of its life. When a stranger steps into the room. It will turn its eyes on it and begin to do analyzing. If the stranger tries to touch or be very close to it, the Robot 2 will become extremely agitated and even hysterical.

Robot 3. It is like a guard for our house. Since more and more data with our personal and secret information has been stored in digital database online or offline. Robot 3 can help us to guard our data. It uses retinal scanning technology to decide who can access to our data. By applying Iris scanning technology, robot 3 can make the decision by asking you to stare into its eyes for a long time. We see the interactivity here is quite similar to face-to-face communication between human beings. And robot 3 also asks if a new form of furniture can be evolved in the future to respond the future technology developments.

Robot 4. It is a very clever robot. Although extremely smart, it needs people to help it to move, because it is trapped in an underdeveloped body. Here the interactivity creates a unequal relationship beyond the common sense of human beings. We all think that robot can help people sometimes human beings is passively receiving the help from the robot. But this one, it needs help. Dunne and Raby also design the possibility for it to evolve so that it can use the language of human beings to communicate when it needs help (Fig. 5).

Fig. 5. 'Technological dreams series: Robots' by Dunne and Raby, from left to right: robot1, robot2, robot3, robot4 2007

From these 4 robots, we can see that technological interactivity and connectivity from the perspective of speculative design emphasize on creating the equal relationship between designed objects and human beings. In the meanwhile, different kinds of technology, which definitely lead to interactivity and connectivity of robots (designed objects) to human beings, become the way of expression of speculation in the future. And these technologies make it possible for robots (designed objects) to evolve as we human beings evolve too.

3.2 Black Mirror

Black mirror is a British anthology television series which is popular in China as well. It explores a diversity of near-future dystopias in individual episodes. And it bases on almost the same principles as speculative design. In each episode, designed fictional objects, interfaces, technical artefacts, scenarios for everyday use in the future can be found. The episode of 'The Entire History of You' is set in a future where a grain technology records people's audiovisual sense, allowing a person to re-watch their memories. In this overhead future world, everyone is implanted with a small memory chip behind their ears. It is called Neural-occular. It can not only store all the memories of the past in details, but also select fragments to project on the screen (see Fig. 6, 7) and share them with others like watching a movie. People can regularly sort out, delete what they don't want, review what they like. The key moments can be replayed for people's own nostalgic or neurotic purpose. We can see clearly that it is social media, smartphones, and surveillance all combined into one 'grain'. Does 'grain', the technology, really help people with their daily life? From different scenes in this episode, we can infer that the result is quite dull. For example, at a dinner party scene, one character discusses the freedom that comes with 'going grainless'. Another character responds with 'I just couldn't do it!' He acts in a suggestive tone of enemas or removing the tongue. Another example is the breakdown of Liam, the layer who is in a downswing career in this episode. Though, it is not the technology of 'grain' cause Liam's breakdown, it only exacerbates his tendencies because it allows for ceaseless recollection of events. We can not deny the interactivity and connectivity of the whole grain system in this episode. We also cannot ignore the similar idea of grain system in the real world such as google glasses, smart-phones, social networks or even the reality TV. In any case, we use lots of technologies which invite us to measure others as the result of their own visible actions, without paying attention to the fact that they are happening now as impossible selves. All the interactivity and connectivity we have designed through technology are actually the attempt to be impossible selves. According to what we have found out in this episode, we should take into account that not every technology will lead us to an integral human enhancement.

Fig. 6. Screen graphics for "The Entire History of You" episode of "Black Mirror" by the courtesy of Clayton McDermott.

Fig. 7. View the content of grain, Screen shot for "The Entire History of You" episode of "Black Mirror"

3.3   The Quantum Parallelograph 2011

The Quantum Parallelograph (see Fig. 8, 9 and 10) is an exploratory public engagement project examining the scientific and philosophical ideas surrounding the theory of quantum physics and multiple universes. The device simulates the experience of users being able to glimpse into their "parallel lives" – to observe their alternate realities. This speculative design work assumes that users will be able to glimpse their own 'parallel life' experiences, an alternative possibility beyond their real life. It is designed to inspire the mind of participants in the exhibition, trying to change their behaviors and break their common way of thinking. Of course, as a quantum device, it is based on the technology such as quantum physics. The participant in the exhibition firstly enters their personal data into the database. And they will turn on the button on the right side of the device. The intensity shown on the device become more and more stronger, it means the bigger difference will be made from the participant's current state. After searching and filtering the data on the internet, the left part of the device which is designed according to the principle of Yong's double slit experiment will start to simulate the evidence of the existence of paralleled world. The device then will print a short description of text when the paralleled world and the world in reality share the same moment. Based on massive personal data on the internet, this piece of speculative design manages to ask questions: Can you accept another you from the paralleled world? Have you ever thought about changing your life or behavior in real world? Do you want to make a change and how to make a change? In this work, we can see that the technological interactivity is executed in a participatory way. It needs the audience to participate and finish the steps of the design. In this sense, technology interactivity in speculation should be participable. Technological connectivity in this case is also very innovative. It enlarges the boarder of design, we can not only design for the existing real world, but also design the possible come-into-being in a paralleled world. How that interesting?

Fig. 8. The Quantum Parallelograph 2011 by studio PSK

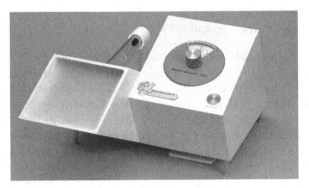

Fig. 9. The Quantum Parallelograph 2011 by studio PSK: the device

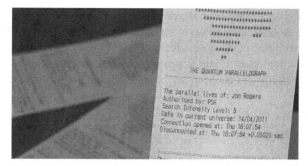

Fig. 10. The Quantum Parallelograph 2011 by studio PSK: the proof of paralleled world

4 Discussion and Conclusions

4.1 New Designers

From the study of the relationship between Art and Design, we can see that there are a bunch of designers using diverse fields of computer sciences, engineering, sociology, psychology…to present their ideas. Different from their predecessors, they have not just applied the technology, they are dealing with implications. They turn away from the commercial side of design, which focuses on the demands of the markets. They engage themselves in a broader context for design, they are proposing future dreams. We call them 'New Designers' [4], who are 'using design as a medium and focus on concepts and artefacts, which, rather than solving problems, they ask questions and open issues to discussion' [4].

From the study of speculative design, we all agree that it is a discursive practice, based on critical thinking and dialogue, which questions the practice of design and its modernist definition. And it is, according to New Designers, one of the most representative examples of the new interactions of different disciplines. New Designers call themselves 'trans-disciplinary, post-disciplinary or even post-designers' [4], that 'do not just produce one thing or type of thing' [5] and sometimes they view themselves as contemporary artists more than modern designers. Because, by speculating, they are rethinking and proposing the alternative products, systems and services just like we have another parallel world.

4.2 Two Paths in Speculative Design

From the above, we can see that there are typically two paths in speculative design. The first one is to do speculations based on the latest technology and its social impact. We can find a few cases since the main purpose is to convey the message of future scenarios to the public today. Museum of the Futures in Dubai has a complete collection in this path. This path is slightly close to what is called conceptualized design in the traditional design world. A case in point is 'grain system' in black mirror. The other path is much more like art piece. It depends on the designers' personal interest and capabilities. The purpose of this path is to educate people through design objects that can provoke the discussion. A case in point is the 4 robots designed by Dunne & Raby. It succeeded in presenting a new perspective on the complex emotions between human beings and domestic robots. And the integration of furniture with the latest technologies gives the light on the possibilities of creating advanced functionality in a familiar appearance. What is the most important thing: it proposes one question to the audience — can technology interactivity and connectivity become strange but still intimate with human beings?

4.3 Design as well as Art

As we discuss the technological interactivity and connectivity in these speculative design objects, we find out that through technology, speculations can create equal relationship between objects and mankind. Or speculations will propose this as a question to ask what if… through imagination and fiction by using design as a medium to propel thinking, raise awareness, provoke actions, open discussions in order to achieve impossible selves of human beings. And it put the audience and the creator together in a participatory way, for example, to design the possible come-into-being in a paralleled world. In this sense, design and art are of no difference. Just as James Auger said that 'one of critiques of this approach (speculative design) is that you get a very particular kind of people that go to galleries anyway. Of course that is an issue but we don't just stop at the gallery, we are often using the media as a gallery space as well, and a lot of these ideas are quite interesting, as is the way we present them, like through photography, video scenarios and a range of other techniques, and they are all good for dissemination, either though web blogs, video materials, newspapers, or magazines. Suddenly, all of these media spheres become a gallery space' [4].

References

1. Dunne, A., Raby, F.: Speculative Everything: Design, Fiction, and Social Dreaming. Massachusetts, Cambridge (2013)
2. Malpass, M.: Critical Design in Context: History, Theory and Practice. Bloomsbury Academic, London (2017)
3. Auger, J.: Speculative design: crafting the speculation. Dig. Creat. **24**(1), 11–35 (2013). https://doi.org/10.1080/14626268.2013.767276
4. Mitrovic, I.: Introduction to Speculative Design Practice—Europia, A Case Study. Croatian Designers Association, Arts Academy, University of Split (2015)
5. Liam Healy. https://liam-h.com/

Study on 3D Print Style in Iris van Herpen Fashion Show Based on Gestalt Theory

RuiTong Gao[1,2(✉)] and SookJin Kim[2]

[1] Shandong University of Arts and Design, No. 1255, College Road, Changqing District, Jinan, China
31808866@qq.com
[2] Sejong University, 209, Neungdong-ro, Gwangjin-gu, Seoul (Gunja-dong), South Korea

Abstract. The etymology of the word Gestalt is "Gestaltung", usually a form, but not simply for "shape", but a "Configuration" for the way things are arranged. This means that Gestalt is not just a form, but composed of more comprehensive and comprehensive meanings. Humans have the characteristics of simplifying the complicated, vague and ambiguous visual information when receiving the information, which means that there is some degree of universality in perceiving visual objects, logically explaining this as the theory of Gestalt psychology. Gestalt theory began with visual research and was applied in various fields of psychology, philosophy, aesthetics, science and more.

This study analyzed the style characteristics of Iris van Herpen's 3D printed clothing based on Gestalt's theory of visual perception. The article through the methods literature research and case analysis, first combing the theoretical background of Gestalt, select the law of Prägnanz, law of Grouping, law of Figure-Ground three rules related to this article for detailed analysis. Subsequently, the concept, principle and type, output mode and shape characteristics of 3D printing were sorted out. By summarizing the 3d printed Style of the Iris van Herpen brand fashion show between 2011 and 2022, the application characteristics of 3D printing of different shapes were compared and analyzed to obtain the modeling characteristics of Iris van Herpen's 3D printed clothing: in the shape of Iris Van Herpen's3d printing style, due to the limitations of materials and printing technology, simplicity theory can be used to build a more accessible overall, and make the design more recognizable. You can also be homogeneous elements, using interval differences, classified into groups, so that the design is change, neat and orderly. It can also use the principles of prospect and background to accurately convey the main body, guide and strengthen the information that designers want to express, and highlight the design theme. This study hopes to provide a feasible design method for 3D print fashion design of modern technology and art.

Keywords: Iris van Herpen · Gestalt · 3D print · Fashion show

1 Introduction

The development of 3D printing technology is bringing technological innovation to medical products, architecture, fashion and other fields. In 2010, a 3D printed dress, featuring

"Crystallization", attracted keen attention from the global fashion world. Therefore, Iris van Herpen has opened a new fashion road and became one of the few fashion designers using 3D printing technology. 3D printing technology has brought unique aesthetic value to the design of Iris van Herpen. Under the general trend of technology intervention in design, people pay more and more attention to 3D printed clothing. However, due to the limitations of materials and printing technology, 3D printed clothing is subject to many limitations in modeling and style shaping. Brands that apply 3D printing to clothing design at home and abroad are still scarce, and Iris van Herpen has become a typical representative of 3D printing clothing design through technological aesthetics. Therefore, the research on Iris van Herpen printing clothing design style may provide a feasible modeling method for 3D printing fashion design, and a feasible style design method for the clothing design with the integration of modern technology and art.

Most of the current studies on 3D printed clothing for Iris van Herpen remain in the shallow form and lack a systematic analysis of its modeling characteristics. In the process of research, the author first collected and sorted out the works released by Iris van Herpen brand. At present, no one has systematically and accurately released the data of the brand, and the collected show information is lack of picture information, inaccurate production method introduction, fuzzy and confusion of time and theme. In order to verify the 3D printed clothing styles appeared in the Iris van Herpen press conference, the author extensively searched the websites, images and book resources at home and abroad, combined with the brand official website, publicity video, foreign network literature, designer interviews, etc., comprehensively sorted out the 3D printed clothing styles in each season of the works from 2010 and so far, and conducted research on this basis.

On the theoretical level, there are limited research materials on the 3D printing style of Iris van Herpen, and relatively few academic research, as mentioned in Hu Jia's "Advantages of 3D printing technology in fashion space modeling design", with the clothing space modeling design as the carrier, take the work from Iris van Herpen2011, Fall/Winter 2022, the advantages and characteristics of 3D printing technology are explored, sorted out the aesthetic connotation [1]. In Song Gina's "This paper takes fashion space modeling design as the carrier to explore the advantages and characteristics of 3D printing technology", The multi-dimensional analysis of the works of designers from the three aspects of materials, technology and art form, and put forward the thinking on the development of fashion in the era of technology [2]. In Liu Xiaohong's "Research on the Method of expression and Aesthetic Image in Iris van Herpen Clothing Design', the author selected the costume show of Iris van Herpen 2015–2018 for research, and focused on analyzing and exploring its costume style from two aspects of creative method of expression and unique aesthetic image [3]. In Zhongyi's "Iris van Herpen-The First Designer to Put 3D Printing to Fashion Week", the interpretation of the designer's autumn and winter works of 2013 mentioned that 3D printing technology has made breakthrough and clothing technology [4]. In Hou Xinzhi's Innovative Application of Clothing Design Based on 3D Printing Technology, the basic situation of 3D printing is reviewed, and the advantages and disadvantages of available 3D printing materials are discussed [5]. In Guo Yanlong's "Research on 3D printed Clothing Design from the Perspective of Bionics", the multi-dimensional, diversified and polymorphic aesthetic laws and inner principles of 3D printed clothing design are discussed from the perspective of bionics [6]. Most of the literature uses Iris van Herpen's 3D printed clothing as some cases to prove the impact of new technologies and new materials on fashion design. To sum up, in terms of the research status, the current research on the brand mainly focuses on the discussion of 3D printing technology and modeling beauty, while the research on the style characteristics and design methods of 3D printing is almost a blank. Under the premise of existing materials and technology, based on the Gestalt theory, the fashion style and design method of the present study discusses 3D printing, and the integration of technology and art, provides feasible innovative design practical methods for 3D printing clothing, and provides new ideas for the future development of clothing design.

2   Theoretical Background

2.1   Background of the Gestalt Theory

The term "Gestalt" first appeared in the auditory field, such as by Austrian psychologist Von Ehrenfels in the 1890s, citing the relationship between note and melody, which vividly explains the concept of "integrity". He believes that the score is composed of multiple note arrangement and combinations, but this does not mean that a piece is only composed of notes, but that there is an inner "gestalt". Different notes can constitute pleasant tunes or noise, which means that music is not only the study of various notes, but also pays attention to its integrity. Thus, he put forward the basic view of gestalt psychology that "the whole is not equal to the sum of parts, the whole is composed of parts, but prior to the part, the part cannot determine the whole" [7].

This theory then became the basis for the research and reference of relevant scholars, including three Germans (Max Wertheimer (1880–1943), Kurt Koffka (1886–1941) and Wolfgang Kohler (1887–1967) fully inherited and developed this theory, after years of experiments and research formed a relatively systematic format the Gestalt theory, become one of the main schools of the modern western psychology. Later, in the United States, Rudolf Arnheim (1904–2007) further extended its theory, and became the main representative figure of Gestalt Psycology, in his book "art and vision" mentioned that the basic principle of Gestalt is the perceptual organization principle is summarized and summary, and further improve and supplement, summed up a series of basic principles, including simplified principles, gestalt principle, graph relationship principle, similarity principle and continuous principle, has made outstanding contributions to the research in the field of visual perception [8]. After the further development and development of Arnheim and others, Gestalt visual perception theory has risen to an unprecedented height, making Gestalt psychology successfully break through the boundaries of psychology and show an important theoretical value in the field of art.

Gestalt theory research is the starting point of "shape", Gestalt psychology believes that human when observing things, visual consciousness has a pursuit of completeness or sexual tendency, Gestalt school research shows that human vision is born to organize "shape" ability, when "shape" size, location, direction and other objective factors, change, the visual cortex of the external stimulus to actively organize and structure, to produce different feelings. Gestalt term started in the visual field of research, but is not limited to the visual field. At present, the research results based on Gestalt theory are widely used in the design field. This paper uses Iris van Herpen's 3D printed clothing example, focusing on the law of Prägnanz, law of Grouping, law of Figure-Ground in the Gestalt theory organization principle [9].

2.2   Organizational Principles of the Gestalt Theory

Law of Prägnanz. The word prägnanz is a German term meaning "good figure. "The law of prägnanz is sometimes referred to as the law of simplicity. This law holds that when you're presented with a set of ambiguous or complex objects, your brain will make them appear as simple as possible. In Fig. 1, when people see the Olympic logo, they are used to calling the five Olympic rings, which means that people see five overlapping circles, rather than various curved, connected lines (Fig. 2).

Fig. 1. Olympic logo   **Fig. 2.** Various curved, connected lines

In contrast, the two graphs overlap more simply than the stitching of several complex graphs. Under the same external outline, producing symmetry in the inside is simpler than asymmetry. In addition, the easier it is to associate, the more recognizable the graph is, and the basis of association is a common natural thing in life.

This shows that, when recognizing the world, individuals have the property of removing complexity and a sense of alienation, and observing reality in the simplest form. According to Gestalt psychology, human visual perception is a metaphysical and abstract process, which can actively integrate the picture information in the field of vision into a unified whole, and simultaneously "simplify" the perceived and complex style into a simple form. It is a simplified abstract processing of the perceptual image, which removes the unnecessary trivial details in the perceptual image, and directly highlights the essential characteristics of things. Arnheim argued that simplification is different from simplicity, "it is often seen as an extremely important feature of artwork" [10].

Law of Grouping. Gestalt psychology believes that people's subconscious automatically integrates shape and color into a whole, which is the grouping principle of Gestalt psychology. The rule of grouping refers to the human cognition of morphology and the tendency to group the location elements of association when processing visual information. Elements with similar visual features are considered more related than elements that do not have similar visual features, and when the physical properties such as shape, size and color of objects are relatively similar, they can easily be organized to form a whole. In Fig. 3, if the black round physical properties of the graph are similar, it is easier to organize and is complete; the same black circles in Fig. 4 are arranged according to positional elements and are usually identified as divided into three groups according to visual tendency.

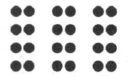

Fig. 3. A set of black circles with similar physical properties

Fig. 4. The same black circle is arranged according to the position element

Gestalt psychology has had a lasting impact on art and design, Witheimer's 1923 paper in Theory of Form, concluded that specific Gestalt is strengthened by our innate ability to assemble, we put seemingly the same elements (called "similar group"), or very similar elements ("similar group"), or structural elements "category" [11]. This ability is innate, not learned. Complex works such as painting, posters, and layout design may intentionally connect using some groups (e. g., color similarity), or using other groups (e. g., distance, or shape, size, and direction differences) [12].

Law of Figure-Ground. Gestalt psychology has such an explanation of the relationship between the graphics and the background: "In the field with a certain configuration, some objects highlight to form the graph, and some objects retreat to the foil status and become the background [13]". The principle of graph bottom relationship refers to the subtle symbiotic relationship between pattern and background. Usually, the stronger the contrast between the "graph" and the "bottom", the easier the previous "graph" will become the center and focus of the vision, and under certain conditions, the relationship between the background and the figure can also be interchangeable. In Fig. 5, observers also often take the graph as the center of visual perception. The background is usually the subjective weakening visual part, which is designed to better reflect the visual form and characteristics of the main figure. However, the relationship between background and graphics can also be interchangeable, making the background the focus of visual perception.

Fig. 5. Interchange of figure and ground

3   Application of Gestalt Theory in Iris van Herpen's 3D Printed Fashion Show

3D printing clothing is a fashion revolution led by technology. It is a clothing design innovation by combining 3D printing characteristics such as clothing CAD technology, VR technology and rapid solidification laser materials [14]. Since Iris van Herpen launched its 3D printed clothing design in 2010, more attention has been paid to 3D printed clothing, and its design applications have been constantly explored. However, due to the limitations of printing materials and technologies, 3D printed clothing has certain limitations in the sense of dress and flexibility. Based on the visual perception theory of Gestalt, this study analyzes the modeling characteristics of Iris van Herpen 3D printed clothing, and explores the feasibility and innovative design method of 3D printed clothing design.

3.1   3D Printing and Principle, Type and Characteristics

3d printing is a kind of additive manufacturing technology, and 3D printing clothing is the design idea of "additive clothing" [15].This study comprehensively examines the commonly used 3D printing and output methods, technical principles and molding characteristics, to provide certain technical support for the development of 3DP products in line with the design intention.

The earliest 3D printer was invented in 1986 by Dr. Charles W. Hull).He founded a company called 3D Systems, and developed and patented 3D printers in the SLA way. At present, the relatively mature 3D printing technology includes Streolithography Apparatus (SLA), Selective Laser Sintering (SLS), Fused Deposition Modeling (FDM), optical curing fast forming technology Polyjet, etc. [16]. The SLA uses UV light to scan the liquid material surface, and each scan creates a very thin layer of slices to accumulate the object. SLS is to heat the powdered material through a high-efficiency laser to shape the object. FDM printing method is to melt the plastic material after heating and solidification by the machine to the established position. Polyjet-is a light curing fast forming technique that sprays the liquid optomymer layer onto the build tray and then solidifies it immediately with UV light without subsequent curing, providing accurate precision, smooth surface and ultra-delicate details [17]. The state-of-the-art PolyJet systems can simulate all details from plastic and rubber to human tissue and produce a full chromatic gamut. The Objet Connex 3D printer is a state-of-the-art PolyJet system that combines different 3D printing materials to the same model by spraying multiple materials simultaneously. This means that designers can selectively place multiple materials in a printed prototype, combining multiple materials to create richer visuals [18]. Due to the different output principles of each technology, it can produce different shapes, with different advantages and disadvantages in shaping the shape (as shown in Table 1).

3D printing is a technology to make 3D objects by laminating (additive manufacturing) of plastic and polymer liquid and powder through CAD model or digital 3 D modeling design (Barnatt 2013/2014). This technique can continuously layer two-dimensional profiles to make items in a printed manner.The 3D printing in the above way is affected by the technology and materials, its output form and size are limited, and its scalability and flexibility are relatively poor, resulting in the visual effect and wearing comfort of 3d printing clothing. And Iris van Herpen uses the clothing design of 3D printing to get

Table 1. Output method (collated by the author)

Types of 3D Printing	Principle of Technology	shape	Characteristics
SLA (Streolithography Apparatus) 1986			• Large objects • Fast lead time •High-quality surface finish • Large space needed
SLS (Selective Laser Sintering)			• Fast lead time • No support rafts • High-quality surface finish • Limited printing size
FDM (Fused Deposition Modeling)			• Rapid prototyping • low-cost • Limited printing size • Various quality levels
PolyJet			• Colour and multiple materials can be combined • High machining precision and good detail • Large loss,

rid of the existing design framework, and combined with effective design methods, to create a changing and shocking visual effect, reflecting the advantages of 3D printing can design three-dimensional complex structure form. Different from other design fields, 3D printing in the field of clothing design is not only an innovation of some technology, but also a breakthrough and discussion of an artistic expression method.

3.2 Analysis of Iris van Herpen 3D Printing Modeling Method Based on Gestalt Theory

In 2010, the 3D print clothing themed "Crystallization" premiered at the spring and summer series of the same Iris van Herpen brand, and was highly recognized by the high fashion industry, thus opening her science and technology fashion road, 3D printing technology has become a unique technique of expression in Iris van Herpen design. This section analyzes the 3D printing works of Iris van Herpen at the brand fashion show in 11 years between 2010 and 2021 (see Table 2 for specific quantities) to explore an effective design method for 3d printing.

Table 2. The 3D print ratio used for the Iris van Herpen fashion show

Number	Year	Theme	Total number (Unit:Piece)	3DP number (Unit:Piece)	3D print ratio
1	2010 F/W	Crystallization	10	1	10%
2	2011 S/S	Escapism	11	4	36%
3	2011 F/W	Capriole	19	3	16%
4	2012 S/S	Micro	15	1	7%
5	2012 F/W	Hybrid Holism	12	1	8%
6	2013 S/S	Voltage	11	5	45%
7	2013 F/W	Wilderness Embodied	11	7	64%
8	2014 S/S	Embossed Sounds	17	2	12%
9	2014 F/W	Biopiracy	26	1	4%
10	2015 S/S	Magnetic Motion	32	10	34%
11	2015 F/W	Hacking Infinity	31	4	13%
12	2016 S/S	Quaquaversal	29	3	10%
13	2016F/W(R)	Lucid	17	7	41%
14	2016F/W(C)	Seijaku	12	1	8%
15	2017 S/S	Between the Lines	16	6	38%
16	2017 F/W	Aeriform	18	5	28%
17	2018 S/S	Ludi Nature	21	1	5%
18	2018 F/W	Syntopia	17	1	6%
19	2019 S/S	Shift Souls	18	0	0%
20	2019 F/W	Hypnosis	19	0	0%
21	2020 S/S	Sensory Seas	21	2	10%
22	2021 S/S	Roots of Rebirth	21	1	5%
Total			404	67	17%

According to the 67 sets of 3D printed clothing works released in the Iris van Herpen11 years, he combines the technical characteristics of 3D printing with innovative materials, shows specific themes through unique modeling and creative techniques, achieve a high combination of art and technology, and constantly explore the combination of art and taking performance. The following paper analyzes the modeling method of Iris van Herpen's 3D printed clothing specifically combined with the law of Prägnanz, law of Grouping, law of Figure-Ground in the Gestalt theory.

Application of the Law of Prägnanz. The law of pragnanz is a visual perceptual principle in gestalt psychology, and is widely used in Iris van Herpen's 3D printing design. As Iris van Herpen showed the "Micro" series of 3D printing works in the spring and summer 2012 (Fig. 6), she was inspired by the form outline of nature (Fig. 7) and extracted from the organic form of wood. According to the output mode and molding characteristics of 3D printing, polyamide 3D printing is equipped with "copper plating" to create a wooden texture. The work summarizes the image of the branch extension into a curved organic form, superimposed and repeated, showing the bionic shape like the ancient wood carving technology. The work is easy to understand, recognizable, and gives people a deep impression. The internal components of the work have the same color, texture and texture, which makes the complex things present a relatively simple object. At the same time, under the simulation of external outline, people's vision is always moving to find its internal relationship and summarize it into a whole, under the action of the visual law, viewers see form is simple, clear, at the same time easy to produce wooden form association, and the basis of association is trees-the common natural things in life. The 3d printed clothing design with the simplified principle can integrate the original independent local information into an overall concept,

Which is highly recognizable, so that the visual audience can clearly interpret the design concept expressed by the designer at the moment they see the clothing. Although the form is simple, it is very delicate.

In July 2014, in Iris van Herpen's "Biopiracy" autumn and winter series (Fig. 8), the thermoplastic elastic material polyurethane, developed by the famous 3D printing company "Materialise", was used as a new material, giving the work a light and rich texture effect. From Fig. 9, we can see that the constituent elements of the clothing are more complex and rich in layers, but the viewer can easily feel the bionic design themes similar to bones and feathers based on the known experience. Using the analysis of the principle of simplicity of Gestalt, when people recognize objective things, they always subjectively notice the obvious elements and unconsciously ignore other redundant elements, which makes the brain see the complex internal form of clothing when the perceptual impression is refined and simplified. Because this automatic "simplification" of graphics by the brain comes from people's experience with feature recognition and cognition [19], viewers can quickly identify feather patterns, stimulate resonance and map design themes.

In 2015, Iris van Herpen, together with Italian architect Niccolo Casas and 3D printing company 3D Systems, launched the "Magnetic Motion" series, creating a new technological revolution in 3D printing fully transparent materials, producing incredible crystal dresses (Fig. 10), with a high level of transparent texture and exquisite texture (Fig. 11). Although the style details are extremely rich, but the visual look and feel is

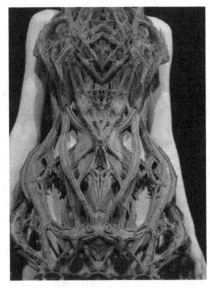

Fig. 6. Iris van Herpen's 3D printing dress (2012.1 S/S Micro) http://shows.vogue.com

Fig. 7. Wood photos (2012.1 S/S Micro) http://shows.vogue.com

Fig. 8. Iris van Herpen's 3D printing dress (2014.7 F/W Biopiracy) http://shows.vogue.com

Fig. 9. Details (2014.7 F/W Biopiracy) http://shows.vogue.com

relaxed and concise. According to the Gestalt concise law analysis, people's vision can actively integrate the picture information into a unified whole, namely "picture integrity", therefore, although 3D printing graphics is more complex and dense, but because of its overall layout symmetry balance, profile is very simple, visual perception will

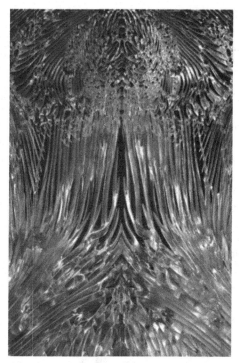

Fig. 10. Iris van Herpen's 3D printing dress (2015.1 S/S Magnetic Motion) http://shows.vogue.com

Fig. 11. Details (2015.1 S/S Magnetic Motion) http://shows.vogue.com

be based on the "decomplexity principle" and combing and organization, eventually its "simplified" for easy to understand form.

In short, in Iris van Herpen's 3D printing design, the designer builds a more easy to understand whole, making the 3D printing design feasible and quickly recognized by the public. Its simplified design is first to highlight the main characteristics, convey the design intention, delete unnecessary trivial details, and secondly, the orderly processing of formal relations is actually one of the ways to simplify and beautify. The the law of Pragnanz analysis of Gestalt found that in the design, the integrity and form simplification of visual experience should be emphasized. When the design theme should be highlighted, the outline of the target should be first be determined, and then the design elements should be constructed according to certain theme characteristics. That is to look at the whole, and then the part, to build a more accessible whole. Using this method, even if the design elements are complicated, the design can be neat and orderly, with a more clear integrity, and then accurately convey the design intention of the designer, and stimulate the resonance of the viewer.

Application of the Law of Grouping. According to the Gestalt grouping principle of viewing objects, visual perception always dynamically seeks the internal organization relationship and summarizes it into a whole, which is widely used in Iris van Herpen's 3D printing design. The grouping principle can be used to form different clusters of elements in the clothing modeling design, to facilitate consumers to understand the chaotic visual elements according to the group, reduce the pressure of visual retrieval, and produce a unified and coordinated and rich in changing form beauty.

Iris van Herpen presents the 3D print line named "Voltage" at Paris Fashion Week in Spring/Summer 2013, caused a huge fashion sensation, this season's work can be more flexible use of 3D printing "fabric", according to the 3D printing output and molding characteristics, Iris van Herpen designed suitable for printing, voltage theme, outward open geometry (see Fig. 12), from the middle tassel form easy to let people produce electric shock resonance. This unit geometry is the basic figure of clothing, they are arranged according to a certain location elements, and because the figure has similar physical attributes (such as shape, size, color, intensity, etc.), according to the visual tendency is usually identified as divided into several groups, through this clever combination, constitute the whole. Reduce the use of volume, make the form more flexible, rich change, neat and orderly, rendering the theme while adding a dreamy color.

Fig. 12. Iris van Herpen's 3D printing dress (2013.1 S/S Voltage) http://shows.vogue.com

The work in Fig. 13 is Iris van Herpen's "skeletal cloth piece" created in 2013.F/W "s" Wilderness Embodied" fashion show. The designer used 3D technology to improve traditional fabrics and make the fabric surface form the texture of skeletal effect. The skeletal "cloth" is designed by computer software, formed with a transparent liquid resin through Materialize Mammoth Stereolithography equipment, and then molded by silicone. This seamless and translucent unique 3D hybrid printing technology has a breakthrough development in clothing technology. The geometry similar to the bone in the figure is arranged and combined according to the formal characteristics of the bone. The formal organization and visual perception are actively constructed. At the same time, due to the collocation of naked material, the bone element becomes beautiful and the shocking visual effect is shown. It is because of this principle of visual organization under specific conditions that the rules and vivid visual forms are constructed, which naturally give people a sense of beauty.

Fig. 13. Iris van Herpen's 3D printing dress (2013.7 F/W Wilderness Embodied) http://shows. vogue.com

In short, in Iris van Herpen 3D printing design, based on the principle of visual organization rules, cleverly used the principle of grouping design method, in the design, in order to highlight the key, strengthen characteristics, improve integrity, designers can refine the theme design elements, and then the same or similar size, color and shape of design elements according to a variety of visual rules, various forms of arrangement combination, make the design theme clear at the same time of change and interesting.

Application of the Law of Figure-Ground. In the recognition of the foreground, the brain generally identifies the smallest object in the composition as the graph, the larger object as the background; the convex elements are more related to the foreground compared to the concave elements [20]. According to the law of prospect and background, the analysis of Iris van Herpen 3D printing clothing design method is to take the most important needs or emotion as the prospect. At the same time, the role of "prospect" and "background" is not absolute, and there is a relationship between mutual existence and virtual and virtual complementarity, and sometimes the phenomenon of prospect and background exchange. For example, in 2011, Iris van Herpen's 3D printed dress work first appeared in Paris Couture Fashion Week. Figure 14 shows her white skeleton dress designed using 3D printing technology, which was named one of the 50 best inventions by Time magazine [21]. As the design subject, the bone becomes a clear cognitive object due to its bright color and convex surface, which is recognized as the foreground according to the visual law, and the form as the foreground is the most clear in human visual feelings, while the rest is regarded as negatives or background items, as the foil of the theme, relatively vague. Using the law of prospect and background, the designer skillfully choose a strong model, more emphasis, highlight the theme, strengthen the three-dimensional sense of strong, very artistic.

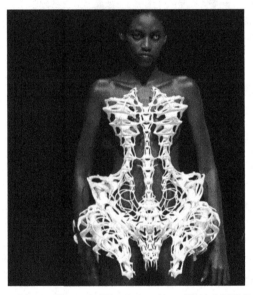

Fig. 14. Skeleton dress-Iris van Herpen's 3D printing dress (2011.7 F/W Capriole) http://shows. vogue.com

In the Iris van Herpen 2016 autumn/winter "Lucid" series of ready-to-wear clothes, there are two sets of 3D printed dresses showing the magma flow form (Fig. 15), using different materials and colors to form the relationship between graphics and background. The two costumes use flat and three-dimensional 3D printing parts with the same pattern respectively. The foreground and background complement each other and complement the virtual and real, forming a visual perception of fabric embroidery. Through the combination of component printing and manual sewing, to enhance the flexibility of the material application and adaptability. Flat print pattern is more real flow, foreground and background are mutual patterns, with exquisite embroidery process; and different color stereo printing components, because of its convex characteristics to enhance the pattern, foreground and background can also be interchangeable, produce different associations.

It can be seen that, as a new form of embroidery, 3D printing can bring infinite possibilities for the presentation of fabrics.

Fig. 15. Iris van Herpen's 3D printing dress (2016.3 F/W Ready-To-Wear Lucid) http://shows. vogue.com

In 2016.1S/S's "Quaquaversal" series (Fig. 16) and 2020 S/S's "Sensory Seas" series (Fig. 17), it can be seen that Iris van Herpen has experienced several years of material exploration and running in with 3D printing technology. Its works have weakened the sense of sculpture, changed from form to detail, with the sense of line and mobility, and began to show female beauty with a more lighter and soft clothing form. At this stage, the work designers creatively use the 3D printer as an embroidery machine. The lines of the 3d printing are more delicate and prominent, and the pattern is coherent with the whole, forming a promising fabric pattern, and becoming a more accurate and efficient new embroidery way.

In short, according to the theory of prospect and background, the designer can put the design points into the design, highlighting the design points, so as to guide the viewer's line of sight, ignore the secondary expression content, and clear the design intention. At the same time, the foreground and background can be replaced with each other and be the main body. Using this feature, we can guide and strengthen the information that designers should be expressed, make the design theme prominent, and increase the design interest and sense of situation.

Fig. 16. Iris van Herpen's 3D printing dress (2016.1S/S Quaquaversal) http://shows.vogue.com

Fig. 17. Iris van Herpen's 3D printing dress (2020 S/S Sensory Seas) http://shows.vogue.com

4   Conclusion

The paper is based on the study of design method in Gestalt theory. Through the analysis, we can draw a conclusion that in the shaping of ris van Herpen 3D printed clothing modeling, due to the limitations of materials and printing technology, it can be combined with the Gestalt theory of the law of Pragnanz, law of Grouping and law of Figure-Ground theory. After studying the modeling characteristics of 3D printing using these three theories, the modeling method of 3D printing is derived.

First, the 3D printing shape of Iris van Herpen presents Pragnanz features. Vision tends to interpret complex objects as simple objects. In the Iris van Herpen 3D printing modeling, when the technical characteristics of 3D printing are used, in the complex information environment, the modeling is built into a more easy to understand whole, so that the design is feasible and recognizable, and quickly recognized by the public and kept in mind.

Second, the 3D shape of Iris van Herpen presents Grouping characteristics. In Iris van Herpen 3D printing modeling, using the characteristics of 3D printing, will constitute clothing modeling elements, by size, color, intensity and other similar physical attributes organization, constitute multiple elements, form a shape or figure can be identified, using the interval difference, classified into groups, make the design simple, orderly and varied.

Third, the Iris van Herpen printing shape presents the Figure-Ground characteristics. The brain generally identifies smaller objects as foreground and larger objects as background; convex elements are more recognizable as foreground relative to concave elements. Iris Van Herpen takes advantage of this kind of "foreground and background" law to use 3D printing modeling through clever design, or accurately convey the subject, or fuzzy cognition, or mutual prospect and background, so as to strengthen the information that designers want to express, highlight the design theme, increase the design interest and sense of situation.

In short, with the help of 3D printing technology, Alice van He puts forward more possible art forms and innovative directions for clothing design. With her unique insights and innovation in art and design, she provides a design method and experience of 3D printing.3D printing fashion design modeling method can be based on the existing technology and materials, combined with the Gestalt psychology of the law of Pragnanz, law of Grouping, law of Figure-Ground theory, using the brain to perceive things and optimize the law of visual information, according to the design intention, analysis, emphasize, reconstruct design elements, to better express the design intention, meet human aesthetic needs and cognitive needs.

Acknowledgment. This work was supported by the faculty research fund of Sejong University in 2022.

References

1. Hu, J.: Advantages of 3D printing technology in fashion space modeling design. Text. Rep. **41**(01) (2022)
2. Song, J.: Crossover and symbiosis: Iris van Herpen's Clothing Design Language Study. Nanjing University of the Arts (2021)
3. Liu, X.: Research on expression technique and aesthetic imagery in Iris van Herpen costume design. China Academy of Fine Arts (2018)
4. Yi, Z.: Iris van Herpen's first designer to bring 3D prints to Fashion Week. Ch. Cloth. **10**, 32–35 (2013)
5. Hou. X.: Innovative application of clothing design based on 3D printing technology. Design **10**(15) (2017)
6. Guo, Y.: Research on 3D print fashion design from the perspective of bionic. Ornament **3** (2018)
7. Koffka K.: Principles Of Gestalt Psychology, vol. 10. Taylor and Francis (2013)
8. Peng, L.: The influence of gestalt psychology on graphic design. Nanchang University (2006)
9. Rudolf, A.: Art and Visual Perception, vol. 12. University of California Press (1974)
10. Rudolf, A.: Art and Visual Perception, p. 66. China Social Sciences Press, Beijing (2008)
11. On Dunkel's lecture at Bauhaus and Wettheimer's influence on Kerry, attend Marianne Teuber, "Blue Night by Paul Klee. In: Henle, M. (ed.) Vision and Artifact, pp. 131–151. Springer, New York (1976)
12. Behrens, R.R.: Illustration as Design. In: Llustration as an Art, Chap. 1. Prentice Hall, Englewood Cliffs (1986)
13. Chandra, P.U.: 3D Surface Geometry and Reconstruction: Developing Concepts and Application, pp. 29–30. Information Science Reference, USA (2012)
14. Guerrero, J.A.: New fashion and design technologies. Bloomsbury Acad. Prof. **148** (2010)
15. Haifei, Q.: Application of 3D printing technology in the loom latitude-opening mechanism. J. Text. **1**, 140–145 (2017)

16. Ivans: Analyse the 3D printer: the science and art of the 3D printer. Cheng Chen translation, pp. 25–40. Machinery Industry Press, Beijing (2014)
17. Michael W.B., Williams, C.B.: Examining variability in the mechanical properties of parts manufactured via polyjet direct 3D printing (2012)
18. Polyjet-Introduction of optical curing fast forming technology (2022). http://www.mohou.com/zhishitang/213.html
19. Rudolf, A.: Art and Visual Perception. China Social Sciences Press, Beijing (2008)
20. Zhang, L.: Analysis and reconstruction of scarf pattern based on format tower principle. Institutes of Technology of Zhejiang (2013)
21. 'The Iris van Herpen couture and ready-to-wear collection (2017). http://zh.orientpalms.com/index

Case Studies to Enhance Collectively Sharing Human Hearing: Ambient Sounds Memory and Mindful Speaker

Risa Kimura[✉] and Tatsuo Nakajima

Department of Computer Science and Engineering, Waseda University, Tokyo, Japan
{r.kimura,tatsuo}@dcl.cs.waseda.ac.jp

Abstract. Our everyday life is filled with a variety of serendipitous and beautiful sounds that are both natural and artificial. We consciously also unconsciously enjoy these sounds. The sounds are one of the most important factor in our daily life, thus it is a promising direction to use such sounds to develop innovative digital services. In this paper, after presenting a brief overview of our digital platform named CollectiveEars, we show two case studies to use CollectiveEars as an underlying platform to exploit to use the captured diverse sounds in the world. The first case study is named Ambient Sounds Memory and the second case study is named Mindful Speaker. These case studies show the feasibilities to use CollectiveEars to develop future innovative digital services.

Keywords: Sharing collective human hearing · More than human · Sharing economy · Virtual and physical 3D sound · Soundscape

1 Introduction

Our everyday life is filled with a variety of serendipitous and beautiful sounds that are both natural and artificial. We consciously also unconsciously enjoy these sounds making our daily life more fruitful. The modern urban life has become very busy and stressful, thus we tend to forget a variety of important issues that contribute to our wellbeing, for example, living in nature or the diverse chance to do so in the future. The various sounds in the world can offer new possibilities that make us aware of our world's diversity and expand our chances to experience diverse new opportunities. The term soundscape refers to the totality of the sounds that can be heard at any moment in any given place [13]. The soundscape offers only what an individual can listen to and not what a collection of people hear. However, using artistic sounds in the world as collective sharing resources has not been well investigated in future smart urban environments. In particular, there is a very few researches to explore to use various sounds in the world for designing soundscape in our daily spaces.

Currently, we are working to develop a digital platform to share collective human hearing named CollectiveEars [10]. The platform captures any sounds in the world and a user listens the sounds anytime, anywhere. CollectiveEars offers a new opportunity that allows people feel novel artistic experiences. However, in the actual world, most of sounds may be meaningless for most of people. For example, in our urban cities, some sounds may be interesting in someone, but usual people feel the sounds a kinds of noise. In this study, we try to develop two case studies developed on CollectiveEars. The first case study is named Ambient Sounds Memory that is a digital service, where daily objects in a living room present sounds captured by CollectiveEars. A user feels that these daily objects offer sounds like living things. The second case study is named Mindful Speaker that is a digital service to offer mindful sounds like a kind of music.

The contribution of the paper is to present our design process of these case studies how to develop them on CollectiveEars. For explaining the design process, we use the novel annotation method that is a method to document structured annotations for creating annotated portfolios, where the structured annotation method is suitable to develop innovative services on an existing underlying platform.

The remaining of the paper is structured as follows. Section 2 shows an overview of CollectiveEars. Section 3 presents the first case study: Ambient Sounds Memory, and Sect. 4 presents the second case study: Mindful Speaker. In Sect. 5, we show the design process of Ambient Sounds Memory and Mindful Speaker on an underlying platform: CollectiveEars based on annotated portofolios. Section 6 shows some related work with this study and finally Sect. 7 concludes the paper.

2   CollectiveEars Digital Platform

CollectiveEars as shown in Fig. 1 is a digital platform with the capability to share a collection of what people are hearing, and enables us to listen to what people are currently hearing, allowing us to enhance our imagination about our world. CollectiveEars gathers sounds heard by people in the world, and present the sounds to any persons. A user can hear any multiple sounds heard by any human in the world in the user's 3D sound space with CollectiveEars.

Fig. 1. A brief overview of CollectiveEars

CollectivEars consists of the following two components. The first component collects the heard sounds captured through people's hearing capabilities around the world and stores all hearing sounds gathered in the component. The current component assumes that the people use wearable microphones such as the eSense device [4, 18] to share their hearing. The second component selects the stored sounds from the shared database based on the selected theme channel and shows multiple sounds selected by the theme channel in a 3D sound space. We adopt Unity [19] to present multiple sounds in a user's 3D listening space. An end-user wears a headphone or is surrounded multiple loudspeakers. The user is equipped with a device containing an acceleration sensor for detecting the user's head gesture and transmits the sensor data through Bluetooth [16].

A user specifies a theme channel [10] to select multiple sounds that are presented around the user, much like a TV channel selector, from stored sounds in the database through the head gesture. The sound focusing [10] function was implemented, where the function makes it possible to loudly hear sounds in the direction one tilts his or her head.

3 Ambient Sounds Memory

Ambient Sounds Memory is a digital service to gather sounds in the world and to present the sounds from any things in a living room as shown in Fig. 2. A user can move the things to any places in the room and the volume of the sounds is automatically configured according to the brightness on the surrounding of the things. He/she can shuffle sounds by touching the things. People consider them as living things so they feel more empathy on them. Therefore, they are more aware of these individual things and want to cherish them. The approach contributes to achieve a sustainable society.

Fig. 2. An overview of ambient sound memory

In the current design, we focus on four things in the room: chairs, books, flowers and cakes. The chairs make mindful sounds, the books make city sounds, the flowers make nature sounds and cakes make sweet sounds. A user wears a headphone and hear 3D sounds from these things. The user can move the things from the current place to a new place, and the position of the sound from a thing is changed according to the current place that the thing is located as shown in Fig. 3. Each thing makes a different sound, so he/she can distinguish the things and their current positions. The user can know where each thing is in the room easily. Because the volume of the sounds is changed according to the surrounding brightness, people may feel that these things are lifelike. Also, the user may consider a new way to have relationship with the things because he/she like to move them according to his/her feeling and mood. Therefore, Ambient Sounds Memory offers new meaning to inanimate.

Fig. 3. Moving daily things in a living room

4   Mindful Speaker

Mindful Speaker is a service to offer mindful sounds to a user. A user is located within multiple loudspeakers that produce different sounds while using Mindful Speaker, where other services to share human hearings to use headphones to produce sounds as shown in Fig. 4. Mindful Speaker specializes the theme channel abstraction to select sounds that a user wants to listen to. The sounds are gathered by people who hear various sounds in the world through the CollectiveEars platform.

The current version of Mindful Speaker offer three themes as theme channels as shown in Fig. 5. The first is Calm, and the second is Ambient and the third is Aesthetic. A user chooses the channel that he/she likes to hear through head-based gestures. After selecting the channel, several sounds are rendered in the 3D sound space and he/she can choose one of them if he/she likes. People need to tag the sounds that they are hearing before registered the sounds in Mindful Speaker. One interesting issue of the approach is that the tagging is determined by human, so the decision of the tagging is based on human' ambiguous perception about the sounds that they hear. Therefore, a user can consider how people think that the current sound is calm, ambient or aesthetic.

Fig. 4. An overview of mindful speaker

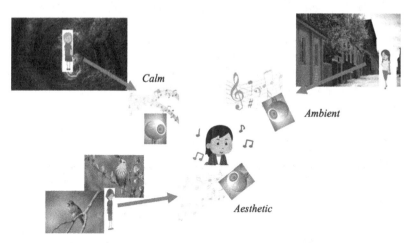

Fig. 5. Theme channels for mindful speaker

5 Exploring Their Opportunities with Annotated Portfolio

5.1 Structured Annotation Method for Documenting Annotated Portfolios

The annotated portfolio method developed by Gaver and Bowers is a method to articulate new knowledge gained from research oriented design practice [2]. The annotated portfolio method is a means for revealing the resemblances and differences that exist in a collection of artifacts. The notion of the method was originally represented by selecting a collection of artifacts, finding their appropriate representations and combining these representations with brief textual and pictorial annotations. The method is a methodology for communicating extracted insights and knowledge in public.

For investigating the abstract qualitative aspects of digital platforms, our annotation strategy for annotated portfolio tried to choose two perspectives to represent the human and material aspects of the platforms. In the first perspective, the sociomateriality aspect makes us to consider both human and material perspectives [11, 12]. Annotations are classified as the domain annotation and interaction annotation in our strategy. The domain annotation named "Domain" represents a set of basic items to identify domain use cases to aim to define a couple of a platform's target goals. The interaction annotation named "Interaction" represents a set of basic items that the platforms offers interaction methods to relate to users. The most important aspect of the annotation method is to introduce the both perspectives explicitly in our structural annotation method.

The second perspective adopted in our annotation method is the four pleasure framework [3]. Describing abstract values for human hearing is essential in our digital platforms. The four pleasure framework makes it possible to classify the abstract values into the four categories: physio-pleasure, psycho-pleasure, socio-pleasure, and ideo-pleasure. Based on the domain and interaction annotation, we investigate what kind of values can be offered by digital platforms. Then, the values are categorized into four pleasures, and described as annotations. The annotations specifying pleasures is named the pleasure annotation. The pleasure annotations are classified into the material side and human side. In the structured annotation shown in the following subsections, the left side shows the pleasure annotation in the material side under the interaction annotation. The right side shows the pleasure annotation in the human side under the domain annotation. The annotations in the material side are colored in red and the annotations in the human side are colored in green. Also, each specific pleasure annotation has a different color to make them visually obvious.

5.2 The Design Process of Ambient Sounds Memory

Ambient Sound Memory was designed to develop on CollectiveEars by focusing on the interaction annotation "Non-Human Agency". Figure 6 presents the structure annotations of Ambient Sounds Memory. In this digital service, we mainly investigated daily artifacts' agency, where Ambient Sounds Memory offers a feeling that presented human hearing is heard from daily artifacts not human. The platform becomes a case study to discuss how new domain use case is investigated by exploiting the materiality of human hearing.

Although Ambient Sounds Memory uses human hearing for presenting sounds from daily artifacts like chairs, a user believes that the captured sounds are delivered from the physical artifacts not human. Therefore, one important aspect of the service is to offer an artifact's agency. The annotations "Feeling Objects' Agency" plays an important role to offer a novel user experience in Ambient Sounds Memory. Each daily artifact autonomously changes the sounds according to its surrounding situation. Therefore, a user feels that the artifact responds to the environmental situations' changes in a living room so he/she feels their own agencies and they offer the sounds to the user based on the artifact's current intention. Ambient Sounds Memory can offer some domain annotations like "Interactive Furniture" and "Room Interior Decoration" can be incorporated by introducing physical daily artifacts. In particular, "Room Interior Decoration" offers a new user experience by arranging the physical artifacts in a living room. The annotations of Ambient Sounds Memory is a good case study to enhance domain use cases by investigating the new material perspective.

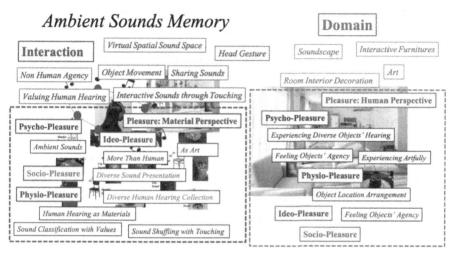

Fig. 6. Annotations for ambient sound memory

In terms of the aspect of the domain annotation "Art", Ambient Sounds Memory captured only natural sounds for investigating the annotation "Mindful Experience". Manually tagging values on sounds by people who gave their hearing enables to capture only mindful sounds. For the purpose, the interaction annotation "Valuing Human Hearing" is customized by valuing only mindful sounds through the customized theme channel.

Ambient Sounds Memory is an example to explicitly incorporate physicality to exploit physio-pleasure from the human perspective by introducing the agency to daily artifacts. The annotation "Object Location Arrangement" labeled as physio-pleasure assumes that the artifacts are physically moved by individual persons. By exploiting the pleasure annotation, the annotation can be changed to socio-pleasure. Thus, arranging the location of each artifact can be performed cooperatively with a user's friends or families. Also, when hearing the same sounds from the daily artifacts in a living room while moving the artifacts together, the annotation "Collective Hearing" can be easily realized by hearing the same sounds from these artifacts.

5.3 The Design Process of Mindful Speaker

Mindful Speaker was also developed on CollectiveEars. Figure 7 presents the annotations of Mindful Speaker. The development of Mindful Speaker focused on the domain annotation "Sounds as Music". For presenting gathered human hearing as music, Mindful Speaker also exploited the opportunity of a physical space for incorporating the annotation "Collective Hearing".

Mindful Speaker chooses only homogeneous mindful sounds for making the composition of the sounds to offer more comfortable user experience like relaxing music, where the annotation "Sound as Music" represents the approach. As shown below, the currently presenting sounds can be changed by anyone, but the changes are small so the composed sounds can be felt as minimal music.

Mindful Speakers focused on the domain annotation "Physical Soundscape", where the platforms offers sounds in a physical space from loudspeakers, although CollectiveEars offers sounds in a virtual 3D sound space through headphones. The advantage to explore using virtual spaces is that a user can easily hear sounds in any places, but the currently hearing sounds are hard to be shared by other people due to using headphones. In the design of Mindful Speaker, the aspect of physical spaces allows us to investigate the domain annotation "Collective Hearing" by explicitly gathering users in a close physical space. Mindful Speaker installs multiple loudspeakers in a small physical space, so multiple users collaboratively listen the same sounds in the physical space, and anyone can change currently presenting sounds by their gestures without noticing other users. The changed sounds can be easily shared by other people in the same space.

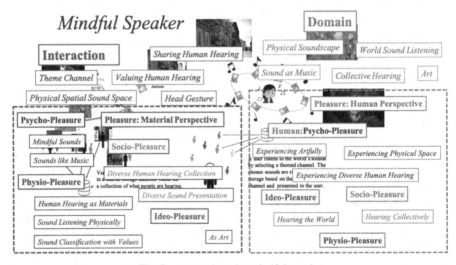

Fig. 7. Annotations for mindful speaker

When investigating the domain annotation "Collective Hearing", we mainly focus on socio-pleasure for incorporate the collaborative aspect. Therefore, the annotation "Hearing Collectively" and "Diverse Sound Presentation" are labeled as socio-pleasure in Mindful Speaker. In other platforms, for investigating the domain annotation "Collective Hearing" or "Collective Seeing", we need to incorporate the agency of people who give their seeing or hearing to make a user to feel others' atmosphere, but in a physical space, people can be easily gathered together and feel others' atmosphere. The discussion makes us aware of the sociality of a physical space. Also, one future possibility is that we can investigate to use Mindful Speaker in public spaces, where the presenting sounds are shared by collective people by replacing their socio-pleasure to ideo-pleasure for the "Hearing Collectivelly" annotation.

6 Related Work

Cities and Memory is a collaborative worldwide project for field recordists, sound artists, musicians and sound enthusiasts who contribute sound recordings collected from various cities in the world [15]. More than 500 contributors have currently contributed to record more than 2,000 audio sounds from over 80 countries around the world on the Web. On the other hand, our services presents multiple sounds from around the world, which are collected from people who use it simultaneously, and users navigate the sounds in their personal listening spaces to hear various sounds in the world.

360 Reality Audio offers a new music experience that uses an object-based spatial audio technology [17]. Individual sounds such as vocals, chorus, piano, guitar, bass and even sounds of the live audience can be placed in a 360° spherical sound field, giving sound artists and creators a new way to express their creativity. Listeners can be immersed in a field of sound exactly as intended by sound artists and creators. The approach will offer our services future directions to locate sounds in a more immersive way in a 3D space.

Audio augmented reality is another direction to enhance the use of sounds. For example, NavigaTone integrates the needed navigational cues into the regular stream of music in an unobtrusive way [1]. Instead of moving the entire track around in stereo panorama, we only move a single voice, instrument, or instrument group. The work uses sounds as design resources to navigate people.

A user interface to music repositories called nepTune creates a virtual landscape for the arbitrary collection of digital music files, letting users freely navigate the collection [5]. Automatically extracting features from the audio signal and clustering the music pieces accomplishes this. The clustering helps generate a 3D island landscape. The interface projects multiple sounds only in a spatial way. Our approach selects preferred sounds through the theme channel abstraction, and uses a similar approach to NepTune if a number of sounds becomes more larger.

Adaptive walk on a fitness soundscape [14] is a new kind of interactive evolutionary computation for musical works. It provides a virtual two-dimensional grid in which each grid point corresponds to a listening point that generates a sound environment. People's localization and selective listening abilities make them walk toward the grid points that generate more favorable sounds. The work also uses sounds as design resources to navigate people.

A digital platform to share collective human eye sights, CollectiveEyes has been proposed [6, 7]. CollectiveEyes offers spatial and temporal multiple view modes similar to Artful CollectiveEars, and the views can be navigated through gaze-based gestures. CollectiveEyes is enhanced for achieving various purposes. For example, In [9], it is enhanced to increase position emotions in our daily life. Also, in [8], it is enhanced as a social watching infrastructure for a citizen science game to help new combinations of protein-protein docking.

7 Conclusion

This paper presented two case studies to use collective sharing human ears to expand the opportunities of innovative digital services. The first case study named Ambient Sounds Memory captures various sounds in the world and shows the talks from daily objects in our living rooms. The second case study named Mindful Speaker arranges natural mindful sounds as a kind of music in a listening space shared by audiences. The current case studies are considered a kind of art works to offer innovative experiences to users. Our approach to use annotated portfolios reveal various potential opportunities as the paper showed some experiences with using the annotated portfolios for analyzing these case studies.

References

1. Heller, F., Schöning. J., NavigaTone: seamlessly embedding navigation cues in mobile music listening. In: Proceedings of the 2018 CHI Conference on Human Factors in Computing Systems (2018)
2. Gaver W., Bowers J.: Annotated portfolios. Interactions **19**(4), 40–49 (2012). https://doi.org/10.1145/2212877.2212889
3. Jordan, P.W.: Designing Pleasurable Products: An Introduction to the New Human Factors. CRC Press (2000). https://doi.org/10.4324/9780203305683
4. Kawsar, F., Min, C., Mathur, A., Montanari, A.: Earables for personal-scale behavior analytics. IEEE Perv. Comput. **17**(3), 83–89 (2018)
5. Knees, P., Schedl, M., Pohle, T., Widmer, G.: Exploring music collections in virtual landscapes. IEEE Multimedia **14**(3), 46–54 (2007)
6. Kimura R. and Nakajima T.: Sharing collective human's eye views for stimulating reflective thinking. In: Proceedings of the 17th International Conference on Mobile and Ubiquitous Multimedia (MUM 2018), pp. 341–349 (2018). https://doi.org/10.1145/3282894.3289724
7. Kimura, R., Nakajima, T.: Collectively sharing people's visual and auditory capabilities: exploring opportunities and pitfalls. SN Comput. Sci. **1**(5), 1–24 (2020). https://doi.org/10.1007/s42979-020-00313-w
8. Kimura, R., Jiang, K., Zhang, D., Nakajima, T.: Society of "citizen science through dancing." In: Novais, P., Vercelli, G., Larriba-Pey, J.L., Herrera, F., Chamoso, P. (eds.) ISAmI 2020. AISC, vol. 1239, pp. 13–23. Springer, Cham (2021). https://doi.org/10.1007/978-3-030-583 56-9_2
9. Kimura, R., Nakajima, T.: Gathering people's happy moments from collective human eyes and ears for a wellbeing and mindful society. In: Schmorrow, D.D., Fidopiastis, C.M. (eds.) HCII 2020. LNCS (LNAI), vol. 12197, pp. 207–222. Springer, Cham (2020). https://doi.org/10.1007/978-3-030-50439-7_14
10. Kimura R. and Nakajima T.: CollectiveEars: sharing collective people's hearing capability. In: The 23rd International Conference on Information Integration and Web Intelligence (iiWAS2021), pp. 104–114 (2021). https://doi.org/10.1145/3487664.3487801
11. Orlikowski, W.J., Yate, J., Okamura, K., Fujimoto, M.: Shaping electronic communication: the metastructuring of technology in the context of use. Organ. Sci. **6**(4), 423–444 (1995)

12. Orlikowski, W.J., Scott, S.V.: Exploring material-discursive practices. J. Manage. Stud. **52**(5), 697–705 (2015)
13. Rudi, J.: Soundscape and listening. In: Rudi, J. (ed.) Soundscape in the Arts. NOTAM (2011)
14. Suzuki, R., Yamaguchi, S.: Adaptive Walk on a Fitness Soundscape. Lecture Notes in Computer Science, vol. 6625 (2011)
15. Cities and Memory. https://citiesandmemory.com/. Accessed 10 Jan 2022
16. McWhertor, M.: Nintendo Switch Joy-Con controller does some amazing things. https://www.polygon.com/2017/1/12/14260790/nintendo-switch-joy-con-controller-features. Accessed 10 Jan 2022
17. 360 Reality Audio. https://www.sony.com/electronics/360-reality-audio. Accessed 10 Jan 2022
18. eSense. https://www.esense.io/. Accessed 10 Jan 2022
19. Unity Platform. https://unity.com/. Accessed 10 Jan 2022

InterestPainter: A Painting Support Tool to Promote Children's Interest in Painting

Jiayu Yao[1]([✉]), Weijia Lin[1]([✉]), Jiayi Ma[1], Jing Zhang[1], Shaogeng Zeng[1], Zheliang Zhu[1,1], Fangtian Ying[2], and Cheng Yao[3]

[1] College of Software Technology, Zhejiang University, Hangzhou, China
{jiayuyao2021,vigalindesign,jiayi2021,jingz2021,zengshaogeng,
22151194}@zju.edu.cn
[2] College of Design, Hubei University of Technology, Hubei, China
[3] College of Computer Science and Technology, Zhejiang University, Hangzhou, China
Yaoch@zju.edu.cn

Abstract. Painting has many benefits for children. But children's interest in painting may decrease as they grow up, resulting in less participation in painting activities. This paper focuses on using mobile technology to enhance children's interest in painting. Informed by a four-phase model of interest development and our formative research, we proposed three specific design strategies: 1) guiding painting activity with personal preference, 2) drawing attention to visual characteristics, and 3) promoting continued engagement with reward mechanism. We deploy these strategies to InterestPainter, a painting support tool, that allows children to extract outlines and colors of objects by taking pictures. Children can use these elements for painting, and apply an animation effect to their paintings. We conduct our experiment with six children aged 7–11 years. The results indicate that Interest-Painter is effective in promoting children's situational interest in painting and offering opportunities to turn the situational interest into individual interest.

Keywords: Children · Painting · Interest development · Painting tools

1 Introduction

Previous studies have shown that participation in painting is beneficial to children's overall development [1, 2]. In specific, painting can support children's abilities including memory, comprehension, logical thinking, and eye-hand coordination [1–6]. These abilities are important for children's growth. Despite the importance of painting for children, there is a general decrease in children's interest in painting as they grow up. According to Vygotsky, children love to express creativity by painting before entering elementary school, but they would lose the passion to paint after entering elementary school when their interest changes to language [7, 8]. As a result of their diminished interest, children become less engaged in drawing activities and may even develop resistance to drawing. Therefore, it is worth exploring how to maintain and promote children's interest in drawing.

N. A. Streitz and S. Konomi (Eds.): HCII 2022, LNCS 13326, pp. 398–410, 2022.
https://doi.org/10.1007/978-3-031-05431-0_27

Joining a growing body of prior research in mobile digital technology for children, our work aims to explore the potential of helping children engage in painting with mobile digital technology. Prior researches recognize that mobile digital technologies can support children's drawing behaviors [9–12]. For example, mobile technology has been used to encourage children's participation in painting by making it easier, such as generating sketches or textures for them [11–14]. However, the majority of these researches focus on the process of painting rather than children's positive attitudes towards painting. We could only find one study that explored the enjoyment of physical interaction in increasing children's painting motivation [15]. And to the best of our knowledge, few prior studies have been systematically designed to evaluate the possibility of using mobile technology to promote children's painting interest.

We extended previous efforts in the field of children's painting by investigating how to design a painting tool to support children's interest development in drawing. Based on the four-phase model of interest development, S. Kawas, S.K. Chase, J. Yip et al. proposed a framework for developing children's interest in nature [16, 17]. Cross-referencing this framework and prior research of children painting [18], we identify three design principles for guiding our study: 1) personal relevance, 2) focused attention, and 3) opportunities for continued engagement. From these principles, we derive design strategies by conducting formative research with children (N = 5). The specific design strategies are 1) guiding painting activity with personal preference, 2) drawing attention to visual characteristics, and 3) promoting continued engagement with reward mechanism.

We introduce InterestPainter, a painting support tool for children developing an interest in painting. It allows children to acquire outlines and colors of surrounding objects by taking pictures. These visual elements, which will be placed in the system, can be used in children's paintings. Besides, children can apply an animation effect to their paintings. In this work, we conducted a user study with children (N = 6) to verify the validity of InterestPainter.

The main contributions of this work are: 1) design strategies for promoting children's painting interest and offering opportunities to turn this situational interest into individual interest, and 2) a painting support tool developed with interest-centered design principles.

2 Literature Review

2.1 Interest

While there is no consensus in the academic community on the definition of interest, the literature generally agrees that interest helps people pay attention to a topic and find enjoyment in it and provides people with a self-motivated engagement [19–21]. Hidi and Renninger define interest as a personal psychological state characterized by concentration and positive feelings while participating in particular content, as well as cognitive and affective motivational predisposition to re-engage with the content over time [16]. They propose an interest development model based on the definition, which divides interest development into four phases: triggered situational, maintained situational, emerging individual, and well-developed individual interest [16, 17]. Although these four phases are considered distinct, some common characteristics are shared in interest progressive development. S. Kawas, S.K. Chase, J. Yip et al. use four of these characteristics - which are personal relevance, focused attention, social interactions, and opportunities for continued engagement - as design principles to trigger children's interest in nature [17].

2.2 Painting Support System for Children

According to prior research, some painting support systems encourage users to partici-pate in painting by reducing difficulty or providing guidance. For example, Painting with Bob [12] provides faded sketches and four different brushes based on photos selected by users and allows them to create paintings within a short time. By using an algorithm to generate a 2.5D mesh from the sketch, Sketch and Shade [22] can help amateur users to paint a better 3D effect. The Drawing Assistant [23] is an interactive drawing tool that helps users to copy pictures. It can automatically extract some structural lines from the pictures to help users observe more details of the pictures, and it can also provide corrective feedback to the user through shape matching. These support systems focus on simplifying the painting process and helping users to create paintings beyond their level. However, they do not improve the enjoyment of the painting process or try to attract users to participate in painting.

There are also painting systems that incorporate real-world physical information into the drawing process to enrich the user's drawing experience. Satoru Tokuihsa and Yusuke Kamiyama believe that the enjoyment of body interaction could increase children's motivation to paint [15], so they design a system that allows users to take pictures to generate a sketch and then use a finger to color on it. And I/O Brush [11] enhances the creativity of digital painting, allowing users to capture colors and textures from - objects with a tangible brush and use it for painting. Similarly, the FingerDraw [24] system encourages users to take and store information from the real world through a camera device on their fingers. The system generates images taken by the user into a pencil sketch, on which they can use the collected colors and textures to draw. All of these studies enhance the interest in painting through interacting with the physical world [9, 11, 15, 24]. We also found that participants in our formative research would gain usable inspiration by observing their surroundings. They observed not only color and texture but also the outlines of objects. Our study showed that some participants would extend drawings based on the outline of the object, and this phenomenon has been paid little attention in previous studies.

3 Interest-Centered Design Framework

We used the interest-centered design principles proposed by Saba Kawas [17] as our design framework. Through formative research with children aged 5 to 10 to identify design strategies. The design strategy is a complementary interpretation of interest-centered design principles in the context of drawing activity (Table 1). And these design strategies will be used to guide the design of mobile technologies that promote children's interest in painting.

3.1 Design Principles

The four design principles proposed by Saba Kawas [17] include personal relevance, focused attention, social interactions, and opportunities for continued engagement. However, painting is more of a personal activity than a social one [18]. And in the core dimensions of interest development proposed by Hidi and Renninger, it was stated that social relatedness is not the determinant of interest development [16]. Therefore, in order to adapt the design principles for children's drawing behavior, we decided to weaken the social relatedness. Next, we would then design with the remaining three interest-centered design principles as a guide.

3.2 Formative Research

Formative research is a kind of developmental research aiming at improving design theory for instructional processes [25]. After determining the design principles, we conducted formative research to establish the design strategies of our project and identify the opportunities and challenges of mobile technology in children's painting interests.

Participants and Procedure. We developed a web-based painting board with one brush tool and eight available colors so that users can paint on a blank canvas (Fig. 1). Five children aged 5 to 10 years (M = 7, SD = 1.9; 2 females, 3 males) were recruited for our formative research. After obtaining written and oral consent, we recorded the entire process. Children were told to use iPad and tablet stylus pen to draw on the canvas. The painting activity lasted 30 min and was video-recorded. Three researchers made records of children's noteworthy behaviors during the drawing process without disturbing them. We gathered the participants' drawings after the activity and conducted one-on-one semi-structured interviews with the children and their guardians. For children, we mainly asked them about their feelings during the drawing process and the reasons for their behaviors observed by researchers. As for guardians, we tried to understand their children's attitudes towards painting and the problems in the process of drawing. The interview responses were all recorded. In the end, all participants and their guardians were compensated with a souvenir worth $5.

Fig. 1. Painting board interface in formative research

Data Analysis. We collected about 3 GB of video and 2 h of voice recording data. Thematic analysis and iterative open coding [26] were used to analyze the data. We focused on children's problems that encountered, changes in attitude, and expectations for drawing activities with Painting board.

3.3 Design Strategies

Table 1. Design principles and strategies to guide the design of InterestPainter.

Interest-centered design principle	Design strategies	Features of InterestPainter
Personal relevance	guiding painting activity with personal preference	Photographing
Focused attention	drawing attention to visual characteristics	Extraction
Opportunities for continued engagement	promoting continued engagement with reward mechanism	Animation

We observed the following throughout the formative research:

1) Most participants tended to paint objects they like or are familiar with.
2) Participants preferred to paint according to their own ideas rather than being asked to paint certain objects.
3) Participants would look for useful inspiration from the surroundings, such as colors and outlines.
4) Participants expected positive feedback during the painting process, for example, their paintings could move.

Combining the above observations and previous studies, the design principles can be explained by the following design strategies: 1) guiding painting activity with personal preference. Participants develop self-motivation as a consequence of interest-driven activities [19, 27]. The design of the drawing activities should take children's preferences as guidance to increase their interest in drawing activities in a self-directed manner; 2) drawing attention to visual characteristics. Visual representations are important to children's painting development. Children use visual media to investigate the lines, shapes, and colors of physical objects [28]. We design to guide children to participate in observational activities with visual characteristics; 3) promoting continued engagement with reward mechanism. Rewards have a stimulating effect on children's interests [29], and appropriate rewards will enhance recurrent participation [30]. We use incentives to maintain children's interest in drawing.

4   Design for InterestPainter

4.1   System Design

The design strategy provides insight into the design of the painting support tool, and the features of InterestPainter (Table 1) are following. 1) photographing: children are free to photograph tangible objects in their surroundings, 2) extraction: the visual characteristics of the objects photographed by children are extracted for painting, 3) animation: children's paintings can take on simple deformation.

InterestPainter is a painting support tool to help children process physical objects and create their paintings. We develope this tool to promote children's interest in painting.

In the design of the painting tool, we make the operation simple and child-friendly. Children can use the camera to take pictures of objects that they are interested in, as shown in Fig. 2(A), to help determine the clarity of the captured object, the photographing interface will guide the child to place an object in the middle circle, and the image around the circle will show the state of blur. After photographing, children would obtain one outline and two colors extracted from the taken picture. The extraction effect is shown in Fig. 2(B). The photo will be displayed on the left, and the extracted characteristics will be displayed on the right side as painting materials for creation. After getting the characteristics, children can drag the outlines in the material bar on the left side of the page and place them at any position on the canvas. Then, they can use the brush tool on the top to choose the extracted color to start painting. They can also use the eraser tool to erase unsatisfied paintings they draw. After finishing the painting, click the animation tool in the top right corner, children can choose any area, and the selected area could move up and down in small increments, as shown in Fig. 2(D).

Fig. 2. The interface of InterestPainter: A) Photographing interface; B) Extracting features interface; C) Painting interface; D) Animation effect interface.

4.2   System Development

InterestPainter is implemented in Vue.js, Python, and PyTorch. This painting support tool has three core functions: color extraction, outline extraction, and animation. For outline and color extraction, images are uploaded to the server after being taken. These images are processed with DeepImageMatting [31] algorithms first, then outlines and colors are generated as output by OpenCV. Finally, outputs are returned to the client. For animation, Konva 2d canvas library is used.

5 Evaluation

5.1 Participants

Table 2. Summary of the participating children in evaluation

ID	Gender	Age (years)	Frequency of after-school painting
C1	Male	7	Seldom
C2	Male	8	Occasionally
C3	Male	9	Occasionally
C4	Male	9	Seldom
C5	Female	10	Frequently
C6	Female	11	Very Frequently

To verify the validity of InterestPainter, we conducted an evaluation test. We invited six children aged 7 to 11 to participate (M = 9, SD = 1.29, 2 females, 4 males) through offline recruitment, with school-age stages from first grade to fourth grade. Before conducting the experiment, children were asked about their usual frequency of painting (Table 2).

5.2 Procedure

The evaluation was conducted in an open space where children could move freely to photograph for drawing element extraction. Two researchers were responsible for keeping the children safe and assisting them in the experiment. Before starting the test, the researchers explained to the children about the painting support tool. Then researchers asked the children about their expectations for the drawing activity and used Smiley-ometer to assess. At the beginning of the experiment, children were asked to observe and photograph objects they were interested in for 10 min with iPads After completing the collection of painting elements, the children started a 30-min drawing process, and the whole process was videotaped (Fig. 3.). They could use the extracted outlines in their drawings and manipulate them by scaling and rotating them. It is also possible to freely switch and use the extracted colors. Participants were also allowed to try out the animation function. After completing the drawing, the researchers conducted a questionnaire interview with each child for about 10 min. A gift worth $5 was given to all participants.

In Sect. 5.3, we would describe the scales we utilized in the experiment as well as the data analysis procedure.

5.3 Data Collection and Analysis

Considering individual interest the deepening of situational interest [1], we collected data mainly for assessing children's triggered situational interest in our experiment. And we

Fig. 3. A child was interacting with InterestPainter

also analyzed whether InterestPainter could offer children the opportunities to develop individual interests. For assessing triggered situational interest, we specifically depended on children's expectations, focused attention, and affective reaction [2]. And we evaluated individual interest development opportunities by asking children's willingness of continued engagement.

Expectation. Before the experiment, we would introduce our system to children first, then used Smileyometer [32] to ask for their expectation of painting with InterestPainter. After the experiment, Smileyometer was used to inquire about their experience. The expectation is possibly the most important step for personal relevance feelings, which is essential for interest development [21]. Smileyometer is designed for measuring children's expected and reported experience based on 1–5 Likert scale. In addition to asking about expectations, we coded children's behaviors and verbal communication as a complement to assess children's feelings of personal-related.

Focused Attention. Given situational interest refers to focused attention and the affective reaction, we analyzed objects and directions children gazed, as well as their facial expressions. Participants' focused attention was analyzed through thematic analysis and iterative open coding [26]. Two research assistants participated in coding and achieved a final interceder agreement of more than 90%.

Affective Reaction. To evaluate affective reaction, we noted observational indicators such as expressed cheerfulness, playfulness, enthusiasm, and excitement, as well as positive verbal statements. Facial expression was a key indicator during the coding process.

Continued Engagement Willingness. We used the Again-Again table [32] and self-report [21] to assess children's continued engagement opportunities. Again-Again table is always used to evaluate children's desire for doing specific activities again. In our Again-Again table, we evaluated InterestPainter and its three features: photographing, outline and color extraction, and animation. Self-report is the most common way in interest evaluation, which includes questions that follow up with other data sources. For example, we asked participants to rate how much they like painting with our system followed by a question that asks what they like about it.

6 Results

6.1 Personal Relevance

InterestPainter made children feel personal related. Specifically, after research assistant described our system, children quickly understood that the outlines and colors are generated from the image they took. Some children (C1, C3, C4) intended to take pictures of objects with the colors they like or want, C4 said," I'm taking this picture because I'm going to paint a watermelon with this red color" Knowing outlines and colors would be generated from pictures, C1 was so excited and even asked us to help him take an image of a toy that is out of his reach. It is noted that we asked for children's expectations for InterestPainter before the experiment, most of the children picked the expectation level over the average (Fig. 4). C2 and C5 said they had high expectations because pictures taken by themselves could determine the generation results, which made them feel involved in the system.

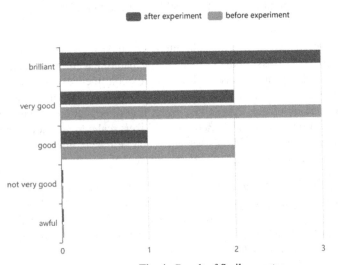

Fig. 4. Result of Smileyometer

6.2 Focused Attention

All children focused on painting during the experiment. Some children's (C1, C3, C4) gaze moved back and forth from InterestPainter to the object. They tried to observe and paint the specific object. While other children's (C2, C5, C6) gaze was on the tablet for the most of time during the experiments, which also could be an indicator of their focusing on painting (Fig. 4). InterestPainter offered a good user experience in general, which support children to focus on painting. But distractions still exist. For example, some children (C1, C3) pointed out that some outlines generated by the system are too complicated, which confused them and interrupted the painting experience to some extent. In addition, though children's attention was drawn effectively when figures were moving by the animation effect, moving figures made some children (C1, C5) anxious. C5 said, "It seems to ruin my painting when the figure's moving, but luckily it will be back to its position soon."

6.3 Opportunities for Continued Engagement

We conducted an Again-Again table and semi-structured interview after the experiment, it is shown (Fig. 5) that InterestPainter and its three features were all given positive feedback in continued engagement. During the experiment, some children (C3, C5, C6) asked the research assistant if they could take one more picture for extra colors. Notably, children (C1, C4) who hardly paint if they are not assigned told us they are willing to paint with InterestPainter, C1 said, "It's just like a toy and I like painting with it." Given children's positive feedback, we argue that continued engagement could be predictable.

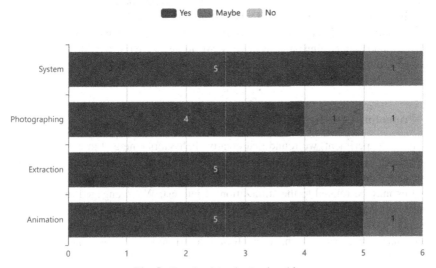

Fig. 5. Result of Again-Again table

6.4 Children's Painting Pattern

We found three painting patterns among all the participants. Some children (C1, C3, C4) tried to paint the objects they had photographed, and they tended to use outlines and colors materials. Another painting pattern was being inspired by outlines and painting something novel. For example, C2 painted one man wearing a suit based on a circle outline generated by our system. Besides, some figures were painted without using outlines, but the color extracted from the image seemed to stimulate this kind of painting pattern.

7 Discussion

The main purpose of InterestPainter is to provide children with a tool to stimulate their interest in painting. It allows children to photograph favorite objects, extract the visual characteristics of objects as painting elements on the canvas, and apply an animation effect to paintings. In the first user study, we learned about children's behavioral preferences and expectations of drawing during drawing activities. Combining these observations and the design principles proposed by previous researchers, we designed and developed InterestPainter, then evaluated it in the second user study to explore InterestPainter's potential of developing children's drawing interest.

7.1 Promote Children's Interest in Painting

We found that InterestPainter can successfully engage children in focused painting activities and stimulate their situational interest. During the use of InterestPainter, children performed the behaviors of taking pictures, extracting, drawing, and applying animation effects (Fig. 3). Some children (C3, C5, C6) wanted to acquire extra drawing elements while drawing. The act of painting and the act of photographing and extracting were mutually promoted, which produced a behavior-driven closed loop in the painting process. The animation effect was considered fun by most children, which also succeeded in motivating and maintaining painting actions. We argue that features guided by the design framework motivate these behaviors and that the interaction between these behaviors makes InterestPainter effective in promoting children's interest in painting.

7.2 Promoting Creative Activity

During our experiment, we found that creative behaviors emerged in children's painting process. After extracting outlines and colors, children (C2) created their paintings rather than paintings of photographed things. We believe that the generation of creative activities may be related to the stimulation of interest. When engaged in activities of interest, children generated feedback including positive affective reactions and repetitive engagement, and these feedbacks may promote children's creativity [33]. This insight may inspire subsequent research on interest and creativity, which is based on mobile technology.

7.3 Limitation

There are two main limitations that should be claimed. In our experiment, we focused on short-term behavioral indicators. Children's behavior and interview demonstrated that InterestPainter was able to promote children's situational interest, which has the potential to develop into individual interest with the support of the system. But it should be clear that a long-term experiment is needed to ensure the validity of our system.

8 Conclusion

In the current study, we show how interest-centered design principles can be applied to the field of children's painting. From these design principles, we derive design strategies applicable to mobile technology. Moreover, we design and develop InterestPainter. In our user study with elementary school children, evidence shows that InterestPainter succeeds in stimulating their situational interest in painting, which may turn into individual interest. We argue that child-centered concepts are needed for promoting a positive attitude in designing painting support tools for children.

References

1. Goodnow, J.: Children Drawing. Harvard University Press (2013)
2. Brooks, M.: What Vygotsky can teach us about young children drawing. Int. Art Early Childhood Res. J. **1**, 1–13 (2009)
3. Fox, J.E., Lee, J.: When children draw vs when children don't: exploring the effects of observational drawing in science. Creat. Educ. **4**, 1114 (2013)
4. Butler, S., Gross, J., Hayne, H.: The effect of drawing on memory performance in young children. Dev. Psychol. **31**, 597 (1995)
5. Drake, J.E., Winner, E.: How children use drawing to regulate their emotions. Cogn. Emot. **27**, 512–520 (2013)
6. Jolley, R.P.: Children and Pictures: Drawing and Understanding. Wiley (2009)
7. Rosenblatt, E., Winner, E.: The art of children's drawing. J. Aesthetic Educ. **22**, 3–15 (1988)
8. Vygotsky, L.S.: Imagination and creativity in childhood. J. Russ. East Eur. Psychol. **42**, 7–97 (2004)
9. Lee, I.-C., Cheng, P.-J.: The influence of different drawing tools on the learning motivation and color cognition of the fourth grade students at the elementary school. In: Stephanidis, C., Antona, M., Ntoa, S. (eds.) HCII 2021. CCIS, vol. 1421, pp. 80–90. Springer, Cham (2021). https://doi.org/10.1007/978-3-030-78645-8_11
10. Couse, L.J., Chen, D.W.: A tablet computer for young children? Exploring its viability for early childhood education. J. Res. Technol. Educ. **43**, 75–96 (2010)
11. Ryokai, K., Marti, S., Ishii, H.: I/O brush: drawing with everyday objects as ink. In: Proceedings of the SIGCHI Conference on Human Factors in Computing Systems, pp. 303–310. Association for Computing Machinery, Vienna, Austria (2004)
12. Benedetti, L., Winnemöller, H., Corsini, M., Scopigno, R.: Painting with Bob: assisted creativity for novices. In: Proceedings of the 27th annual ACM symposium on User interface software and technology, pp. 419–428. Association for Computing Machinery, Honolulu, Hawaii, USA (2014)
13. Follmer, S., Ishii, H.: KidCAD: digitally remixing toys through tangible tools. In: Proceedings of the SIGCHI Conference on Human Factors in Computing Systems, pp. 2401–2410 (2012)
14. Zhang, C., et al.: Bio sketchbook: an AI-assisted sketching partner for children's biodiversity observational learning. In: Interaction Design and Children, pp. 466–470. (2021)
15. Tokuhisa, S., Kamiyama, Y.: The world is Canvas: a coloring application for children based on physical interaction. In: Proceedings of the 9th International Conference on Interaction Design and Children, pp. 315–318 (2010)
16. Hidi, S., Renninger, K.A.: The four-phase model of interest development. Educ. Psychol. **41**, 111–127 (2006)
17. Kawas, S., Chase, S.K., Yip, J., Lawler, J.J., Davis, K.: Sparking interest: a design framework for mobile technologies to promote children's interest in nature. Int. J. Child-Comput. Interact. **20**, 24–34 (2019)
18. Anning, A.: Learning to draw and drawing to learn. J. Art Des. Educ. **18**, 163–172 (1999)
19. Renninger, K.A., Hidi, S., Krapp, A., Renninger, A.: The Role of Interest in Learning and Development. Psychology Press (2014)
20. Ito, M., et al.: Connected Learning: An Agenda for Research and Design. Digital Media and Learning Research Hub (2013)

21. Renninger, K.A., Hidi, S.E.: The Power of Interest for Motivation and Engagement. Routledge (2015)
22. Parakkat, A.D., Joshi, S.A., Pundarikaksha, U.B., Muthuganapathy, R.: Sketch and shade: an interactive assistant for sketching and shading. In: Proceedings of the Symposium on Sketch-Based Interfaces and Modeling, Article 11, pp. 1–2. Association for Computing Machinery, Los Angeles, California (2017)
23. Iarussi, E., Bousseau, A., Tsandilas, T.: The drawing assistant: automated drawing guidance and feedback from photographs. In: Proceedings of the 26th Annual ACM Symposium on User Interface Software and Technology, pp. 183–192. Association for Computing Machinery, St. Andrews, Scotland, United Kingdom (2013)
24. Hettiarachchi, A., Nanayakkara, S., Yeo, K.P., Shilkrot, R., Maes, P.: FingerDraw: more than a digital paintbrush. In: Proceedings of the 4th Augmented Human International Conference, pp. 1–4. Association for Computing Machinery, Stuttgart, Germany (2013)
25. Frick, T., Reigeluth, C.: Formative research: a methodology for creating and improving design theories. Inst.-Des. Theories Mod. New Paradigm Inst. Theory 2, 633–652 (1999)
26. Braun, V., Clarke, V.: Using thematic analysis in psychology. Qual. Res. Psychol. 3, 77–101 (2006)
27. Azevedo, F.S.: The tailored practice of hobbies and its implication for the design of interest-driven learning environments. J. Learn. Sci. 22, 462–510 (2013)
28. Matthews, J.: Drawing and Painting: Children and Visual Representation. Sage (2003)
29. Eisenberger, R., Armeli, S.: Can salient reward increase creative performance without reducing intrinsic creative interest? J. Pers. Soc. Psychol. 72, 652 (1997)
30. Berridge, K.C., Kringelbach, M.L.: Affective neuroscience of pleasure: reward in humans and animals. Psychopharmacol. 199, 457–480 (2008)
31. Xu, N., Price, B., Cohen, S., Huang, T.: Deep image matting. In: Proceedings of the IEEE Conference on Computer Vision and Pattern Recognition, pp. 2970–2979. (2017)
32. Read, J.C., MacFarlane, S., Casey, C.: Endurability, engagement, and expectations: measuring children's fun. In: Interaction Design and Children, pp. 1–23. Shaker Publishing Eindhoven, (2002)
33. Greene, T.R., Noice, H.: Influence of positive affect upon creative thinking and problem solving in children. Psychol. Rep. 63, 895–898 (1988)

On the Experience Design of Interactive Installations in Public Space

Mu Zhang$^{(\boxtimes)}$

Shandong University of Art & Design, NO. 02, Nineteen floor, Unit 1, Building 5, NO.187, Jingliu Road, Huaiyin, Jinan, China
153962234@qq.com

Abstract. The social gregarious nature of human beings determines that public space is a stage with social groups and tribes as its image. Considering and treating the public environment from the artistic point of view is an important aspect for human beings to optimize their living conditions and their own situation. In the 1960s, The National Art Foundation of America and the Public Service Administration have carried out a series of activities such as art in the public domain and art percentage, during which the concept of public art was born. People began to think about how to create art in public space, how to bring the installations in the exhibition hall or paintings into life. Public art emphasizes that its characteristics must have public nature, and its artistic creation needs to show human history or major events in specific areas. Public art must also have the characteristics of openness, and the forms and contents of artistic expression need to be integrated into the public life, with a wide audience. Public art also needs both materiality and spatiality. While using a variety of artistic expressions, it integrates into space and its cultural connotation. With the rapid development of science and technology in the 21st century, virtual reality, augmented reality and other technologies make it easy for people to get spiritual satisfaction in the virtual world, and people are willing to lock themselves in the compiled programs, revise it over and over again to achieve the effect of imitating reality. The ability of communication interaction has been weakened. How to re-establish interpersonal communication and enhance mutual communication has become an important issue in today's society. The artistic creation of new media in public space, especially the design of interactive installation can not only improve the economic benefits brought by the passenger flow in public places, but also enhance the emotions between people and shorten the distance between them. The interactive installation not only meets people's demands for art, but also weakens the inequality caused by cognitive differences, effectively explains the characteristics of artistic creation in public space, and uses unique artistic expression, become a popular art form. Taking the Yuanmingyuan night tour project as an example, this paper summarizes the experience of the integrated development of interactive devices and public space by analyzing the design process of interactive devices in the park. Combining the theories of user experience and psychology, this paper studies the concrete methods of improving user experience by interactive installation in public space.

Keywords: Public space · Interactive installation · User experience · Public art · Interactive art

1 Development of Public Art at Home and Abroad

The concept of public space can be explained from two aspects: narrow sense and broad sense. In terms of the narrow sense, public space refers to the places for daily leisure and life, where people can enter freely with communication and interaction. The facilities and space in these places can be used together by the public. It can be divided into indoor and outdoor parts. Streets, parks, squares and sports venues are involved in the outdoor spaces, while the indoor spaces include public transport, schools, restaurants, shopping centers, exhibition halls, etc. For the broad sense, public space includes people in the space and the cultural exchange and emotional interaction based on the space more than physical meaning, which contains entertainment, cultural exchange, production, religious and political gatherings, etc.

1.1 Development of Public Art Abroad

As the development of science and technology as well as the progress of human civilization, people's cognition of public space begins to shift from ordinary functionality to the construction of culture and the exploration of art, also from social education to daily aesthetics, which is prone to equal communication and interaction with art. This shift brings great changes to public art, making it more than just the creation simply moved indoor to outdoor; Moving from an art gallery to a public space also makes it no longer be a work of art created for a specific space or group of people. Artists are seeking a new breakthrough in art, or in public art. As the modern art, especially the post-modern art, rising, conceptual art and installation art have become the protagonists in the spotlight. Western society began to vigorously promote the large-scale development of public art. For example, the new public art method in Berlin, Germany, in 1987; The "public art development trust agency" in Britain in the 1980s; 1% of the buildings used for the public art in Japan at the same period. These are all the governmental support and assistance of the western world for public art [1] (Fig. 1).

1.2 Development of Public Art in China

Since the reform and opening-up, China's politics, economy, science and culture have developed by leaps and bounds. In the 1990s, the concept of "public art" came to China, appearing in urban space as the sculpture and murals, which set off a vigorous urban sculpture movement in China. With the development of urban construction and the promotion of cultural needs, public art gradually becomes popular in the new century [2]. Over the past 20 years, public art has been through the process of being accepted, explored and re-recognized. From the external form to the academic system, it derives many new types and ways that meet the social demands and reflect the characteristics of the times through constant adjustment under the mutual promotion of practice and theory. Public art is integrated into the multiple relationships of society, ecology, humanities and history for overall conception, so as to realize urban cultural innovation to promote the development of city (Fig. 2).

Fig. 1. 2017 Milan plant design week

Fig. 2. Wuhan optics valley plaza

2 Interactive Installations Design in Public Art

The art form of public space has begun to change from simplification to diversification in the nearly 20-year development process. Nowadays, whether in squares and streets, or at stations and supermarkets, the art works in public space cannot be just murals and sculptures at all. The rapid development of science and technology makes virtual reality, augmented reality and other technologies become a part of life. Besides, it also makes intellectualization and digitization exist in the new era as the label of public art. Developed countries like Europe and the United States began to try digital interactive art works in public space in the 1990s.

Daniel Rozin, a new media artist born in New York, creates an unusual "magic mirror" through computer programming and mechanical power installation, which is constituted by thousands of pieces of wood. Under each piece of wood, there is a stepping motor hidden. After the camera captures the environmental image, the computer adjusts the inclination angle of the wood through the programming instruction. Different angles of wood can bring light and shade changes. If each piece of wood is regarded as a single pixel, a "black-and-white screen" can be formed when all pieces of wood are put together. Daniel uses a camera to capture the image of visiting audience, and the captured image is played out in real time with this "wood screen", which has the effect as a mirror. Kimchi and Chips is an art studio in Seoul, founded by Elliot Woods (UK) and Mimi Son (Korea). Their interactive installation, Halo, is located in the Edmund J. Safra fountain courtyard of Somerset House in London, England. There are 99 smart steering gear making mirrors follow the sun like sunflowers all day, which are arranged on two 5-m-high towers and a 15-m-long track. Each mirror shoots a beam of sunlight into a water mist. The beams are computationally aligned to form a bright circle in the air. The mechanism of installation interaction completely depends on the existence of the sun, which explores the possibilities and limitations of technology to capture what cannot be touched. The halo can only appear at the moment when wind, sun, water and technology cooperate, creating a form between material and non-material. The interactive installation Reflect created by American new media artist Jen Lewin is an immersive, multi-sensory public art interactive work, which is inspired by the dynamic mode created by organic systems in the nature. This 2400 ft^2 sculpture consists of three concentric circles, and each circle has an interactive platform to respond to the footsteps of visitors, making the splash of light, so as to create a constantly changing composition. This interactive installation can encourage New Yorkers to stop to think and discover, connecting to the city when it enters a new era of hope and rejuvenation (Figs. 3 and 4).

Over the past 10 years, Chinese artists have begun to try to add interactive elements to public art, exploring public art through digitalization. For the Aranya church on the coast of Hebei Province, artist Wang Zhigang uses images to express his thoughts with "tide" as the theme, exploring the value of reincarnation between the rising and falling. As a multimedia art work in the "Cross-border Art" unit of Aranya Drama Festival, The Tide brings the audience a spiritual meditation more than a diversified artistic experience. The building absorbs energy during the day and releases slowly as light and shadow when the night falls, like the carrier of memory, comforting our souls with nowhere to place in the endless murmur of iteration and recursion. The Aranya church by the

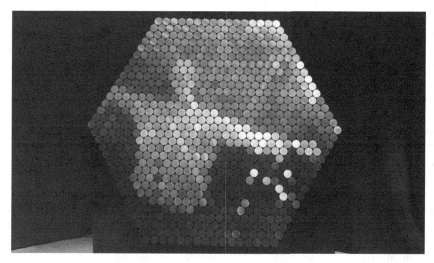

Fig. 3. Magic mirror

Fig. 4. HALO

sea, like a spiritual Utopia, can always show unique peace in impermanence after the ups and downs of the tide and the change of day and night. The work, Ink Reveries, created by a new media artist, Zhang Hanqian, show the climate change in 63 years with a bamboo forest composed of 63 ink bamboos. Scientists have been collecting carbon dioxide data through modern industrial methods since 1958, and the content of carbon dioxide in the atmosphere has increased at an annual rate of nearly 100 times that recorded during the last ice age in the past 63 years. The color of the ink bamboo surface changes with the temperature, bringing the faded landscape through the heating installation driven by carbon emission data. When the visitors touch, it can also change the appearance of the bamboo forest, symbolizing the impact of human intervention on the surrounding environment. Through the interactive effect of data visualization, the visitors can experience to reflect on the relationship between human and nature and the possibility of coexistence in the future. Beautiful Algorithm is a digital interactive installation created by Zhang ZhouJie team of Tongji University, which is located at the intersection of Chifeng Road in Shanghai, opposite the "Tongji Academy". In such a scholarly atmosphere, Zhang ZhouJie chose to express the installation works in a minimalist way: a standing long column, which is also the embodiment of the number "1". "One creates all things, and all things ends one". This also expresses the artist's long-standing artistic creation concept: the work can be shown in a simple and pure way, so that people cannot just focus on the surface of the, but it can arouse everyone to pay more attention to the content and significance of the work itself, as well as the nature and humanities it reflects. As a part of NICE2035 Chifeng Road Project of School of Design and Creativity in Tongji University, Zhang ZhouJie conveys his vision for the future through this work: he hopes that the "algorithm" can always have a positive significance to the society, making our life better and better (Fig. 5).

Fig. 5. Beautiful algorithm

3　Case Analysis of Night Tour in Yuanmingyuan

The Yuanmingyuan was first built in 1707 (the 46th year of Kang Xi). It covered an area of 3.5 km^2, with a construction area of 200000 m^2 and more than 150 scenes, which was originally a garden given by Emperor Kang Xi to his fourth son, Yinzhen. Kang Xi gave the title of "Yuanmingyuan" and "Yuanming" was the religious name of Yong Zheng.

After Yong Zheng ascended the throne in 1722, he expanded the original park, and built the Zheng Da Guang Ming Hall and Qin Zheng Hall in the south of the park, as well as many duty rooms of the cabinet, the Sixth Department and the military department, in order to "hold court with no noise" in summer. During the reign of Emperor Qian Long, in addition to the partial construction and reconstruction of the Yuanmingyuan, Chang Chun Garden was built in the east and Wan Chun Garden was in the southeast. The pattern of the Yuanmingyuan was basically done, and it was repaired and expanded many times during the years of Jia Qing and Dao Guang. During the second Opium War in 1860, the Yuanmingyuan was looted by the British and French allied forces and burned down in order to destroy the evidence. The former site is now the Yuanmingyuan Park. The Yuanmingyuan night tour project aims to improve the number of tourists and the viscosity of the park visiting through the design and planning of interactive installations in the park, so as to increase the economic benefits (Fig. 6).

Fig. 6. Yuanmingyuan

3.1 Preliminary Research

The project team began to conduct a comprehensive investigation and analysis on the history, positioning and current situation of the Yuanmingyuan in early 2019. From the perspective of history, the Yuanmingyuan was a large imperial garden in the Qing Dynasty, with a history of more than 300 years. Yuanmingyuan was located in Haidian District, Beijing. It was founded in 1707 (the 46th year of Kang Xi in the Qing Dynasty), which was composed of Yuanmingyuan and its attached gardens, Chang Chun Garden and Qi Chun Garden (later renamed Wan Chun Garden), thus, it was also called Three

Gardens of Yuanming, which was known as the "Garden of Gardens". The emperors of the Qing Dynasty came here to spend the summer and hold court every midsummer. So, it was also called "Summer Palace". After more than 150 years of establishment and operation in the Qing Dynasty, the Yuanmingyuan was famous in the world for its grand regional scale, outstanding construction skills, exquisite architectural scenery, rich cultural collection as well as broad and profound national cultural concept. Therefore, it was known as "the model of all gardening art", moreover, it was also known as "the model of ideal and art" by the French writer Victor Hugo (Fig. 7).

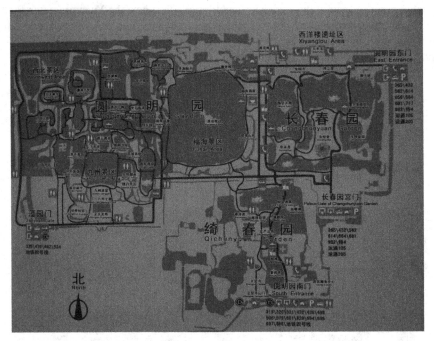

Fig. 7. Yuanmingyuan

Nowadays, the Yuanmingyuan is positioned as a patriotism education center, a national heritage park and a leisure and entertainment center. First of all, it is of great significance to strengthen patriotism education. In 1860, the British and French allied forces invaded Beijing, burning the Yuanmingyuan. In 1900, the Eight-Power Allied Forces looted the park, completely destroying the buildings and ancient trees in it. The Yuanmingyuan has witnessed the history of poverty and weakness in modern China, which is also a historical witness of imperialist aggression against China and making China a colony and a semi colony. Therefore, in March 1995, the Ministry of Civil Affairs of the People's Republic of China identified the Yuanmingyuan Park as the first batch of 100 patriotism education bases. Over the past 20 years, Yuanmingyuan Park has always adhered to patriotism, which is the glorious tradition of the Chinese nation. It has guided people, especially teenagers, to establish correct ideals, beliefs, view of life and values as a basic project to improve the overall quality of the whole nation, doing a lot of work to promote the rejuvenation of the Chinese nation. Second, as a large imperial garden of the imperial dynasty, the Yuanmingyuan has important archaeological value, which plays an important role in inheriting Chinese traditional garden art. One of the characteristics of Chinese gardens is reflected in the mountain, water and vegetation techniques. Therefore, the Yuanmingyuan after environmental restoration can provide people with a place to understand and learn Chinese traditional garden art, which is of great significance to inherit and carry forward Chinese traditional garden art. Furthermore, it plays a significant role in the development of tourism in Beijing. At present, only the Chang Chun Garden, Qi Chun Garden and a small part of Yuanmingyuan are open to the public, but most areas of the Yuanmingyuan have only completed the relocation of residents and units in the park, the construction of walls as well as some garden roads. Most areas are in disorder with basically no landscape effect. Necessary renovation and restoration shall be carried out for these plots to restore the mountain, connect the water system and conduct greening. Expanding the open area of the Yuanmingyuan through the exploitation of these tourism resources can make an important contribution to the development of tourism in Beijing.

3.2 Project Planning

With preliminary investigation and research, the project team introduced the concepts of "seed" and "net" based on the three positioning of the Yuanmingyuan, which are used to design the interactive installations in the park.

From the perspective of the positioning of patriotism education base, "seed" means breeding and growth, which indicates that patriotism will take root and sprout from this land. Starting from the archaeological excavations and national sites, "seed" refers to the dissemination and inheritance, which is not only the inheritance of Chinese traditional garden skills, but also the dissemination and development of Chinese traditional culture. In terms of the leisure and entertainment center, the interactive installation will be designed based on the concept of "seed", which contains the element and connotation of seed in the modeling and interactive experience. While the "net" represents exchange and intercommunication. We need to add interactive functions in public art installations to increase the viscidity of tourists and the time of visiting. The most important feature of interactive installation is the interaction and participation of more people. In the installation design, interaction design is a key link to connect tourists in the park and even outside the park with the user experience design through the concept of "net", which is an important strategy to improve the interactivity. Through the above two concepts, it is expected to integrate the three aspects of patriotism education center, national heritage park as well as leisure and entertainment center into the Yuanmingyuan night tour project (Fig. 8).

The factor analysis of the preferred places of visitors in Yuanmingyuan Park shows that the green space with beautiful scenery and diverse plants is the most preferred place for visitors. The reason why it can deeply attract tourists to stay is that Yuanmingyuan Park has various green landscapes, such as rich landscape plants, exquisite landscape structure combined with terrain, and man-made garden landscaping surpassing nature. The water body and waterfront landscape that can be enjoyed, loved and played in the Yuanmingyuan are the characteristics of the park and also an important factor of

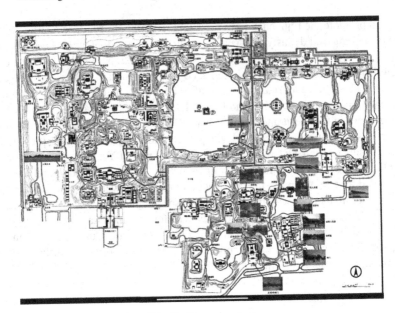

Fig. 8. Yuanmingyuan

its recreational attraction. The scenic spots around Fuhai are most popular. The rich imperial garden cultural relics of the Yuanmingyuan are also scenic spots that tourists like to visit. The charm of the cultural heritage of the Yuanmingyuan is also one of the main reasons for its popularity. The scenery of "plant + waterscape + sites" makes the core attraction, which can create the main impressive and popular sightseeing space of the park.

3.3 "Seed" Interactive Installation Design

With the preliminary research and planning, we decided to use the shape of dandelion as the carrier of "seed" interactive installation. Dandelion symbolizes courage and self-confidence, and every seed represents the promotion of patriotism and the inheritance of traditional culture. The whole installation contains luminous LED components and power base, and each seed of dandelion is an LED bulb. The luminous LED uses the contact charging mode, which is sucked into the base slot with magnet adsorption. The LED components have many forms, such as cone, mountain, etc. and many colors like red, blue, etc. Thus, it can be designed with a variety of combinations through extending the shape and color of the "seed" (Fig. 9).

The interaction mode adopts natural interaction, which means that different LED lights are placed next to the base, and users can take them at will for installation experience. Users directly participate in the appearance and color design of the device to interact with the device emotionally at will through free imagination. For example: cross installation with cold and warm color, or with trapezoidal and conical. The interactive experience mode can also take a variety of other forms. For example, it can be combined with lidar. After detecting an object, the LED light radiates around with a corrugated

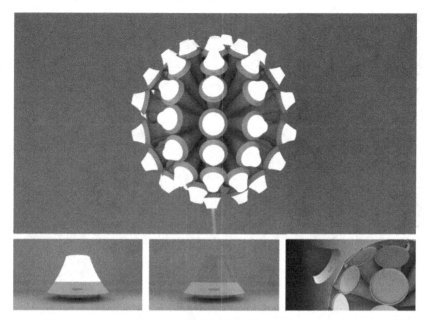

Fig. 9. Seed

shape. The contour of tourists can be generated on the device through capturing with lidar for detection. Visitors can design the interactive wall by themselves. The above methods can freely plug in and out, which not only reduces the learning cost of users, but also increases the types of feedback and user experience. The effect of the interactive design of this installation is to change the interactive feedback of the whole device with one of the combination modes of colors or forms changing, so as to achieve the great design goal with little effort (Fig. 10).

The luminous LED uses the contact charging or power-on mode to suck into the base slot with magnet adsorption. This technology is widely used in the current market, such as charging headphones, electric toothbrushes, etc. This charging technology has been relatively developed, and products with the same principle have entered the market. Xiaomi YEELIGHT night lamp adopts magnetic adsorption combined with base, charging by contact wireless technology. The power supply mode of the installation can adopt the same charging mode as Xiaomi YEELIGHT night lamp, with built-in polymer battery. Alternatively, power-on mode with magnetic adsorption can be carried out without built-in battery, thus, it can power on when adsorbing and power off when separating. The luminous LED lights can be managed with anti-theft buckle design. Different LED lights are placed next to the ground device, and users can take them at will for installation experience. Security check doors are set at the entrance and exit. The anti-theft buckle built on all LED lights will be alarmed if someone goes out with LED.

Fig. 10. Interaction mode

The LED with personalized "seed" can also be sold for commemoration. Users can collect exhibition materials or badges as souvenirs after participating in activities or visiting exhibitions. LED lights can be sold to users at a low price as a souvenir through their collection psychology. Additional printing of company advertisements can be carried out on the LED lights, such as the logo of the exhibition and the company logo. Therefore, the cultural concept of the enterprise can be rooted in the hearts of the people through the method of taking the seed away.

3.4 "Net" Interactive Installation Design

The shape of the "net" device adopts pyramid structure, and the outer side of the vertebral body is covered with mirror material, which means the moral of embracing nature and walking into nature. The vertebral body refers to the "growth" with upward feeling. The whole-body mirror reflects the surrounding light with the sense of science and technology, making it well integrated into the environment. When approaching, they need to pass through an area of mirror, which not only increases the ritual sense of the installation, but also gives the user a psychological hint that you have come to another place, so that they can focus on the installation. When it is lighting, the whole device exists in the shape of a diamond, as if floating on the ground, which can add more sense of ritual (Fig. 11).

Fig. 11. Pyramid

There are two concepts of "tangible net" and "intangible net" in the interactive design of the "net". "Tangible net" is composed of various devices distributed in the park. As shown in the figure below, the red area is better for playing area, and all devices can be evenly distributed in the whole scenic area. The best distance between the devices is more than 50 m, which is connected by four side-by-side LED cold light bands. It is a tangible huge net when viewed from a distance. Each device has four luminous energy stage, and the device does not light up without interaction. The whole device is hidden in the dark because of the dim light at night and the mirror reflection on the surface. The chip tickets bought or received for free by each visitor before entering the park can also be designed into small souvenirs of various shapes. Users with e-ticket can keep it as a souvenir through their collection psychology. Tickets can be designed with unique shapes with additional printing of company advertisements. For example, the logo of the exhibition and the company can increase the effect of advertising. When the user approaches the device with an e-ticket, the device will be brighter. So, when four users approach the device at the same time, the brightness can reach the strongest level 4. When users leave, the device will reduce the brightness level one by one. Each additional brightness level will light up an LED light band at the same time. The LED light band is connected to another device 50 m away to guide the audience. When the brightness reaches the maximum, all four LED cold light bands are on. When the users leave, one LED light band will be off in turn. The connection between the e-ticket and the device adopts NFC induction technology, which can light up the device as long as you are close to it, while the light goes off when you leave. Near-field communication (NFC) can provide short-range wireless connection, so as to realize two-way interactive communication between electronic devices. On the other hand, the "intangible net" is carried out through the interaction of mobile APP, which loads the map of Yuanmingyuan and the location of all devices. Through GPS positioning technology, users can view their position in the park and the number of devices they have lighted up in real time. The lighted devices will be connected into a net, the intangible net. When a certain number of devices are lighted up, users can enter the APP store for reward exchange. When all devices are lighted up, a complete "net" will appear and you can win the final reward. The devices can be placed in areas where visitors rarely arrive, so as to encourage users to light up all devices, which increases the experience time of the device, moreover, it also helps the scenic spot reverse the flow of people (Fig. 12).

Fig. 12. Interaction mode

People can only pay attention to one point at any time, thus, we integrate the interaction process with sightseeing through the design of the "net", so as to avoid the phenomenon that the audience has no time to take into account the "interaction" when "appreciating". At the beginning of the experience, there needs to be a point that can attract the visitors immediately. So, the light of the device can be changed four times, starting from scratch then becoming brighter and brighter, which makes the audience try to explore. It grasps the curiosity of the visitors at the beginning of the interaction, keeping them in the device experience. Three elements can be perceived by the visitors: the brightness of the LED, the number of lights on the LED band and the guiding direction of LED band, which comply with Miller's Law, 7 ± 2 Principle. The number of tourist concerns shall not exceed 5. There are two choices for the audience to make during the experience: the one is whether to close the e-ticket to the device, and the other is to move to the guiding direction, lighting up the next one. This kind of design avoids the phenomenon that too many choices will affect the interactive experience. As closing to the designated area, it can be lightened with low learning cost. The light band can guide visitors to the next device (Fig. 13).

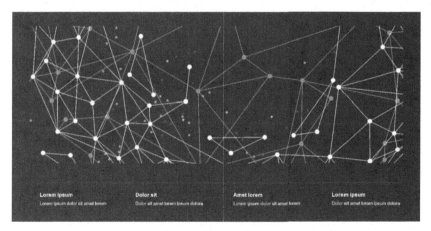

Fig. 13. Interaction mode

4   Conclusion

The Yuanmingyuan night tour project is an attempt to design interactive installations in public space. We have accumulated rich experience through this project, proving that interactive installation art in public space can not only integrate into public life, but also have materiality and spatiality. The installation is well integrated with the culture of the space. The interactive installations in public space do not lose the function of carrying cultural connotation while increasing the interactivity and reflecting the sense of science and technology. This attempt well explains the role and significance of interactive installation art in public space under the background of new technology. Furthermore, it accumulates experience for the future interactive installation design projects in public space.

References

1. Zhang, C.: Application of Digital Media Technology in Urban Public Space – Based on Optical Media. Jiangnan University, Jiangsu Province (2014)
2. Liu, H.: Image Installation Art and its Application in Public Space. Beijing Institute of Fashion Technology, Beijing City (2012)

Author Index

Printed in the United States
by Baker & Taylor Publisher Services